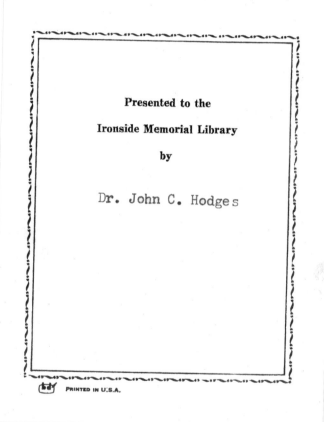

THE DEVELOPMENT OF
THE AMERICAN SHORT STORY

THE DEVELOPMENT
OF THE AMERICAN
SHORT STORY

AN HISTORICAL SURVEY

BY

FRED LEWIS PATTEE

BIBLO and TANNEN
NEW YORK
1966

Printed in U.S.A. by
NOBLE OFFSET PRINTERS, INC.
NEW YORK 3, N. Y.

26761

CONTENTS

THE DEVELOPMENT OF
THE AMERICAN SHORT STORY

THE DEVELOPMENT
OF THE AMERICAN
SHORT STORY

CHAPTER I

WASHINGTON IRVING

I

The American short story began in 1819 with Washington Irving. Short fiction there had been in America before *The Sketch Book,* some of it written by men of significance—Franklin, Freneau, Charles Brockden Brown—but from the standpoint of the modern short-story form none of it need detain us. Franklin wrote anecdotes with didactic intent; Freneau threw off narrative propaganda, some of it in verse; Brown, as in his posthumously collected *Carwin the Biloquist, and Other American Tales and Pieces,* produced not short stories, but abortive romances, tales begun as novels and abandoned; others, especially in the magazines of the decade before *The Sketch Book,* wrote imitations of the Hannah More and Maria Edgeworth moral tracts which were so popular in England after the "great religious awakening." All of it is negligible: none of it influenced the evolution of the short story. A study of the form in its American phases begins with Irving.

II

The first observation to be made upon Irving concerns the fact that he was born in New York City of British parentage, and therefore was untouched by New England. The Puritan age had been introspective, and the New England of the early nineteenth century was still basically Puritan; the eighteenth century of

1

Addison and Fielding and Goldsmith had been circumspective, and the New York of Irving's boyhood was a prolongation of it: worldly, cosmopolitan, it was even then absorbed in an all-engrossing present; the romantic age that was to dominate the opening years of the new century was to be retrospective, unmindful of voices within and clamor without, while it created for itself an ideal world out of its dreams of a vanished past. Of all that savors of introspection and New England Puritanism, Irving had no trace. The grim shadows of conscience and that chilling religious atmosphere which in New England killed all early attempts at fiction and which in later days could render pale and often unearthly the work of a genius like Hawthorne, touched him not at all. Like Cooper, he could be lawless without a qualm. It is worth while to dwell upon this: it was inevitable that American fiction should have had its beginnings in New York, and especially inevitable was it that the short story should have sprung from its soil. It would have withered and died in the shadow of early New England Brahminism, for it is a thing of this world; it breathes worldliness or it perishes.

Irving's birth in New York had another effect. Unlike the Boston of the period, the city had no intellectual atmosphere, no traditions of a scholarly past, no Brahmin caste, and as a result the lad, naturally bookish, was forced in upon himself and in upon his father's library, which had stopped growing at a period antedating the Revolution. To the eager boy, marooned in a literary desert, the volumes of the eighteenth-century writers came as something new and vital. The then comparatively recent advice of Dr. Johnson to give one's days and nights to the volumes of Addison was authoritative and compelling. As a result Irving prolonged the eighteenth century. Ignorant of the new literary tides that were rising to sweep away old things, he began deliberately to write as Addison would have written had he been born into the New York of the dying eighteenth century. The Jonathan Oldstyle papers, which appeared in the *Morning Chronicle* when Irving was nineteen, are of the age of Queen Anne rather than of the second decade of the lusty young American Republic. So, too, with the *Salmagundi* papers that followed in 1807. This basis of classicism, which in a way he had been forced upon, was, as we see it now, tremendously important to the young writer: it came first, it came in his impressionable years; he never wholly left it. It gave him stability while others went to extremes, it compelled restraint, it rendered impossible anything save beauty of style and perfect clearness, and it made him observant of men and manners and times.

But the eighteenth century was dead: even while Irving was writing his Oldstyle papers the reaction against all it had stood for had become a revolution. Already had come what Carlyle was terming "the sickliest of recorded ages, when British literature lay all puking and sprawling in Werterism, Byronism, and other sentimentalism, tearful or spasmodic (fruit of internal wind)." That the impressionable young New-Yorker sooner or later should have been affected was inevitable. How the new forces laid hold upon him and modified his classicism is a problem tremendously important, for it is at this point, where in him the Addisonian Arctic current was cut across by the Gulf Stream of romanticism, that there was born the American short story, a new genre, something distinctively and unquestionably our own in the world of letters.

III

The second observation about Irving concerns his ancestry: Scotch and Cornwall-English, prevailingly Celtic. The father was a restless soul from the Orkneys, a sailor on the North Sea, a fighter in the armada against the French, an emigrant to America in the period before the Revolution. The dash of Celtic accounts for the mercurial temperament of the man, his affinity for romance, his love of the picturesque, his kinship with Scott, his swiftly changing moods. He was as temperamental as Dickens. Only when the mood was upon him would he write: for months and years and decades would he lie fallow. The mood was upon him only in periods of serenity: hence the uniform serenity of his product; hence also the surprisingly small bulk of his writings—in twenty years and in the prime of his life only five volumes, all of them small. From his temperament came, too, his habits of work: he wrote by spurts and dashes, a story at a sitting. Bancroft visited him in 1821: "He took me to his room, and read to me what he had written at one sitting. I remember it to this day: It was his 'St. Mark's Eve,' from the words, 'I am now alone in my chamber,' to the end." A part of his "Rural Funerals" "was written at Miller's, where he stopped in at early dawn, feverish and excited, after having been all night at a dance, and borrowed pen and paper to jot down his 'thick coming fancies.'" Easily was he discouraged, easily deflected. In Dresden he became interested in dramatics and translated German operas like "Abu Hassan"; later in Paris he worked with John Howard Payne upon adaptations from the French—"Richelieu," "Charles II," and the like. For months he thought apparently of nothing else. Then suddenly he plunged into a series of "American Essays," finished two or three, but at a hint from the Spanish minister threw them away and was off to Madrid to work on a life of Columbus. This biography well started, he dashed it aside to begin on *The Conquest of Granada*. Such a temperament will express itself, if it turns to fiction, not in long, patiently wrought novels, but in narrative dashes—sketches.

His indolence, too, must be noted. He was the youngest of eleven, precocious, vivacious, the pet of the family, a bit spoiled. His abortive novel "Mountjoy" possibly may have in it an element of autobiography. His brothers attended Columbia College, but not he: "He was more alive to the drudgery than the advantage of a course of academic training." Threatened with consumption, his life became for a long period a series of health excursions, which culminated at twenty-one in a year and a half in southern Europe. It turned his attitude toward life into that of the convalescent who has been watched with anxiety and whose every wish has been anticipated. His brothers sacrificed for him, idolized him. "It is with delight," wrote William, "we share the world with you; and one of our greatest sources of happiness is that fortune is daily putting it in our power thus to add to the comfort and enjoyment of one who is so very near to us all." A little later his brothers established a hardware business, Irving to receive one-fifth of the profits, though contributing nothing to the capital stock. "It was not expected by the brothers," writes the nephew biographer, "that he would pay any attention to the business, their object in giving him an interest in their concern being mainly to provide for his subsistence and leave him at liberty to cultivate his general talents."

For a decade he did practically nothing. In high spirits, caused partly by his sense of humor, partly by the joy of hoaxing the public, he dashed off in 1809 his *Knickerbocker's History of New York*, but for years afterward he lived in idleness. "The spur of necessity," continues his biographer, "was needed to quicken and invigorate his literary ambition, which gradually wore off under the temptations to ease and idleness, until at last he settled down into a sort of gentleman of leisure." In 1817, his friend Ogilvie wrote to him that it was a shame that in the flower of his youth and possessing higher literary reputation than any of his countrymen had ever claimed, esteemed and beloved by all, he could allow indolence to overcome him and render him sterile. Position after position was offered him—a secretaryship of legation in London, a clerkship in the Navy Department, an editorship offered by Scott, another by Murray with a salary of a thousand guineas, and still another as contributor to the *Quarterly* at one hundred guineas the article, but he declined them all. His reply to Scott is enlightening:

My whole course of life has been desultory, and I am unfitted for any periodically recurring task, or any stipulated labor of body or mind. I have no command of my talents such as they are, and have to watch the varyings of my mind as I would a weathercock. Practice and training may bring me more into rule; but at present I am as useless for regular service as one of my own country Indians or a Don Cossack.

In 1815 he had gone to England, but, contrary to what is taught in the text-books, he had not gone in connection with the family business. His nephew biographer records it thus: "Yielding to a roving propensity, 'the offspring of idleness of mind and a want of something to fix the feelings,' he had pulled up anchor in New York . . . to drift about Europe in search of novelty and excitement, ready, as he expressed it, 'to spread his sails wherever any vagrant breeze might carry him.'" His married sister lived in Birmingham, and with her he resided in idleness until his brother Peter's serious illness compelled him to enter the business house that so long had supported him. Until his brother recovered he did the work as best he could, for several months, indeed— months that filled his letters with superlatives: "I would not again experience the anxious days and sleepless nights which have been my lot since I have taken hold of the business to possess the wealth of a Crœsus." And yet he had but taken temporarily his brother's usual load.

After some months of recuperation in his sister's home he started again on his wanderings, visited Campbell and Scott, toured the Highlands of Scotland, and undoubtedly would have drifted on and on over Europe had he not been arrested by a sudden catastrophe: early in 1818 his brother's firm was forced into bankruptcy and Irving was cut off without funds. By sheer necessity he was forced into literary work. His thoughts centered at length upon another *Salmagundi*, to be issued when the mood was upon him and to be stopped at will. The result was *The Sketch Book*, issued in numbers like a magazine and varied in contents. The instant success of it changed the current of his life: whenever he needed money he would write a book—a feverish period of literary effort to be followed by a year or two of serene leisure in England, or Germany, or France, or Spain. He had found his profession.

Again we may observe that such a temperament will never write a novel. If it write at all, it will produce brevities, dashes while the mood is on, embodied emotions, impressions, tales to be told at a sitting. The adjective *desultory* best describes his earlier work—he used it himself in his letter to Scott. With the one exception of *Knickerbocker's History*—itself a loosely bound mass of materials—all he wrote until he was forty-five may be classed as miscellanies—temperamental dashes, sketches. *Bracebridge Hall*, to which he placed the subtitle "a medley," contains fifty different pieces. His very title, "The Sketch Book," has apology in it, for a sketch book is a random receptacle for first impressions, materials collected *for* work and not the work itself. He apologized at the close of it; his friends, he says, had expostulated with him, but he had decided to ramble on as he had begun. In *Tales of a Traveller*, he defends himself with the ingenious argument that if his tales "prove to be bad, they will at least be found short; so that no one will be wearied long on the same theme. 'Variety is charming,' as some poet observes."

His writing of short pieces is thus naturally accounted for. He did not deliberately choose the shortened form: he fell into it automatically because of his temperament, his natural indolence that forbade long-continued efforts, his powerful yet volatile emotions, and his early literary training in the school of Addison and Goldsmith and Dr. Johnson. To realize how unfit he was for long-sustained forms of fiction one has but to read his amorphous "Buckthorne" and "Mountjoy" and "Ralph Ringwood," all of which started elaborately as novels, moved with increasing effort for a time, and then either stopped abruptly or else exploded into fragments.

IV

It is needless to dwell upon Irving's debt to Addison and to Goldsmith. The debt to Goldsmith he himself acknowledged in all its fullness. In his introduction to his life of the poet he wrote that he could say of Goldsmith what Dante said of Vergil in the "Inferno." The lines, which he quoted in the original were translated thus by Longfellow:

> Thou art my master, and my author thou;
> Thou art alone the one from whom I took
> The beautiful style that has done honor to me.

The debt is evident to all who read even carelessly any of his earlier work; it is more important that we trace within him the growth of the new romantic spirit that so profoundly was to affect his later writings.

One notes first of all that between 1809 and 1819 lies a fallow decade in his life. On one side of it lies *Salmagundi*, which Richard Henry Dana had reviewed with the discerning sentence, "It has to do with the present and the real, not the distant and the ideal"; and the *Knickerbocker's History*, which had reminded the early *North American Review* of Sterne, and Scott of Dean Swift: "I never read anything so closely resembling the style of Dean Swift as the annals of Diedrick Knickerbocker." On the other side lie *The Sketch Book, Bracebridge Hall*, and *Tales of a Traveller*, books redolent of the romantic revolt. On the one side the eighteenth century, on the other the nineteenth; on the one side the boy marooned in his father's library and saturating himself with books as out of date as a sedan chair, on the other the Washington Irving that we know—Irving the romanticist, whose literary life was a processional from romantic area to romantic area: from old Dutch New York to the England of his dreams; thence on to the lands of the Rhine; thence on to France and Arabesque Spain and the Alhambra; and thence still on to the plains of western America and the picturesque trading posts of the primitive Northwest.

What had happened during the decade? He had come in contact with Scott. The transition from Irving the classicist to Irving the romanticist had been caused by that great Jupiter of the North which had deflected from their orbits all the fiction writers of a generation. In August, 1810, while idling at Mr. Hoffman's summer retreat on the Hudson, Irving had read "The Lady of the Lake," a copy of which he had secured from the American publishers in advance of its publication. In the words of his biographer, "All eagerness to devour it, he had stolen forth with his secret treasure to have the first reading to himself. More than once have I heard him descant upon the delight of this stealthy perusal, and the surprise with which he started to his feet at the unexpected dénouement,

> 'And Snowden's knight is Scotland's king.' "

Soon was to come a more intimate experience. His friend Brevoort, who was abroad, had presented Scott with a copy of *Knickerbocker*, and now he forwarded Scott's glowing letter of acknowledgment to the author of the book. It came as a veritable breath from the wonderland of romance. "Let me know," it said, "when Mr. Irving takes up his pen again; for assuredly I shall expect a very great treat." No wonder it set him to dreaming. During the next two years he read widely and in the current literature of the time. For the *Analetic Magazine* he reviewed the poetry of Byron and prepared an appreciative paper on Campbell, who had been influenced, he said, by the "richer and more interesting field of German *belles-lettres*." In the early summer of 1815 he sailed for England, and during the next four years was in the full current of British literature.

It was the period of the metrical romance, of that luxuriant growth that had been seeded by "Marmion" and "The Lady of the Lake," by Byron's "Bride of Abydos," "The Corsair," and "Lara," by Coleridge's "Christobel" and Keats's early poems, by Moore's "Lalla Rookh," Hunt's "Story of Rimini," and Southey's "Roderick, the Last of the Goths." It was the period, too, of the Waverley Novels and their exciting mystery of authorship. In August, 1817, Irving wrote his brother, "I find it pretty generally believed that Scott is the author of these novels, and Verplanck tells me he is now traveling about collecting material for *Rob Roy*." Shortly afterward he was himself in Scotland, quoting "Marmion" and excited and eager before the landmarks that had figured in "The Lady of the Lake," which he knew by heart. Armed with a letter from Campbell, he made bold to call upon

Scott, and received a royal welcome. Scotland in reality was his fatherland—at least it was his father's land—and in the Scotch romancer he found a kindred soul. For a week he lived in the world of the Waverley Novels and was swept beyond his power of words: "I have rambled about the hills with Scott; visited the haunts of Thomas the Rhymer, and other spots rendered classic by border tale and witching story, and have been in a kind of dream or delirium. As to Scott, I cannot express my delight at his character and manners."

Remembering that Scott had begun his romanticism after translating Bürger's "Lenore" and "Der Wilde Jäger," and Goethe's "Götz von Berlichingen," we may note that Irving's visit to Scott was followed by a wild effort to take German by storm. "At this time," remarks his biographer, "Washington had shut himself up from society and was studying German day and night." To Brevoort he wrote in May, 1818: "I have been some time past engaged in the study of the German language, and have got so far as to be able to read and splutter a little. It is a severe task, and has required hard study; but the rich mine of German literature holds forth abundant reward."

Whatever the reason may be, we know that the first number of *The Sketch Book*, which appeared just a year later, was a contribution to the new literature of romanticism, and that in many ways it is a landmark in the history of the movement. By temperament Irving was inclined toward the romantic: his predisposition to indolence unfitted him for realism, which always is scientific and based upon research. His early isolation, too, had made of him a dreamer: cut off from the lands of culture and fed during his boyhood from the memories of his parents, he had idealized the lands of their childhood and had thrown over them the dreamy softness of romanticism.

He went to no extremes—his early training forbade that. One may even be doubtful whether in the case of *The Sketch Book* the balance falls on the side of the eighteenth or on the side of the nineteenth century. We to-day, to whom it is a classic familiar from our earliest years, cannot realize how novel and fresh it was to its earliest readers. To them it was a revolutionary book. Lady Lyttleton wrote in 1820 to Mr. Rush that she had no patience with the rumor then current that it had been written by Scott, for "the style and nature of the book are so new and peculiar that it puts me out of all patience to hear the surmise." Even the quotations at the head of the sketches were revolutionary. They set the pitch for the collection:

> Here's a few flowers! but about midnight more:
> The herbs that have on them cold dew o' the night
> Are strewings fitt'st for graves—
> You were as flowers nor wither'd; even so
> These herblets shall, which we upon you strow.

> He that supper for is dight,
> He lyes full cold, I trow, this night!
> Yestreen to chamber I him led,
> This night Gray-Steel has made his bed.

> A pleasing land of drowsy head it was,
>   Of dreams that wave before the half-shut eye,
> And of gay castles in the clouds that pass,
>   For ever flushing round a summer sky.

> May no wolfe howle; no screech owle stir
> A wing about thy sepulchre! etc.

Such texts, though common enough in the eighteen-thirties, were startlingly new in 1819 and 1820, despite Monk Lewis and his *Tales of Terror* and despite the German fragments that everywhere were appearing in the English and even the American magazines. In 1804 a translation of "Lenore" had appeared in the Philadelphia *Portfolio*, and three years later it was followed by a parody upon the poem. Irving even before his contact with Scott undoubtedly had traveled widely in this infectious area of literature.[1]

This softened light that was spreading from Germany over all Europe shimmers everywhere through *The Sketch Book* and makes it notable in the history of English romanticism. One finds it, still more softened and still more vaguely dim, in the next book, *Bracebridge Hall*. Here there is nothing of the present, so much so, indeed, that its first English readers found it a thing apart from life, at least from any life that they themselves had experienced.

---

[1] See "German Literature in American Magazines Prior to 1846." Scott Holland Goodnight. Bulletin of the University of Wisconsin, No. 188.

Blackwood's complained that "the great blemish of the work is, that it is drawn not from life, but from musty volumes."

Irving had approached England as the romantic poet approaches the object of his dreams, as Tieck and Wackenroder, when in 1793 they had wandered over Germany, had approached Nuremberg, the city of Albrecht Dürer and Hans Sachs, and had thrown over it the soft light of the Middle Ages. He had seen England not with his physical eyes, but with his brooding imagination, and he had developed it in the true Tieck-Wackenroder atmosphere of romantic sentiment, impressionistic art, a softened literary atmosphere glimmering through a medium of books—old books mellowed by time. His early reading had made of him a classicist, but Scott had awakened within him his true soul and had made of him, almost in spite of himself, an original force in the movement of his day.

In a footnote to "The Historian" in *Bracebridge Hall*, Irving makes mention of the fact that several of his critics had discovered that the tale "Rip Van Winkle" "was founded on a little German tradition,"[1] and explains it by saying: "In a note that follows that tale, I had alluded to the superstition on which it is founded, and I thought a mere allusion was sufficient, as the tradition was so notorious as to be inserted in almost every collection of German legends. I have seen it myself in three." That the author had made use of an old German story is nothing, but that he had

[1]Grimm's tale "Peter Klaus, the Goatherd" appeared in Otmar's collection of German legends published in 1800. Tending his goats on a hillside near his native village of Sittendorf, Peter is accosted by a young man who silently beckons him to follow. Following the mysterious stranger, he is led at length into a deep dell inclosed by rocky precipices where he finds twelve ancient and knightly men playing at skittles. None of them speaks a word. Gazing about him, Peter espies a can of wine and, approaching it, perceives that it breathes a delicious fragrance. Drinking deeply from it, he is inspired with new life, but at length he is overpowered by sleep. When he awakes he is again on the hillside, but rubbing his eyes, he can see neither his goats nor his dog. Trees appear where he had never seen trees before; everything is changed. Descending the mountain and entering the village, he meets no one but strangers. At length he finds his daughter, who he finds has grown suddenly old. Neighbors, also strangely old, drop in to visit him, and he finds at length to his consternation that he has been asleep twenty years. That Irving had read this tale is unmistakable. In Grimm's tale Klaus thinks he hears his name called, but, looking about, sees only a raven; in Rip it is a crow that answers, but it is needless to trace the parallelisms. Undoubtedly "The Legend of Sleepy Hollow" was influenced by Bürger's "Der Wilde Jäger." In this latter legend the headless horseman hurls at his fleeing victim not a pumpkin, but a huge piece of meat.

written the tale, after having examined three collections of German legends, is something indeed, especially when every page of the story reflects the romantic spirit and atmosphere of the German *Sturm und Drang*.   Joseph Jefferson, dramatizing the tale in 1859, felt that the romantic atmosphere was its central motif, and therefore made it the central motif of his play.   At the climax he could find no accompanying music so fully in accord with his theme as was the ballad song to which had been set Heine's "Die Lorelei."   Curtis in an "Easy Chair" paper has thus described the climactic moment of the play:

The drop had just fallen, and the scene on the mountains was about to open.   The house had been darkened, and as the clear, quiet, unforced tone of Rip, yielding, not remonstrating, to the doom that we all knew and he did not, fell upon the hushed audience, the eyes of men and women were full of tears; while the orchestra murmured, *mezzo voce* during the storm within and without the house, the tenderly pathetic melody of the "Lorelei":

> "I know not what it presages,
>   This heart with sadness fraught;
> 'Tis a tale of the olden ages
>   That will not from my thought."

It is the full voice of German romance.   "Rip Van Winkle" is a *Märchen* of the "Lorelei" type, blended with the softly tinted style and the clearness of Goldsmith, and the kindliness and whimsical humor of Irving himself.

That Irving did not consciously surrender to the German school is evident to all who read his sketches.   Everywhere he has sly hits at its extravagances.   "The Stout Gentlemen," introduced as it is with a page of melodramatic circumstance ending with the sentence: "I think it has all the elements of that mysterious and romantic narrative so greatly sought after at the present day," is in reality a travesty.   "The Spectre Bridegroom," too, was written perhaps in the spirit of travesty.   It ends with a caper.   Undoubtedly, before he wrote it he had read the same wild romance that had inspired Bürger to the creation of his "Lenore." To Irving, however, the legend brought no serious inspiration: it aroused within him rather the same impish spirit that had called forth the *Knickerbocker's History of New York* after he had read the pompous guide book.   Then too it may be argued that the unexpected, sprawly ending of this tale and of many others like it came from his lack of dramatic power. He started his story in all seriousness, as an impressive romance, went on strongly for a time, found himself powerless to arrive at an adequate dénouement, and then suddenly turned the whole thing into a joke. It is an ingenious conjecture, surely.

V

That the *Märchen* world of Germany had laid powerfully hold of the imagination of Irving is shown by the fact that at the first possible opportunity he visited the Rhine lands and remained in Germany for a period exceeding a year. In July, 1822, after the publication of *Bracebridge Hall*, he entered the country at the "little old ghost-ridden city" of Aix-la-Chapelle, as he termed it, worked leisurely up "the haunted stream," visited the chief cities, including Mayence, Frankfort, Darmstadt, Heidelberg, Ulm, Munich, Salzburg, Vienna, at each of which he remained from three days to a month, and then, in November, arrived at Dresden, where he resided until the next July.

The German biographer of Irving, Herr A. Laun, was of the opinion that he had been naturally drawn to Germany because "he found there so much that was attractive to his soul and his imagination, which reveled in myths and legends and was inclined toward the dreamy, the mystical, and the romantic. Dresden, the German Florence, appeared to him, and justly so, as the place which, so far as art, literature, and conviviality were concerned, could offer him all that he wished." And again he notes that "in addition to studies in Italian and French, he seems to have busied himself seriously with the learning of German. He took private lessons in the language, but that he ever penetrated deeper into German literature than into those romantic, fabulous, and legendary areas which attracted him, the occasional citations from Schiller in his writings and his single reference to the works of Jean Paul do not prove.[1]

Certainly he could not have been ignorant of the work of E. T. A. Hoffman, whose death, just as Irving was entering Germany, had brought his work into new prominence, so much so, indeed, that *Blackwood's* in 1824 could say, "His romances and tales are at present about the most popular of all books among the light

[1] *Washington Irving. Ein Lebens- Und Charakterbild.* A. Laun. Berlin, 1870.

readers of Germany." Irving must have read at least a part of the collection of tales and sketches entitled *Serapionsbrüder*, first issued in 1819–21, for Part I of his *Tales of a Traveller* has much in common with it both in structure and in atmosphere. In Part II also, Irving uses his acquaintance with the literary art world much as Hoffman had used his knowledge of music as material for "Der Dichter und Der Komponist." Since Irving, however, had begun his "Buckthorne" as early as 1820, he may have derived his "kunstroman" idea, as did perhaps Hoffman, from Goethe. *Blackwood's* in 1824 declared "Buckthorne" to be an attempt at an English *Wilhelm Meister*. Again, the banditti tales of Part III are pitched to the German note, though not with the wild extravagance of Hoffman, as are also the Knickerbocker tales of Part IV. There were other influences. That Irving was aware of the folk tales of Musæus we know. Mrs. Foster has this in the diary which she kept during the tour from Dresden through the Hartz:

Old châteaus visited, all of which had some legends connected with them more or less curious, recorded by Musæus, whose work in many volumes was our evening study, when stopping for the night. It was in German, but Mr. Irving would get us to translate it for him.

That England expected a German book to follow *Bracebridge Hall* is evident from the reviews of *Tales of a Traveller*. The suggestion undoubtedly had come from Irving himself. From Paris, whither he had gone after his year in Germany, he had written his brother:

I have been thinking over the German subjects. It will take me a little time to get hold of them properly, as I must read a little and digest the plan and nature of them in my mind. There are such quantities of these legendary and romantic tales now littering from the press, both in England and in Germany, that one must take care not to fall into the commonplace of the day. Scott's manner must likewise be widely avoided. In short, I must strike out some way of my own, suited to my own way of thinking and writing.

His plan for a two-volume novel to be entitled *Buckthorne and His Friends* fell through quickly. He made another start: "Tried to commence work on Germany, but could not do anything." Then later, "Toward twelve o'clock an idea of a plan dawned on me—made it out a little, and minuted down heads of it. Felt more encouraged—felt as if I should make something of it." According to his biographer, this plan was "to mingle up the legendary superstitions of Germany, in the form of tales, with local descriptions and a little of the cream of traveling incidents." Some weeks later he could record, "I think I have run into a plan and thrown off writings which will be more novel and attractive."

What this plan was undoubtedly appears in Parts I and III of *Tales of a Traveller*. The plan undoubtedly was better than the execution. The book is loose and ragged, wanting in unity, even the unity that was possible with his loose and rambling plan. What he might have done and what he undoubtedly had in mind as he planned his work, Hauff afterward did in his *Das Wirtshaus im Spessart* (1827), a book clearly inspired by Irving's[1] indeed, as were also parts of Heine's *Die Harzreise*. As it was, it became four issues of a periodical, each totally distinct from the others, and the second part a mere mass of chaotic materials from his abandoned novel, *Buckthorne*.

Like all of Irving's work, it is a mixture, partly classical, partly romantic. Scott in his "On the Supernatural in Fictitious Composition," a review of Hoffman's Tales, could mention "The Bold Dragoon" as the only example of the Hoffman type of the fantastic at that time in English literature, and yet one cannot feel that Irving was sincerely romantic as he wrote it.[2] "The Bold Dragoon" is not genuinely fantastic; in a way it is as much a travesty upon romanticism as was "The Stout Gentlemen." Irving's grotesque humor, broad here even to coarseness, spoils the effect of the piece as a bit of romanticism. "The Story of the German Student," too, ends with a Knickerbocker caper.

Tales of a Traveller failed in England. The public was looking for another *Knickerbocker's History* in which the Germans were to be made as ludicrous as the New York Dutch had been, and instead they had been given what to them seemed, to quote Irving's own words, a mere "commonplace of the day." "The author has cribbed from the German books he has been dabbling

[1] *Washington Irving's Einfluss auf Wilhelm Hauff.* Otto Plath. In *Euphorion, Zeitschrift fur Literaturgeschichte.* Leipzig, 1913. It is worth noting, perhaps, that Hauff's tale "Das Kalte Hertz" is but a German variation of Irving's "The Devil and Tom Walker."

[2] "On the Supernatural in Fictitious Composition." *Foreign Quarterly Review*, July, 1827.

in"; "It is becoming daily a more dangerous thing to pillage the Germans"—such was the burden of the reviews. Even as early as 1822 the *Edinburgh Review* had criticized "The Student of Salamanca" as dealing with "the commonplaces of romantic adventure."

What Irving might have written had he remained longer in the German atmosphere we may not say. As it was, all in a moment he found himself in another area of romance, one strangely kindred yet strangely remote—the half oriental twilight of Spanish legend. In January, 1826, Alexander H. Everett, United States minister at Madrid, attached him to the American legation and in the same letter proposed his translating Navarrete's *Voyages of Columbus,* which was about to appear. Irving's prompt acceptance marks the opening of what we may call the last period in his evolution as a romanticist.

VI

As to the extent that Spanish literature and legend had affected him in his earlier periods one must be content with conjecture. That there was an early Spanish influence we have his own words: "From earliest boyhood," he wrote in his later years, "when on the banks of the Hudson I first pored over the pages of an old Spanish story of the wars of Granada, that city has ever been a subject of my waking dreams,and often have I trod in fancy the romantic halls of the Alhambra." Howells, who as a boy found *The Sketch Book* for a time a dominating passion, considered the influence of Spain upon Irving radical: "I did not perceive then that Irving's charm came largely from Cervantes and the other Spanish humorists yet unknown to me, and that he had formed himself upon them almost as much as upon Goldsmith." External evidence is almost wholly lacking. That Irving had applied himself at various times to the study of French and German and Italian his biographer does not leave us in doubt, but nothing is said of his learning Spanish. Yet almost a year before the call to Spain he had written his nephew in the tone of one who is a specialist in the subject: "The Spanish language is full of power, magnificence, and melody. To my taste it excels the Italian in variety and expression. It has twice the quantity of words that the French has. I do not know anything that delights me more than the old Spanish literature. . . . The old literature of Spain partakes of the character of its history and its people; there is an Oriental splendor about it." Moreover, the fact that he was called by the American minister to translate antique manuscripts and that he performed the task quickly and to the satisfaction of Navarrete himself, who spoke of him as "erudite," able to evaluate his collection of old papers and "to examine them critically," proves that Spanish to him was no new acquisition. More specific than this we may not be.

Whatever be the cause, we know that in his next collection of tales and sketches, *The Alhambra*, Irving is completely Spanish in his romanticism. The book is an Arabesque, as redolent of the Orient as the tales of Scheherezade. No more travesty, no more romance tempered with rollicking humor verging at times upon coarseness, as in "The Bold Dragoon." His surrender was complete: "For my part, I gave myself up, during my sojourn in the Alhambra, to all the romantic and fabulous traditions connected with the pile. I lived in the midst of an Arabian tale, and shut my eyes, as much as possible, to everything that called me back to everyday life." As a result no other American has caught so richly and so completely the full spirit of the Oriental story-world.

It must be confessed that there was little that was new in the material that Irving presented. Scott in 1827 had complained that the public "had been inundated, *ad nauseam*, with Arabian tales, Persian tales, Turkish tales, Mogul tales, and legends of every nation east of the Bosphorus"; Carlyle the same year declared that German literature was dwelling "among wizards and ruined towers, with mailed knights, secret tribunals, monks, spectres, and banditti . . . moonlight and mossy fountains." *The Edinburgh Review*, March, 1831, complained of

The irruption of these swarms of publications now daily issuing from the banks of the Danube, which, like their ravaging predecessors of the darker ages, though with far other and more fatal arms, are overrunning civilized society. Those readers whose purer taste has been formed on the correct models of the old classic school, see with indignation and astonishment the Huns and Vandals once more overpowering the Greeks and Romans. They behold our minds, with a retrograde but rapid motion, hurried back to the reign of Chaos and old Night, by distorted and unprincipled compositions, which in spite of strong flashes of genius, unite the taste of the Goths with the morals of Bagshot.

The literature of France also was gorgeous during this period with an Orientalism that culminated in 1829 with Hugo's *Les Orientales*; poems almost flamboyant in their extravagance. Hugo had been in Spain and had been fired by its romance. Irving, caught in this tide of Gothic extravagance, did not surrender to it. He fought constantly against what he called "the manner of the times." Restrained by his early training in the school of the eighteenth century, he went to no extremes. His is a softened and subdued Gothic and Arabesque art, a blending of humor and pathos and naturalness with the extravagance of romanticism, and the result was something all his own. No one has better expressed it than Frederick H. Law, who selects as the best of the tales "The Rose of the Alhambra":

Here is pure romance fancifully localized and definitely related to history. The dainty Spanish damsel, Jacinta, is ingeniously made descendant of romantic ancestors; the ever-watchful aunt, Fredegonda, is one of the living characters that make the pages of Irving so vivid; Ruiz de Alarcon and Zorahayda are mediæval and dreamlike. There are touches of humor and good-natured satire throughout the story, with a pensive kind of melancholy appropriate to a legend of the old tower of the Infantas. Most remarkable of all, it is a richly sensuous effect created by flowing rhythms, poetic descriptions, and suggestive words. The word "rose," the key word of the tale, is repeated again and again, giving an atmosphere of fragrance.

The tale is one of summer-evening fancy and enchantment, one of the sweetest that ever ennobled an ancient building. Old-fashioned, aromatic, redolent with charm, "The Legend of the Rose of the Alhambra" is truly a flower of the long ago, plucked in the rich gardens of the Alhambra, pressed in the pages of Irving's book, and stirring us with the memories of other days.

VII

Excluding such rambling character sketches as "The Wife" and the "Widow and Her Son" in *The Sketch Book*, and such abandoned fragments as "Buckthorne" and "Ralph Ringwood" in his later collections, Irving wrote something like forty-eight narrative pieces that, in a general way, we may call short stories. Roughly we may classify them under four heads: first, sentimental tales in the conventional manner of the time, like "The Pride of the Village," "Annette Delabre," and "The Widow's Ordeal";

second, seven Knickerbocker tales—"Rip Van Winkle," "The Legend of Sleepy Hollow," "Dolph Heyliger," "The Devil and Tom Walker," "Wolfert Weber," "The Adventure of the Black Fisherman," and "Guests from Gibbet Island"; third, other tales touched by German romance, like "The Spectre Bridegroom" and Parts I and III of *Tales of a Traveller;* and, fourth, Arabesque tales and sketches of Spanish romance, like those in *The Alhambra, Legends of the Conquest of Spain,* and *Wolfert's Roost.*

Arranged in chronological order, the tales reveal an evolution that is most instructive. The *Salmagundi* papers are of the eighteenth century: only one of them by any stretch may be called a short story. "My Aunt" is a whimsical anecdote, "My Uncle John" is an Addisonian sketch of character and manners, but "The Little Man in Black" has elements in it that are new: it is the transition link between the *Spectator* sketches of the book and the Germanized "Rip Van Winkle" that was to follow ten years later. So redolent of the eighteenth century is it that John Neal could declare it a direct imitation of Goldsmith's "Man in Black" in No. 26 of *The Citizen of the World,* yet it is not a study of manners or of character, and it is not an apologue—it has no moral. It is a graphic picture—the man is alive and he is presented not to make the reader think, but to make him feel. It has dialogue, characterization, but no development of character, and it has verisimilitude. The author's whole object is to entertain: to surprise, indeed, the reader. The little man is the first shadow of the coming Knickerbocker, and the first shadow also of the coming of the romantic into its author's work. In the story there is first a mystery, then a seeming solution, then a surprise-ending almost of the modern type: the little man is no other than a descendant of the erudite Linkum Fidelius who has been so whimsically and so ponderously quoted through the volume just as the Little Man in Black runs through *The Citizen of the World* to be revealed at the end. A stupendous tome, the labor of a lifetime, has been left in the hands of the author and the source of his learned quotations is now plain. The reader is left with the impression that the tale was told with no other purpose than to set the stage for this surprise.

The Sketch Book, which came a decade later, after Scott and romanticism had come into Irving's life, marks the boundary line between the new and the old. The first critic clearly to recognize that a new literary form had arisen was Prescott, the historian, who under the title "Essay Writing" made, in *The North American Review* as early as 1822, this remarkable analysis:

> *The Sketch Book* certainly forms an epoch in the history of this kind of literature; for, although of the same generic character with the British essayists, it has many important specific peculiarities. The former were written . . . with a direct moral tendency, to expose and to reform the ignorance and the follies of the age. *The Sketch Book*, on the other hand, has no direct moral purpose, but is founded on sentiment and deep feeling. . . . In one word, the principal object of the British essayists was to instruct, so they have for the most part given a picture of common life, in simple language; while the principal object of *The Sketch Book*, being to delight, scenes only of exquisite emotion are selected, and painted in the most exquisite, but artificial language.

Irving touched the eighteenth-century apologue with emotion, stripped it of its obvious moral, and reduced it from the general to the particular. Addison saw the type, Irving the individual; Addison aimed at the head, Irving at the heart; Addison lighted his work with flashes of wit, Irving suffused his with the mellow glow of humor.

From *The Sketch Book* the progress of Irving into the full stream of romantic fiction was rapid, until, indeed, his *Alhambra* sketches are all picture, all emotion, sentiment, entertainment. Save in their restraint, their beauty of style, their clearness and simplicity, there is little in all of his later tales to remind us that their author had once been completely under the spell of the eighteenth century.

VIII

For the short story as we know it to-day Irving performed perhaps nine distinctive services:

1. He made short fiction popular. He was peculiarly endowed for writing the shortened form and he used it exclusively. After the sensational triumph of *The Sketch Book*, a success that stirred greatly the imagination of the younger seekers for literary recognition, sketches and tales became the literary fashion in America, and in such volume did they come that vehicles for their dissemination became imperative. The annual, the gift book, and lady's books like *Godey's* and *Graham's*, and the various popular magazines that sprang up in the 'thirties and 'forties—nurseries for the short

story—were thus indirectly the fruit of Irving's success as a sketch writer. He set the bells ringing.

2. He was the first prominent writer to strip the prose tale of its moral and didactic elements and to make of it a literary form solely for entertainment. Knowing the fashions of his day, he was constantly apologizing for his lack of didactic basis. "I have preferred addressing myself to the feeling and fancy of the reader more than to his judgment," he wrote Brevoort in 1819. "My writings, therefore, may appear light and trifling to our country of philosophers and politicians." His apology in the introduction to *Bracebridge Hall* is facetious and characteristic. No more clever explanation is to be found in English literature. The suggestion that there might be a moral to his tales aroused his mirth. "I was once," his biographer tells us, "reading aloud in his presence a very flattering review of his works, which had been sent him by the critic in 1848, and smiled when I came to the sentence 'His most comical pieces have always a serious end in view.' 'You laugh,' said he, with that air of whimsical significance so natural to him, 'but it is true. I have kept that to myself hitherto, but that man has found me out. He has detected the moral of *The Stout Gentleman.*'"

3. He added to the short tale richness of atmosphere and unity of tone.

4. He added definite locality, actual American scenery and people. Though only seven of his forty-eight tales are native in setting, these seven have been from the first his best loved and most influential work. They were the result of no accident. Deliberately he set out to create for his native land that rich atmosphere which poetry and romance had thrown over the older lands of Europe, or, to quote his own words, "To clothe home scenes and places and familiar names with those imaginative and whimsical associations so seldom met with in our new country, but which lie like charms and spells about the cities of the Old World." He was the pioneer, therefore, in that new school that demanded an *American* literature, an art that would work in native materials in an original manner.

5. He was the first writer of fiction to recognize that the shorter form of narrative could be made something new and different, but that to do it required a peculiar nicety of execution and patient workmanship. To quote his own words:

There is a constant activity of thought and a nicety of execution required in writings of the kind, more than the world appears to imagine. It is comparatively easy to swell a story to any size when you have once the scheme and the characters in your mind; the mere interest of the story, too, carries the reader on through pages and pages of careless writing, and the author may often be dull for half a volume at a time, if he has some striking scene at the end of it; but in these shorter writings every page must have its merit. The author must be continually piquant; woe to him if he makes an awkward sentence or writes a stupid page; the critics are sure to pounce upon it. Yet if he succeed, the very variety and piquancy of his writings—nay, their very brevity, make them frequently referred to, and when the mere interest of the story is exhausted he begins to get credit for his touches of pathos or humor; his points of wit or turns of language.

6. He added humor to the short story and lightness of touch, and made it human and appealing. A pervasive humor it was, of the eighteenth-century type rather than of the pungent American type that was to be added by Aldrich and his generation, but nevertheless something new and something attractive.

7. He was original: he pitched the short story in a key that was as new to his generation as O. Henry's was to his. He constantly avoided, as he expressed it, the "commonplace of the day": "I choose to take a line of writing peculiar to myself, rather than to fall into the manner or school of any other writer." And again, "It is true other writers have crowded into the same branch of literature, and I now begin to find myself elbowed by men who have followed my footsteps; but at any rate I have had the merit of adopting a line for myself, instead of following others."

8. Though his backgrounds may often be hazy, though the complaint of the early *Blackwood's* critic that there is "no reality about his Yorkshire halls" has a basis of truth, his characters are always definite individuals and not types or symbols. Rip Van Winkle and Ichabod Crane are more vividly real as human personages to-day than is George Washington, their contemporary. Even "Mountjoy," a complete failure as a short story, has a character in it that is most decidedly alive, that is, indeed, a study in adolescence worthy even of a Henry James.

9. And finally, he endowed the short story with a style that was finished and beautiful, one that threw its influence over large areas of the later product. To many critics this was Irving's

chief contribution to American literature, and to some New Englanders at least it was his only contribution. To Emerson, Irving was "only a word-catcher." Perhaps he was, and yet it is by no means a calamity that our pioneer short-story writer should have begun with a literary style that has been the despair of all of his followers. It would have been well if many others who have practiced the art, especially some in recent days, could have learned Irving's secret of a distinctive and beautiful style.

But in many respects Irving was a detriment to the development of the short story. So far as modern technique is concerned he retarded its growth for a generation. He became from the first a model followed by all: unquestionably he was in America the most influential literary figure of the nineteenth century. To him as much as even to Scott may be traced the origin of that wave of sentimentalism and unrestrained romance that surged through the annuals and the popular magazines for three decades. Longfellow received his first inspiration from *The Sketch Book*. His *Outre-Mer*, and many other books of the early period issued in parts, like Dana's *Idle Man*, came as direct results of Irving's work. Bryant wrote tales of the *Sketch Book* type; the young Whittier planned a novel which was to be in style "about halfway between the abruptness of Laurence Sterne and the smooth gracefulness of Washington Irving," and even Thoreau began his literary life with a "meditative description" in the manner of Irving. Everywhere in the midcentury the softness and sentiment of this first great leader, as notably in Mitchell's *Reveries of a Bachelor*, and *Dream Life*, and Curtis's *Lotus Eating, Prue and I*, and the "Easy Chair" papers. One may skip a generation and still be in the presence of the great romancer: Harte, the leader of the new school of short story writers after the war, began by writing legends modeled after the legends of the Hudson. Poe was powerless in the 'thirties and 'forties in his attempts to change the technique of the form. His careful analysis was either unread by his generation or else unheeded because it was a revolt from Irving.

Of form as we know it to-day the tales of Irving, even the best of them, have little. He had begun as an eighteenth-century essayist, and according to Dr. Johnson an essay is "a loose sally of the mind; an irregular, undigested piece; not a regular or orderly composition"; he had ended as a romanticist, and romanticism may be defined as lawlessness. His genius was not dramatic. He delighted to saunter through his piece, sketching as he went, and chatting genially about his characters. "Rip Van Winkle" has six pages of material before there is any movement. The well-known stage version of the tale has little in it of Irving's material. "The theme was interesting, but not dramatic." Jefferson tells us in his Autobiography: "The silver Hudson stretches out before you as you read, the quaint red roofs and queer gables of the old Dutch cottages stand out against the mist upon the mountains; but all this is descriptive. The character of Rip does not speak ten lines. What could be done dramatically with so simple a sketch?" A study of what the dramatist added to the tale and what he left out will reveal how far it falls short of modern short-story requirements. There is lacking sprightly dialogue, movement unimpeded by description or exposition, additional characters with more collisions and more contrasts, and finally a swift culmination involving all the *dramatis personæ*.

To Irving plot seemed unessential. He had evolved with deliberation a form of his own that fitted him perfectly. In a letter to Brevoort he explains its characteristics:

For my part, I consider a story merely as a frame on which to stretch my materials. It is the play of thought, and sentiment, and language; the weaving in of characters, lightly, yet expressively delineated; the familiar and faithful exhibition of scenes in common life; and the half-concealed vein of humor that is often playing through the whole—these are among what I aim at, and upon which I felicitate myself in proportion as I think I succeed.

Of "The Legend of Sleepy Hollow" he could say: "The story is a mere whimsical band to connect descriptions of scenery, customs, manners, etc."

But there is a more serious indictment. *Blackwood's* mentioned it as early as 1824. About all of Irving's writings, the reviewer had complained, there is a languorous softness that relegates them almost to the realm of feebleness, and he added, "Nobody has ever taken a strong hold of the English mind whose own mind has not had for one of its first characteristics manliness." Expressed in modern phraseology, it means that Irving lacked robustness, masculinity, "red-bloodedness." He was gentle to the verge of squeamishness. Mrs. Foster, who knew him intimately in

Dresden, noted that "he looks upon life as a picture, but to catch its beauties, its lights—not its defects and shadows. On the former he loved to dwell. He had wonderful knack at shutting his eyes to the sinister side of anything." Beyond a doubt this lack of robustness in Irving must be reckoned with as one cause of the general effeminacy and timid softness that characterized so much of American fiction during the greater part of the century.

But criticism of Irving's defects is thankless labor. It is best to overlook his faults and be profoundly thankful for him, for with him began American literature. He brought with him wholesomeness and distinction of style and careful workmanship; he introduced to us the form that has become our most distinctive literary product; and, in the words of his earliest critic, Dana, he took our crude American materials and turned them "all to beauty like clouds shone on by the moon."

BIBLIOGRAPHY

A Chronology of Irving's Short Stories

1807. *Salmagundi.*
    1. The Little Man in Black. November, 1807.

1819–20. *The Sketch Book.*
    2. Rip Van Winkle. May, 1819.
    3. The Spectre Bridegroom. November, 1819.
    4. The Pride of the Village. March, 1820.
    5. The Legend of Sleepy Hollow. March, 1820.

1822. *Bracebridge Hall.*
    6. The Stout Gentleman. September, 1821.
    7. The Student of Salamanca.
    8. Annette Delarbre.
    9. Dolph Heyliger.

1824. *Tales of a Traveller.*
    10. The Hunting Dinner.
    11. The Adventure of My Uncle.
    12. The Adventure of My Aunt.
    13. The Bold Dragoon. February, 1824.
    14. The Adventure of the German Student.
    15. Adventure of the Mysterious Stranger.
    16. The Story of the Young Italian.
    17. The Inn at Terracina.
    18. The Adventure of the Little Antiquary.

19. The Belated Travellers.
20. The Painter's Adventure.
21. The Devil and Tom Walker.
22. Wolfert Weber, or Golden Dreams.
23. Adventure of the Black Fisherman.

1832.   *The Alhambra.*
24. Adventure of the Mason.
25. Legend of the Abrabian Astrologer.
26. Legend of Prince Ahmeid Al Kamel.
27. Legend of the Moor's Legacy.   1829.
28. Legend of the Three Beautiful Princesses.
29. Legend of the Rose of the Alhambra.
30. The Governor and the Notary.
31. Governor Manco and the Soldier.
32. The Legend of the Two Discreet Statues.

1835.   *Legends of the Conquest of Spain.*
33. The Legend of Don Roderick.   1829.
34. Legend of the Subjugation of Spain.   1829.
35. Legend of Count Julian and His Family.   1829.
36. The Widow's Ordeal.   *Cunningham's Annual.*   1829.

1839–41.   *Knickerbocker's Magazine.*
37. Mountjoy.   1839.
38. Adelantado of the Seven Cities.   1839.
39. Legend of Don Munio.   1839.
40. Guests from Gibbet Island.   1839.
41. Pelayo and the Merchant's Daughter.   1840.
42. The Grand Prior of Minorca.   1840.
43. Legend of the Engulfed Convent.   1840.
44. Abderahman.   1840.
45. The Taking of the Veil.   1840.
46. The Count Van Horn.   1840.
47. Don Juan: a Spectral Research, 1841.
48. The Abencerrage.   *Wolfert's Roost.*   1855.

CHAPTER II

I

The unprecedented success of Irving's *The Sketch Book* and of Cooper's *The Spy*, which appeared a year later, brought a pressure upon the literary vehicles of America that is often overlooked by students of the period. A new literary generation was coming on. J. K. Paulding, G. C. Verplanck, R. H. Dana, Edward Everett, Bryant, and John P. Kennedy already had won literary recognition; Miss Sedgwick, Prescott, Robert C. Sands, Grenville Mellen, Robert Montgomery Bird, and William G. Simms were just beginning to write, and Longfellow, Hawthorne, Willis, and Poe, still in school or college, were dreaming of literature as a lifework. All of them had been touched by the magic of Scott, and all of them had been stimulated by the almost unbelievable success of their two young countrymen. As to whether Irving or Cooper was the greater influence upon this group is an open question. Griswold in 1846 was inclined toward Cooper: "*The Spy* gave an extraordinary impulse to literature in the country. More than anything that had occurred, it aroused the people from their feeling of intellectual dependence." Concerning the influence of Irving a volume of testimony might be collected. His effect upon Longfellow may be cited as typical:

Every reader has his first book; I mean to say, one book among all others which in early youth first fascinates imagination, and at once excites and satisfies the desires of his mind. To me, this first book was *The Sketch Book* of Washington Irving. I was a schoolboy when it was published, and read each succeeding number with ever-increasing wonder and delight, spellbound by its pleasant humor, its melancholy tenderness, its atmosphere of revery,—nay, even by its gray-brown covers, the shaded letters of its titles, and the fair clear type, which seemed an outward symbol of its style.

As a result of these influences came all at once a flood of Irving-like sketches, essays, tales, and an increasing number of Scottlike, Cooper-like historical romances, among the earliest of which were Mrs. Child's *Hobomok*, and *The Rebels*, John Neal's *Logan* and *Seventy-Six*, Paulding's *Konigsmarke*, and Timothy Flint's *Francis Berrian*. But publication channels were limited. It was more profitable for publishers of books to pirate Scott and his English contemporaries than to pay for the crude first attempts of their unknown countrymen.

The young writer who would essay to write fiction had open for him the literary column of the weekly newspaper and to a limited extent the pages of a few struggling magazines like the New York *Mirror and Ladies' Literary Gazette*, but they offered small reward for his efforts. Bryant contributed his earliest attempts at fiction to the *United States Review and Literary Gazette*, William Austin's "Peter Rugg, the Missing Man" first appeared in Buckingham's *New England Galaxy*, and Hawthorne a decade later was forced to use the columns of a newspaper as obscure as the Salem *Gazette*. But even this outlet was limited: the papers and magazines of the period could publish only a fraction of what the new group was eager to produce.

Some writers solved the difficulty by issuing their collected material at their own expense. Thus in 1821, in Baltimore, appeared *Tales of the Tripod; or a Delphian Evening*, by Pertinax Particular [Dr. Tobias Watkins]; in Trenton, N. J., in 1827, *Village Tales*, by Oliver Oakwood [Stacy Gardner Potts]; and in Portland, Maine, the same year, *Tales of the Night*, by a Lady of Maine [Mrs. Sally Saywood Wood].

Others, emboldened by the success of *Salmagundi* and *The Sketch Book*, published what in reality were little magazines of the modern type, pamphlet miscellanies issued at irregular periods according to the author's whim, to be continued as long as material held out or as the work succeeded. Thus in 1818–19, in Baltimore, John P. Kennedy and Peter Hoffman Cruse issued in fortnightly numbers *The Red Book* the literary organ of the Delphian Club, a lively organization, among whose members were such well-known men as John Neal, Jared Sparks, John Pierpont, Francis Scott Key, Samuel Woodworth, and William Wirt; in Boston, in 1820, William Hickling Prescott and other young Harvard men put forth four issues of *The Club Room*; and a year later, in New York, Richard Henry Dana published in six or eight numbers his *The Idle Man*, all of these periodicals, like *The Sketch Book*, being finally republished as books. Often the series first appeared in a newspaper, to be finally collected and published, like Potts's *Village Tales*, which first appeared in the Trenton *Emporium*, or to rest undisturbed like the "Lay Monastery" series which Longfellow while in college wrote for the *United States Literary Gazette*, or like the melange which he and his friends a year later contributed to the Portland *Advertiser*.

As late as 1827, when the "Literary Confederacy," led by William Cullen Bryant, Gulian C. Verplanck, and Robert C. Sands, organized itself in New York to take the castle of literature by storm, it could think of no weapon more formidable than a book of miscellanies of the eighteenth-century type. Their publisher, Dr. Elam Bliss, however, sensing the new spirit of the times, advised them to issue their material as an annual properly embellished, and the result was *The Talisman* and success beyond their dreams. "When I committed to the press last year a miscellaneous selection from my unpublished writings," Bryant wrote in his second preface, "I had no idea of commencing a series of volumes to appear annually in the same form": "the flattering reception given to the first" volume had changed all his plans. *The Talisman* ran for three years—1828, 1829, 1830,—was reissued later in three volumes as a gift book with the title *Miscellanies*, and in 1832, with a larger corps of contributors, was followed by *Tales of Glauber Spa*, a short-story gift book which was not continued beyond the first volume.

Thus at the moment when the success of Irving in Europe and of Cooper in America was filling young Americans everywhere with the desire also to produce sketches and tales in prose, and when the demand for a vehicle had become imperative, came the annual, a fashion new from Europe, and all at once it became their market place and their book of models. Until the rise of the great magazines in the middle of the century, all of the American short-story writers—Hawthorne, Poe, Miss Sedgwick, Willis, Mrs. Child, Leggett, Hall, Simms, Longfellow—owed much of their success to the encouragement given their early work by this popular literary vehicle. Poe may be cited as a single example. As late in his literary career as 1834 Carey & Lea, the publishers, would make him no offer for his *Tales of the Folio Club*, and "not from want of merit in the production," as John P. Kennedy wrote him, "but because small books of detached tales, however well written, seldom yield a sum sufficient to enable the bookseller to purchase a copyright. He recommended, however, that I should allow him to sell some of the tales to the publishers of the annuals. He has, accordingly, sold one of the tales to Miss Leslie for *The Souvenir* at a dollar a page."[1] It was the one market that could be depended upon, and without it many who later achieved success might have surrendered in their discouragement and ceased to write.

II

The first "annual proper" published in America was *The Atlantic Souvenir; a Christmas and New Year's Offering*, issued at Philadelphia late in 1825 for the year 1826. The idea had been borrowed from abroad; the editors acknowledged it at the start. "On the Continent of Europe," they explained, "such a volume has long been the attendant of the season, and the shops of Germany and France abound every winter with those which are suited to every age and taste." But the idea was the only thing they borrowed. From the start they used American material exclusively, and their example was followed by practically all of the later annuals. We are "relying," wrote the editor in the preface to the second volume, "solely on our countrymen, both in the literature and the embellishments of the volume." From this policy it never once departed during the seven years of its existence and its successor followed in its footsteps.

The idea of *The Atlantic Souvenir* undoubtely had been borrowed from London, though even there the fashion was a new one. In December, 1821, *Blackwood's* had reviewed *The Literary Pocket Book or Companion for the Lover of Nature or Art*, for 1822, as a novelty, but two years later, reviewing *The Graces or Literary Souvenir, an Annual Pocket Book Volume*, it could say, "November is cheered by a whole carnival of minute volumes" of its kind. The fashion had been an importation from Germany and had been adopted wholesale and at once. "The Germans," it went on to explain, "of all men the wisest in their literary generation, have led the way in this species of performance," and "our neglect of so interesting a mode of authorship is among the more striking instances of the tardiness with which ingenuity sometimes crosses the sea."

[1] Kennedy to Poe, December 22, 1834. Virginia edition of Poe's Works, Vol. XVII.

In Germany the annual had had a long history. At first it had been a miscellany of poetic and elegant extracts, but after Schiller had used it for his "Maid of Orleans" and Goethe for his "Herman and Dorothea," it had become so favorite a vehicle for original articles that H. Payne in 1826, in *The North American Review*, could say, "An author whose subject is within the intellectual reach of general readers, and who wishes to be soon and widely read, is more sure of being so in Germany, by contributing to a *Taschenbuch*, than by any other mode in which he can give his works to the world. Among the French, however," he added, "they do not seem to be general, except for mere external ornament."

Especially was the annual adapted for the short prose tale, and from the first in England it relied largely for its interest upon this variety of work. The reviewer of *The Graces or Literary Souvenir*, 1823, notes that it contains a "Spanish tale of considerable length, a melancholy narrative." Hoffman in Germany had made use of it constantly for his weird tales. One finds them in the *Taschenbuch zum geselligen Vergnügen* for 1819 and 1822, in the *Taschenbuch der Liebe und Freundschaft* for 1819, 1820, 1821, and 1823, in *Urania* for 1819, in the *Berliner Taschenkalender* for 1820, and the *Reinisches Taschenbuch* for 1821.

The arrival of the annuals in America marks the beginning of a new period. They came at a critical moment and their coming more than any other single influence determined the direction American literature was to go. *The North American Review*, April, 1829, was the first to remark upon their importance; it was even inclined to point to these "little golden specks which are just glimmering above the dim horizon as the twilight dawn of American literature."

These little works [it went on], made up of short articles of poetry and prose, seem especially suited to the instant genius of our land. The body of our writers are yet young. Few of them have acquired experience and strength enough to venture alone into the world. Here seems to be a fair and pleasant field for them to exercise together, to prove their powers and to prepare them for future and nobler exertions. Not that we would allow our young men to devote their time or talents exclusively, or even to any considerable degree, to work like these. [They are] literary toys. They serve as a kind of sampler, on which they may practice those niceties and beauties of expression, hereafter to be worked in upon more enduring materials; or, to use a more dignified figure, they answer as the cartoons of the Indian artists, on which may be figured in small those creations of fancy and devices of thought, which may afterwards be applied to the more matured and nobler fresco.

The leading annuals of the 'twenties, the ones which exerted the greatest influence upon the short-story form, were *The Atlantic Souvenir*, 1826; *The Token*, edited by S. C. Goodrich, Boston, 1828; *The Legendary*, edited by N. P. Willis, Boston, 1828; *The Talisman*, New York, 1828; and *The Western Souvenir*, edited by James Hall, Cincinnati, 1829. The first of these, after seven issues, was absorbed by its Boston rival, and until 1842 was published annually as *The Token and Atlantic Souvenir*. The fashion spread rapidly until by 1830 the gift book with its sentimental title and its gold and vellum bindings and its elaborate and expensive embellishments had become one of the leading Christmas commodities. Almost every writer of the period from Willis to Edward Everett Hale at one time or another in his career was the editor of at least one of these gorgeous creations. Publishers vied with one another to produce the most attractive specimen, and hardly a city of any size in the country but sometime during the period added at least one to the number. Frederick Faxon has listed nearly two thousand different annuals and gift books, issued in English during the period, more than half of them in America, and there are volumes that escaped his notice.[1] So far as quantity is concerned, the high tide on this side of the ocean came in the mid 'forties. In 1844 the London *Athenæum*, reviewing *The Gift*, could say,

Fashion in literature and works in prose and verse when transplanted to America, continue there to circulate, and even to increase in influence, long after they are forgotten in England. Annuals that have seen their day with us are commencing it with them.

But the annual in 1844 had ceased to be a power; the magazines had begun to come in strongly, and the gift books had become *merely* gift books—articles of merchandise sold not to readers, but to buyers of showy presents. To make them profitable the publishers, and among them even the editor of *The Token*, had begun to take liberties with their customers that may fairly be called unscrupulous. *The Magnolia* for 1836, for instance, between the

[1] *Gift Books and Annuals.* Frederick Faxon. 1910.

time of its first publication and the year 1854, was reissued no
less than twelve times, with twelve different bindings, and twelve
different arrangements of the literary contents, though often
with new illustrations.   It was issued as *The Morning Glory*, as
The Coral, as *Friendship's Token*, as *Memory*, as *The Gift of
Affection*, as *The Snowflake*, as *The Aloe*, and each revamping of
the old material was advertised and sold as a new book.   This
never could have happened had the books been bought to be read,
but after their first decade they seem to have exerted less and less
influence upon the reading public.   William Leete Stone in the
preface of his *Tales and Sketches*, 1834, notes that, "Although
everybody buys the annuals, it is said nobody reads them.   They
only look at the binding and the pictures."   Poe, reviewing
Simms's *The Wigwam and the Cabin*, remarked that "the volume
is a collection of tales most of which were written for the annuals,
and thus have failed in circulating among the masses of the
people."   In one of Miss Sedgwick's tales, "Cacoëthes Scribendi,"
the "hero," in Boston "at the periodical inundation of annuals,"
bought two of the prettiest he could find as a present for his
sweetheart, and, "Poor simple girl! she sat down to read them,
as if an annual was meant to be read."   The result of this reading,
according to Miss Sedgwick was indeed disastrous; the girl was
immediately ruined both in body and in soul.

At best they were a makeshift, a temporary relief during a
transition period that was full of discouragement for the new literary generation, but they played an important part during the
brief time they were in power.   They gave for the first time an
adequate outlet for the writing of the new group, they paid prices
that were remarkable, they insisted upon native themes and
native authors, and thus helped to create a distinctively American
literature, and they suggested and made possible the popular
literary magazine which was to be such a power during the latter
half of the century.   That they were but a temporary expedient,
a bridge to something better, was recognized from the first.[1]

[1] Paulding satirically pictures a book auction in 1829: "The English
annuals were struck off to a picture virtuoso who declared his intention of
cutting out the plates, and throwing the rest away.   The American souvenirs
were knocked on the head by an unlucky observation from a spruce gentleman, who observed that they had not cost one-tenth as much as 'the keepsake' which had been got up at an expense of eleven thousand guineas.   The
fortunate purchaser of the Keepsake, on hearing this, fancied he had got

Only two years after the first *Atlantic Souvenir*, we find *The North American Review* pointing out their fundamental weakness: "We hope the time is not far distant when those among us who are capable of assisting in the great work of building up a national literature may not be compelled to seek for readers through a medium which must depend, in a great measure, for its popularity upon the arts of publication, and upon the selection of a season to secure general circulation." Until this medium did come, however, the annuals bore the burden, and despite all their failings they deserve praise.

III

Excluding the work of Irving, only three short stories produced in America before 1826 have any merit as judged by modern standards: "Recollections," by Franklin Dexter, 1820; "The Adventures of a Watchman," by Dr. Tobias Watkins, 1821; and "Peter Rugg, the Missing Man," by William Austin, 1824.

In 1818, under the leadership of William Hickling Prescott, there had sprung up in Boston a club of congenial souls, for the most part young Harvard graduates, who, though already in their professions—theology, law, medicine—still had dreams of a literary career. The papers read before this club seem to have been so unusual that, as in the case of the Delphian Club in Baltimore at about the same time, it was proposed to publish them in *Sketch-Book*-like numbers, Prescott to be the editor. The result was *The Club Room* (1820), the four numbers of which contain what to-day may fairly be classed with the curiosities of American literature.[1] Among the varied contents, for instance, there is a short story by Edward Everett, a preacher-like production; there is an explained ghost story by Prescott, "Calais," which is said to have made a great impression upon Washington Allston, though it is hard for us to understand why; and there is the first well-told ghost story written in America, "Recollections," by Franklin Dexter (1793–1857), a writer who soon surrendered himself to the law and was lost to American literature.

---

possession of a treasure, though he had only gained the sweepings of English literature, sanctioned by popular names, and embellished with a parcel of engravings from worn-out plates."—"Memoir of the Author" in *Tales of the Good Woman*.

[1] Reviewed by W. H. Prescott under the title, "Essay Writing," in *The North American Review*, April, 1822. An account of the Delphian Club and its members may be found in Scharf's *History of Baltimore*, page 642.

The story, which purports to be told from a manuscript received from a Tyrolese student, who in turn had received it from a friend in the University of Königsberg, depends for its effect not so much upon the culminating sequence of its happenings as upon its unity of atmosphere and its emotional intensity. It begins in the sunshine: "The sun was hastening to a glorious setting as I gained the last hill that overlooks the forest." For a paragraph there is a description of the "glories of the western sky," but as the sun disappeared, the teller of the story, Herman, turned his back upon the glorious scene, "and leaving the moon behind the hill, entered the long dark shadow it threw over the wood at its foot. It was gloomy and chill . . ." and from this chilliness and gloom the story never again emerges. Late at night in the forest he comes to "a large and ruinous structure, which had once been a castle."

I knocked long before I was admitted; at last an old man came to the door with a lantern, and, without a word of welcome, led my horse to the stable, leaving me to find my way into the house. The spirit of the place seemed to have infected its inhabitants. I entered a kitchen, whose extent I could not see by the dim firelight, and, having stirred the embers, sat down to warm me. The old man soon returned, and showed me up the remains of a spacious staircase, to a long hall, in a corner of which was my bed. I extinguished the light, and lay down without undressing; but the thoughts and scenes of the evening had taken strong hold of my mind, and I could not sleep.

He went to the window and looked for a long time out into the night coldly lighted by the moon, and then

My attention was suddenly recalled by a low but distinct sound of some one breathing near me—I turned with a sudden thrill of fear, and saw nothing; and, as the sound had ceased, I readily believed it was a fancy. I soon relapsed into my former train of thought, and had forgotten the circumstance, when I was again startled by a sound I could not mistake— there was some one breathing at my very ear—so terribly certain was the fact, that I did not move even my eyes; it was not the deep regular breath of one asleep, nor the quick panting of guilt, but a quiet gentle respiration; I remained listening till I could doubt no longer and then turned slowly round that I might not be overpowered by the suddenness of the sight, which I knew I must meet—again there was nothing to be seen—the moon shone broad into the shadow on the corners, I am sure nothing visible could have escaped the keenness of my gaze, as I looked again and again along the dark wainscot. My calmness now forsook me, and as I turned fearfully back to the window, my hand brushed against the curtain whose deep folds hid the corner near which I was standing—the blood gushed to my heart with a sharp pang, and I involuntarily dashed my hands forward—they passed through against the damp wall, and the tide of life rolled back, leaving me hardly able to support myself. I stood a few moments lost in fear and wonder—when the breathing began again, and there—in the bright moonlight—I felt the air driven against my face by a being I could not see.   I sat down on the bed in great agitation, and it was a considerable time before I could at all compose my mind—the fact was certain, but the cause inscrutable.

The fleeting vision of his lost Gertrude; her half-heard whisper, "But one year more!" his voluntary impulse to go the next day to Underwalden, the home of Gertrude; his arrival just as she was being lowered into the grave, and his departure for Rome for preparation for his death—and the story closes abruptly: "I have watched the fall of the last leaves in Underwalden; I shall return to see them put forth once more, but when they fall again, they will cover the grave of Herman." There is no moral; there is crudeness in parts and unnecessary material, but viewed against the background of its times it is a remarkable tale, the work of one who had a sense of artistic effect, one who, had he given himself wholly to literature, could not have failed to have produced distinctive work.

"The Adventures of a Watchman," one of the tales in Dr. Watkins's *Tales of the Tripod*, "was taken," as the author explains in his preface, "from an anonymous German correspondent of the 'Lesefrüchte.'[1]   It pleased me and I did it into English, expressly to amuse the Delphian Club."   Since it was the fashion of the time to publish anonymously and to attribute the authorship of one's tale or book to some mythical source, the reader of such an explanation is inclined to be cautious.   This, however, was no hoax: the tale is a faithful translation of Heinrich Zschokke's "Das Abenteuer der Neujahrsnacht."   It is the quality of the translation as viewed against its times that makes it worthy of consideration.   It was the first bit of American fiction, original or otherwise, that has sprightliness of style, rapidity of movement by means of conversation, and sparkling dialogue.   Good dia-

[1]Undoubtedly *Lesefrüchte von Felde de neusten Literatur*, gesammelt und herausgegeben von J. C. Pappe. Hamburg, 1816–30.

logue came late into our literature. The conversational parts of Cooper are wooden and stilted, and even Irving failed whenever he made his characters speak. But Dr. Watkins's version is more sprightly even than the original German, more sprightly and sparkling indeed than Parke Godwin's translation of the tale a generation nearer our own day. From this point of view the story is remarkable. It shows that even in the America of *The Spy* and *The Sketch Book* there was at least one writer who could appreciate adequate dialogue. That his work made any impression, however, upon the Delphians who heard it read or upon the readers who bought the book there is no evidence. We know that it made no permanent impression upon its own author, for the other tales of his collection are more wooden even than the average of his day. Had Cooper or Irving made the translation and put it into the fierce light that beat upon all of their early writings, it might perhaps have changed the style of much of our later fiction.

The third notable bit of work of the early period is "Peter Rugg, the Missing Man," a tale that stands in curious solitude amid the fiction of the New England 'twenties.[1] Its author, William Austin, a graduate of Harvard in the class with William Ellery Channing and Longfellow's father, and in later years a successful lawyer, is included among the writers of fiction because of this single piece. Two other short stories he is known to have written: "The Late Joseph Natterstrom," *New England Magazine*, 1831, and "Martha Gardner," *American Monthly Magazine*, 1837, but both of them are deservedly forgotten. His "Peter Rugg," however, made an impression from the first. Buckingham, who first published it, says in his *Personal Memoirs*, "This article was reprinted in other papers and books, and read more than any newspaper communication that has fallen within my knowledge." Interest in the story has been revived from time to time until now it is everywhere recognized as one of the strongest of the early American short stories.

From the standpoint of artistic form it is not at all above the average of its day. It has no single thread of action and interest

---

[1] *The Literary Papers of William Austin* were published in Boston in 1890. Higginson's "A Precursor of Hawthorne" appeared in the *Independent*, March 29, 1888. See also *The Outlook*, January 26, 1907, and Baldwin's *American Short Stories*, page 59.

leading to a climax; it is not condensed and rapid of movement; it contains rather a series of glimpses by various persons of one Peter Rugg, a mysterious driver of a mysterious chaise and a miscellany of evidence about him and his movements.   The story is in two parts, for after his first success the author added a sequel, following a plan so loose that he might have expanded it into a book with indefinitely added adventures and testimony of witnesses.   Moreover, the two parts have motifs that are different: The first is the Wandering Jew motif: for a single blasphemous outburst,—"I will see home to-night in spite of the last tempest, or may I never see home!"—he is condemned to spend the years in an agonizing attempt to find Boston and his home, driving wildly over the roads and always in the wrong direction.   It suggests also "The Man Without a Country" of later years.   In the second part there is the "Rip Van Winkle" motif: Peter Rugg finally gets to his home, only to find everything changed and all who knew him gone.   The supernatural element is suddenly dropped and he becomes a pathetic, Rip-like figure.

Then spake a voice from the crowd, but whence it came I could not discern: "There is nothing strange here but yourself, Mr. Rugg.   Time, which destroys and renews all things, has dilapidated your house, and placed us here.   You have suffered many years under an illusion.   The tempest which you profanely defied at Metonomy has at last subsided; but you will never see home, for your house and wife and neighbors have all disappeared.   Your estate, indeed, remains, but no home.   You were cut off from the last age, and you can never be fitted to the present.   Your home is gone, and you can never have another home in this world."

It is the "Rip Van Winkle" of New England literature, a folk legend with its roots in the supernatural.   It was this that gave it its popularity among the people of the region it describes.   Its strength as a short story lies in its atmosphere and in its skillful maneuvering along the narrow No Man's Land which divides the seen from the unseen.   Everywhere there are suggestions of Hawthorne, and that Hawthorne, who was a college student when it was published, had read the tale we know from the curious melange which he called "A Virtuoso's Collection."   Here the Virtuoso, who proves to be the Wandering Jew, has as his door-keeper Peter Rugg; and as the romancer enters to view the collection he is greeted dolorously at the portal: "'I beseech you, kind sir,' said he, in a cracked, melancholy tone, 'have pity on the most unfortunate man in the world. For Heaven's sake, answer me a single question: Is this the town of Boston?'"

To compare the story with the other tales contemporary with it is to realize its unique quality. Charles Brockden Brown, with whom Austin is often compared, never lets go of the actual world: he must deal with the accountable, with somnambulists, ventriloquists, and with varieties of insane people. "Peter Rugg" leaves its reader tantalizingly uncertain to the end and then leaves him uncertain. It creates an atmosphere but it explains nothing. That Hawthorne derived anything from his early reading of "Peter Rugg" is improbable, and yet among all the work written before the period of the great romancer there is nothing that offers so many points of resemblance as does this early tale.

IV

The leading annual of the pioneer period of the annuals was *The Atlantic Souvenir*—1826-1832—issued from Philadelphia. During the seven years before it was merged with *The Token* it published no less than forty-seven short stories, or an average of over six to each volume. Thirteen of these tales must be marked anonymous, but the others were written by thirteen different authors, of whom six—James Kirke Paulding, Richard Penn Smith, Godfrey Wallace, Catharine Maria Sedgwick, William Leete Stone and Lydia Maria Child—contributed more than one tale. These six and the *Talisman* group, and *The Token* group of Boston led by Sarah Josepha Hale, Samuel Griswold Goodrich, and Nathaniel Parker Willis, constitute the leading short-story writers of the period before the rise of Hawthorne and Poe.

Of these the two of most import to the readers of the decade were Paulding and Miss Sedgwick. Paulding had furnished three tales for the first volume of *The Atlantic Souvenir* and eleven for the entire seven volumes. Beginning his literary career with Irving as co-editor of *Salmagundi*, during the two following decades he had poured out a surprising amount of material—no less than twenty volumes in almost every possible literary form, a great amount of it material which has never been collected. Emulous of Irving, he tried Knickerbocker sketches and volumes, Spanish romantic tales, broad humor and satire mostly in prose, historical novels, essays, and a biography of Washington. He lacked Irving's restraint; he entered too many fields. His many short stories, though free from the floridness of the times and containing often really brilliant narrative and description, as in "The Yankee Roué," for instance, yet fail completely as wholes. Some are overromantic, some oversatiric, all are rambling and unconvincing. He was witty rather than humorous, satirical rather than sympathetic. Hardly one of the tales is remembered to-day. His story, "The Ghost," a sea tale, at first seems convincing, but when we learn that the specter is a Kanaka sailor who swims all day and part of the night the most of the time under water in the wake of the vessel, to climb aboard at midnight for food, we lose interest.

Miss Sedgwick, however, was the most popular short-story writer of the decade. At a time when most work in annuals and magazines was published anonymously, her name or her signature, "by the Author of *Redwood*," always appeared at the head of her tales. She was considered as a financial asset to any annual or other periodical that was fortunate enough to secure her work. She was the most prominent contributor to the first and second volumes of *The Atlantic Souvenir*, though it was edited at Philadelphia, and she furnished the opening tale for *The Legendary* and for Bryant's *Tales of Glauber Spa*. Unlike Paulding, she refused to be hastened, and the amount of her work is comparatively small.

In the history of New England fiction she must be rated as a significant figure. When she began to write there was everywhere about her a sharply defined antagonism to all save the moral tale or the eighteenth-century apologue essay; when she died in 1867 New Englanders were reading everywhere not only *The Lamplighter*, but Robert Bonner's New York *Ledger* with its extreme Sylvanus Cobb type of melodramatic romance. Miss Sedgwick's work marks the beginning of the transition. She began with Hannah More religious tracts, and during all her life at intervals she produced such moral and didactic fiction as that in her "Stories for Young Persons." At the same time she wrote highly colored tales of the Middle Ages full of revengeful monks, mad queens, wandering knights, and superlatively fair maidens—tales suggested, perhaps, by Scott and Irving, but often running as completely into the melodramatic as Anne Radcliffe's *Udolpho*. That Catharine Sedgwick wrote the tale was enough for many of her generation. Even the daughters of the Puritans did not scruple to read "Le Bossu," though its author had dared boldly to announce that she wrote romance simply to amuse, "without any purpose or hope to slay giants or to supply mediocre readers with small moral hints on various subjects that come up in daily life." Paulding, her leading rival in the world of the annuals and gift books, considered her one of the leading literary forces of her time, and summed her up as having "wit, and keen observation of life and manners, based on good sense." There has been no better summary.

Her place, however, is not with the short-story writers. Her pen was constantly in demand by annuals and lady's books, but the work she furnished was miniature novels rather than short stories. Like Scott and Cooper, she was impatient of restraint; her lawless romanticism needed unlimited room, and she struck out without thought of bounds. "Le Bossu," written for *Tales of Glauber Spa*, proceeds like a romance for thirty thousand words, then ends in a huddle as if time had been called. One of her early biographers naïvely explains that her *New England Tale* (1822) was begun as a religious tract, but, expanding in her hands "beyond the limits of such publications," it was finally made into a novel. Despite the fact that her tales appear in all the leading annuals and magazines during a generation, she must be classed with the romancers and the novelists and not with the short-story writers.

V

Miss Sedgwick was not alone in this peculiarity. That there was any difference between the novel and the tale save in the one attribute of length no one of the gift-book school seems to have suspected. *The Token*, volume four, complained of the undue length of all the material submitted to it. Dana's explanation in number five of his *Idle Man* is amusing to-day: "A story," he complained, "will sometimes run to a greater length than was intended." He had begun "Paul Fenton" as a tale, but it had grown in his hands until it crowded out all the other material that he had intended to use and made of the number a huge affair almost as large as all the others put together. Sands halts the movement of his story, "Mr. Green," to explain that it was "a plain tale, which *might* make two volumes duodecimo, but must here be restricted to a nouvelette of some fifty pages."

Undoubtedly the short story of the annuals was greatly affected by the Review type of essay fashionable at the time. In 1817, a writer in *The North American Review* after having used four pages on topics only remotely connected with his subject, makes a fresh start:

> But enough of this; and now to our author. He must excuse us, for even reviewers, like the ladies, must follow the fashion; and a review, nowadays, without a dissertation at its head, would look about as singular as a slender maid of sixteen, in close rapt muslin and simple smoothly plaited hair, amidst expanded hoops and storied headdresses, on a St. James Court-day.

It was felt by many that tales should follow the same fashion. Bryant, for instance, in his "The Marriage Blunder" begins with a lengthly dissertation upon marriage, then tells with detail of a journey he once made into the Red River country, describes a peculiar man he encountered there, and then, after twelve pages, or one-third the total number of words, have been used, proceeds to the tale proper as told him by this man. John Neal in his tale, "Otter-Bag," uses twenty of his sixty pages for describing the habits and general history of the North American Indians.

It was a time, too, of ornate diction and flamboyant figurative language, "the expanded hoops and storied headdresses" of the literary fashion. Prescott attributed the fact to the widespread influence of Irving. His work "is the very worst model in the world for the imitation of writers, especially of young writers, who, wanting genuine sensibility, will only expose the beggarly condition of their thoughts the more by arraying them in this gorgeous apparel." Another, writing at the same time, offered another explanation: "The general tone of our popular compositions has been showy and declamatory, a natural result of the influence of free and independent forms of government upon the buoyant spirits of a young, enterprising, and prosperous people."[1]

Whatever the cause, it is certain that this gorgeousness of style is a leading characteristic of almost all the members of the gift book school of fiction. A straightforward statement of fact seems

[1] An opinion repeated in later years by Thomas Wentworth Higginson: "Literature in a new country naturally tends to the florid, as had been shown by the novels of Charles Brockden Brown, or even so severe a work as Bancroft's History of the United States."—*A Reader's History of American Literature.* 1903. P. 143.

to have been regarded by this generation of writers as an unliterary thing to be avoided. Everything is elaborately ornate. "Ulrick Guyon, in the morning of life, basked beneath fortune's sunshine," begins the tale, and not once does it descend to lower levels. It is as if the characters were quoting constantly from a book of elegant extracts. One of Sand's lovers has proposed and as a reward gets this response from his inamorata: "My father's will must be law to me. Want of filial piety is a bad omen for matrimonial felicity." Dana in his tale, "The Son," speaks of one of his characters not as a negro, but as one having "affinity with that gallant race, by the conquest of whom Scipio earned his distinguishing appellation," and the author of "The Son of a Gentleman," volume two of *The Token*, instead of locating the tale in the year when the Erie Canal was completed, explains that it was the year "when the gentle maiden Erie stretched forth her long slender arm and was wedded to the boisterous Atlantic." Even Bryant, who in later years could place among his rules for young writers: "Call a spade by its name, not a well-known oblong implement of manual labor; let a home be a home, not a residence; a place, not a locality"—even he, in his *Talisman* story, "The Whirlwind," instead of saying that a Baptist minister was traveling to Lexington to baptize some converts, explained that he was on his way "to perform beside the translucent streams and under the venerable trees of that fine region, those picturesque solemnities of his sect, to which they love to point as a manifold emblem of purification from moral pollution, and of the resurrection from the death of sin and the sleep of the grave."

Another prevailing weakness in the tales of the period is in characterization. The characters do not reveal themselves: they are revealed; the author does all the work. The shrewish widow meets the choleric Frenchman and sets her cap for him:

She was weary of having nobody but servants to govern; besides, she was a lady of spirit, and she felt herself moved by a noble ambition of taming so intractable a creature as Monsieur Du Lac. She, therefore, began to treat him with extreme civility and deference, inquired, with the tenderest interest, the state of his health, sent him prescriptions for his maladies and good things from her well-stored pantry, and whenever they met, accosted him with her mildest words and softest accents, and chastened the usual terror of her eye into a catlike sleepiness and languor of look, etc.

Monsieur Du Lac, delighted at the prospect of securing "so accomplished a nurse in the midst of his increasing infirmities, offered her his hand, and after a proper exhibition of coyness, hesitation, and deliberation, was accepted," etc. Then came the storm, but it is simply described objectively.

There is no dialogue: all is exposition. We do not once hear the virago's voice, or feel her or even see her. A later writer, like Miss Wilkins, for instance, or George W. Cable, would have made her a veritable presence, that would haunt us even after we had laid down the book.

And yet there is much to be praised in the gift books. There are tales whole pages of which are worth quoting. Here and there are well-drawn characters, excellent specimens of dialogue, well-handled situations. Bryant's tale, "Medfield," for instance, has a theme which, had it been better handled, would have made it one of the select few tales in American literature. It was an early precursor of Maupassant's "Le Hula" and Bierce's "The Damned Thing." The author prepares his reader by scientific exposition after the manner Poe was to use in later years:

Of all the senses the touch is the least liable to delusion and mistake. I never heard of an instance in which the touch became subject to an illusion while the eye remained faithful to reason and the truth of things. In all the idle and silly stories of ghosts and apparitions, in which I believe as little as you do, the supposed supernatural visitor always addresses himself to the eye or the ear; the haunted person sees its form or distinguishes its voice; he rarely ever feels its substance.

The writer then, in the first person, informs us that he is a man subject to violent paroxysms of anger at the least opposition to his will, and that after the death of his gentle wife, the only restraining influence he had ever known, he once, as he was losing control of his temper, felt a firm grasp upon his arm. Exploring for the cause, he had recognized his wife's hand by the feeling of the ring he had given her, but he could see nothing. This had been repeated until it had ceased to move him, but at last had come the day when rage was about to destroy him: in a whirlwind of passion he was about to strike a man dead when he felt himself suddenly seized and pinioned by unseen forces that felt like bony arms. Groping with his hands for the cause, he discovered that he was held as in a vise by two skeletons, invisible

yet fearfully real to the touch. When his rage had given place to
terror, he was released, and as suddenly as he had been seized.
There is no explanation and no comment.

The failures of the story come at the points where most of the
other tales of the period fail. The materials are excellent, but
they are not handled with effect. The narrative is wordy; the
introduction is too long and it is not skillfully joined to the second
part. Despite the scientific approach, there is lack of verisimilitude. It does not strike the reader as a real experience: it does
not grip and convince as a story of the kind must do if it is to be
told at all. The flood of horror that would surge over one who
felt such a hand upon his arm should be communicated to the
reader, but the reader of "Medfield" does not shudder; on the
contrary, when there enter the two skeletons, hired, doubtless, by
the wife on account of their superior strength, he is inclined to
smile. Then suddenly at the close comes the suspicion, one cannot explain why, that the final intent of the story is ethical, that
it is a craftily concealed sermon.

The short stories of the gift-book period, then, may be summed
up in general as lacking in constructive art, as lacking compression, as lacking in simplicity and naturalness and verisimilitude, as lacking, indeed, most of those elements which in later
years followed the realization that the short story is not a novel
in miniature, but an independent art form with laws definite and
compelling. Yet, despite all these imperfections, even in 1830
Miss Mary Russell Mitford could declare that American "lighter
fiction" surpassed anything of the kind in Great Britain, and could
deem it worth while to issue three volumes of it for the edification
of her countrymen. Her introduction is a document in the history
of the American short story:

To remedy this deficiency in our own literature by presenting to the
English public some specimens of the shorter American stories, is the
intention of the following work. The selection has been made partly
from detached tales, but principally from a great mass of Annuals, Magazines, and other periodicals, embracing many of the most popular
productions of the most popular living writers of the Western world.
Amongst these I am chiefly indebted to Messrs. Verplanck, Paulding,
Hall, Neal, Barker, Willis, and Stone, and, though last, far from least,
to Miss Sedgwick; some of the pieces are altogether anonymous, and of
some the signature is entirely fictitious. . . . In fixing on the different

pieces, my principal aim has been to keep the book as national and characteristic as possible. Many a clever essay have I rejected because it might have been written on this side of the Atlantic.

It is noteworthy that she published no selections from the work of Irving. Her reason is also noteworthy: "In spite of a few inimitable sketches of New York in its Dutch estate, his writings are essentially European, and must be content to take their station amongst the Spectators and Tatlers of the Mother Country."

It is noteworthy also that ten years later, in 1840, there should have been established in London what in reality is the first American short-story magazine, *The American Miscellany of Popular Tales, Essays, Sketches of Character, Poetry, and Jeux D'esprit by Transatlantic authors*, published weekly on Saturdays. The first volume of it, a book of 460 pages, containing above fifty tales and as many "popular sketches," is a notable document in the history of American shorter fiction. As did Miss Mitford, it excluded the work of Irving as not American, but it republished nearly everything else of notable American short fiction and sketch work produced before 1840. Tales with peculiarly native background were frequent in its issues, as, for example, Mrs. Child's "Chicorua's Curse," Mrs. Hale's "The Emigrant," Flint's "The Indian Fighter," Mrs. Kirkland's "Romance in the Forest," and several of John Neal's. The editors seemed even more attracted by tales of the *Lady's Book* type, such as those by Mrs. E. C. Embury, Ann Stephens, H. W. Herbert, Mrs. Seba Smith, Miss Leslie, Caroline Orne, and a dozen others. Especially emphasized was the wild tale, "Datura Fastuosa, Translated from the German of Hoffman by an American," and "Elsie Armand. From the German," by Mrs. Ellet. The quality of the literary art of these stories was constantly held up as the basis of choice of material. Such "elegant" and elevated styles as are found in Willis's "Unwritten Poetry," Dana's "Filial Affection," D. L. Hillhouse's "The Beggar of Florence," and E. Maturin's "The Death of Nero" seem to have been especially attractive to the editors.

Thus it was the American short story, crude affair though it was in its earlier forms, that first won its way in England as literature distinctively and uniquely American. Cooper was "the American Scott," Irving was "the American Addison," and Bryant was "the American Wordsworth," but the native writers of short fiction for the annuals and the periodicals were producing something that had no prototype in the older lands, a literary form that was to grow in excellence with every decade until it could serve at last as the model for the story-tellers of the rest of the world.

BIBLIOGRAPHY

LEADING SHORT STORIES OF THE 'TWENTIES

The Red Book, John P. Kennedy. Baltimore, 1818–19.

The Club Room [William H. Prescott]. Boston, 1820.
  "Lake George," W. H. Gardner; "Recollections," Franklin Dexter; "Calais," W. H. Prescott; "Memorial," Edward Everett.

Tales of the Tripod; or, a Delphian Evening. Pertinax Particular [Dr. Tobias Watkins]. Baltimore. 1821.
  "Adventures of a Watchman," and others.

The Idle Man, Richard H. Dana. Boston, 1821–22.
  "The Son," "Edward and Mary"; "Thomas Thornton"; "Paul Fenton."

Carwin the Biloquist, and Other American Tales and Pieces. Charles Brockden Brown. London, 1822.
  "Carwin the Biloquist"; "Stephen Calvert"; "Jessica."

Buckingham's *New England Galaxy.* Boston, 1824.
  "Peter Rugg, the Missing Man," by William Austin.

The Atlantic Souvenir for 1826. Philadelphia.
  "The Eve of St. John," James K. Paulding; "The Catholic Iroquois," Catharine M. Sedgwick; "A Tale of Mystery; or, the Youth That Died Without a Disease," James K. Paulding; "The Spanish Girl of the Cordillera," James K. Paulding; "A Revolutionary Story," L; "The Wardstellen."

The Atlantic Souvenir for 1827. Philadelphia.
  "Modern Chivalry," Catharine M. Sedgwick; "The White Indian," James K. Paulding; "The Green Mountain Boy," J. N. Barker; "The Little Dutch Sentinel of Manhadoes," James K. Paulding; "The Rival Brothers," Lydia M. Child; "The Trials of the Troth," Grenville Mellen; "A Legend of the Eusons."

Village Tales, or Recollections of By-Past Times. Oliver Oakwood [Stacy Gardner Potts]. Trenton, N. J., 1827.

Tales of the Night. By a Lady of Maine [Sally Saywood Wood]. Portland, Maine, 1827.

The Philadelphia Monthly Magazine. 1827-28.
"The Ice Island," "The Spirit of the Reeds," "The Phantom Players,"—all by Robert Montgomery Bird.

The Atlantic Souvenir for 1828.
"Heaven and Earth"; "Prediction," Richard Penn Smith; "The Poet's Tale," J. K. Paulding; "The Stepmother"; "Cobus Yerks," J. K. Paulding; "The Young West Indian," Lydia M. Child; "The Rifle," William Leggett.

The Legendary for 1828.   Boston, N. P. Willis, editor.
Vol. I. May. "Romance in Real Life," C. M. Sedgwick; "The Indian Wife," Lydia M. Child; "Unwritten Poetry," N. P. Willis; "The Frontier House."
Vol. II. November. "Extracts from a Sea Book," S. Hazard; "The Camp Meeting"; "Leaves from a Colleger's Album," N. P. Willis; "Unwritten Philosophy," N. P. Willis.

The Talisman for 1828, 1829, 1830.   New York.   W. C. Bryant, editor.
"Adventure in the West Indies," "The Cascade of Melsingak," "Recollections of South Spain," "A Story of the Island of Cuba," "The Indian Spring," "The Whirlwind," "The Marriage Blunder," "Legend of the Devil's Pulpit"—all by W. C. Bryant; "Mr. Viellecour and His Neighbours," Sands and Verplanck; "The Peregrinations of Petrus Mudd," "Major Egerton," and "Gelyna, a Tale of Albany and Ticonderoga," by Verplanck; "The German's Story," Sands or Verplanck.

The Token for 1828.   Boston.
"Some Passages in the Life of an Old Maid"; "The Fair Pilgrim"; "The Mysterious Rival"; "Anne Herbert"; "A Moonlight Adventure"; "The Legend of Mt. Lamentation"; "The Voyage of the Philosophers"; "The Hidden Treasure"; "The Hermitess"; "A Bridal in the Early Settlements"; "The Lone Indian"; "The Adventure of the Raindrop"; "The Recluse of the Lake"; "A Canadian Legend."

Sad Tales and Glad Tales.   By Reginald Reverie [Grenville Mellen]. Boston, 1828.
"The Palisadoes"; "The Spy and the Traitor"; "The Meeting of the Planets"; "The Presidency in 1825"; "The Tale of an Aëronaut."

The Atlantic Souvenir for 1829.
"The Esmeralda," Godfrey Wallace; "Benhadir," J. K. Paulding; "The Emigrant's Story," Richard Penn Smith; "The Methodist's Story"; "Narantsauk"; "The Catholic."

The Token for 1829.

"The Seaman's Widow," Grenville Mellen; "The Son of a Gentleman"; "Retrospections"; "Ma Petite Pupille"; "The Ruse," N. P. Willis; "The Drowned Alive," William Leete Stone; "Otter-Bag, the Oneida Chief," John Neal; "The Blind Boy"; "The Emigrant," Sarah Josepha Hale.

Tales of the Good Woman by a Doubtful Gentleman. James K. Paulding. New York, 1829.

"The Yankee Roué"; "The Drunkard"; "Dyspepsia"; "Old Times in the New World."

Chronicles of the City of Gotham. James K. Paulding. New York, 1830.

The Atlantic Souvenir for 1830.

"A Romance of the Border," William Leete Stone; "Reconciliation"; "Cacoëthes Scribendi," Catharine Maria Sedgwick; "The Ghost," James K. Paulding; "The Village School," Richard Penn Smith; "The Fawn's Leap"; "Love's Falconrie"; "A Legend of the Hurons," Samuel S. Boyd; "Early Impressions. A Fragment," Charles Sealsfield [Carl Postl]; "The Heroine of Suli," Godfrey Wallace.

The Token for 1830.

"The Doomed Bride," Grenville Mellen; "The Young Provincial," possibly Hawthorne; "The Captain's Lady," James Hall; "The Country Cousin," Catharine M. Sedgwick; "The Wag-Water," Samuel Hazard; "Chocorua's Curse," Lydia M. Child; "The Utilitarian," John Neal; "The Indian Fighter," Timothy Flint.

Tales and Sketches by a Cosmopolite. James Lawson. 1830.

"Flora McDonald"; "The Dapper Gentleman's Story"; "A Legend of Kent"; "The Spendthrift."

Sketches of American Character. Mrs. Sarah J. Hale. Boston, 1830.

Stories of American Life. By American Writers. Edited by Mary Russell Mitford. Three volumes. London, 1830. Introduction signed January 28, 1830.

Vol. I. "Otter-Bag," John Neal; "The French Village," James Hall; "The Country Cousin," Miss Sedgwick; "The Sick Man Cured"; "Mr. De Viellecour and His Neighbours," Verplanck; "The Esmeralda," Godfrey Wallace; "The Tutor," James Hall; "The Indian Hater," James Hall.

Vol. II. "Pete Featherton," James Hall; "The Drunkard," James K. Paulding; "The Marriage Blunder," William Cullen Bryant; "A Romance of the Border," William Leete Stone; "The Ghost," James K. Paulding; "The Seaman's Widow," Grenville Mellen; "Unwritten Philosophy," N. P. Willis; "Scenes in Washington."

Vol. III. "The Catholic Iroquois," Miss Sedgwick; "The Peregrinations of Petrus Mudd," Verplánck; "Unwritten Poetry," N. P. Willis; "The Captain's Lady," James Hall; "The Isle of Shoals"; "The Idle Man," R. H. Dana; "Cacoëthes Scribendi," Miss Sedgwick; "The Fawn's Leap"; "Reminiscences of New York"; "The Little Dutch Sentinel of the Manhadoes," Paulding; "The Rifle," William Leggett.

The Atlantic Souvenir for 1831.
"Giles Heaterly, the Free Trader," Godfrey Wallace; "Three Score and Ten"; "A Day in New York a Century Since"; "The Dead of the Wreck," William Leete Stone; "The First Born," Richard Penn Smith; "The Eve of St. Andrew," James K. Paulding.

The Token for 1831.
"Sights from a Steeple," Nathaniel Hawthorne; "The New England Village"; "The Village Musician," James Hall; "Mary Dyre," Catharine M. Sedgwick; "Lord Vapourcourt"; "Te Zahpohtah," William J. Snelling; "The Fated Family," possibly Hawthorne; "The Adventurer," J. D. H.; "The Haunted Quack," Joseph Nicholson [Nathaniel Hawthorne].

The Spirit of the Annuals for 1831. Philadelphia. E. Littell, 1831.

The Atlantic Souvenir for 1832.
"The Haunted Man," John Neal; "The Mortgage," Godfrey Wallace; "A Night of Peril," William Leete Stone; "The Indian Bride"; "The Dunce and the Genius," James K. Paulding.

The Token for 1832.
"The Indian Summer"; "The Gentle Boy," Nathaniel Hawthorne; "Roger Malvern's Burial," Hawthorne; "David Whicher"; "My Cousin Lucy," James Hall; "My Wife's Novel"; "The Bashful Man"; "A Sketch of a Blue-Stocking," Catharine M. Sedgwick; "Wives of the Dead," Nathaniel Hawthorne.

Tales of Glauber Spa. Bryant and Others. New York, 1832.
"Le Bossu," Catharine M. Sedgwick; "Childe Roeliff's Pilgrimage," James K. Paulding; "The Skeleton's Cave," Bryant; "Medfield," Bryant; "The Block-house," William Leggett; "Mr. Green," Robert C. Sands; "Selim," Paulding; "Boyuca," R. C. Sands.

The Book of Saint Nicholas. Translated from the original Dutch of Dominie. Nicholas Segidius Oudenarde [James Kirke Paulding]. 1836.

American Stories for Young People. Edited by Mary Russell Mitford. 1832.

Lights and Shadows of American Life, edited by Mary Russell Mitford. In three volumes. London, 1832.
Vol. I. "The Politician," Paulding; "Elizabeth Latimer"; "The

Squatter," Leggett; "Pinchon," Snelling; "The Devil's Pulpit, a Legend," Bryant; "The Binnacle."

Vol. II. "The Young Backwoodsman," Flint; "Major Egerton," Verplanck; "An Adventure at Sea," William Leggett; "The Green Mountain Boy, a Tale of Ticonderoga," J. N. Barker; "Cobus Yerks," Paulding; "The Wag-Water," S. Hazard.

Vol. III. "The Azure Hose," Paulding; Weenokhenchah Wandeetteekah," Snelling; "The Three Indians"; "Modern Chivalry," Sedgwick; "The Isle of Flowers, a Canadian Legend"; "The Last of the Boatmen," Neville.

CHAPTER III

I

The decade and a half after *The Sketch Book* and *The Spy* may be termed the period of flamboyant Americanism in our native literature. It was "the era of good feeling," the era of "Spread-eagle" Fourth-of-July oratory, the era of national expansion. The success of Scott with his native backgrounds, of Miss Edgeworth with her Irish fiction, of Irving with his American legends, and Cooper with his American historical romance, had suggested the idea of a native literature in America which should make use of the rich stores of legend and history that lay everywhere undeveloped. Sydney Smith's taunt had had its effect. On all sides were heard voices crying for distinctively American productions. In 1822, William H. Gardiner in a review of *The Spy* filled five pages of the conservative old *North American Review* with a resonant demand for native romance. Materials for it, he declared, lay all about in embarrassing profusion: "In no one country on the face of the globe can there be found a greater variety of specific character than is at this moment developed in this United States of America." Thereupon he proceeded to give a catalogue a page long of the various human types peculiar to America, from the Yankee peddler and the wild boatman of the Ohio to the aristocrat of the southern plantation and the cosmopolitan merchant of New York.

Irving, more than anyone else, had set Americans to thinking of legends. Quickly the collecting of old traditions, like the Peter Rugg legend for instance, became a fad. It was discovered that America was full of such picturesque material. "No inch of our ground," declared a contemporary reviewer, "is without its peculiar association, its appropriate legend; and it seems hardly more than filial affection to gather and garner up these little mementoes of our fathers' joys and trials before time shall have marked them as alms of oblivion." The annual edited by Willis in 1829 took as its name "The Legendary" and added as its subtitle, "original pieces in prose and verse; tales, ballads, and romances chiefly illustrative of American history, scenery, and manners."

It was the period when the Indian was believed to be the leading subject for American romance. For a generation every young writer who essayed either poetry or fiction tried his prentice hand upon an Indian legend. There is a whole shelf of such material: *Yamoyden, Hobomok, Mog Megone,* and the rest. In reviewing the novel *York Town, A Historical Romance,* in 1827, *The American Quarterly Review* could speak of the Indian as the leading romantic topic in America:

> If a writer in this country wishes to make its history or its traditions the subject of romantic fiction, high wrought, obscure, and somewhat extravagant, agreeably to the taste of the times, he must go back to the aborigines. It is there that the materials of character, situations, and superstitions are to be found in abundant profusion; it is among them that life is full of romance and adventure.

As late as 1836 N. P. Willis wrote in his tale, "The Cherokee's Threat": "The wrongs of civilization to the noble aborigines of America are a subject of much poetical feeling in the United States and will ultimately become the poetry of the nation." From the first it was a favorite theme with the writers of native tales. Hardly a gift book but had its Indian legend in which the "noble redman"—a white man really, daubed with vermilion—was made either pathetic or else heroic.

The annuals from the first insisted upon exclusively native material. The initial number of *The Atlantic Souvenir* announced that "every article is the production of our own citizens," and, following this lead, hardly an issue of any of the leading gift books but boasted that not only was its written work strictly home-made, but its engravings and embellishments as well. The editor of the second volume of *The Token* (1829) could even congratulate his readers upon the opening of a new era in American literature:

> We are happy to observe that a new era in literature and the arts has dawned upon our country. Our writers of historical fiction now present the world with tales into which are woven our own rivers, lakes, hills, mountains, meadows, and prairies—our own spring and summer, autumn

and winter—our own heroes and our own society; thus adding to the national interest felt in "our own, our native land," the finer associations of poetry and romance.

But for a new era in literature far more is needed than mere native materials. The *Keepsakes* and the *Books of Beauty* of England were swarming with Byronic romance. There must be a hero, and he must come from the Greek archipelago or from the recesses of the Alps or the Apennines, and there must be bandits and corsairs and castles and dark forests. The Puritanic Miss Sedgwick, who at times could be the Hannah More and the Miss Mitford of her native Berkshires, delighted to let her imagination run Scott-like upon such mediæval themes as "Le Bossu" and "The White Scarf," and Paulding, who with Irving was the keeper of the Dutch traditions of the Hudson, liked to let himself go in such tales as "The Eve of St. John" and "The Spanish Girl of the Cordillera." Even in a publication as aggressively American as *The Western Souvenir* there is a *Tale of the Greek Revolution*. Such romance was in the air; readers demanded it. It was modified by the new interest in American history and tradition, but, as we shall see, it emerged in the midcentury as a tide that for a time swept over all landmarks.

It dominated even the American materials of the early patriotic annuals. The central figure of the legendary tale might be an Indian, but he was quickly romanticized out of all lifelikeness, and made an aboriginal count or baron or bandit. The heroine of Miss Sedgwick's tale, "The Catholic Iroquois," is made an Indian Joan of Arc. The materials and the workman may have been American, but all else was English.

II

The attention of the East was first called to the trans-Allegheny region as a background for sketches and tales by a story in *The Atlantic Souvenir* for 1828, entitled "The Rifle, by the author of *Leisure Hours at Sea*." The writer was William Leggett, a New Yorker who had gone West with his father at seventeen and for three years had lived as a settler on the newly opened frontier in Illinois. The prairie setting of the tale, sketched in by one who was known to have first-hand knowledge of what he wrote, and the descriptions of frontier crime and of frontier methods with criminals, struck the reading public as something new. Later in *The New York Mirror*, of which he became the editor, he published other tales of western life notably "The Squatter," and in 1829 he issued a collection entitled *Tales of a Country Schoolmaster*.

It is very evident to-day that Leggett, who later became a national figure as an editor of *The Evening Post* with Bryant and as an abolitionist, has been overpraised for this pioneer material. The novelty of his backgrounds concealed from his early readers, his almost total failure as a story-teller, but even his backgrounds, as we see them now, are sadly lacking. Everything is general. With a few changes the tales might be transferred to New England or even to Russia. The narrative is sprawly and full of digressions; the dialogue is theatrical. The squatter and his wife, even in the seclusion of their home, talk to each other in sentences like these:

"Look not so wildly, William," replied his wife, "nor attach so much importance to the aimless curiosity of yonder lawyer. His visit will doubtless be brief; and whatever be its object, it cannot be possible that any suspicion ——"

"Do not name that dreadful, that hateful occurrence," said he, interrupting her. "Do not name it, Eleanor, lest the winds should reveal the secret, and I should yet meet the fate so narrowly avoided. It is not for myself—not on my own account, my best beloved,—that my heart has grown so feverish and faint," etc.

Much better is he as a teller of sea yarns. In such tales as "The Main-Truck or a Leap for Life," and "Charles Maitland, or the Mess-Chest," he may be compared to advantage even with Cooper.

The real pioneer in Western fiction was not Leggett, but Judge James Hall of Vandalia, Illinois, who in 1828 issued *The Western Souvenir* for 1829, a gift book as elegant in make-up as anything that had yet been produced in the East. The purpose of the new work was set forth in the preface:

We have endeavored to give it an original character by devoting its pages exclusively to our domestic literature. It is written and published in the Western country, by Western men, and is chiefly confined to subjects connected with the history and character of the country which gives it birth. Most of the tales are founded upon fact, and, though given as fiction, some of them are entitled to the credit of historical accuracy.

Hall was born in Philadelphia in 1793. At the outbreak of the War of 1812 he left his legal studies, entered the army, and for several years saw much active service, taking part in the battles of the Niagara campaign and later on in the campaign against the Barbary pirates. He continued his legal studies in Pittsburgh, where he had been given military duties, and in 1820, "in search of adventure," as he himself expressed it, he resigned his commission and boarded an Ohio River "keel-boat" for Shawneetown in the newly made state of Illinois.

The rest of his life is bound up with the history of his adopted region. As prosecuting attorney for ten counties and then as circuit judge, he was for twelve years almost constantly traveling from court to court through some of the most primitive and picturesque regions of the new state. No story writer ever had more abundant opportunity for collecting original material. "He took notes," observes his biographer, "not from books, but from men and things." His industry was tireless. He edited at various times several newspapers and in 1830 established *The Illinois Magazine*, the pioneer literary monthly of the state. Three years later, in Cincinnati, Ohio, he became editor of the new *Western Monthly Magazine* and succeeded in making of it a periodical worthy to be compared with anything then published in the East. The magazine in 1834 accomplished a feat that alone was enough to bring fame to any periodical—it discovered a new writer, Miss Harriet Beecher, then a resident in Cincinnati. Her tale, "A New England Sketch,"[1] was awarded the fifty-dollar prize which had been offered for the best sketch or tale, and its publication in the magazine was the beginning of a literary career destined to exert great influence upon the history of American fiction.

Judge Hall's own contributions were numerous. In 1832 he issued his *Legends of the West, Sketches Illustrative of the Habits, Occupations, Privations, Adventures, and Sports of the Pioneers of the West*, following it almost immediately with his *The Soldier's Bride and Other Tales*. Later he published other collections, all of them dealing with pioneer life in the West in the period of the first settlement. His object as his first title indicates was primarily to preserve the history and the traditions of his adopted state. With the exception of *Harpe's Head*, an historical novel, all

[1] Republished in her volume, *The Mayflower*, 1845, with the title "Uncle Lot."

of his fiction—and in bulk alone it may be compared with that of
Hawthorne and of Poe—is short, but it can hardly be called a
collection of tales in the sense that Poe's narratives may be called
tales. It is rather a series of historical sketches, made short for
the convenience of the magazines and annuals in which they first
appeared, and given "the form of fiction in order to attract readers."

There is, however, much of real value in the collection and its
influence was considerable. The material and the background
were decidedly fresh and new and its author had a Cooper-like
way of giving movement to his narrative and of holding his readers
to the end. Moreover, at times he could surpass Cooper in the use
of dialogue and equal him in graphic description. His "The
French Village," "a *genre* study," "has in detail," in the words of
Dr. Charles S. Baldwin, "a delicacy and local truth not unworthy
the material of Cable." Here and there among his voluminous
output one may find a tale that conforms in some degree even to
modern requirements as to structure, "The Silver Mine," for
instance, the story of a furious race through the woods to the land
registry office by rival parties each eager to be the first to register
land on which they have discovered silver, only to discover that
the metal is not silver at all. "The New Moon," also—the tale
of a trader who married an Indian girl—would require but few
changes to make it a really effective modern short story.

But little more can be said for Hall. His work is typical of the
literary product of a whole school of Western writers of the period.
Like all of his generation East and West, he lacked constructive
power. Like Cooper, he was discursive rather than condensed,
historical and picturesque rather than dramatic. His material
dominated him; he got under way slowly, and he paused often
to show striking things not at all needed for the movement of
his tale.

In its review of *The Soldier's Bride* (1833), *The United States
Gazette* spoke approvingly of the author, since "He never loses
sight of the true and legitimate purpose of fiction, the elevation of
the taste and the moral character of his readers." But it is at this
very point that Hall—and with him his whole school of tale writers
—most signally failed: he was thinking more of the taste and
morals of his reader than he was of the truth and naturalness of the
scenes and actions that he was recording. He was not in sympathy with his material; he had gone into the West after all his

preconceptions and tastes and standards had hardened into forms that nothing new could greatly modify. *The North American Review* as early as 1836 spoke the last word about him as a writer of Western tales: "He wants the intellectual openness which would enable him to catch the spirit of society. His mind is shut up in its own ways of thinking and feeling, and his writings, in consequence, give no true reflection of Western character." He recorded the unique society of the border, not as it actually was, crude, raw, often disgustingly coarse, but as it looked through his literary lenses softened and tinted by his reading of older romance. He sought, indeed, "the elevation of the taste" of his unpolished Western neighbors, but to him such elevation meant the elegant phrasings and flowery circumlocutions of the polite eighteenth-century writers. The ignorant and superstitious frontiersman, Pete Featherton, for example, in the tale of the bewitched gun, does not load his rifle, but "he commenced certain preparations fraught with danger to the brute inhabitants of the forest." This done, his "keen eye glittered with an ominous lustre as its glance rested on the destructive engine." Again, in the tale, "The Silver Mine," the company does not go fishing. Instead, they "were distributed in quietness along the shore angling for the finny tribe, which sported, unconscious of danger, in the limpid element."

Contemporary with Hall and in many ways parallel with him as a writer of pioneer Western fiction was the Rev. Timothy Flint, who in the early 'twenties crossed the Alleghenies in search of health and for years was a wanderer in the most picturesque regions of the middle West. He had finally settled in Cincinnati, where in 1827 he founded *The Western Magazine and Review*, in the first number of which as editor he published his literary creed: "Our literary creed is included in one word, *simplicity*. Our school is the contemplation of nature." In his adherence to this creed he surpassed Hall; he surpassed him, too, in the use of dialogue and in sprightliness of narrative. Miss Mitford singled out his tale, "The Young Backwoodsman," as the gem of her collection of American short stories, declaring it "a remarkable instance of literary merit, almost equal to Defoe." He had certain defects, however, that were well-nigh fatal even in the day in which he wrote. He poured out such a profusion of fiction when once he had begun to write, that parts of it are almost without form and void. He out-Coopered even Cooper. He wrote chiefly historical novels, but he wrote also a large number of tales, the most of them still in the magazines to which they were first contributed, tales that with a little more care in their construction he might have made worthy to have come down in collections even to our own day.

III

The work of Hall and Flint represents a transplanted literature, an Eastern stock flowering in the wilderness. But side by side with it there was to grow a native variety, a unique evolution, product of the new Western soil, a variant to be reckoned with. It was inevitable that it should have come. Always on the westward-looking borders spring up originality, uncontrolled individualism, and wild freedom lapsing into license. On the flatboats and the rafts of the great rivers, and in the raw settlements along the frontier, there had grown up a peculiar type of humanity—half savage, fiercely individual, intoxicated with its own physical vitality. To cross the Alleghenies and to come with appealing force to men like these, a convention had indeed to be strong. Of literature in its refined essences they knew nothing and cared nothing, but they could tell stories with effectiveness, and they had stories worth the telling—stories often overcolored and overstrong, full of exaggerations and unheard-of metaphors, tales of Indian fights and wild beasts, stories of unrecorded tragedies, of mighty wrestlings with forces that made demigods of the men who won. From the Western river bottoms and plains, from the camp fires of hunters and westward-moving settlers, from flatboats and rafts floating at night down the great rivers, came a race of story-tellers, how expert one may learn from books like Herndon's life of Lincoln or Mark Twain's early volumes.

The most insistent literary demands of the pioneer magazines were for stories. Many of them offered prizes for tales and sketches. Hunt's *Western Review*, in its initial number, 1819, begged for narratives of "heroic and sanguinary conflicts with Indians," and it threw its door wide open: "Gentlemen who are not in the habit of writing for the public and who are not accustomed to composition of any sort are still solicited to communicate, in the plainest manner, the facts within their knowledge." A crude native *genre* was the result. Side by side with the work of Judge Hall and Harriet Beecher one finds this native stuff—unliterary bits of local history, unpolished sketches of unique types, like "Mike Shuck" in the Missouri *Intelligencer*, 1822, or Mike Fink, in "The Last of the Boatmen," or like "Colonel Plug" the river wrecker, in the Missouri *Intelligencer*, in 1829.

The first definite name to emerge from this uncharted region of story-telling was that of Morgan Neville, whose sketch, "The Last of the Boatmen," first appeared in Hall's *Western Souvenir*, 1829. In the history of American literature he holds a unique position: He was the first notable writer of fiction to be born west of the Alleghenies—he was born in Pittsburgh in 1783—and he was the first to bring prominently before Eastern readers the new Western humor and those new Western methods of local characterization, which were to be used so freely by later writers.

He can hardly be called a man of letters. In true Western fashion he was at various times lawyer, sheriff, newspaper editor, and secretary of a life-insurance company, and though Brackenridge, who knew the whole school, could count him as the one undisputed genius among Western writers, he wrote little and only for his own diversion, and he made no attempt to collect his work. A few of his tales are still to be found in old annuals and magazines, like "The Chevalier Dubac," and two in the *Gift* annual—"The Lady of Blennerhasset, or the Despoiled Island" and "Poll Preble, or the Law of the Deer Hunt"—but the most that he wrote has disappeared probably forever in the anonymous columns of ephemeral local newspapers. Doubtless it is for the best. In a strict sense he was not at all a short-story writer, so formless was his work and so discursive was his style. But nevertheless he deserves great credit. He was the pioneer in what may be called the "Mike Fink" school of short fiction, that school which in 1835 published in the East its first collection of tales: *The Big Bear of Arkansas, by T. B. Thorpe, and Other Tales by Various Writers*. Just what its quality was one may judge better from a single fragment than from a page of description. In the year of Mark Twain's birth this was what was coming as literature from the Southwest:

The timid little man near me inquired if the bear in Arkansaw ever attacked settlers in numbers.

"No," said our hero, warming with the subject; "no, stranger, for you see it ain't the natur of bar to go in droves; but the way they squander about in pairs and single ones is edifying. And then the way I hunt them—the old black rascals know the crack of my gun as well as they know a pig's squealing. They grow thin in our parts—it frightens them so, and they do take the noise dreadfully, poor things. That gun of mine is a perfect epidemic among bar: if not watched closely, it will go off quick on a warm scent as my dog Bowieknife will: and then that dog— whew! why the fellow thinks the world is full of bar, he finds them so easy. It's luck he don't talk as well as think; for with his natural modesty, if he should suddenly learn how much he is acknowledged to be ahead of all other dogs in the universe, he would be astonished to death in two minutes. Stranger, that dog knows a bar's way as well as a horse jockey knows a woman's: he always barks at the right time, bites at the exact place, and whips without getting a scratch. I never could tell whether he was made expressly to hunt bar, or whether bar was made expressly for him to hunt: anyway, I believe they were ordained to go together as naturally as Squire Jones says a man and woman is, when he moralizes in marrying a couple. In fact, Jones once said, said he, 'Marriage according to law is a civil contract of divine origin; it's common to all countries as well as Arkansaw, and people take to it as naturally as Jim Doggett's Bowieknife takes to bar.'"

In this same year of Mark Twain's birth and of the publication of the first volume of the "Mike Fink" school, appeared Augustus B. Longstreet's *Georgia Scenes,* a collection of sketches describing life in the primitive regions of early Georgia. So realistic were they and so true to the coarse, fighting, swearing, horse-swapping, gander-pulling society of the Southern mountains that their author, who in later life became a preacher and the president at various times of four Southern colleges, tried to secure and destroy all copies of the book. It was republished, however, without his consent and it has been widely read and much laughed over. It is worth recording, perhaps, that Poe once laughed inordinately over its pages.

It remained for a foreigner to write what is, perhaps, the best specimen of this Southwestern type of sketches. Karl Postl, a native of Austria, escaped in 1822 from a strict religious order in Prague and made his way to America, where at length he became a naturalized citizen, taking the name Charles Sealsfield. He traveled widely throughout the West, owned at one time a plantation in Louisiana, and made explorations in Texas, varying his Western life by frequent visits to Germany where he published voluminously, his final edition filling thirty-five volumes. His

Indian romance, *Tokeh, or the White Rose* (1829), we may pass by, merely remarking that it was one of the influences that later brought forth the "dime novel," but he wrote an abundance of sketches and tales of Western life fresh and vigorous and even to-day very readable.   Few foreigners have ever mastered the English language more completely.   As a type of his tales, we may take his "A Night on the Banks of the Tennessee," first published in *The New York Mirror* and republished in *The Atlantic Club Book*, in 1835, for its period a remarkable tale, not only in its truth to local conditions but to a degree in its form and its freedom from digression.   It begins with abruptness and introduces its characters without exposition:

"And can you tell us whether we are right in our way to Brown's ferry?" I demanded from a man on horseback, who came pacing towards us, in a narrow cart track on the banks of the Tennessee.

It was growing dark; the mists hung gray and heavy over the woods and waters, and gave to the landscape a bewildering chaotic appearance, so as to render it impossible to discern any object at more than three yards' distance.   Nearly as long as this digression was the pause of the rider.   At last he answered in a tone which from its singular modulation, I think must have been accompanied with a shake.

"Way to Brown's ferry?   Mayhap you mean Coxe's ferry?"

"Well then, Coxe's ferry," replied I, with some impatience.

"Why now you are five miles off, and may as well turn your horse's head.   I guess you are strangers in this part of the country?"

"The devil," whispered my friend R——ds, "we are in the hands of a Yankee.   He guesses already." etc.

A decade or so later the Boston *Daily Advertiser* made the discovery that in a continuation of Frederick Schlegel's *History of Literature* a writer by the name of Sealsfield was declared to be the leading American author, and described as "the great national painter of the characteristics of his native land, who has unfolded the poetry of American life and its various relations yet better than Cooper and Irving," and instead of laughing at the typically Teutonic statement, took it with tragic seriousness and refuted it with the conclusive argument that no one in all Boston, even in the Athenæum library, had ever even heard the name Sealsfield.

More gentle studies of the West and the South there were, notably John P. Kennedy's *Swallow Barn*, a book that is not a novel—"I have had the greatest difficulty," complains the author

in his preface, "to keep myself from writing a novel"—but a kind
of Virginia *Bracebridge Hall*, sketches of people and manners in
the Old Dominion of the South. Longstreet chose for his subject
the picturesque, half-savage mountaineers of Georgia, ancestors
of the poor whites of to-day, unique evolutions from our own soil;
Kennedy chose the more refined types and manners of the Virginia old regime—retired lawyers, fox hunters, defenders of the
code, and the like, portrayed with Addisonian finish and grace.
Longstreet presented the more realistic and the more uproariously
funny picture; Kennedy the more idealistic and genuinely humorous, yet of the two Longstreet's work has had the greater influence
upon later writers.

IV

Life in the extreme West, in the vast Indian country of the Rocky
Mountain region, was for the first time adequately depicted in
fiction by William Joseph Snelling (1804-48), and by Albert
Pike (1809-91).

Snelling was perhaps the most picturesque literary figure of his
period. He had in youth been a fur trapper in the Missouri
mountains, had joined the army, and as an under officer had seen
much of wild life at various stations in the Northwest. About
1830 he had settled down in Boston as a literary free-lance,
issuing at first his *Tales of the Northwest*, and then throwing himself with vigor into the field of sensational journalism. At one
time he declared war upon gamblers, and in preparation for the
enemies which for a time sought his life converted his office into
a veritable arsenal. The following year he aroused the anger of
his fellow authors by publishing a slashing *Dunciad* poem, *Truth,
a New Year's Gift for Scribblers*, in which he spared no one. For
a short period he edited *The New England Galaxy*, to which, as
well as to other periodicals, he contributed freely.

His Indian stories are undoubtedly the best written during the
early period. As one reads them, time and again one is reminded
of Parkman: the same rapid incisive style and the same flash-
light glimpses into Indian life. It is impossible to escape the conviction that the author of *The Oregon Trail* read the book in his
boyhood and unconsciously was influenced by its style.

In his preface Snelling expressed his contempt for "the Indian
tales, novels, etc., which teem from the press and the circulating

libraries, in which the savages are dragged from their graves to be murdered and scalped anew," a fling undoubtedly at Cooper and his followers, and put forth one of the earliest calls for realism ever made in America, for to write an adequate tale of Indians, he declared, "a man must live, emphatically *live*, with Indians; share with them their lodges, their food, their blankets, for years." That he himself had done this is evident on every page of his tales. One may open almost at random and find such graphic pictures as this:

The camp of the Hohay nomads was pitched in a little oasis in the midst of a boundless plain. Toward the skirts of the wood, horses were browsing on the elm branches. A few children at play on a slight rising ground, were the first to perceive the approaching company. The alarm was given, and mounted warriors were soon seen riding to and fro, reconnoitering the party advancing. Okhonkoiah dismounted, and made some signals with his robe that were perfectly understood by the others, for they immediately came forward to meet him, and all rode into the camp together. Dogs barked and women scolded, while the others looked on in silence. Not a few children screamed with affright at beholding Gordon's complexion, and ran to their mothers for protection.

Having given the horses in charge to the women, Ohkonkoiah led the way to his lodge. A buffalo robe was spread for the visitor to sit upon, and his moccasins were taken off as he sat, by his cousin's wife. Presently a wrinkled old woman entered, and placing her hand on his head, cried aloud and wept bitterly. The substance of her lament was the death of her daughter. Anon her tears ceased to flow and her notes became joyful. She had now a son, she said, to take care of her in her old age; to provide meat, and steal horses for her.

A dog was killed, and when its hair had been singed off, it was cooked and set before our hero and his friends. Before he had swallowed three mouthfuls of this savory repast, he was summoned away to a feast in another lodge, and then to another, and another, and another.

His weakness is the weakness of all the short-story writers of his time: he lacked constructive art. Had his mastery of plot and of motif been equal to his picturing power, his rapidity of movement and his incisive style, he would have deserved a commanding place in the history of the American short story.

Pike was a New England school-teacher of the roving type, who in 1831 walked most of the way to St. Louis, joined there a band of forty men bound for the Santa Fe region, and after several years of adventure in the wildest regions of the Northwest with trappers and Indian fighters, settled finally in Little Rock, Ark., first as a newspaper editor and then as a lawyer. He was first of all a poet, and much of all he wrote is in poetic form, but he produced several notable sketches and tales of life in the Indian country and cannot be neglected by the student of early Western fiction. All of his tales have the nervous energy and the convincing power that comes from an abundant first-hand knowledge of vivid new materials. His work, like Snelling's, in free from the literary affectations of Hall and the Eastern group, but more one cannot say. His narratives can hardly be called tales in the modern sense of the word. They are facts rather than fiction, a series of stirring episodes that actually happened, narratives that in reality are chapters in the early history of the West.

V

No literary crop so quickly exhausts the soil as that dependent for its materials upon life in sparsely settled and savage regions. The Indian as a subject for romance was found to be a failure. There was no perspective, no adequate background, no richness of life. The social system of the wilderness allows the novelist no room for complicated effects. The idea of a fading race is romantic, but there is little material beyond the idea. Indian fights, Indian massacres, Indian wigwam scenes, offer little variety. The story-writer runs quickly into ruts: over and over we find in the early border tales variations of the "shot in the eye" motif, the story of the settler who after the massacre of his family devoted himself to Indian slaughter; of the Indian lover's leap motif; of the Indian cunning foiled by white-man cunning motif, and the rest. For use as short-story stuff the border material became threadbare even in the hands of its discoverers. None who knew the Indian perfectly treated him as romantic material, and realism soon exhausted the subject.

Then came a Western literary cyclone, sudden, unforeseen, obliterating. In 1845 appeared the first book bearing the name of "Ned Buntline," the product of an adventurer from the East by the name of E. C. Z. Judson. Following him came Emerson Bennett and a whole school of others. The old Indian and wild adventure material sprang into life with a melodramatic roar— the era of the dime novel had begun.

BIBLIOGRAPHY

1828. *Tales from the West, by the Author of Letters from the East.*

1829. *The Western Souvenir*, Cincinnati.
"Oolemba in Cincinnati," Timothy Flint; "A Tale of the Greek Revolution," Lewis R. Noble; "The French Village," "The Bachelor's Elysium," "The Forest Chief," "The Billiard Table," "The Indian Hater," "The Massacre," "Pete Featherton," all by James Hall; "The Descendants of Paugus," S. S. Boyd; "The Last of the Boatmen," Morgan Neville.

1829. *Tales and Sketches by a Country Schoolmaster.* William Leggett.
"The Squatter"; "A Burial at Sea"; "The Stanton Ghost"; "The Steel Clasp"; "The Lie of Benevolence"; "The Rifle"; "Near-Sighted"; "A Watch in the Main-Top"; "White Hands"; "The Mistake."

1830. *Tales of the Northwest; or, Sketches of Indian Life and Character.* By a Resident Beyond the Frontier [William Joseph Snelling].
"The Captive"; "The Hohays"; "The Devoted"; "Payton Skah"; "Charles Hess"; "The Bois Brûlé"; "Weenokhenchah Wanddeeteekah"; "La Butte des Morts"; "Pinchon"; "The Lover's Leap."

1832. *Swallow Barn; or, a Sojourn in the Old Dominion.* John P. Kennedy.

1832. *Legends of the West.* James Hall.
"The Backwoodsman"; "The Divining Rod"; "The Seventh Son"; "The Missionaries"; "A Legend of Carondelet"; "The Intestate"; "Michael de Coucy"; "The Emigrants"; "The Barrack-Master's Daughter."

1833. *Transatlantische Reiseskizzen.* Charles Sealsfield.

1833. *The Soldier's Bride and Other Tales.* James Hall.
"The Soldier's Bride"; "Cousin Lucy and the Village Teacher"; "Empty Pockets"; "The Captain's Lady"; "The Philadelphia Dun"; "The Bearer of Despatches"; "The Village Musician"; "Fashionable Watering Places"; "The Useful Man"; "The Dentist"; "The Bachelor's Elysium"; "Pete Featherton"; "The Billiard Table."

1834. *Naval Stories.* William Leggett.
"The Encounter"; "A Night at Gibralter"; "Merry Terry"; "The Mess-Chest"; "The Main-Truck; or A Leap for Life"; "Fire and Water"; "Brought to the Gang-Way."

1834. *Novellettes of a Traveller; or Odds and Ends From the Knapsack of Thomas Singularity, Journeyman Printer.* Edited by Henry Junius Nott.
"Biographical Sketch of Thomas Singularity"; "The Andalusian Rope-Dancer"; "The Solitary"; "Cock Robin"; "The Shipwreck"; "The Counterfeiters"; "The French Officer."

1834. *Tales and Sketches—Such as They Are.* William Leete Stone.
"Mercy Disborough"; "A Romance of the Border"; "Lake St. Sacrament"; "The Withered Man"; "The Dead of the Wreck"; "The Grave of the Indian King"; "The Murdered Tinman"; "A Sparkling Vision"; "The Mysterious Bridal"; "The Skeleton Hand"; "A Night of Peril"; "The Drowned Alive."

1835. *Legends of a Log Cabin.* By a Western Man.

1835. *Georgia Scenes*, Characters, Incidents, &c., in the First Half Century of the Republic. By a Native Georgian. Augustus Baldwin Longstreet.
"The Dance"; "The Horse-Swap"; "A Native Georgian"; "The Fight"; "The Song"; "The Turn Out"; "The 'Charming Creature' as a Wife"; "The Gander Pulling"; "The Ball"; "The Mother and Her Child"; "The Debating Society"; "The Militia Drill"; "The Turf"; "An Interesting Interview"; "The Fox Hunt"; "The Wax-Works"; "A Stage Conversation"; "The Shooting Match."

1834. *Prose Sketches and Poems.* Written in the Western Country. By Albert Pike.
"A Mexican Tale"; "The Inroad of the Navajo"; "Refugio."

1836. *The Bachelors and Other Tales, Founded on American Incidents and Characters.* Samuel Lorenzo Knapp.

1837. *Charcoal Sketches, or, Scenes in a Metropolis.* Joseph Clay Neal.

1839. *Wild Scenes in the Forest and Prairie.* Charles Fenno Hoffman.
"The Ghost-Riders. A Legend of the Great American Desert"; "Petalesharoo"; "The Missionary Bride"; "The Inn of Wolfswald"; "The Dead Clearing"; "Ko-rea-ranneh-neh; or, The Flying Head"; "The Major's Story"; "A Sacondaga Deer-Hunt"; "The Twin-Doomed"; "Otne-Yar-Heh; or, The Stone Giants. A Legend of Tseka Lake"; "Rosalie Clare"; "A Night on the Enchanted Mountains"; "The Last Arrow."

1839. *Tales and Sketches of the Queen City.* Benjamin Drake.
"The Queen City"; "The Novice of Calrokin"; "Putting

a Black-leg on Shore"; "The Baptism"; "The Yankee Colporteur"; "The Grave of Rosalie"; "The Burial of Moonlight"; "A Kentucky Election"; "A Visit to the Blue Licks"; "Trying on a Shoe"; "The Battle of Brindle and the Buckeyes"; "The Buried Canoe"; "The Flag Bearer."

1839.   *Major Jones's Courtship.*   William Tappan Thompson.
1843.   *Major Jones's Chronicles of Pineville.*   William Tappan Thompson.
1845.   *Wigwam and Cabin.*   William Gilmore Simms.

"Murder Will Out" [declared by Poe to be the best story he ever read]; "The Two Camps"; "The Last Wager"; "The Arm-Chair of Tustenugge"; "The Snake of the Cabin"; "Oakatiblee"; "Jocasse."

CHAPTER IV

THE RISE OF THE LADY'S BOOKS

I

Though the annual and the gift book in America persisted even to the time of the civil war, reaching their maximum in quantity as late as 1845, they had in quality and influence reached their height a decade before. From the publisher's standpoint they had been very profitable. The editor of the English *Forget Me Not* for 1827 announced in his preface that, "though nearly ten thousand copies of the last volume were printed, yet so rapid and extensive was the demand that this large impression was exhausted some time before Christmas, and the publisher received orders for thousands more than he was able to supply," a statement that had immediate effect on this side of the water. By 1830 the news stands of America were covered with gift books, and every publisher was planning new volumes for the coming season.

It was at this point that an enterprising publisher in Philadelphia, Lewis A. Godey, conceived what proved to be a revolutionary idea: the annuals were published primarily as presents for ladies; they succeeded because of their feminine appeal—why not issue them oftener than yearly? why not issue them monthly, with strong emphasis upon those features that would attract feminine attention? Such a thing was by no means new in America. Periodicals with titles like *The Lady's Magazine, or Entertaining Companion for the Fair Sex,* made attractive with poems and moral tales and engravings and even with colored fashion plates had sprung up every year for two decades, usually to perish after a few excited issues.[1] *Godey's Lady's Book,* however, the first

[1] Some of the more prominent among these may be mentioned *The Weekly Visitor and Ladies' Museum,* New York, 1817; *The Ladies' Literary Cabinet,* New York, 1819; *The Ladies' Magazine,* Savannah, Georgia, 1819; *The New York Mirror and Ladies' Literary Gazette,* 1823, Woodworth and Morris, editors; *The Album and Ladies' Weekly Gazette,* Philadelphia, 1826; *The Philadelphia Album and Ladies' Literary Portfolio,* 1827; *The Casket; or, Flowers of Literature, Wit, and Sentiment,* Philadelphia, 1827; *The Ladies' Magazine and Literary Gazette,* Sarah Josepha Hale, editor, Boston, 1828.

number of which appeared in January, 1830, had been prepared for
by the annuals: it was in reality a monthly gift book, a distinct
stage in an interesting literary evolution. It had an elaborately
embellished title page after the approved style of *The Token* and
The Legendary, it had finely executed steel engravings of romantic
maidens and Apennine landscapes, it had expensive colored fashion
plates, and in each monthly number nine or ten tales, as many
poems, several pages of miscellany, and often a popular selection
of music. Its editor was described by the Philadelphia *Gazette*
of 1836 as a man "having a felicitous knack of hitting the taste
of the times." What this taste was in 1830, especially in its
feminine manifestations, a brief examination of the magazine
makes clear. At first the editor depended largely upon English
annuals and magazines for his literary supply; it cost him nothing;
and it is interesting to note that with the whole mass of British
fiction to draw from gratis he chose tales with such titles as
"Isabel of Angoulesme," "Rupert de Lindsay," "The Suicide's
Last Carouse, a Tale of Fashionable Life," "A Scene in the Star
Chamber," and "Anna and Eudosia, a Polish Story"—the most
of them written by women.

That Godey did indeed know the taste of his time is shown by
results. By 1836 the *Lady's Book* was on the high tide of prosperity, issuing editorial notes like these: "The magazine has a much
larger circulation than any other monthly in the country"; "The
publisher of this work, with a view of securing original contributions
for its columns, will give for such articles as he may approve and
publish the highest rates of remuneration offered by any periodical
in this country." The following year it was able to absorb its Boston rival *The American Ladies' Magazine and Literary Gazette*, and
take over its editor, Mrs. Sarah Josepha Hale, who was destined
to direct its literary policy for forty years. This was her salutatory:

Ours is the only periodical in the Republic devoted solely to the mental,
moral, and religious improvement of women. We have the assistance of
many of our best female writers. We offer a field where female genius
may find scope; where the female mind may engage in its appropriate
work—that of benefiting the female sex. . . .

It is our aim to prepare a work which, for our own sex, should be
superior to every other periodical. To effect this, ours must differ in
some important respects from the general mass of monthly literature.
It must differ as do the minds of the sexes.

More and more as the magazine prospered native material began to dominate, until in the January number, 1834, the entire seven tales, one of them as we know now, written by Poe, were marked "Original." The editor insisted that all fiction must be short. Once in 1836 he allowed a tale to run through two installments, but he apologized roundly for doing it, and later he issued this ultimatum: "We have again to ask for shorter stories from our contributors. We shall commence the new year with rejecting all articles that we cannot publish entire." Mrs. Hale had very definite ideas as to what constituted effectiveness in short fiction. In December, 1839, she issued these instructions to her contributors:

Redundancy is a serious fault in our writers for periodicals. . . . Not infrequently we have sent us a single story, essay, or poem, which would if inserted entire, nearly fill the monthly number. If the article is divided it loses considerable of its interest, the reader is vexed and scolds, the writer disappointed and frets, and both join in laying all the blame on the poor perplexed editors.

We want short, racy, spirited essays; stories and sketches that embody pages of narrative and sentiment in a single paragraph, and by a few bold touches paint rather than describe, the characters they exhibit for the instruction and entertainment of our readers. Such stories may be called *too short*, but that usually implies they are very popular.

Though many men contributed to the *Lady's Book*, among them such favorites of the time as Richard Penn Smith and William Leete Stone, and though here and there one finds startling material, as, for instance, one of the first tales published by Poe, a short story by Horace Greeley, and in 1835 a translation of E. T. A. Hoffman's "The Sandman," the greater part of the fiction—all of it single installment tales—was written by women. In January, 1840, the publisher, advertising with pride his list of contributors, does not include a single masculine name:

No periodical publisher in our own country or in England has ever presented a list of contributors equal to that now presented to the subscribers of the *Lady's Book*. Such names as Mrs. Emma C. Embury, Mrs. Seba Smith, Mrs. Cornwall Baron Wilson, Mrs. H. Beecher Stowe, Mrs. E. F. Ellet, Mrs. Mary Russell Mitford (her first contribution we believe to an American magazine), Miss A. M. F. Buchanan, Mrs. M. H. Parsons, Miss Juliet H. Lewis, Mrs. F. S. Osgood, Miss C. H. Waterman,

Miss A. D. Woodbridge, Mrs. St. Leon Loud, Miss H. F. Gould, Miss Mary H. Hale, Mrs. Hoffland, Mrs. Sarah J. Hale, Mrs. Lydia H. Sigourney—are seldom presented in the same work.   The English magazines do not equal ours in enterprise. . . . We are proud of our success, and justly so.   We were the first to introduce the system of calling forth the slumbering talent of our country by offering an equivalent for the efforts of genius.   We have found our reward in so doing. . . . Our subscription list will double the actual list of any other magazine in America.

This calling forth of "slumbering talent" by the *Lady's Book* was, therefore, the assembling of a school of feminine writers, a school, indeed, which was to have more widespread results than even the sanguine Godey could dream.   It marked the beginning of that feminine uprising which, so far as fiction is concerned, is seen to-day to have been a distinctive reaction.   The stronger part of the Irving influence and the hope of a new Western *genre*, to be tamed at length and made artistic, perhaps, disintegrated in a swiftly rising tide of sentimentalism and dreamy unreality and servile imitation of extreme types of English romance—that "elegant" literature, in short, so much talked about during the midyears of the century.   The movement was natural and inevitable.   Woman in America during the early nineteenth century was beginning to emerge.   She had been repressed; she was adolescent in her views of life, given to extremes of emotionalism, prudish, sentimental, full of dreams and idealism, addicted much to exaggeration and often to gloom.   The clear-headed Mrs. Hale understood her perfectly and had an explanation: "When woman," she wrote in the 1837 *Godey's*, "enjoys the advantages of education in a manner appropriate to her character and duties, proportionally with man, she will no longer deserve or incur from him the epithet of 'romantic animal.'"

Thanks to Mrs. Hale, who for years used her magazine as propaganda for female education, and to others who worked with her, this consummation was at length to come, but in the meantime the increasing group called into being by the *Lady's Book* and the host of imitators that followed it, began to deluge America with sentimental fiction.   The rigid requirements of the periodicals decreed that the most of it was to be short, but after *The Wide Wide World* (1850) and *Uncle Tom's Cabin* and *The Lamplighter*, feminized novels began to cover the bookstands.   It was our sentimental era.   As one traces the stream of the short story from its origins down through the nineteenth century one almost loses it for a time in this marsh of emotionalism, and mawkish romance.

By 1846, Margaret Fuller deemed this statement not too strong:

The style of story current in the magazines is flimsy beyond any texture that was ever spun or even dreamed of in any other age or country. They are said to be 'written for the seamstresses.' . . . Take them generally, they are calculated to do a positive injury to the public mind, acting as an opiate, and of an adulterated kind, too.

II

The lady's books were by no means the sole cause of the era, though by giving unlimited outlet for the products of feminine pens they gave it substantial aid. The fundamental causes lay far deeper. Thomas Wentworth Higginson, defining sentimentalism as "a certain rather melodramatic self-consciousness, a tender introspection in the region of the heart, a kind of studious cosseting of one's finer feelings,"[1] thought Byron might have been the cause, or more probably Rousseau. All Europe had been affected. The German literature of the period before had been saturated with emotionalism. Goethe with *Die Leiden des jungen Werther*, Schiller with *Die Räuber*, Lamartine, and Jean Paul had started a new emotional movement in literature. In England there had been Mackenzie with his *Man of Feeling*, and now there were Moore, Mrs. Hemans, Miss Norton, and L. E. L. For a generation two novels set the emotional pitch on both sides of the water: Bulwer-Lytton's *Pelham* and Disraeli's *Vivian Grey*. In the latter "all the heights of foppery and persiflage did but set off what was then regarded as the unsurpassable pathos of Violet Fane's death." Even transcendentalism had its sentimental side: no wonder that American fiction for a period went to extremes.

There were many honest attempts to keep literature in the old sober channels. Mrs. Hale, literary director of *Godey's*, in her own short-story work stood for truth and morality: "If an impression favorable to the cause of truth and virtue is left on the mind of the reader the author will be satisfied." Eliza Leslie, too, sister of the famous English artist, Charles Robert Leslie, who with her short

[1] "The Decline of the Sentimental." T. W. Higginson. *Independent*, November 3, 1887.

story, "Mrs. Washington Potts," won a much-advertised prize contest conducted by *Godey's* after which she became the most prolific of tale writers, was also a steadying influence. Her stories in the *Lady's Book* and later in *Miss Leslie's Magazine*, issued at length in three collected editions, were decidedly above the average of her day. She had a mastery of detail and a facility for sketching in backgrounds that at times reminds one of the subtle art of Miss Mitford. Caroline M. Kirkland, too, was a writer who refused to be swept along in the conventional tide. A native of New York, she had gone West with her husband in 1842 and three years later had published her *Western Clearings*, realistic tales and sketches, the most sustained and artistic short-story work that had come out of the West. She was, she tells us in one of her prefaces, indebted to Miss Mitford for the form of her sketches of village life, but otherwise she was a pioneer: "I have departed," she records in her *A New Home* (1839), "from all rules and precedents in these wandering sketches of mine." Without the conventional elegance of Hall, or the merely historical motif of Snelling, she told the vigorous truth concerning life in the pioneer settlements, and in addition she told it with simplicity and refinement and to a considerable degree, with artistry. Of all the group of feminine tale writers of the mid-century she alone has done work that may be studied with profit to-day. It is noteworthy that her son, Joseph Kirkland, with his realistic novel *Zury: the Meanest Man in Spring County* (1887), was a pioneer of the local-color school, and the leading influence, perhaps, that turned Hamlin Garland to realism and veritism.

To counteract the growing influence of the lady books counterfires were resorted to—"gentleman's magazines" were started, periodicals that in their prospectuses declared war upon the "Julianas and Florellas of Feebledom." *The American Magazine of Useful and Entertaining Knowledge* (1834) had this note in its prospectus:

During the last four years the increase and multiplication of magazines and periodicals of every character has been without a parallel. Yet some of them are strikingly defective in one respect—the subjects of which they treat are almost exclusively of foreign growth.

and it informed its readers that it was to be the leading object of the magazine to correct this defect.

Three years later William E. Burton, of Philadelphia, approached the problem from another angle: his new *Gentleman's Magazine* was to be conducted on so high a plane that it would be worthy of a place "upon the parlor table of every gentleman in the United States." Four years later, in 1841, came *Graham's Magazine*, a curious marriage of the distinctive feminine *Casket* and the avowedly masculine *Gentleman's Magazine*, and it started out with the policy of paying its contributors prices that would secure the best that America had to offer. For a time it was highly successful. For eighteen months Poe was its editor, and during his period it exerted an influence more widely reaching than was exerted by any other periodical before the Civil War. In it appeared some of the best tales of Hawthorne and Poe, and some of the most distinctive poetry and essays of the New York and the New England schools. Yet strong as it was on the more substantial side, it dared not exclude those lighter and more sentimental elements that pleased the larger part of its subscribers. It published work by Washington Allston, Cooper, Paulding, Halleck, Bryant, Hawthorne, Poe, Longfellow, Lowell, W. W. Story, Tuckerman, R. H. Dana, E. P. Whipple, and many others as substantial, yet it defended vigorously its copious infusion of "light" literature. In 1844 this was its note:

It has become the fashion among a certain set, a very small one, to sneer at the "light" magazines—as if the literature of a young and growing nation must be heavy to be good, or would be popular if it were. The light magazines are but so many wings of a young people panting for a literature of their own. They are training a host of young writers and creating an army of readers, who are urging on a happier day.

In every way it was a compromise, leaning ever to the popular side. That it sought to run with the hare and course with the hounds is evident in its very title page: "*Graham's Ladies' and Gentleman's Magazine (The Casket and Gentleman's Magazine United), embracing every department of literature; embellished with engravings, fashions, and music arranged for the piano forte, harp, and guitar.*" It might in later months print on its title page a list of its eminent contributors, but the lady-book features so ruled the magazine that Poe left it in disgust. To Thomas in May, 1842, he wrote:

My reason for resigning was disgust with the namby-pamby character of the magazine—a character which it was impossible to eradicate. I allude to the contemptible pictures, fashion plates, music, and love tales.

Even *Sartain's Magazine,* founded later for the encouragement of the highest excellence in American art and literature, and boasting that it had "sedulously excluded from its pages the whole brood of half-fledged witlings with fancy names—the Lilies and the Lizzies—the sighing swains and the rhyming milkmaids of literature," dare not cut loose from fashion plates and sentimental steel engravings.

Boston, says Tassin in his *The Magazine in America,* considered all three of the Philadelphia magazines, *Godey's, Graham's, Sartain's,* "vapourish and simpering," but even Boston had had for a period its *Ladies' Magazine,* though it was exceedingly staid and religious, like its editor, Mrs. Hale, and later it had had its *Boston Pearl, a Gazette of Polite Literature.* Then in 1841, the year *Graham's* was started, it yielded again to the current of the times and launched *The Boston Miscellany,* with Nathan Hale as editor. Like his contemporary, Graham, Hale catered to the unliterary democratic mass even to the limit of Parisian fashion plates— the subscription list demanded it—but he sought on the other hand to placate literary Boston by advertising an impressive list of Brahmin contributors. "Nathan raged at the ignominious clog of fashions which dangled from the hind leg of his soaring steed, yet it is probable that on account of it his Pegasus was permitted to continue its flight to the middle of the second year."[1] He sought, as did Graham, to appease the elect few who enjoyed "solid literature" by arguing that the age demanded more and more the "light" literature that they affected to despise:

Of the large demand in our country for an elegant literature, the number and circulation of the already established magazines furnishes at least some indication. It is a late day to undertake any defense of what is called light-reading—it has defended itself. It needs no wild belief in the glories or the truth of the ideal at the expense of the real to bid us enjoy and cultivate an acquaintance with artificial lives.

Edward Everett Hale, brother to Nathan, the editor, wrote the epitaph of the magazine. In the preface to one of the *If, Yes, and*

[1] *The Magazine in America.* Algernon Tassin, p. 75.

Perhaps stories, 1868, he sums up the episode, characteristically freeing Boston from the stigma of a suspicion that it once supported a lady's book, and generously taking upon his own family the blame for the literary crime, offering as an excuse their extreme poverty.

III

Holmes was the first prominent American writer to protest against the rambling, sentimentalized, moralizing fiction of the 'twenties and the 'thirties and to plead for the pointed, shortened, compact form of story-telling—in short, for the modern short story. In his first *Autocrat of the Breakfast Table* paper, published in the *New England Magazine* in 1832, he satirized the fiction of the time, first by telling a story as it should be told, and then indicating how a writer of the period would have handled it. Here is his suggested model of a story short enough to be told in crackling sentences over the morning coffee:

It was in the course of the last year that a post chaise drove up furiously to the door of an inn in a little Russian village. A melancholy-looking gentleman got out, went into the house, and called for the landlord. "Has the cholera left this place?" said the stranger. "The Lord forbid," said the landlord—for he only understood one dreadful word in the sentence, which was spoken in French. The question was made intelligible. "It has been gone a fortnight." "In what direction?" "Toward the north."

The stranger thereupon plunged out to his chaise and started furiously in pursuit, mumbling the while of a faithless Héloïse who had made life for him impossible. With him he had his gravestone and upon it a tiny cupid and an inscription which would melt all who saw it to tears and break for the faithless one her heart. "He said a good deal more in this strain, but French sentiment makes English fustian." Then quickly to the final sentence:

Ten days from this time he came up with the cholera, and a month afterwards, by a strange coincidence, I found myself cracking a filbert on his gravestone. I remember I hit my thumb, which was unpleasant, and I broke a little out of the cupid, which was unfeeling.

Now suppose, instead of telling this singular tale while you were finishing your first cups of coffee, I had felt the inclination to make a long story of it and sent it to a periodical. I think I have a practical plan to stretch this or anything like it into a tolerable length. Write down your facts, leaving after each an interval of two, four, or six times its own space. Shuffle in descriptions, reflections, and discussions, as may be appropriate and convenient. There is nothing like system for a hack writer. Liberal stuffing will bolster out anything; you may cram a starveling until he would split the jacket of Hercules.

That New England in general, however, had no sympathy with "light" or even "elegant" literature, and that until even the latter half of the century it considered the short story a trivial and a negligible literary form, is shown by its treatment of N. P. Willis, in some respects the most important figure in the American mid-century school of fiction. That Willis should have been born in New England from Puritan ancestry seems like a paradox—the springing up of a tropic palm tree in a northern herb garden. Naturally brilliant, florid of temperament, volatile, he had all that was artificial and frivolous within him precociously forced into flower before he was out of his boyhood. While yet an undergraduate at Yale he was hailed as one of the leading poets of America. Literature as a profession was to him a foregone conclusion: he thought of nothing else. Leaving college at twenty-one, he was given employment in the office of S. C. Goodrich, first as editor of the two volumes of *The Legendary*, then of *The Token* for 1829, but in April of that year he broke away from all restraint to start a periodical of his own, *The American Monthly Magazine*, the most of the contents of which were destined to come from his own pen.

Willis had found his profession: by ancestral inheritance—his father and grandfather had been journalists—by temperament, and by the quality of his genius he was a magazinist. The past did not appeal to him; Scott and Irving did not touch him; he cared nothing for legends and little for books; but he was overwhelmingly interested in the contemporary human spectacle, especially in all that pertained to the world of the aristocratic, to the embroideries and the pomp and the gilded machinery of what he termed "high life." He was frivolous and given to dandyism, he was sentimental, and he was as impressionable as a debutante, and as excited and undisillusioned. Not only was he essentially a creature of this world, but he was essentially of his own day and moment: or, in the words of his critic, Woodberry, "he was gigantic in his contemporaneousness."

During the two years and a half of his Boston editorship he let himself go with all the extravagance and romantic abandon of adolescence. He poured out tales sophomoric in their adjectived elegance, tales that he never republished, though Miss Mitford selected two of the earliest specimens for her book of illustrative American prose sketches and tales. Willis himself in later years republished only fragments from this flamboyant period, scattering them among his later tales. Boston critics were not slow in reproving his lightness. They treated caustically his debonair sentimentality, his coxcomb affectations, and his literary dandyism. At first he defended himself, but subscriptions began to dwindle, and at last in high disgust he shook the Boston dust from his dapper boots and departed, leaving behind him some three thousand dollars' worth of unpaid bills as a souvenir of his attempt to bring lightness into the literature of the American Athens.

In New York city instantly he found his level. Scarcely a month after the failure of his magazine *The New York Mirror* announced that it had united with itself the *The American Monthly Magazine* and had taken over its editor, the editorial board now to consist of George P. Morris, Theodore S. Fay, and Nathaniel P. Willis. With *The Mirror* and its successor, *The Broadway Journal*, Willis was to be associated the rest of his life.

Immediately he was sent abroad as a special correspondent with a contract to write weekly a penciling by the way. The move was a wise one. During the next four and a half years he fluttered airily over Europe, seeing and recording in gossipy detail an enormous area of the surface of its social activities. In imitation of Lord Byron, he cruised among the islands of Greece, visited Constantinople, and peered, according to popular belief, into seraglios and slave markets, and told tales of what he saw that were heavy with Oriental perfumes and rich with the mystery and romance of the East. Arriving in London, he found himself famous. He was lionized like an Indian prince and eagerly importuned by publishers. He published *Pencilings by the Way*, gathered hastily from *The Mirror*, then a book of poems, and in the meantime poured into the English magazines a series of short stories written under the pseudonym "Philip Slingsby." In March, 1836, he had enough material for a volume, *Inklings of Adventure*, thirteen tales, which by some are considered his most characteristic literary product. Four years later in America he issued his second book of fiction, *The Romance of Travel*, tales which had appeared in various American magazines, then, in 1845, *Dashes at Life with a Free Pencil*. With this collection, though he now and then dashed off a tale for the magazines, his short-story writing really came to a close. It had covered a period of scarce ten years, yet in that time he had produced a volume of tales larger than Poe's and larger than Hawthorne's. He wrote, for example, no less than forty tales and sketches between the years 1842 and 1844.

Sentimental though he was, effeminate, and dandified, Willis was by no means wanting when it came to the details of his profession. As a magazinist he has been surpassed by few Americans. With the sure instinct of the journalist he gave his readers precisely what they wanted, and in doing so he prospered. He was alert, and he was equipped to take advantage of every wind that blew. He was the best paid magazinist of his generation: in 1842 he was receiving from four magazines $100 a month each for tales and sketches and he had other literary income nearly as large. He knew how to market and re-market and re-re-market his literary wares in new editions and combinations. For example after 1850, he republished all of his tales in a totally new arrangement in three volumes: *People I Have Met; Life Here and There;* and *Fun Jottings*, as if it was all new material.

According to his own classification the stories may be gathered under four heads: romantic tales of Europe and the Orient; tales of English high life; tales of American fashionable life, laid for the most part at Saratoga and other watering places; and "fun jottings." Upon the first three he did what he considered to be his most serious work. They are elaborate "pencilings by the way," presented in story form, with plot and romantic atmosphere. His biographer, Beers, has well characterized them: "They are crowded with duels, intrigues, disguises, escapades, masked balls, lost heirs, and all the stock properties of the romancer's art." They are redolent of Byron, of Bulwer, and of Disraeli, and they were pitched at every point for the readers of Mrs. Norton and the American *Godey's*.

For the most part, they are condensed novels, divided into chapters, and furnished with all the novel machinery save only length. That he was not allowed to spin them out to their natural limits Willis considered a real grievance. To be compelled to write fragments when he should be producing wholes, was the penalty, he believed, of having been born in a perverse generation. His tale, "Violanta Cesarini," he complained, was but the ghost of what it might have been had he been allowed to exercise the full compass of his art:

This tale of many tales should have been a novel. You have in brief what should have been well elaborated, embarrassed with difficulties, relieved by digressions, tipped with a moral, and bound in two volumes, with a portrait of the author.

Again and again he let it be known that he wrote his stories in shortened form simply because he was compelled by the times. In his preface to *Dashes at Life*, 1844, he makes the matter perfectly clear. The short story as an independent literary form did not exist for Willis:

Like the sculptor who made toys of the fragments of his unsalable Jupiter, the author, in the following collection of brief tales, gives material, that, but for a single objection, would have been molded into works of larger design. That objection is the unmarketableness of American books in America, owing to our defective law of copyright. The foreign author being allowed no property in his books, the American publisher gets for nothing every new novel brought out in England. Of course, while he can have for publication, *gratis*, the new novels of Bulwer, D'Israeli, James, and others, he will not *pay* an American author for a new book, even if it were equally good. The consequence is, that we must either write books to give away, or take some vein of literature where the competition is more equal—an alternative that makes almost all American authors mere contributors of short papers to periodicals.

The romantic nature of the American people which had expressed itself in the outburst of tales of the *Lady's Book* type, he attributed to the same cause. In an editorial in *The Mirror* he voiced it thus:

Throughout all the middle and lower classes of American life, everything except toil and daily bread is looked at through the most sentimental and romantic medium. In their notions, affections, and views of life the Americans are really the most romantic people on earth. We do not get this from our English forefathers—the English are as much the contrary as is possible. We do not get it from our pursuits—what can be more unromantic than the daily cares of an American? We do not get it from our climate—it is a wonder how romance, fled from the soft skies of Spain and Italy, can stay among us. We get it from books—from the hoisting of the floodgates of copyright—from the inundation of works of fiction. . . . Fifteen millions of people, all ductile, imitative, and plastic—all, at some moment or other, waiting for a type upon which to mould their characters—and all supplied, helter-skelter, at a shilling the pair, with heroes and heroines made to sell—the creatures God has first created in his own image, taken soft from his hand, and shaped, moulded, and finished by De Kock and Bulwer. Who is there, high or low, who is not reached by these possessing and enchanting spirits? We are sure we do not overrate their power. In our own case, a novel of Bulwer's, read in a day, possesses us exclusively and irresistibly for a week, and lingers in our brain for many a day after.

Willis undoubtedly would have defended his own fiction with the plea that his first object was the imparting of information. For his American readers he would reproduce the European spectacle, for his English readers he would show the backgrounds and the manners of America. His stage settings everywhere dominate the action. In the tale "F. Smith" the first third is a "penciling by the way," with Nahant as the subject, then naïvely, before a single character is introduced, the author observes: "I am not settled in my own mind whether this description of one of my favorite haunts in America was written most to introduce the story that is to follow, or the story to introduce the description. Possibly the latter."

The America of his day was hungry for the romance of European travel, and he fed them to the full. He gave them all the stock properties of the romance his readers desired, and he mingled with them copious extracts from his journals and his memories of travel. Never was there writer more discursive. A tale like "Edith Lindsey" is a *mélange*. The story lights airily, whimsically, here and there, like a butterfly on a meadow, but the chief thing is the meadow: and such a vastness of variety of meadow—America and Europe, scenery, manners, anecdotes, poems, sermons, essays, parentheses numberless, digressions in every paragraph. He runs on like a rattle at a tea party, and always is he calling himself back: "I have no idea why I have digressed this time," and "I scarce know what thread I dropped to take up this *improvista* digression (for, like Opportunity and the Hour, I never look back), but let me return to the shadow of the thousand elms of New Haven." The rules for the short story as Poe evolved them or as we to-day conceive of them, Willis seems to have known no more about, or at least to have cared no more about, than the cracker-box narrator in a village store.

But not only was Willis lacking in dramatic sense, he was lacking in sense of reality, and in truthfulness as well. To open his tales is to enter the world of the rococo and the artificial. Nothing is real, not even the backgrounds. It is a sentimental world with heroes and heroines, fountains and moonlight, castle interiors richly furnished, nightingales and bulbuls, and lovers breathing their vows to the accompaniment of soft music. Every noun has its adjective and even its sentence of description or embellishment. The episode takes place after sunset—there must be a sentence describing the night: "The night was breathless, and the fragmented light lay on the pavement in monotonous stars, as clear and definite in their edges as if the 'patines of bright gold' had dropped through the trees, and lay glittering beneath my feet." It is a literary effect solely, and it serves no purpose save gaudy decoration. Everywhere mere prettiness:

The gold of the sunset had gilded up the dark pine tops and disappeared, like a ring taken slowly from an Ethiop's finger.

Von Leisten had lost, by death, the human altar on which his heart could alone burn the incense of love.

The whippoorwill had chanted the first stave of his lament; the bat was abroad, and the screech owl, like all bad singers, commenced without waiting to be importuned, though we were listening for the nightingale.

Clearly the picture in this last was not made to illustrate: it adds no touch of truth, for in no earthly clime are whippoorwills and nightingales equally indigenous. It was added simply as a literary touch to add prettiness.

Undoubtedly Willis was a victim of his times. He was through and through colored with melodramatic romance, and always is the romantic spirit careless as to orderliness and form. Moreover, with the journalistic instinct that was large within him he wrote what his age demanded and what it would most surely buy. If it demanded prose embroidery and short-story tatting he could produce it in more elegant designs than could even Fanny Fern or Grace Greenwood. In one respect he could outdistance them all: he had himself actually lived Old World romance and he had handed in countesses to dinner in the most ancient and exclusive baronial halls of Europe. It was only natural that he should make the most of his opportunity and in the form that was most in demand.

IV

To Willis the light prose narrative shortened for popular magazine purposes was a "sketch"; it was a thing too trivial to be termed a tale or a story. In the preface to his *Fun Jottings* he makes it clear that he does not consider the collection a book of tales:

To value or merit in the sketches which follow, the author makes no definite pretension. They record, under more or less of disguise, turns of event or of character, which have amused him. In recompiling his past writings into volumes, these lighter ones have been laid aside, and they are now trusted to take their chance by themselves, appealing to whatever indulgence may be in store, in the reader's mind, for a working pen at play.

And in one of them he pauses in the midst of the narrative to assure the reader that he is presenting a "sketch, for it can hardly be called a story."

It is very evident that to Willis a short story differed from a novel only in length (a fact which accounts for the muddle in which the most of his short stories end), and in elaborate machinery, and in elevated characters, and serious treatment. Yet it is in these very "fun jottings" which he considered the mere chips from his literary table that his really valuable work in the domain of the short story may be said to lie. All unconsciously to himself he discovered a new variety of tale and worked in it with skill, a skill that, had he but realized his powers and realized the value of his discovery, would have placed him high among the short-story masters of the century. In these light, sketchy studies of manners, touched with satire and illuminated with flashes of wit, unconventional even to lawlessness, and sparkling at every point, he has had few superiors even in later days. In his own time he was as new and startling a phenomenon as was even O. Henry at the end of the century. At the very moment when the tremendously serious Transcendental school was holding Boston, and Emerson and Longfellow and Whittier and the rest were putting forth their most typical work, Willis could begin a sketch like this:

Sit back in your chair, and let me babble! I like just to pull the spiggot out of my discretion, and let myself run. No criticism if you please, and don't stare! Eyelids down, and stand ready for slipslop.

I was sitting last night by the lady with the horn and the glass umbrella, at the Alhambra—I drinking a julep, she (my companion) eating an ice. The water dribbled, and the moon looked through the slits in the awning, and we chatted about Saratoga.

And so babblingly on and on to the end. There is much to remind one of O. Henry in this *Fun Jottings* section of Willis—so much, indeed, that one feels that it could not have been accidental. In this area of his work Willis was himself. He was seeking no literary effect, catering to no romantic audience. He dropped his diffuseness and his sandal-wood-scented adjectives, and ceased to watch his feminine audience as he wrote. Note the O. Henry-like openings of some of these tales:

Mabel Wynne was the topmost sparkle on the crest of the first wave of luxury that swept over New York.

Most men have two or more souls and Jem Thalimer was a doublet, with sets of manners corresponding.

A grisette is something else beside a "mean girl" or a "gray gown," the French dictionary to the contrary notwithstanding. Bless me! you should see the grisettes of Rochepot!

After opening his tale with a beruffled series of sentences, he starts a paragraph like this:

And now, dear reader, having paid you the compliment of commencing my story in *your* vein (poetical), let me come down to a little everyday brick-and-mortar, and build up a fair and square common sense foundation.

In all of this section of his work one feels that deep in his heart the writer had contempt for his sentimental readers, that he had written his elaborate lady-book tales simply as a good piece of business. To judge from these *Fun Jottings*, "The turns of event or of character, which amused him," to quote from his preface, were really the very things that he had dwelt upon as the subject and characters of his own more elaborate tales. Thus he opens his "Nora Mehidy; or, the Strange Road to the Heart of Mr. Hypolet Leathers":

Now, Heaven rest the Phœnicians for their pleasant invention of the art of travel.

This is to be a story of love and pride, and the hero's name is Hypolet Leathers.

You have smiled prematurely, my friend and reader, if you "think you see" Mr. Leathers foreshadowed, as it were, in his name.

(Three mortal times have I mended this son of a goose of a pen, and it will not—as you see by the three unavailing attempts recorded above— it *will not* commence for me, this tale, with a practicable beginning.)

The sun was rising (I think this promises well)—leisurely rising was the sun on the opposite side of the Susquehanna.   The tall corn endeavored to lift its silk tassels out of the sloppy fog,—etc.

And in what is perhaps the best of all the tales in this volume of his work, "The Spirit Love of 'Ione S——,'" he satirizes the whole school of lady-book fiction writers.   This is the opening paragraph:

Not long ago, but before poetry and pin money were discovered to be cause and effect, Miss Phebe Jane Jones was one of the most charming contributors to a certain periodical now gone over "Lethe's Wharf." Her signature was "Ione S——!" a neat anagram, out of which few would have picked the monosyllable engraved upon her father's brass knocker.   She wrote mostly in verse; but her prose, of which you will presently see a specimen or two, was her better vein—as being more easily embroidered, and not cramped with the inexorable fetters of rhyme. Miss Jones abandoned authorship before the *New Mirror* was established, or she would, doubtless, have been one of its *paid* contributors—as much ("we" flatter ourselves) as could well be said of her abilities.

The tale proceeds much as O. Henry would have told it:

Gideon Flimmins was willing to take her on her outer inventory alone. . . . he made industrious love to the outside and visible Phebe.

But

Phebe believed that in the regions of space there existed, "wandering but not lost," the aching worser half of which she was the "better"— some lofty intellect, capable of sounding the unfathomable abysses of hers.

The plot culminates, as romance should, at midnight:

It was inky night.   The moon was in her private chamber.   The stars had drawn over their heads the coverlet of clouds and pretended to sleep. The street lamps heartlessly burned on. . . . On tiptoe and with beating heart, Phebe Jane left her father's area.

There is a surprise ending of a decidedly modern type. Everywhere in the tales readers of O. Henry are on familiar ground:

> Greville Seville, of New York, had all the refinement that could possibly be imported. . . . He wore a slightly restrained whisker and a faint smut of an imperial, and his gloves fitted him inexorably.
>
> She was as tall as a pump and riotously rosy like a flowering rhododendron.
>
> Her teeth were white and all at home.
>
> Miss C. Sophy's autograph had not long been an object of interest at the bank.

Before telling the tale of "Count Pott's Strategy" he informs the reader of what is before him: Two aunts and a guardian angel *vs.* an evil spirit and two lovers—Miss Onthank's hand the (well-covered) bone of contention.

> Her black curls swung out from her bonnet like ripe grapes from the top of an arbor; her dark eyes were bent upon her knees, as if to warm them (as unquestionably they did).

No one in his generation, not even Poe, knew magazine values better than Willis. He was the first to put vivacious, rapid-firing, "light," humorous values into the short story. He added to the form unexpectedness, an element defined by Poe as "matters brought into combination which not only have never been combined, but whose combination strikes us as a difficulty happily overcome." He was master of an instrument that until he introduced it had never been played with effect in the varied orchestra of American fiction. Lacking the dramatic and the serious elements, he never in any period could have taken a place beside such writers as Hawthorne and Poe, yet he deserves great credit for discovering and exploring the area that to-day is one of the most tilled fields of American fiction. That he did not blunder upon this field and exploit it, not knowing what he did, we have his own words. His ideal of what the short story should be he has set forth in the preface to his *Rural Hours*:

> No one who has not tried this vocation can have any idea of the difficulty of procuring the light, yet condensed—the fragmented, yet finished,— the good-tempered and gentlemanly, yet high-seasoned and dashing, papers necessary to a periodical. A man who can write them can, in our country, put himself to a more profitable use—and does.

The failure of Willis came from the fact that he was a journalist, that he catered to the taste of his day, and gave, though he despised it, namby-pamby sentimentalism, and romanticized travelogues, and "hurrygraphs." The greater number of his tales are to be classed with *Pencilings by the Way*, the gossip of the grand tour, "the romance of travel." But if he is to be remembered at all it will be on account of that lighter third of his work, composed of tales and only tales, such light and vivacious jottings as "Mrs. Passable Trott," "The Spirit Love of 'Ione S——'," "Nora Mehidy," "The Inlet of the Peach-Blossoms" (classed by its author as a *"Fun Jotting"*), "The Belle of the Belfry," "The Female Ward," and "Mabel Wynne"—ephemeral bubbles upon which to build a permanent reputation, but none the less substantial material when seen to be pioneer work in an area now overbuilt and decidedly overcrowded.

BIBLIOGRAPHY

1830. *Godey's Lady's Book*. Philadelphia.

1832. *Knickerbocker's Magazine*, New York.

1832. *Dreams and Reveries of a Quiet Man*. Theodore S. Fay.

1833. *The Book of My Lady. A Mélange*. By a Bachelor Knight.
[William Gilmore Simms.]
"Chatelard"; "Ponce De Leon"; "The Venetian Bridal"; "The Death of a Fairy"; "A Story of the Sea"; "The Broken Arrow"; "Haiglar, a Story of the Catawba"; "The Mental Prism"; "Missouri, the Captive of the Pawnee"; "La Pola"; "The Children of the Sun"; "A Tale of Fearie"; "A Legend of the Pacific"; "A Scene of the Revolution"; "The Choctaw Criminal"; "The Spirit Bridegroom. From the German"; "The Festival of Isis."

1833. *Outre-Mer; a Pilgrimage Beyond the Sea*. Henry Wadsworth Longfellow.
"Martin Franc and the Monk of Saint Anthony"; "Jacqueline"; "The Baptism of Fire"; "The Notary of Perigueux" [and other sketches].

1833. *Crayon Sketches by an Amateur*. William Cox.

1833. *Pencil Sketches; or, Outlines of Character*. Vol. I. Eliza Leslie. Vol. II, 1835; Vol. III, 1837.

1834. *Tales and Essays*. Lydia H. Sigourney.

1835. *Traits of American Life*. Sarah Josepha Hale.

1835. *Tales and Sketches.* Catharine M. Sedgwick.
"A Reminiscence of Federation"; "The Catholic Iroquois"; "The Country Cousin"; "Old Maids"; "The Chivalric Sailor" ["Modern Chivalry"]; "Mary Dyre"; "Cacoëthes Scribendi"; "The Eldest Sister"; "St. Catharine's Eve"; "Romance in Real Life"; "The Canary Family."

1836. *Inklings of Adventure.* Nathaniel Parker Willis. London.
"Pedlar Karl"; "The Cherokee's Threat"; "F. Smith"; "Edith Lindsey"; "Scenes of Fear"; "Incidents on the Hudson"; "The Gypsy of Sardis"; "Tom Fane and I"; "Larks in Vacation"; "A Log in the Archipelago"; "The Revenge of the Signor Basil"; "Love and Diplomacy"; "The Madhouse of Palermo"; "Minute Philosophies."

1836. *The Actress of Padua, and Other Tales.* By the author of "The Forsaken" [Richard Penn Smith].
"The Actress of Padua"; "The Campaigner's Tale"; "The Last of His Tribe"; "The Old Story"; "Retribution"; "Madness"; "The Sea Voyage"; "The Leper's Confession"; "The First Born"; "Prediction"; "The Man with a Nose"; "Apologue"; "The Apparition"; "The Emigrant's Daughter"; "The Daughter"; "A Tale of Hard Scrabble"; "The Pauper and His Dog"; "The Old Maid's Legacy."

1838. *Carl Werner, an Imaginative Story, with Other Tales of Imagination.* William Gilmore Simms.

1838. *Peter Pilgrim; or, a Rambler's Recollections.* Robert Montgomery Bird.

1839. *The Little Frenchman and His Water Lots.* George Pope Morris.

1839. *Pictures of Early Life; or, Sketches of Youth.* Emma Catharine Embury.

1840. *Scenes from Real Life.* Lucy Hooper.

1840. *The Romance of Travel; Comprising Tales of Five Lands.* Nathaniel Parker Willis. New York.
"Lady Ravelgold"; "Paletto's Bride"; "Violanta Cesarini"; "Pasquali, the Taylor of Venice"; "The Bandit of Austria"; "Condor Hoofden"; "The Picker and Piler."

1841. *Graham's Magazine.* Philadelphia.

1841. *Sketches from a Student's Window.* Samuel Griswold Goodrich.

1841. *Rambles and Reveries.* Henry Theodore Tuckerman.

1843. *The New Mirror.* George P. Morris and N. P. Willis, editors.

1843. *The Mayflower and Miscellaneous Writings.* Harriet Beecher Stowe.

"Uncle Lot"; "Love *versus* Law"; "The Tea Rose"; "Trials of a Housekeeper"; "Little Edward"; "Aunt Mary"; "Frankness"; "The Sabbath"; "Let Every Man Mind His Own Business"; Cousin William"; "The Ministration of Our Departed Friends"; "Mrs. A. and Mrs. B.; or, What She Thinks About It"; "Christmas; or, The Good Fairy"; "Earthly Care a Heavenly Discipline"; "Conversation on Conversation"; "How Do We Know?"; "Which Is the Liberal Man?"; "The Elder's Feast"; "Little Fred, the Canal Boy"; "Feeling"; "The Seamstress"; "Old Father Morris"; "The Two Altars"; "A Scholar's Adventures in the Country"; "'Woman, Behold Thy Son'"; "The Coral Ring"; "Art and Nature"; "Children"; "How to Make Friends with Mammon"; "A Scene in Jerusalem"; "The Old Meeting House"; "The New-Year's Gift"; "The Old Oak of Andover"; "Our Wood Lot in Winter."

1845. *Dashes at Life with a Free Pencil.* Nathaniel Parker Willis. London. Stories of European Life:

"Leaves From the Heart Book of Ernest Clay"; "The Marquis in Petticoats"; "Beauty and the Beast"; "Brown's Day with the Mimpsons"; "Mr. and Mrs. Follett"; "The Countess Nyschriem and the Handsome Artist"; "My One Adventure as a Brigand"; "Miss Jones's Son"; "Lady Rachel"; "The Phantom Head Upon the Table"; "Getting to Windward"; "The Wife Bequeathed and Resumed"; "A Revelation of a Previous Life"; "Flirtation and Fox-Chasing"; "The Poet and the Mandarin"; "Beware of Dogs and Waltzing"; "The Inlet of the Peach-Blossoms"; "The Belle of the Belfry"; "Kate Credfield."

Stories of American Life:

"Meena Dimity"; "The Power of an Injured Look"; "Count Pott's Strategy"; "The Female Ward"; "Two Buckets in a Well"; "Light Vervain"; "Nora Mehidy"; "The Pharisee and the Barber"; "Mrs. Passable Trott"; "The Spirit Love of 'Ione S——'"; "Mabel Wynne"; "The Ghost Ball at Congress Hall"; "Born to Love Piga and Chickens"; "The Widow by Brevet"; "Those Ungrateful Blidgimses."

1846. Western Clearings. Mrs. C. M. Kirkland.

"The Land-Fever"; "The Ball at Thrain's Huddle"; "A Forest Fête"; "The Bee-Tree" [and eleven other tales].

1849. *Greenwood Leaves: a Collection of Sketches and Letters by Grace Greenwood.*

CHAPTER V

NATHANIEL HAWTHORNE

I

The short story was an exotic in New England, deemed a trivial thing, a sap shoot from the trunk of serious literature. Mrs. Child and Mrs. Hale had potted it and coaxed it into coy bloom, Miss Sedgwick and N. P. Willis had brought it a few times into tropic efflorescence, but by most New Englanders it was considered as a thing unworthy of a man's best powers, a feminine diversion to be tolerated like the fashions, or at best to be turned into harmless forms for the moral instruction of children. In 1834 *The New England Magazine* had this to say of T. S. Fay, who with Willis was leading the New York school of writers of light sketches and tales:

We fancy he writes in a little study, on little paper, with a little pen, for his style is little, his stories are little, his thoughts are little, his images are little, and his sentences and subjects are little. Yet he writes agreeably. His productions are excellent things to while away an hour with, if one wishes to occupy his mind in soothing meditation of pleasing nothingness. Mr. Willis—but he is so notorious that it would be absurd to say much on so stale a celebrity.

This was the New England attitude from the first toward the short story written merely for entertainment. Hawthorne, when in 1842 he moved with his bride into the Old Manse at Concord, the first lay occupant in the history of the venerable structure, felt that the place rebuked him, the mere teller of little tales in the seat of the Brahmins, and resolved to do something worthy: to write a moral treatise or a history like Bancroft's, or even a novel. A story-teller in the Old Manse is symbolic in true Hawthorne style: he was the first to bring the romantic tale into the old areas of Puritanism and to have it accepted and dignified, the first to make the unacclimated exotic grow in the cold New England soil. Pale and unreal it was at first, unworldly even to

91

ghostliness, a weird growth of the darkness brought out into the sun, but at length it became vigorous and at last it was to be found as if native in every New England garden.

The fact that Hawthorne was born in Salem, one of the few places in the vast newness of America over which hangs the shadow of an old tragedy, that his ancestors had been prominent Puritans, and that one of them, a judge, had dealt harsh injustice to Quakers and witches, one of whom had cursed him even to the unborn generations of his children, kindled his imagination as a boy, and later colored the texture of his brooding years of solitude, as did also the fact that many of the family in later days had followed the sea as captains of merchant ships. The really dominating factor, however, in his line of descent was his mother, a woman of intellect and culture, but abnormally sensitive and so intense of temperament that after the death of her husband at sea she immolated herself to his memory, retiring for the rest of her life into a seclusion that was almost complete.

The strangeness of the family régime under which the boy was reared made an impress upon him that time never erased. His mother took all her meals in her room alone, and his two sisters grew into lives almost as strange. The record of the family life is like a fragment from Mrs. Wilkins-Freeman's studies in New England abnormality. G. P. Lathrop, son-in-law of the romancer, gives us this glimpse into the period after Hawthorne had returned from college:

He had little communion with even the members of his family. Frequently his meals were brought and left at his locked door, and it was not often that the four inmates of the old Herbert Street mansion met in family circle. . . . It was the custom of this household for the members to remain very much by themselves: the three ladies were perhaps as rigorous recluses as himself.

Though reared in the city, Hawthorne was never a boy among boys. He was tutored privately at home and for long periods, sometimes of years, he was sent to his uncle's large estate on the shores of Sebago Lake. "I lived in Maine," he once told James T. Fields, "like a bird of the air, so perfect was the freedom I enjoyed. But it was there I got my cursed habits of solitude." Such a childhood had thrown him in upon himself into a world within created by his reading. An accident in early boyhood for a long period had deprived him of the use of one of his feet, and, confined to his room, he had read almost continuously, the books of his choice being *Pilgrim's Progress*, Shakespeare, *The Castle of Indolence*, Spenser, and others from the same shelf. Especially did he pore over the *Faerie Queene*—it was the first book he ever purchased with his own money. Poetry was his favorite reading, and next to poetry, romance. Not many details of the period have come down to us, but all agree as to his omnivorous reading. In a letter to his sister, written in 1819, he announces that he has read "'*Waverley*,' '*The Mysteries of Udolpho*,' '*The Adventures of Ferdinand Count Fathom*,' '*Roderick Random*,' and the first volume of '*The Arabian Nights*.'" A year later, while serving for a time as secretary to his uncle, he writes:

I have bought the *Lord of the Isles* and intend either to send or to bring it to you. I like it as well as any of Scott's other poems. I have read Hogg's *Tales*, *Caleb Williams*, *St. Leon*, and *Mandeville*. I admire Godwin's novels, and intend to read them all. I shall read *The Abbott*, by the author of *Waverley*, as soon as I can hire it. I have read all of Scott's novels except that. I wish I had not, that I might have the pleasure of reading them again. Next to these I like *Caleb Williams*. I have almost given up writing poetry. No man can be a poet and a book-keeper at the same time.

Two years with a private tutor at Salem, four years at Bowdoin College—years that gave him one or two lifelong friends and a mastery of Latin and English—and he was ready for his work. Like his classmate, Longfellow, he had dreams of literature as a profession, dreams that had come to him even before he entered college. Longfellow had abandoned his ideal early. "There is not enough wealth in this country," his father had told him, "to afford encouragement and patronage to merely literary men," and reluctantly the young dreamer had turned to the law. But Hawthorne was free to work his own will. "We were in those days," wrote his sister Elizabeth, "almost absolutely obedient to him." His uncle, who had largely furnished the money for his education, would have turned him to a profession, but deliberately the young graduate, partly because of his habits of solitude and his sensitive nature that shrank from the material grossness of the life about him, and partly from a defiant individualism, by no means lessened by his years in the provincial little college with its sturdy ideals, which made possible freedom to follow his own bent—deliberately he sat down to be a man of letters without encouragement and without prospects.

His apprenticeship was twelve years long—twelve years of seclusion almost total, twelve years of defiance of public opinion such as few men have had the courage to face. In his "Passages from an Abandoned Work" he has given us a glimpse of what the step really meant:

I, being heir to a moderate competence, had avowed my purpose of keeping aloof from the regular business of life. This would have been a dangerous resolution anywhere in the world; it was fatal in New England. There is a grossness in the conceptions of my countrymen; they will not be convinced that anything good may consist with what they call idleness; they can anticipate nothing but evil of a young man who neither studies physic, law, nor gospel, nor opens a store, nor takes to farming, but manifests an incomprehensible disposition to be satisfied with what his father left him. The principle is excellent, in its general influence, but most miserable in its effect on the few that violate it.

Now it was that Hawthorne did the greater part of that reading so amazingly suggested in his fantasy, "A Virtuoso's Collection." "It was said in those days," writes a contemporary, "that he had read every book in the Athenæum library in Salem." And he read studiously: his sister is authority for the statement that "he read a great many novels; he made an artistic study of them." And as he read he wrote: his afternoons he devoted to writing. And he wrote and rewrote, and burned his failures, or else buried them unconnected with his name in ephemeral periodicals. Doubtless his burnings were but the destruction of early drafts of tales which finally found form. He hoarded his material and finally used it all. There was no lavish pouring out of material in the manner of Scott and Cooper; it was rather the tardy presenting of material that had been brooded over with introspective searchings until it sometimes had a pale and sickly cast, material that had been finished to the limits of its creator's power, and then put forth with timidity, as if dreading to have even the children of his imagination appear bold faced and unannounced amid the throng of the public streets. Not until *Twice-Told Tales* appeared in 1837 was his name printed in connection with any of his writings. Few in the history of literature have served so severe an apprenticeship; few have been so long and so steadily true to their literary dreams without recognition and without encouragement.

II

In college Hawthorne unquestionably dreamed of the novel as his literary field. It was the novel era: prose romance was engrossing the attention of the reading world. During Hawthorne's four years at Bowdoin (1821–25) Scott issued seven of the *Waverley* series, including such masterpieces as *Kenilworth* and *The Talisman*, and the American Cooper became an international figure with his *The Spy, The Pilot, The Pioneers,* and *Lionel Lincoln.*

At just what period Hawthorne himself began to produce fiction we do not know, but there is evidence that he left college with two books more or less ready for publication: a novel and a collection of stories and sketches with the title, "Seven Tales of My Native Land." Neither of them found a publisher. Of the literary experiences of their author during the next three years we know little, but in 1828 we know that at his own expense he issued *Fanshawe. A Tale,* a novel in one volume in a day when novels were published in two and three volumes. Its brevity undoubtedly may be accounted for by the condition of its author's purse. Despite its title page, it is by no means a tale. It records the doings of less than two days, and yet it has all the machinery of a *Waverley* novel: two groups of characters, one high and the other low; two lines of action given in alternate chapters; and a leisurely movement in the earlier parts as if the space for the narrative were unlimited. The influence of Scott is unmistakable. There are too many characters for a tale; there is not room for the development of Fanshawe, the hero, and he becomes a mere abstraction, flitting here and there without much vital connection with the plot. None of the characters save the old landlord perhaps, are really vital. They are of books bookish, the creations of one who has dreamed of life over volumes of romance. One cannot believe that there ever was a time when an American college student, seeing a trout in a pool, would say in seriousness to the girl with whom he was walking, that he wished he had a "piscatorial instrument of death." Vastly superior as it is to the slovenly work of many of his contemporaries, it is not to be wondered at that its author in the splendid later days of his full powers should have tried to destroy all traces of the book. We are grateful that he failed, for otherwise we should have had nothing that was surely from his prentice hand, and would be unable to study the influences that molded him and made possible his art.

The failure of *Fanshawe* seems to have turned him completely from novel writing. It was the high-water period of the annual and the gift book. If a writer was to market his literary wares with success, he must become a magazinist like Willis and Poe. It compelled him to think of fiction not in terms of plot, but in terms of situation. The *American Note Books* are full of jottings not of plots nor of architectonic designs, but of single strokes of thought, climaxes, culminating moments, antitheses sharply drawn, paradoxes, moral culminations to be embodied in little room. It regulated his literary pace; it formed in time his habitual literary unit of measure: he would cover a limited area with intense focus; he would sketch picturesque angles, not landscapes. The habit so took possession of him that it rendered difficult his work as a novelist in later years. The *Scarlet Letter* is in many respects of short-story texture, to use Hawthorne's own words, "keeping so close to its point as the tale does, and diversified no otherwise than by turning different sides of the same dark idea to the reader's eye." *The Marble Faun* is seriously weak in plot. His failure in his last period of unfinished work came largely from the fact that he took what really were short-story situations and tried to expand them into novels. It was an attempt to do the impossible. The germs of these fragmentary romances, as he had jotted them down in his notebooks, were distinctively of twice-told-tales compass. To try to expand them into complete romances was to work against his own art habits learned in the slow school of years.

His apprentice period, too, came in the decade when American themes, American legends, American backgrounds were the dominating literary fashion, and that Hawthorne was conscious of the fact appears from the titles of some of his abandoned volumes: *Seven Tales of My Native Land, Provincial Tales, Old Time Legends*. From one popular native field he was barred completely by his own fastidious taste. In his *Sketches From Memory* (1835) he records:

It has often been a matter of regret to me that I was shut out from the most peculiar field of American fiction by an inability to see any romance, or poetry, or grandeur, or beauty in the Indian character, at least till such traits were pointed out by others. I do abhor an Indian story.

The logic of the period with its romanticism, the influence of Scott, the example of Irving and Cooper, and undoubtedly the quality of his own genius, impelled Hawthorne to select native themes. Unlike Irving and Longfellow, he resided abroad in the later years of his career when his work was practically done. He knew only New England, and he cared to enter no wider field. "New England," he wrote in later years, "is quite as large a lump of earth as my heart can readily take in." To center upon so narrow and so provincial an area meant intensive work. He who would cultivate New England legends finds himself in a cold region of abnormalities of conscience, of tragedies of repression, of inflexible ideals hardened in the course of time into fanatical intolerance. The few bits that he gives of legendary lore are seldom narratives of mere happenings in the material world: they record cold tragedies of the inner life.

Not only did he know the externals of his New England, its seasons and flowers and birds, but he knew its history and its innermost soul. He had lived his whole life in the Puritan atmosphere—it was all the life that he knew. And his knowledge and his imagination had been intensified by his four years at Bowdoin, with its self-contained isolation, its paternal government, and its firmly set belief that it is the duty of a college to enrich the life within and to make of its students men apart from the unthinking crowd. The passage in *Fanshawe* describing Harley College is autobiographic:

If this institution does not offer all the advantages of elder and prouder seminaries, its deficiencies were compensated to its students by the inculcation of regular habits, and of a deep and awful sense of religion, which seldom deserted them in their course through life.

His brooding years in solitude made him naturally introspective: he lived in a world within. His almost total isolation gave his imaginings at length an unworldly atmosphere, that peculiar lucidity one finds in the writings of the blind, in Milton and in Prescott. For years, at the height of his powers, he despaired of being recognized, yet he worked on for the joy of the creating.

"Ever since my youth," he could say as late as 1851, "I have been addressing a very limited circle of friendly readers without much danger of being overheard by the public at large." He hovered over his work and finished it and retouched it, and, returning to it again and again, gave it finality. Poe chose the word "repose" to describe his style. His very lack of recognition for so many years increased the richness of his style: it made him the most finished prose writer that America has yet produced. He complained at times of his countrymen's neglect, yet he refused to be popular. He kept himself anonymous, and even when he contributed to the popular annuals he brought always his work up to the highest artistic standards that he knew. His recognition at last came from the few rather than from the many, from Longfellow and Poe, and a select circle of discerning critics. Year after year he sat alone "the obscurest man of letters in America," and dreamed over the old poets of the richer days and brooded and perfected his art. And as a result he became a soul detached, the perfect antithesis of Willis and the lady's books, an anomaly in the midcentury, seemingly without forbears, and, for a time at least, seemingly without followers.

III

When, early in 1837, Hawthorne, with the help of his classmate, Bridge, was enabled to issue a collection of his writings, he had, if we count only material unquestionably his, some fifty tales and sketches from which to choose—fifty small pieces, the work of twelve years given almost uninterruptedly to literature as a profession, or on the average, four pieces for each year. From these fifty he selected the eighteen which he considered his best, and published them as *Twice-Told Tales*, a title breathing a hint of bitterness, as if he had been compelled by circumstances to come before the public at first through an unworthy medium.

It is impossible to study with accuracy the growth of Hawthorne's art. Very many, if not most, of the early links in the chain of his development have disappeared. The notebooks do not begin until 1835, and they shed light only on certain phases of his work. His acknowledged writings, when arranged in the order of first publication, are not necessarily arranged in the order of composition. According to his own testimony, the most of his apprentice work he destroyed and much which he published in the newspapers and annuals undoubtedly remained for a long period in manuscript. In the preface to his collection of 1851 he wrote: "Some of these sketches were among the earliest that I wrote, and after lying for years in manuscript, they at last skulked into the Annuals or Magazines and have hidden themselves there ever since." Others had gone "quite out of my own remembrance, and whence no researches can avail to unearth them."

A study of these fifty or more sketches and tales in the best sequence we now possess is the necessary preliminary approach to Hawthorne. Poe, the first to analyze this earlier work, pointed out the obvious fact that some of the pieces are "pure essays" and the others are "tales proper," for the most part allegorical. In quantity the two elements are almost perfectly balanced: if the fifty pieces were published in two volumes, the first could be entitled "Sketches," the other "Tales." Each volume could be subdivided into three parts. The first would contain *Historical Sketches* like the biographical studies, and "Old News," and "Doctor Bullifant," the second would contain *Travel Sketches*, personal experiences mostly in New England, like the "Notch of the White Mountains," "A Visit to Niagara," "Old Ticonderoga," and "The Ontario Steamboat," and the third might be entitled *Studies in Personality*, observations upon moving sections of life during a typical hour with intense focus, the procession that files by a solitary man who records what he sees and draws what conclusions he may, even to the discerning of plot and dénouement. This last variety is peculiarly the creation of Hawthorne; in the use of it he was completely himself: he never tired of it, as appears from the jottings in his notebooks. It exerted its influence even upon his allegorical tales; for instance, upon "David Swan." "Sights From a Steeple" may be taken as the most carefully wrought example of it, and after it may be named such sketches as "The Seven Vagabonds," "The Village Uncle," "Little Annie's Ramble," "A Rill from the Town Pump," "Sunday at Home," and in later years, "Toll Gatherer's Day," "Footprints on the Seashore," and "Night Scenes Under an Umbrella."

That the essay form predominates in the earlier period of Hawthorne's work may be accounted for, perhaps, by the influence of Irving. In none of his pieces may be found direct evidence that Hawthorne had ever seen *The Sketch Book*, and yet one cannot but feel that the two groups of sketches are very closely related. They are dissimilar only as the two men who wrote them were dissimilar. Both wrote short studies of men and manners and environment, but Irving was interested primarily in picturesque externals, in the genially human, and in all that makes for romantic sentiment; Hawthorne, on the contrary, would search below the surfaces of life and find morals and motives and spiritual interpretations. "The artist—the true artist—," he wrote in his "The Prophetic Pictures," must look beneath the exterior. It is his gift, his proudest, but often a melancholy one—to see the inmost soul." Only a few times did Irving deal with his native Knickerbocker region, but Hawthorne restricted his work almost exclusively to New England subjects. So intensely did he focus upon the region that he knew and so thoroughly did he study its records and its traditions that whenever he has touched with his pen an episode in its history the work is definitive. The trial scene in "Anne Hutchinson," for instance, is unsurpassed in graphic description by anything in Macaulay. Unquestionably, had he centered his powers upon historical composition, he could have said the last word concerning at least the New England area of early American history.

The second division of his work, the "tales proper" as distinguished from the "pure essays," falls also into three subdivisions. The first, the *New England Legends*, is the complement of the Knickerbocker, or "Rip Van Winkle," group of legends. That they lack the genial humor, and the warmth, and the infectious bonhomie of Irving's creations comes not alone from Hawthorne's personality; it comes also from the nature of the materials used. He who would reproduce the atmosphere of Puritan days must approach his task with all religious seriousness. For Hawthorne, in the shuddery half light of this grim period, caricature and levity were impossible. All the legends of New England are cold and gloomy, and they center about personalities that were abnormal and deeds that can be told with truthfulness only in hushed tones. The best of these legends, undoubtedly, is "The Gray Champion," a most impressive tale on the highest levels of patriotism. Others are half historical, like "The Gentle Boy" and "The May-Pole of Merry Mount." In later collections he added others like "Endicott and the Red Cross" and the four "Legends of the Province House."

In the second subdivision fall what may be called *Plain Tales*, stories told with merely narrative intent without allegory or moral or historical bearing. They are few in number even if we assemble all of the variety that he ever wrote, but among them, from the mere standpoint of short-story technique, are some of Hawthorne's best work. The typical four of the earlier period are "The Wives of the Dead," "Mr. Higginbotham's Catastrophe," "The White Old Maid," and "Mrs. Bullfrog." Of these the last comes the nearest to modern standards of technique. It has humor and lightness, and a surprise ending of the O. Henry order. That its creator was working in the New England atmosphere which forbade such frivolity appears in an entry in the *American Note-Books* (1841): "As to Mrs. Bullfrog, I give her up to the severest reprehension. The story was written as a mere experiment in that style; it did not come from any depth within me—neither my heart nor mind had anything to do with it." But "The White Old Maid" undoubtedly *did* come from depths within him. It is one of the most intense of all his tales, and, though it covers a period of years, it is one of the most compact. The opening and the closing scenes are laid in the same somber room with the same rays of the moon illumining a dead face. "The Wives of the Dead" opens at the climax of a long and somewhat scattered series of happenings, and its action, which covers but a single night, concentrates upon a single phase of the culminating situation.

The third subdivision is the most important of all: The *Allegories and Parables*. Hawthorne himself affixed to some of the pieces in this group such classifying tags as "A Fantasy," "An Apologue," "A Morality," "A Parable"—the last in connection with "The Minister's Black Veil," and for one collection, never published, he suggested the name "Allegories of the Heart." The most distinctive of these tales, arranging them in the order of first publication, are "The Hollow of the Three Hills," the earliest published of all the tales and sketches which can with certainty be ascribed to Hawthorne, "Young Goodman Brown," "Wakefield," "The Ambitious Guest," "The Minister's Black Veil," "The Great Carbuncle," "The Prophetic Pictures," "David Swan," "Fancy's Show Box," "The Man of Adamant," "Dr. Heidegger's Experiment," "The Shaker Bridal," "Egotism, or the Bosom Serpent," "The Birthmark," "Rappaccini's Daughter," and "Ethan Brand." Concerning the quality of this area of his work no one has spoken more illuminatingly than Hawthorne himself:

They have the pale tint of flowers that blossomed in too retired a shade—the coolness of a meditative habit, which diffuses itself through the feeling and observation of every sketch. Instead of passion there is sentiment; and, even in what purports to be pictures of actual life, we have allegory, not always so warmly dressed in its habiliments of flesh and blood as to be taken into the reader's mind without a shiver. Whether from lack of power, or an unconquerable reserve, the author's touches have often an effect of tameness; the merriest man can hardly contrive to laugh at his broadest humor; the tenderest woman, one would suppose, will hardly shed warm tears at his deepest pathos. The book, if you would see anything in it, requires to be read in the clear brown, twilight atmosphere in which it was written; if opened in the sunshine, it is apt to look exceedingly like a volume of blank pages.

IV

The eighteen tales, ten of them from *The Token*, which Hawthorne in 1837 selected for the first issue of *Twice-Told Tales*, were the pieces he had wrought with greatest care, the ones nearest his heart, the ones uniquely his. A study of them in connection with those he rejected is profitable. The most of them are tales rather than sketches; all of them are highly imaginative, highly serious, and written on the plane of poetry rather than of prose. They remind us of the dictum of Yeats that "Poetry is the voice of the solitary man." It was the poetic element within them that called out Longfellow's glowing tribute in *The North American Review* (1837), the first prominent notice Hawthorne's work had ever received. "The book, though in prose," Longfellow had declared, "is written, nevertheless, by a poet." He selected his illustrative extracts all of them to show the author's "bright poetic style," and the marvelous beauty of his descriptions. Margaret Fuller, also writing in Hawthorne's obscurest days, believed that, had he "written 'Roger Malvern's Burial' alone, we should be pervaded with the sense of the poetry and religion of his soul."

Undoubtedly Hawthorne's genius was lyric rather than epic or dramatic. "Much poetry," said Tieck, "is only prose gone mad; much prose is only crippled poetry." The phrase describes

Hawthorne's early work, the work he brooded over in his solitary chamber—"crippled poetry." Longfellow chose as his favorite selection "The Great Carbuncle," and Hawthorne in his "Sketches from Memory" had written in 1835: "There are few legends more poetical than that of the 'Great Carbuncle' of the White Mountains." He had opened the tale as if it were a German romantic ballad:

At nightfall once in the olden time.

The sentences are everywhere on the high romantic level, and everywhere near to the rhythm of poetry. At the climax the two who had discovered the gem threw their arms around each other

And trembled at their own success,
For as the legends of this wondrous gem
Rushed thick upon their memory they felt
Themselves marked out by fate,
And the consciousness was fearful. Often
From Childhood upward they had seen
It shining like a distant star, and now
This star was throwing its intensest luster on
Their hearts. They seeméd changed to one
Another's eyes in the red brilliancy
That flamed upon their cheeks while it lent
The same fire to the lake, and rocks and sky
And to the mists which had rolled back before
Its power.

"Crippled poetry" manifestly, but, nevertheless, poetry rather than prose. Everywhere in the volume one finds oneself moving in rhythmical measures on the high levels of the poetic:

Where would be Death's triumph
If none lived to weep?

The sweeping sound of the funeral train
Faded away like a thin vapor, and the wind
That just before had seemed to shake
The coffin pall, mourned sadly round the verge
Of the hollow between three hills.

In some happier time
The Rosebud may revive again, with all
The dewdrops in its bosom.

His hour is one
Of darkness and adversity and peril,
But should domestic tyranny oppress us
Or the invader's step pollute our soil,
Still may the Gray Champion come.

At the culminating scene of "The Hollow of Three Hills," the movement becomes funereal and sobbingly broken, like the "Bridge of Sighs," its monotonous time-beat at length pounding upon the heart of the reader like the dead march at an execution:

Then came a measured tread
Passing slowly, slowly on,
As with mourners with a coffin
Their garments trailing on
The ground. . . .
Before them went the priest
Reading the burial service
While the leaves of his book
Were rustling in the breeze.
And though no voice but his
Was heard to speak aloud
Still there were revilings
And anathemas
Whispered but distinct
From women and from men,
Breathed against the daughter
Who had wrung the aged hearts
Of her parents, and the wife
Who had betrayed the trusting
Fondness of her husband,
The mother who had sinned
Against natural affection
And left her child to die.

To read the work of Irving is to be conscious of eighteenth-century prose; to open Hawthorne is to be in the presence of the poets, of Thomson most of all. A sketch like "Toll-Gatherer's Day" has in it the atmosphere and at times even the rhythms of *The Seasons*. Spenser, too, is in the tales, in their allegorical bearings, their tendency to fantasy, their dim, mysterious light, their harmonious beauty.

Hawthorne wrote in the period when American authors tended

toward the grandiose in style and diction. The writer of romance, as none better than he understood, galloped constantly on the brink of absurdity, and most of the American writers fell hopelessly over, but *Twice-Told Tales* and the others which followed it are never extravagant, never ornamented for the sake of ornament, never, even when viewed in the cold light of to-day, ridiculous. They were uninfluenced by the popular material by which they were surrounded. Many of them were written while the Dickens wave was sweeping over English fiction, but there is no slightest trace of Dickens in Hawthorne. So far as style is concerned his tales might have been written in the eighteenth century. His was a style that had been molded by an early knowledge of Greek and Latin classics, of the English Bible, which seems to have been read aloud daily in the Hawthorne home, and of the early English masterpieces brooded over for years in solitude. It is a classical style: finished yet seemingly spontaneous; artistic, yet simple even to childlikeness.

Poe in 1847 professed to have found the secret of Hawthorne in Tieck, even declaring that all who called him original betrayed their own ignorance, "their acquaintance not extending to the German Tieck, whose manner in some of his works is absolutely identical with that habitual with Hawthorne"—certainly a sweeping statement. A calmer and more truthful criticism came five years later in the British *New Monthly Magazine* from a reviewer to me unknown: "His stories have been likened to Tieck's in their power of translating the mysterious harmonies of nature into articulate meanings, and to Töpffer's, in high finish and purity of style."

One may indeed "liken" Hawthorne's work to Tieck's and even to Töpffer's, but it is doubtful if one may go much farther. Certainly one finds in him Tieck's brooding, poetic fancy, his tendency at times to symbolism and allegory, and his conception of romantic art as the ability to "lull the reader into a dreamy mood." Both, moreover, handled the *Mährchen*, or legendary tale, in the poetic manner and both in some instances made use of the same materials. Tieck's tale "The Klausenburg," for instance, is a study of the workings in a later generation of a curse launched by a gypsy upon one in power who had condemned her to cruel punishment. "Feathertop" in a vague way is like Tieck's "Die Vogelscheushe," and H. A. Beers in his *English Romanticism* finds traces in Hawthorne's work of Tieck's "The Elves," "The Goblet," and "The Runenberg." Carlyle in 1827 had indeed published these three, together with two others, "The Fair-Haired Eckbert" and "The Trusty Eckart," and it is not improbable that Hawthorne read the translation, though internal evidence of the fact is small. That he may have heard much of Tieck at Brook Farm in 1842 and even have heard readings from his tales is also not impossible. Margaret Fuller was volubly enthusiastic over the German writers, especially Tieck, and George William Curtis was spending his afternoons reading Novalis and *Wilhelm Meister*. That Hawthorne read the tales in the original, however, is quite another matter. It is safe to say that during the period in which he wrote the most of his shorter work he had no knowledge of the German language. Even the leading transcendentalists were not much influenced by the German until well into the thirties. Says James Freeman Clarke of Margaret Fuller:

Margaret began to study German early in 1832. Both she and I were attracted toward this literature, at the same time, by the wild bugle call of Thomas Carlyle, in his romantic articles on Richter, Schiller, and Goethe, which appeared in the old *Foreign Review*, the *Edinburgh Review*, and afterwards in the *Foreign Quarterly*.

In 1843 Hawthorne in his *Note Books* records his struggle with one of Tieck's tales in terms of one who has to make his way laboriously with a "phrase book:" "Went on with Tieck's tale slowly and painfully, often wishing for help in my difficulties" . . . "I again set to work on Tieck's tale and worried through several pages" . . . "Plodded onward in the rugged and bewildering depths of Tieck's tale till five o'clock" . . . "Till dinner time I labored on Tieck's tale"—this in 1843, after the most of his tales had been written and after his manner of writing had long since, to quote Poe, become "habitual."

The likeness between the two came from similarity of soul and from the fact that both were working in an atmosphere charged with the German romantic spirit. Like his own artist in "Prophetic Pictures," Hawthorne worked not in life, but in an idealization of life. "A subdued tinge of the wild and wonderful is thrown over a sketch of New England personages and scenery, yet . . . without entirely obliterating the sober hues of nature." It is the very essence of the later romanticism and both romancers made full use of it, Tieck often with wild abandon, Hawthorne always sanely and with due reverence for the essential Puritan foundations from which his feet never wandered.

V

Despite Poe's elaborate formulation of the rules governing the art of the *Twice-Told Tales*, it is to be doubted if Hawthorne had any theory of the short story or any suspicion that the tale differed from the novel save in the one attribute of length. A few of the tales obey in full the laws of Poe, but they are so few they may be counted as exceptions, so few, indeed, that they seem accidental rather than intentional. Hawthorne was most at home in the sketch, the rambling essay type of reminiscent description, as in "The Old Manse" and the introduction to *The Scarlet Letter*, and in expository analyses of situations or personalities or mental states. Everything had seemed to turn him to the shorter varieties of prose—the demands of the magazines, the uncertain market for American novels, the nature of his own genius, which was more inclined to brood over moral situations than to plan elaborate structures of plot—and in his solitary chamber he wrote to please himself, using for models, if he used any at all, the older classics, the dramas of Shakespeare, and the English novel which, according to his sister's testimony, he had studied for its technique. As a result his tales, from the standpoint of form, show surprising merits and, on the other hand, equally surprising defects. Poe was the first to formulate the former, and A. P. Peabody, in a review some ten years later, the first to dwell upon the latter. "The most paltry talemaker for the magazines or the newspapers," Peabody had declared, "can easily excel him in what we might term the mechanical portion of his art. His plots are seldom well devised or skillfully developed . . . the conversations are not natural," and so on with other details. It is not hard now, in the light of modern rules, to point out Hawthorne's failures: his leisurely, expository openings; his frequent discursiveness; his characters which for the most part are as abstract and bloodless as Spenser's creations; his distance from the warm currents of actual life; his moralizing endings. But these defects, serious as some of them may be, are overbalanced by equally important excellencies, even in technique, for if we are to judge him by his work, by a dozen or more tales universally admitted now to be masterpieces, tales like "Rappaccini's Daughter," "The Birthmark," "The Great Stone Face," "The Wives of the Dead," "The Great Carbuncle," "The White Old Maid," "The Minister's Black Veil," "Ethan Brand," the four "Legends of the Province House," "The Snow Image," and a few others, we shall find that even in the matter of form Hawthorne was a pioneer, in advance of all his contemporaries save Poe.

He conceived of his tales in terms of culminating action; there is always a dramatic moment for which everything before has been a preparation. One may most easily illustrate this from his jottings for tales in his notebook. It reveals his habit of mind:

A sketch to be given of a modern reformer—a type of the extreme doctrines on the subject of slaves, cold water, and other such topics. He goes about the streets haranguing most eloquently, and is on the point of making many converts, when his labors are suddenly interrupted by the appearance of the keeper of a madhouse, whence he has escaped. Much may be made of this idea.

The scene of a story or sketch to be laid within the light of a street lantern; the time, when the lamp is near going out; and the catastrophe to be simultaneous with the last flickering gleam.

Two persons, by mutual agreement, to make their wills in each other's favor, then to wait impatiently for one another's death, and both to be informed of the desired event at the same time. Both, in most joyous sorrow, hasten to be present at the funeral, meet, and find themselves both hoaxed.

Perhaps his emphasis of a single climactic moment rather than of a growing series of happenings in chronicle form came from the sermonic habit, which, like every other indigenous New-Englander, he had inherited from his Puritan ancestors. His tales came to him as texts to be illustrated and driven home. "On this theme," he observes after one of his notebook jottings, "methinks I could frame a tale with a deep moral." He wrote "Wakefield" "trusting there will be a pervading spirit and a moral, even if we should fail to find them done up neatly and condensed into the final sentence."

In the second place, Hawthorne had a keen eye for situation. Here again was he a pioneer, the first prominent writer whose tales may be defined in terms of situation. So far as I have been able to find, the first to perceive and record this fact was the English *National Review* in 1861:

All his tales embody single ideal situations, scarcely ever for a moment varied in their course. . . . His longer works are ideal situations expanded by minute study and trains of closely related thought into the dimensions of novels. . . . He prefers to assume the crisis past and to determine as fully as he can the ideal situation to which it has given rise when it is beginning to assume more of a chronic character.

No one has expressed more clearly than this what Hawthorne really added to the short story. If it be true—and no one has disputed it—then the author of the *Twice-Told Tales* rather than Poe stands as the father of the American short story. At least he was the first to direct it into its modern form.

Hawthorne was the first in America to touch the new romanticism with morals, at least the first to touch it in the department of its fiction. His situations are almost invariably moral culminations, and for presenting them he had several devices. Often he sought for a symbol that would grip and shake the reader's imagination. This from his notebooks:

Meditations about the main gas pipe of a great city,—if the supply were to be stopped, what would happen? How many different scenes it sheds light on? It might be made emblematical of something.

A snake taken into a man's stomach and nourished there from fifteen years to thirty-four, tormenting him most horribly. A type of envy or some other evil passion.

The result of the latter was "Egotism, or the Bosom Serpent." Sometimes the situation is presented in order to study the psychological reactions of the victim and to probe into the depths of personality, as in "Wakefield." Most often of all, the situation is presented in order to point out a fundamental characteristic or a subtle besetting sin of humanity. In his notebook he writes this:

A person to be in possession of something as perfect as mortal man has a right to demand; he tries to make it better, and ruins it entirely;

which is his tale, "The Birthmark," reduced to its lowest terms. If each of his tales were cut to bare single-sentence texts, as their severe unity renders it possible to do, as, for example:

In every heart there is secret sin, and sad mysteries which we hide from our nearest and dearest, and would feign conceal from our own consciousness.—"The Minister's Black Veil";

Does it not argue a superintending Providence that, while viewless and unexpected events thrust themselves continually athwart our path, there should still be regularity enough in mortal life to render foresight even partially available?—"David Swan";

In the solitude of a midnight chamber or in a desert, afar from men or in a church, while the body is kneeling, the soul may pollute itself even with those crimes which we are accustomed to deem altogether carnal.—"Fancy's Show Box";

Would all who cherish wild wishes but look around them, they would oftenest find their sphere of duty, of prosperity and happiness, within those precincts and in that station where Providence itself has cast their lot.—" The Three-Fold Destiny";—

if all his tales were so reduced and the resulting texts were gathered into a chapter, it would be a fairly complete summary of the best elements of his philosophy. His stories, the best of them, are, therefore, sermons, each with a text to which its author rigidly adheres, made vivid by a single illustration dwelt upon lingeringly, presented from new angles again and again until it becomes a haunting presence that lays its hands upon one's very soul.

VI

Hawthorne, therefore, did four things for the short story: he turned it from its German romantic extravagances and frivolity and horrors into sane and moral channels; he made of it the study of a single intense situation; he deepened it and gave it beauty; and he made it respectable even in New England, a dignified literary form, admitted as such even by the most serious of the Transcendentalists. After *Twice-Told Tales* and *Mosses From an Old Manse* the short story had no longer to apologize for its existence and live a vagabond life in the corners of weekly papers and the pages of lady's books and annuals: it had won so secure a place that even before Hawthorne had died *The Atlantic Monthly*, the constituted mouthpiece of the Brahmins of New England, could print seventeen specimens of it in its first volume.

BIBLIOGRAPHY

HAWTHORNE'S TALES AND SKETCHES

COLLECTIONS

1. Twice-Told Tales, 1837.
2. Twice-Told Tales, Second Series, 1842.
3. Mosses From an Old Manse, 1846.
4. The Snow Image and Other Twice-Told Tales, 1851.
5. True Stories From American History and Biography, 1851.
6. The Wonder Book, 1851.
7. Tanglewood Tales, 1853.
8. The Dolliver Romance and Other Pieces, 1876.
9. Fanshawe and Other Sketches, 1876.

TALES AND SKETCHES CHRONOLOGICALLY ARRANGED

1. The Hollow of the Three Hills (1), *Salem Gazette*, 1830.
2. Sir William Phipps (9), *Salem Gazette*, 1830.
3. Mrs. Hutchinson (9), *Salem Gazette*, 1830.
4. An Old Woman's Tale (8), *Salem Gazette*, Dec., 1830.
5. Doctor Bullivant (8), *Salem Gazette*, Jan., 1831.
6. Sights From a Steeple (1), *Token*, 1831.
7. The Gentle Boy (1), *Token*, 1832.
8. My Kinsman, Major Molineux (4), *Token*, 1832.
9. Roger Malvin's Burial (3), *Token*, 1832.
10. Wives of the Dead [The Two Widows] (4), *Token*, 1832.
11. The Canterbury Pilgrims (4), *Token*, 1833.
12. Sir William Pepperell, *Token*, 1833.
13. The Seven Vagabonds (2), *Token*, 1833.
14. The Story-Teller, No. I [Passages From a Relinquished Work] (3), *New England Magazine*, Nov., 1834.
15. The Story-Teller, No. II (3), *New England Magazine*, Dec., 1834.
16. Mr. Higginbotham's Catastrophe (1), *New England Magazine*, Dec., 1834.
17. Alice Doane's Appeal, *Token*, 1834.
18. The Haunted Mind (2), *Token*, 1835.
19. The Village Uncle [The Mermaid, A Reverie] (2), *Token*, 1835.
20. Little Annie's Ramble (1), *Youth's Keepsake*, 1835.
21. The Gray Champion (1), *New England Magazine*, Jan., 1835.
22. My Visit to Niagara (8), *New England Magazine*, 1835.
23. The Colonial Newspaper (4), *New England Magazine*, Feb., 1835.
24. The Old French War (4), *New England Magazine*, March, 1835.
25. Young Goodman Brown (3), *New England Magazine*, April, 1835.
26. The Old Tory (4), *New England Magazine*, May, 1835

27. Wakefield (1), *New England Magazine*, May, 1835.
28. The Ambitious Guest (2), *New England Magazine*, June, 1835.
29. Graves and Goblins (8), *New England Magazine*, June, 1835.
30. A Rill From the Town Pump (1), *New England Magazine*, June, 1835.
31. The White Old Maid [The Old Maid in the Winding Sheet] (2), *New England Magazine*, July, 1835.
32. The Vision of the Fountain (1), *New England Magazine*, Aug., 1835.
33. The Notch of the White Mountains (3), *New England Magazine*, Nov., 1835.
34. Our Evening Party in the White Mountains (3), *New England Magazine*, Nov., 1835.
35. The Devil in Manuscript (4), *New England Magazine*, Nov., 1835.
36. The Canal Boat (3), *New England Magazine*, Dec., 1835.
37. The Wedding Knell (1), *Token*, 1836.
38. The Minister's Black Veil (1), *Token*, 1836.
39. The May-Pole of Merry Mount.   A Parable (1), *Token*, 1836.
40. Old Ticonderoga (4), *American Monthly Magazine*, Feb., 1836.
41. The Ontario Steamboat, *Magazine Useful Knowledge*, 1836.
42. Sunday at Home (1), *Token*, 1837.
43. The Great Carbuncle (1), *Token*, 1837.
44. The Prophetic Pictures (1), *Token*, 1837.
45. David Swan, a Fantasy (1), *Token*, 1837.
46. Fancy's Show Box, a Morality (1), *Token*, 1837.
47. The Man of Adamant, an Apologue (4), *Token*, 1837.
48. Mrs. Bullfrog (3), *Token*, 1837.
49. Monsieur du Miroir (3), *Token*, 1837.
50. Dr. Heidigger's Experiment (1), *Salem Gazette*, March, 1837.
51. A Bell's Biography (4), *Knickerbocker's*, March, 1837.
52. Fragments From the Journal of a Solitary Man (8), *American Monthly Magazine*, July, 1837.
53. Edward Fane's Rosebud (2), *Knickerbocker's*, Sept., 1837.
54. Toll Gatherer's Day (2), *Democratic Review*, Oct., 1837.
55. Endicott and The Red Cross (2), *Salem Gazette*, Nov., 1837.
56. Night Sketches Beneath an Umbrella (2), *Token*, 1838.
57. Peter Goldthwaite's Treasure (2), *Token*, 1838.
58. The Shaker Bridal (2), *Token*, 1838.
59. Sylph Etherege (4), *Token*, 1838.
60. Footprints on the Seashore (2), *Democratic Review*, Jan., 1838.
61. Time's Portraiture, *Salem Gazette*, 1838.
62. Jonathan Cilly (9), *Democratic Review*, 1838.
63. Thomas Green Fessenden (9), *American Monthly Magazine*, 1838.
64. Snowflakes (2), *Democratic Review*, Feb., 1838.
65. The Three-Fold Destiny (2), *American Monthly Magazine*, March, 1838.

66. Howe's Masquerade (2), *Democratic Review*, May, 1838.
67. Edward Randolph's Portrait (2), *Democratic Review*, July, 1838.
68. Chippings With a Chisel (2), *Democratic Review*, Sept., 1838.
69. Lady Eleanore's Mantle (2), *Democratic Review*, Dec., 1838.
70. Old Esther Dudley (2), *Democratic Review*, Jan., 1839.
71. The Sister Years (2), *Salem Gazette*, Jan., 1839.
72. The Lily's Quest (2), *The Southern Rose*, Jan., 1839.
73. John Inglefield's Thanksgiving (4), *Democratic Review*, March, 1840.
74. A Virtuoso's Collection (3), *Boston Miscellany*, May, 1842.
75. The Old Apple Dealer (3), *Sargent's New Monthly Magazine*, Jan., 1843.
76. The Antique Ring (8), *Sargent's*, Feb., 1843.
77. The Hall of Fantasy (3), *Pioneer*, Feb., 1843.
78. The New Adam and Eve (3), *Democratic Review*, Feb., 1843.
79. Egotism, or the Bosom Serpent (3), *Democratic Review*, March, 1843.
80. The Birthmark (3), *Pioneer*, March, 1843.
81. The Procession of Life (3), *Democratic Review*, April, 1843.
82. The Celestial Railroad (3), *Democratic Review*, May, 1843.
83. Buds and Bird Voices (3), *Democratic Review*, June, 1843.
84. Little Daffydowndilly (4), *Boys' and Girls' Magazine*, Aug., 1843.
85. Fire Worship (3), *Democratic Review*, Dec., 1843.
86. The Intelligence Office (3), *Democratic Review*, March, 1844.
87. The Christmas Banquet (3), *Democratic Review*, Jan., 1844.
88. Earth's Holocaust (3), *Graham's*, March, 1844.
89. The Artist of the Beautiful (3), *Democratic Review*, June, 1844.
90. Drowne's Wooden Image (3), *Godey's*, July, 1844.
91. A Select Party (3), *Democratic Review*, July, 1844.
92. A Book of Autographs (8), *Democratic Review*, Nov., 1844.
93. Rappaccini's Daughter (3), *Democratic Review*, Dec., 1844.
94. P's Correspondence (3), *Democratic Review*, April, 1845.
95. The Old Manse (3), 1846.
96. Main Street (4), *Æsthetic Papers*, 1849.
97. The Great Stone Face (4), *National Fra*, Jan., 1850.
98. The Snow Image (4), *International Magazine*, Oct., 1850.
99. Grandfather's Chair (5).
100. Famous Old People (5).
101. The Liberty Tree (5).
102. The Gorgon's Head (6).
103. The Golden Touch (6).
104. The Paradise of Children (6).
105. The Three Golden Apples (6).
106. The Miraculous Pitcher (6).
107. The Chimæra (6).
108. Ethan Brand (4), *The Dollar Magazine*, May, 1851.

109. Feathertop (3), *International Magazine*, Feb., March, 1852.
110. The Wayside (7).
111. The Minotaur (7).
112. The Pygmies (7).
113. The Dragon's Teeth (7).
114. Circe's Palace (7).
115. The Pomegranate Seeds **(7).**
116. The Golden Fleece (7).

CHAPTER VI

EDGAR ALLAN POE

I

The chief literary contemporary of Hawthorne in America, his earliest adequate critic, and his most able colleague in the development of the short-story form, was Edgar Allan Poe. The two began their literary career at almost the same moment, they contributed to the same periodicals, they worked in the same atmosphere of romanticism—the wild German *Mährchen* world which had been dignified by Scott and sentimentalized by Byron and Bulwer and Disraeli, and both were destined permanently to enrich that shortened form of fiction which circumstances had placed in their hands: yet in spite of all this the two men were as absolutely unlike as North and South.

Hawthorne fundamentally and unalterably was a New-Englander. As completely as even Poe was he a romanticist and a worshiper of beauty, and yet so redolent was he of his native region that he could make of romanticism a thing accepted by even the straitest sect of the Brahmins, and do it, moreover, in the form of short fiction. Never was he able to forget that everything, even art, must have its moral connotations. To him, sensitive with inherited conscience and trained from childhood to peer beneath the surfaces of life, into the sources of action, into the recesses of the heart, a tale was a problem in the mathematics of human living, with its a and b and x and its inevitable resultant.

From this point of view no man could have been farther away than Poe. He was anti-Puritanical, anti-New England and all its content. His inheritance and training had been the direct opposite of Hawthorne's. He was nomadic, restless, temperamental— it was in his blood. His grandfather, born in Ireland, became a general in the American Revolutionary War, and later settled in Baltimore; his father, when not yet of age, had thrown down his law books, joined an itinerant company of actors, and had married the sprightly little variety artist of the troupe, an English

115

girl of theatrical antecedents, born in mid-ocean, educated from infancy on the stage, and with her had lived the excited, unnatural life of the nomadic actor.

Before their child Edgar was old enough to remember them, both of his parents were dead, leaving him nothing save a miniature of the young mother, an elfish thing—it "accompanied the poet through all his wanderings"—the original, one might easily believe, of his Ligeias and Eleonoras and Ulalumes, a creature to haunt the boy's imagination, petite, elfin-eyed, exquisite as the nymphs she delighted to impersonate on the stage and as guiltless of soul. Nothing else of mother influence or of home sentiment ever seems to have touched the boy. From the first he was anchored to nothing and grounded in nothing save the intellectual. The Allan family, which made him a part of their household—austere, Scotch, materialistic—understood him little and gave him not at all the training that should have been his. During the years from six to eleven, the peculiarly impressionable years, he was transplanted to England and placed in a school, first in London, then in Stoke Newington, a plucking up of whatever of roots may have formed in his early Virginia environment. Then for five years, or until he was sixteen, he was in a Richmond school, a select establishment, preparing for college. A year in the University of Virginia, brilliant in scholarly results, but unfortunate in all others, served still further to unsettle his soul. Gambling debts exceeding two thousand dollars are seldom looked upon with complacency by the fathers or even the foster fathers of freshmen. Mr. Allan withdrew him and sought to induct him into a business career.

One might laugh, were it not pathetic, at the blindness of the well-meaning old merchant into whose staid household had come this surprising elf child to upset it. The boy disappeared. Shortly afterward in Boston appeared a thin volume *Tamerlane and Other Poems. By a Bostonian,* and its author, by what impulse we can only conjecture, possibly in emulation of his favorite poet, Coleridge, celebrated the event as a soldier regularly enlisted in the United States army. A military life of two years followed, at every point blameless, until Mr. Allan, learning in some way of his whereabouts, secured for him an honorable discharge and a cadetship at West Point. If he was to be a soldier he should enter the army as a gentleman. Again a burst of poetry—*Al Aaraaf,*

Tamerlane, and Minor Poems, by Edgar A. Poe, issued at Baltimore in his twentieth year.

He was at West Point a year and a half. At first his record was creditable and even distinctive. Then had come the remarriage of Mr. Allan—Poe's foster mother had died early in 1829—and the full realization on the part of Poe that he was no longer a rich man's sole heir, but a dependent who might at any time be cut off with nothing. A little later he was to realize his worst fears: trained in all the tastes and instincts of a gentleman he was to be left, like an English second son, penniless without trade or profession, and, moreover, with an aristocratic pride that made manual toil impossible. How deeply this cut into his life appears from a letter he wrote several years later, after the death of his foster father:

Brought up to no profession and educated in the expectation of an immense fortune (Mr. Allan having been worth $750,000), the blow has been a heavy one, and I had nearly succumbed to its influence, and yielded to despair.

The army as a profession lost whatever charm it had ever had for him. Without money, as Poe himself later explained it, there was little hope for a worthy military career, and deliberately he disobeyed orders, absented himself from classes, and neglected duties until in March, 1831, he was dropped from the academy rolls. Again he celebrated his new freedom with a volume of poetry—*Poems by Edgar A. Poe*, bearing, like the *Lyrical Ballads* of a generation before, a preface that defined and explained and defended his poetical canons.

He was twenty-two, practically the same age as Hawthorne, when he left Bowdoin, and, like him, he also retired into a seclusion almost total. For nearly three years little is known of his life. The most probable conjecture is that he lived at Baltimore with his father's sister, Mrs. Clemm, and that, like Hawthorne again, he gave himself over to reading and study and literary creation. He worked, we know, at a drama entitled *Politian*, and he wrote tales, some of which he may have published early, even as did Hawthorne, anonymously and in obscure papers. He once noted, for instance, that the "MS. Found in a Bottle" had been first published in 1831, two years before it won the prize that was to make him known.

The first tale, however, concerning which we have positive data is his "Metzengerstein," which appeared anonymously in the Philadelphia *Saturday Courier* in January, 1832. Four other tales, also anonymous—"Duc de L'Omelette," "A Tale of Jerusalem," "Loss of Breath," and "Bon-Bon"—appeared in the same paper during the year. That the *Courier* in 1831 had offered a prize of $100 for the best story submitted before December 1, a prize awarded Miss Delia S. Bacon, of the State of New York, author of *The Tales of the Puritan*, etc., for her story, "Love's Martyr," a story printed the week before "Metzengerstein," and that the publishers had announced that all stories submitted were to become the property of the paper, perhaps accounts for the publication of the five tales.[1]

We can be more positive concerning Poe's next publication. In the summer of 1833 the Baltimore *Saturday Visiter* offered a prize of fifty dollars for the best tale submitted, and this prize Poe won, his "MS. Found in a Bottle" being selected as the best of the six tales he had put in competition under the general heading *Tales of the Folio Club*. The tale duly appeared in *The Visiter*, October 19, 1833. Just a week later the paper announced that a volume of tales to be entitled *The Folio Club* was "being put to press." The announcement is worth reproducing:

> The prize tale is not the best of Mr. Poe's productions. Among the tales of The Folio Club there are many possessing uncommon merit. They are all characterized by a raciness, originality of thought, and brilliancy of conception which are rarely to be met with in the writings of our most favored American authors. In assisting Mr. Poe in the publication of The Folio Club, the friends of native literature will encourage a young author whose energies have been partially damped by the opposition of the press, and, we may say, by the lukewarmness of the public in appreciating American productions. He has studied and written much—his reward rested on public approbation—let us give him something more substantial than bare praise.

One week later, November 2, the announcement was withdrawn. Mr. Poe had decided to bring out the book in Philadelphia.[2] The book was not published. After holding the manuscript

---

[1] These facts were first brought out by John C. French in his "Poe and the Saturday Evening Visiter," Modern Language Notes, May, 1918.

[2] A few Notes on Poe's Early Years. Killis Campbell. *The Dial*, Feb. 17, 1916.

apparently for a year, Carey & Lea finally refused it, adducing
as their reason that "small books of detached tales, however
well written, seldom yield a sum sufficient to enable the bookseller to purchase a copyright."

The book refused by the Philadelphia firm contained sixteen
tales: the six offered for *The Visiter* prize, the five previously
published by *The Saturday Courier*, and in addition "Berenice,"
"Morella," "Hans Pfaal," "King Pest," and "Shadow—a
Parable." From *The Visiter* announcement of October, 1833,
it may fairly be inferred that all of these sixteen tales, save perhaps "Hans Pfaal," had been written before the time of the
contest, and that at least some of them had received a cold reception at the hands of editors and publishers and even readers.

The next period in Poe's life is connected with the *Southern
Literary Messenger* of Richmond. Through the influence of
Kennedy he became a contributor, and, after July, 1835, the
editor, of this periodical, and in a few months by the brilliancy of
his work he placed it among the most successful of American
magazines. He wrote during the period of his editorship little
save criticism, but he printed in its pages the greater number of
the Folio Club Tales and several of his earlier poems. Suddenly
in January, 1837, he left Richmond for no reason that has adequately been explained, and settled in New York City induced
possibly by the promises of the editor of the New York *Review*, a
journal that soon became one of the victims of the panic year.
For several months he worked upon his novel *The Narrative of
Arthur Gordon Pym*, which Harper and Brothers brought out in
July, 1838, and then some time during the summer he moved to
Philadelphia, where he remained for six years.

The rest of Poe's life may be passed over rapidly. He was a
magazinist, flitting from magazine to magazine, now as editor,
now as contributing assistant, now as hack writer and literary
adventurer. It must not be forgotten that during the entire
period of his literary life he dreamed of founding a magazine of
his own, one in which he could be free to lift to his own level the
standard of American poetry and prose, in which he might review
fearlessly the books of his period, and in which he might work
out to completeness his system of literary criticism. Often for
months at a time he was just at the point of launching his *Penn
Magazine* or his *Stylus*, often even reaching the stage where he had

already a list of subscribers, but always the project fell through at the last moment for want of funds. The effect upon American literature, especially upon its fiction and its criticism, had Poe been financially supported and been enabled to have realized to the full his dream, can only be conjectured. As it was, he was compelled to live the life of a Grub Street magazinist, doing to a large extent not what he would, but what he must. Discouraged, cursed by hope deferred, maligned and belittled, neglected even when he had put forth some of the most distinctive work of his period, he never once turned his back upon literature. Unlike all the rest of his literary contemporaries, he earned never a dollar in his life save with his pen.

The Philadelphia period was undoubtedly the golden era of his genius, especially in the field of prose. Here he wrote the most of those distinctive tales that are now to be found in books of selections. Only a part of the time was he actually connected with any magazine. For a year beginning July, 1839, he was assistant editor of Burton's *Gentleman's Magazine;* for another year, from April, 1841, he was editor of *Graham's Magazine*, at its period of highest influence; and he seems in 1843 to have had some connection with the weekly *Saturday Museum.*

During the rest of his life, from April, 1844, he was a resident of New York City. In the autumn of that year he became a subeditor of Willis's *Evening Mirror;* in February of the following year he was made co-editor with C. F. Briggs of the weekly *Broadway Journal;* and, in October of the same year, he became its editor and proprietor. The paper died, however, the following January, Poe's finances being in such a condition that failure was inevitable. In 1845 appeared his poem, "The Raven," the first piece of his work to gain universal recognition. But disaster was upon him; his child wife, whom he idolized, died amid surroundings of utter poverty, and Poe himself fell into an illness that for weeks held him near to death. Never again was he to be fully himself. In November, 1845, he wrote Duyckinck: "I really believe that I have been mad—but indeed I have had abundant reason to be so." The rest of the story it is needless to tell. He died wretched and alone in Baltimore, October 7, 1849.

II

Poe's first period as a short-story writer produced the sixteen *Tales of the Folio Club*, all of them probably written during the penumbral years between 1831 and 1835. Possibly some were of earlier date. He wrote tales, we know, while in the University of Virginia and read them to his classmates, and he may have written them while at West Point, but so far as we know none have survived. The sixteen tales represent all that is known of his early fiction. There is a gap of years between them and the next group, for, during the *Messenger* period, he wrote only criticism; the stories that appeared in nearly every issue of the magazine were all drawn from the earlier collection. In the case of Hawthorne we have *Fanshawe*, we have self-revealing paragraphs concerning his obscure years, and after 1835 we have notebooks, but for a study of Poe's 'prentice years we have only these tales, and of these we know only the probable sequence of first publication, certainly not the order in which they were written.

Kennedy, the literary godfather of Poe, writing him February 9, 1836, concerning the eight tales already published in the *Messenger:* "Berenice," "Morella," "Lionizing," "The Visionary," "Bon-Bon," "Loss of Breath," "The MS. Found in a Bottle," and "Metzengerstein"—characterized them as "bizarreries." His first impressions of the tales, gained in the atmosphere of the time and in full knowledge of the fiction then being produced, has peculiar value. He wrote Poe:

You are strong enough now to be criticized. Your fault is your love of the extravagant. Pray beware of it. You find a hundred *intense* writers for one *natural* one. Some of your *bizarreries* have been mistaken for satire—and admired, too, in that character. They deserved it, but *you* did not, for you did not intend them so. I like your grotesque—it is of the very best stamp, and I am sure you will do wonders for yourself in the comic, I mean the *serio tragi comic*.

Poe replied that he *had* intended the tales to be satires:

Most of them were intended for half banter, half satire—although I might not have fully acknowledged this to be their aim even to myself. "Lionizing" and "Loss of Breath" were satires properly speaking—at least so meant—the one of the rage for Lions, and the facility of becoming one—the other of the extravagances of Blackwood.

Almost at the same moment, March 3, 1836, Paulding was writing to White, the proprietor of the *Messenger*, explaining that the publishing house of the Harpers had declined to bring out the tales, first, because they already had appeared in the *Messenger*, and therefore would be "no novelty," but

Most especially they object that there is a degree of obscurity in their application, which will prevent ordinary readers from comprehending their drift, and consequently from enjoying the fine satire they convey. It requires a degree of familiarity with various kinds of knowledge which they do not possess to enable them to relish the joke: the dish is too refined for them to banquet on.

The Harpers, however, agreed that if Mr. Poe would "lower himself a little to the ordinary comprehension of the generality," they would be glad to publish his work. Paulding thereupon offered this advice:

Suggest to him to apply his fine humor and his extensive acquirements to more familiar subjects of satire: to the faults and foibles of our own people, their peculiarities of habits and manners, and above all to the ridiculous affectations and extravagances of the fashionable English Literature of the day, which we copy with such admirable success and servility. His quiz on Willis, and the Burlesque of "Blackwood," were not only capital, but, what is more, were understood by all. For Satire to be relished, it is necessary that it should be leveled at something with which readers are familiar.

It would seem, therefore, that Poe by his own confession and in the judgment of those of his contemporaries best fitted to speak upon the matter considered these early tales, including even "Berenice" and "Morella," as satires upon the philosophical vagaries of the time and upon the extravagances of current prose romance.

To Poe, in this earlier period, literature was poetry, and poetry with him was "not a pursuit, but a passion." If he must live by his pen, as fate had decreed, he must write prose, and marketable prose in 1831 meant short stories for the annuals and the lady's books. The quality of this commodity in the period when Poe began his work we have seen. Irving a decade before had spoken of wild tales of the German type as even then "the commonplace of the day." By 1830 they had grown wilder and had invaded even a periodical as staid as *Blackwood's*. That Poe was a reader of the *Blackwood's* of this period we have plenty of evidence. He read William Mudford's "The Iron Shroud" in the January, 1831, number, and later made use of its idea and atmosphere for "The Pit and the Pendulum." In one of his later critiques he showed familiarity with the gruesome series entitled "Passages From the Diary of a Late Physician." The nature of these tales one may learn from their titles: "The Murder Hole," "The Murderer's Last Night," "The Dance of Death. From the German," "The Pandour and His Princess. A Hungarian Sketch," and "The Bracelets. A Sketch From the German."

The American echoes of the school we have studied. *Godey's* and its tribe became increasingly full of *mélanges* of sensation and horror—flamboyant with adjectives and tremulous with sentimentality. That Poe was aware of this literature and its vogue, and that it ran counter to all his conceptions of literary art is evident to all who read him. To his "Loss of Breath" travesty in the *Messenger* he gave the subtitle "à la Blackwood," and at a later period he wrote "How to Write a Blackwood Article" and to it he appended a burlesque beyond which travesty may not go.

It is but fair to Poe to believe that only a few of these tales chorded with his own highest literary ideals. Three of his early sketches undoubtedly he wrote upon the highest planes he knew: "Silence—a Fable," "Shadow—a Parable," and "Assignation." It is the prose that has beauty in its soul, prose that is near to poetry in its elevation of style. That Poe was embittered by his failure to market this really remarkable type of work is not improbable and that he thereupon launched out into travesty and satire and banter there can be no question.

The literary prototype of the man was Daniel Defoe. There are similarities in the two almost startling: the same journalistic instinct, the same sardonic humor, the same love for hoaxing the reading public, the same genius for seizing upon the latest discovery or scientific inference and pressing it to its conclusion, and the same mastery of verisimilitude by the use of minute details. "Hans Pfaal" and "Arthur Gordon Pym," "The Balloon Hoax" and "The Facts in the Case of M. Valdemar," "The Journal of Julius Rodman" and "Von Kempelen and His Discovery," read as if from the pen of the author of *Robinson Crusoe* and *The Apparition of Mrs. Veal*. A letter written by Poe to Duyckinck as late as March, 1849, throws light upon Poe's habit of mind at this point:

If you have looked over the Von Kempelen article which I left with your brother you will have fully perceived its drift. I meant it as a kind of "exercise" or experiment, in the plausible or verisimilar style. Of course there is *not one* word of truth in it from beginning to end. I thought that such a style, applied to the gold excitement, could not fail of effect. My sincere opinion is that nine out of ten (even among the best informed) will *believe* the quiz (provided the design does not leak out before publication) and that this, acting as a sudden, although, of course, a very temporary, check to the gold fever, it will create a *stir* to some purpose. . . .

I believe the quiz is the first deliberate literary attempt of the kind on record. In the story of Mrs. Veal, we are permitted, now and then, to perceive a tone of *banter*. In *Robinson Crusoe* the design was far more to please, or excite, than to deceive by verisimilitude, in which particular merely, Sir Edward Seaward's narrative is the more skillful book. In my "Valdemar Case" (which *was* credited by many) I had not the slightest idea that any person should credit it as anything more than a "Magazine paper"—but here the whole strength is laid out in verisimilitude.

No one can read the *Folio Club* tales straight through without feeling that Poe wrote the most of them in the hoaxing spirit—"half banter, half satire." The public was reveling in the *Blackwood's* type of tale steeped in "Germanism and gloom"; the metaphysical cult, especially in New England, was discussing Swedenborgian mysticism and metempsychosis, and the various intricacies of the German mysticism: he would write tales that would out-Herod Herod. In "Loss of Breath" he presses the popular manner to its extreme; Peter Schlemihl lost his shadow, Undine lived without a soul, Hauff's Dutch Michael did very well without a heart, Faust and Tom Walker disposed of their souls—he would tell of the man who lost his breath. His hero is maimed, mangled, crushed, hanged, buried alive, but, being without breath, it is impossible for him to breathe his last breath. Consigned to the tomb, he industriously opens all the coffins, sets in view their contents, finds in one of them his lost breath, and, taking possession of it, is rescued, none the worse for his adventures. Satire can go no further.

It is to be doubted if "Metzengerstein" is to be taken with complete seriousness, fine as are some of its art effects. For the second printing of it in 1836 Poe added the subtitle, "A Tale in Imitation of the German." The horse in the tapestry that comes ferociously to life, and the final destruction of the castle with the fiery ascension of the beast, are both of *Otranto* texture, and the metempsychosis motif is a fling at the subtleties of German philosophy. It is not hard to believe that even "Berenice" and "Morella" have in them much of banter and satire. Poe was trying his 'prentice hand. German mysticism and the marvels of psychology were vaguely understood among the generality of readers: he would, in Defoe fashion, make use of the interest in them for tales that would arouse wonder and even amazement, just as later he did it with mesmerism for the "M. Valdemar" tale.

How much German Poe actually knew is open to question, but in French he had been carefully trained, and he had read enough of it to catch to perfection the French lightness and finesse. Kennedy, writing him in September, 1835, advised him to devote himself to the writing of "farces after the manner of the French vaudevilles." Undoubtedly he had been reading "The Duc de l'Omelette," "Bon-Bon," and "A Tale of Jerusalem"; all of them French after the Disraeli manner.

To study these early travesties and youthful exercises is to discover the genesis of certain elements in Poe's art. In all of them invariably there is unity of tone, there is freshness and novelty of treatment, and there is a carefully prepared dénouement. "The Duc de l'Omelette" is essentialy French in its art. The "Duc," who has "died of an ortolan," has fallen, in the approved manner of the time, into the hands of Mephistopheles, but he proves superior to his Majesty in finesse and beats him in a game of cards for his soul, flinging down the winning trump with a smartly turned epigram. Nothing could be more French in style and feeling. In "Bon-Bon" his Majesty discourses wittily with his victim, recounts with gusto parallel cases—"Quintus Flaccus— dear Quinty! as I called him when he sung a seculare for my amusement, while I toasted him in pure good humor, on a fork"— and finally works him to a neatly turned climax in the crackling, epigrammatic, French-paragraph style.

Everywhere it is the work of an artist who plans and proportions and who shapes all to the culmination. Such a craftsman naturally will be out of sympathy with the clumsy work of those about him, with the crude color-splashing and overdone effects and straggling proportions of the lady's book fiction everywhere so popular. His contempt he expressed with unusual bitterness at the beginning of his *Messenger* editorship, the first chance he had had to take a public stand. The novel *Norman Leslie* he dubbed "the most inestimable piece of balderdash with which the common sense of the good people of America was ever so openly or so villainously insulted." The plot is a "monstrous web of absurdity and incongruity." "The characters have no character." They are, "one and all, vapidity itself." "All the good ladies and gentlemen are demigods and demigoddesses, and all the bad are—the d—l." "As regards Mr. Fay's style, it is unworthy of a schoolboy—he has been a-Willising so long as to have forgotten his vernacular language."

It was an attack upon far more than Theodore S. Fay, its author, and on far more than the New York *Mirror*, of which Fay was an editor, it was a blow at the whole lady's book school of the mid-century. *Norman Leslie* was a type not only of the fashionable novel of the time, but of the Willis variety of the short story. The attack was none too severe. He had begun with the rapier, but the age that enjoyed Willis and *Godey's* could understand only the bludgeon.

Had *Tales of the Folio Club* been published, as Poe did his best that they should be, in 1833 or even in 1836, they would have been, by their author's intention at least, a book primarily humorous, a book surprising in its originality and variety, brilliant in its workmanship, a book of carefully wrought hoaxes, of burlesques and imitations, and, in addition to these lighter elements, a book containing two or three serious pieces that are near to poetry, as, for example, the sketch, "Silence." Its soul would have been critical and intellectual rather than spontaneous, deliberate rather than emotional.

III

Almost the first critical comment ever published on Poe's tales connected them with "Germanism." To "Berenice" in the March, 1835, issue of the *Messenger*, Mr. White, the editor, added the note: "Whilst we confess that we think there is too much German horror in his subject, there can be but one opinion as to the force and elegance of his style." Four years later, after the appearance of "The Fall of the House of Usher," James E. Heath wrote Poe:

The editor "doubts whether the readers of the *Messenger* have much relish for tales of the German school, although written with great power and ability, and in this opinion I confess to you frankly, I am strongly inclined to concur. I doubt very much whether tales of the wild, improbable and terrible class can ever be permanently popular in this country.

Charles Dickens, it appears to me, has given the final death blow to writings of that description.

In the preface to *Tales of the Grotesque and Arabesque* (1839), Poe denied the German influence. He had been charged, he declared "with Germanism and gloom," but,

> The truth is that, with a single exception, there is no one of these stories in which the scholar should recognize distinctive features of that species of pseudo-horror which we are taught to call Germanic, for no better reason than that some of the secondary names of German literature have become identified with its folly. If in many of my productions terror has been the thesis, I maintain that terror is not of Germany, but of the soul—that I have deduced this terror only from its legitimate sources, and urged it only to its legitimate results.

The title of his book was against him, as was his allusion to his tales as "Fantasy-pieces," a Hoffman term, and yet the burden of proof lies heavily upon any critic who would maintain that Poe was wrong in his statement.[1]

That he had more than a slight acquaintance with the German language is doubtful, so doubtful, indeed, that it is safe to make the assertion that he knew German literature only in translation. This by no means would mean ignorance of the literature. There were, even in the early 'thirties, translations of the work of most of the German romanticists. By 1826, for instance, at least five of Hoffman's books had been done into English. Scott had reviewed Hoffman at length in the *Foreign Quarterly Review* in 1827; a collection of *Tales From the German* had appeared in 1829; and isolated tales like "The Lost Reflection," *Boston Athenæum*, 1826, "The Fair Eckbert," *New England Magazine*, 1832, and "The Sandman," *Godey's*, 1834, were appearing in the magazines.[2]

---

[1] German books were exceedingly rare in America during the 'thirties. Edward Everett Hale has written: "As late as 1843 I could buy no German books, even in Pennsylvania, but Goethe and Schiller and the Lutheran hymn book."—*A New England Boyhood.* xxiii.

[2] For studies of Poe's German indebtedness see "Edgar Allan Poe und die deutsche Romantik," Paul Wächtler, Leipzig, 1911; "Poe's Knowledge of German": (1) *Publications of the Modern Language Association*, Vol. XIX, No. 1, by Gustav Gruener; (2) *Modern Philology*, Vol. II, 1904. "Influence of E. T. A. Hoffman on the Tales of E. A. Poe," Palmer Cobb. *Studies in Philology*, Vol. III, 1908, published at the University of North Carolina by the Philology Club; "Die Romantische Bewegung in der Amerikanischer Literatur." Walter Just. Berlin. 1910: "Poe and Hoffman," Palmer Cobb, *South Atlantic Quarterly*, January, 1909.

As to the extent with which Poe was acquainted with such translations it is not easy to determine. He was for a year in contact with a leading German specialist in the University of Virginia, and could not have failed to be aware of his enthusiastic studies and translations, but there is no evidence that he was at all influenced by the man. His early title, "Tales of the Folio Club," may have been suggested by the "Serapionsbrüder," but there is little else of Hoffman's book in the collection. The title might just as reasonably have been suggested by Dr. Watkins's Baltimore book of tales of the Delphian Club. The source of all his German allusions and quotations may be located in the current magazines of his time. As an editor he had access to the most of the periodicals of his day, both American and foreign, and it is probable that nearly all of his reading after his editorial career began was confined to this literary area. Instead of being thoroughly acquainted with the German writers, therefore, he may have gathered his knowledge from such careful reviews as that on German literature in *The American Monthly Magazine* (1833), or the review of Heine's "Die Romantische Schule," in *The North American Review* (1834), or the review of Heine's "The Present State of German Literature" in *The American Monthly Magazine* (1836).

If any of Poe's tales contains Germanism, it came not from Germany, but from the grotesque English reflections of the German school found in Walpole and Monk Lewis and their later followers. "The MS. Found in a Bottle" derives from "The Ancient Mariner;" the superman tales like "Morella" and "Ligeia," derive from Byron and Disraeli. Poe's master, however, in this early period was Bulwer-Lytton, and back of Bulwer was *Gil Blas*. From this school of fiction writers he learned the secrets of vaults and dungeons, of bizarre luxury and magnificence of setting, and of those shadowy high-born heroes and heroines who are found only in the dreams of adolescence. "The Assignation," for instance, owes nothing to Hoffman's "Doge and Dogaressa"— there is scarcely a point of similarity: whatever debt it owes is to the Bulwer of the *Pelham* period. Note a passage like this from the *Godey's Lady's Book* version of the tale, January, 1834, a passage, with others like it, carefully edited out in later years:

There was low melancholy music, whose unseen origin undoubtedly lay in the recesses of the red coral trellice work which tapestried the ceiling. The senses were oppressed by mingled and conflicting perfumes reeking up from strange Arabesque censers which seemed actuated with a monstrous vitality as their particolored fires writhed up and down, and around their extravagant proportions. The rays of the rising sun poured in upon the whole, through windows formed each of a single pane of crimson-tinted glass and from their cornices like streams of golden silver, mingled at length, fitfully with the artificial light, and lay weltering and subdued upon a carpet of rich, liquid-looking cloth of gold. Here then had the hand of genius been at work—a wilderness—a chaos of beauty was before me; a sense of dreamy and incoherent grandeur took possession of my soul, and I remained speechless.

That Poe was acquainted with the work of the brothers Schlegel, as would appear from frequent quotations, accounts perhaps for some of his standards in criticism and his knowledge of some of the German writers. He charged Hawthorne with imitation of Tieck's manner with the air of one who himself *knew* Tieck's manner. His allusions to Hoffman in his criticism bear the stamp of knowledge. In 1836, in a review of the novel *Conti the Discarded*, he analyzes one of Hoffman's peculiar innovations:

The Art Novels—the Kunstromanen—books written not so much in immediate defense, or in illustration, as in the personification of individual portions of the Fine Arts—books which, in the guise of Romance, labor to the sole end of reasoning men into admiration and study of the beautiful by a tissue of *bizarre* fiction, partly allegorical and partly metaphysical. In Germany alone could so mad—or perhaps so profound—an idea have originated.

In 1839 he reviewed at length and with unqualified commendation Fouque's *Undine,* and in another review he called Longfellow's *Hyperion* a mixture of ingredients, among them "one or two of the Phantasy Pieces of the Lorrainean Callot." There are unmistakable traces of Hoffman's "Das Marjorat" in "The Fall of the House of Usher," and there is a trace of the Hoffman style in several others of the tales. So far we may go with certainty: the rest is conjecture.

That Hoffman and Poe were kindred souls unquestionably is true. Both were abnormally sensitive, neurotic, subject to *doppelganger* illusions, as in Poe's "William Wilson" and "Ulalume," and both at last were near to insanity. Hoffman's pathetic entry in his diary, "Why, in sleeping and waking, do I, in my thoughts, dwell upon the subject of insanity? The outpouring of the wild ideas that arise in my mind may perhaps operate like the breathing of a vein," might have been as well a notation by the author of "The Haunted Palace." Hoffman might have posed as the original of Usher in Poe's weird tale, and Poe might have been one of the unique four that formed the Serapion Club. Both worked with the same temperament, with the same materials in the same atmosphere of romance, Hoffman with lawless creative genius, Poe with a deliberate art that in its field is well-nigh perfect.

IV

Poe was made a romanticist by his times; fundamentally he was not romantic: he was scientific. He was turned to the short story of the Germanized grotesque and arabesque type by necessity: circumstances demanded it. He had tried to enter the field of literature by way of poetry, issuing three books of verse before he was twenty-two. Driven to produce literary wares that would sell, he turned to sketches and tales to be submitted for cash prizes, but with no conviction that he was producing serious work. It had been his ideal to enter the profession with dignity by means of books. Kennedy in a letter to White, dated April, 1835, noted that Poe was basing his expectations upon a book that had been for a year in the hands of a Philadelphia publisher, but that he had advised the young man to turn all his powers into the magazines. "He is very clever with his pen—classical and scholarlike. He wants experience and direction. . . . I told him to write something for every number of your magazine. . . . He is at work upon a tragedy, but I have turned him to drudging upon whatever may make money."

Poe as a writer of tales undoubtedly was created by the magazines, and the magazine movement to a large extent had been brought about by copyright conditions. "The want of an International Copy-Right Law," Poe wrote in the seventh number of the *Broadway Journal*, "by rendering it nearly impossible to obtain anything from the booksellers in the way of remuneration for literary labor, has had the effect of forcing many of our best writers into the service of the Magazines and Reviews." His own literary life had opened just at the moment when the magazine in America had become a dominating force, and he found himself swept along irresistibly by the current of it. In New England, as proved by the case of Willis, the advent of the lighter types of literature provided by the magazines, was looked upon with concern, but Poe, well outside of the conservative area, was quick to feel the momentum and meaning of the new movement. By 1840 he could declare that "the whole tendency of the age is magazine-ward"; but the period of the quarterly reviews which discussed "only topics caviar to the many" was over: "In a word, their ponderosity is quite out of keeping with the rush of the age. We now demand the light artillery of the intellect; we need the curt, the condensed, the pointed, the readily diffused— in place of the verbose, the detached, the voluminous, the inaccessible."

More than once he expressed himself that an era had come that forced men "upon the curt, the condensed, the well-digested, in place of the voluminous—in a word, upon journalism in lieu of dissertation."

We need now the light artillery rather than the "Peace-makers" of the intellect. I will not be sure that men at present think more profoundly than half a century ago, but beyond question they think with more rapidity, with more skill, with more tact, with more method and less of excrescence in the thought. Besides all this, they have a vast increase in the thinking material; they have more facts, more to think about. For this reason, they are disposed to put the greatest amount of thought in the smallest compass and disperse it with the utmost attainable rapidity. Hence the journalism of the age; hence, in especial, magazines.

In a letter to Professor Anthon, June, 1844, Poe had written that "before quitting the *Messenger*" he had had a vision of the supreme possibilities of the American magazine and had determined to found one himself after his own ideals:

I perceived that the country, from its very constitution, could not fail of affording in a few years a larger proportionate amount of readers than any upon earth. I perceived that the whole energetic, busy spirit of the age tended wholly to Magazine literature—to the curt, the terse, the well-timed, and the readily diffused, in preference to the old forms of the verbose and ponderous and inaccessible. I knew from personal experience that lying *perdu* among the innumerable plantations of our vast Southern and Western countries were a vast host of well-educated men peculiarly devoid of prejudice who would gladly lend their influence to a really vigorous journal.

It was in this letter that Poe described himself as one who had written no books, but had been "so far a magazinist . . . a mere magazinist." It is evident that he considered the magazine article in a class by itself. Of his "M. Valdemar" hoax he had written, "I had not the slightest idea that any person should credit it as anything more than a 'Magazine-paper.'" The object of such a paper was to entertain, to hold the attention of a reader pleasantly for a limited period. It must be of a quality that would attract instantly, and its first requisite, therefore, must be novelty. "What the public seek in a Magazine," Poe wrote in 1849, "is what they cannot elsewhere procure." This point he had emphasized as early as 1836 in his "Peter Snook": "How rarely are we struck with an American magazine article, as with an absolute novelty—how frequently the foreign articles so affect us. . . . We are lamentably deficient not only in invention proper, but what is more strictly Art."

Next to novelty he sought variety: "Variety has been one of my chief ends," Poe wrote to Anthon. Again and again he iterated this canon of "diversity and variety." Of tales, he declared, "there is a vast variety of kinds and, in degree of value, these kinds vary—but each kind is equally good of its kind. . . . I do not consider any one of my stories *better* than another." Defoe-like, he would touch his reader ever at the point of his greatest curiosity, giving him always something new, something fitted skillfully into the newnesses of the time. As a result the tales of Poe are marvelous in their diversity: the work of few men is so difficult to classify.

The third requisite that Poe required of the magazine paper was Art. The tale of the German type, the work even of Hoffman and Tieck, was clumsy and lumbering, diffuse, and often disjointed, but with Poe constructive art was a prime requisite. Once the province of the magazine article was understood, the need of constructive art was obvious, but, curiously enough, few who had used the form had perceived this. To Poe all that was not "curt, and condensed, and well digested" was unfitted for magazine publication, and yet the magazines everywhere were full of such work:

It is, however, in the composition of that class of Magazine papers which come properly under the head of *Tales*, that we evince the most remarkable deficiency in skill. If we except first Mr. Hawthorne—

secondly, Mr. Simms—thirdly Mr. Willis,—and fourthly, one or two others, whom we may as well put mentally together without naming them—there is not even a respectably skillful tale-writer on this side the Atlantic. We have seen, to be sure, many well-constructed stories—individual specimens—the work of American Magazinists; but these specimens have invariably appeared to be happy accidents of construction; their authors, in subsequent tales, having always evinced an incapacity to construct.

Margaret Fuller in 1846 had had much the same opinion:

The most important part of our literature, while the work of diffusion is still going on, lies in the journals. . . . Among these, the Magazines take the lowest rank. Their object is principally to cater for the amusement of vacant hours, and, as there is not a great deal of wit and light talent in this country, they do not even this to much advantage.

Poe would supply this obvious lack: he would bring Art to the Magazine-paper. To him Art was a deliberate thing. The tale writer should write not from his emotions or from his inspirations, but coldly and deliberately from his intellect. A tale should be made as an architect plans a building. First, the purpose of the structure should be determined: the merit of the tale, to use Poe's own terms, lies in its "being perfectly adapted to its purposes."

Most authors sit down to write with *no* fixed design, trusting to the inspiration of the moment; it is not, therefore, to be wondered at, that *most* books are valueless. Pen should never touch paper, until at least a well-digested *general* purpose be established. In fiction the dénouement—in all other compositions the intended effect—should be definitely considered and arranged, before writing the first word; and *no* word should be then written which does not tend, or form a part of a sentence which tends to the development of the *dénouement* or to the strengthening of the effect. Where plot forms a portion of the contemplated interest, too much preconsideration cannot be had. *Plot* is very imperfectly understood, and has never been rightly defined. Many persons regard it as a mere complexity of incident. In its most rigorous acceptation, it is *that from which no component atom can be removed, and in which none of the component atoms can be displaced, without ruin to the whole;*[1] and although

---

[1] In an epic or a tragedy, the plot, which is an imitation of an action, must represent an action that is organically unified, the structural order of the incidents being such that transposing or removing any one of them will dislocate and disorganize the whole. Every part must be necessary, and in its place; for a thing whose presence or absence makes no perceptible difference is not an organic part of the whole.—ARISTOTLE's *The Art of Poetry.*

a sufficiently good plot may be constructed, without attention to the whole rigor of this definition, still it is the definition which the true artist should always keep in view, and always endeavor to consummate in his works.

As early as 1836, while still editor of the *Messenger*, Poe had discovered that the novel and the short story are essentially different art forms: "Unity of effect, a quality not easily appreciated or indeed comprehended by the ordinary mind, and a desideratum difficult of attainment even by those who can conceive it—is indispensable in the 'brief article'"—he was reviewing the short sketches of Dickens—"and not so in the common novel." The novel, he declared, "from the length of the narrative, cannot be taken in at one view of the reader," and therefore always fails as a whole. If it is admired at all, it "is admired for its detached passages, without reference to the work as a whole."

Poe, therefore, had discovered the principle of the short story through his study of poetry, his theories concerning which he had first formulated in 1831 for the third edition of his poems. He had discovered that the tale is akin in its art to the ballad, the requirements of which he had set forth in his review of Longfellow's poems. Of the ballad he had written, "its effect will depend in a great measure upon the perfection of its finish, upon the nice adaptation of its constituent parts, and especially upon what is rightly termed by Schlegel the unity and totality of interest." He defined poetry always in terms of lyricism, of emotionalism, and the emotional unit necessarily is short. The tale, he now discovered, was also dependent upon emotion, a lyrical unit, a single stroke of impressionism, the record of a moment of tension.

Having made this discovery, the rest was easy. His experience as an editor, working always in terms of space, seeking always the maximum of effect with the minimum of material, helped him to formulate his art to completeness. By 1842 he was ready to formulate his canons of the short story into something like a system. His universally quoted review of Hawthorne's *Twice-Told Tales* should be given at length in every study of the American short story. It is the leading document in the history of the form:

V

The tale proper, in our opinion, affords unquestionably the fairest field for the exercise of the loftiest talent, which can be afforded by the wide domains of mere prose. Were we bidden to say how the highest genius could be most advantageously employed for the best display of its own powers, we should answer, without hesitation—in the composition of a rimed poem, not to exceed in length what might be perused in an hour. Within this limit alone can the highest order of true poetry exist. We need only here say, upon this topic, that, in almost all classes of composition, the unity of effect or impression is a point of the greatest importance. It is clear, moreover, that this unity cannot be thoroughly preserved in productions whose perusal cannot be completed at one sitting. We may continue the reading of a prose composition, from the very nature of prose itself, much longer than we can persevere, to any good purpose, in the perusal of a poem. This latter, if truly fulfilling the demands of the poetic sentiment, induces an exaltation of the soul which cannot be long sustained. All high excitements are necessarily transient. Thus a long poem is a paradox. And, without unity of impression, the deepest effects cannot be brought about. Epics were the offspring of an imperfect sense of Art, and their reign is no more. A poem *too* brief may produce a vivid, but never an intense or enduring impression. Without a certain continuity of effort—without a certain duration or repetition of purpose— the soul is never deeply moved. There must be the dropping of the water on the rock. De Béranger has wrought brilliant things—pungent and spirit-stirring—but, like all immassive bodies, they lack *momentum*, and thus fail to satisfy Poetic Sentiment. They sparkle and excite, but, from want of continuity, fail deeply to impress. Extreme brevity will degenerate into epigrammatism; but the sin of extreme length is even more unpardonable. *In medio tutissimus ibis!*

Were we called upon, however, to designate that class of composition which, next to such a poem as we have suggested, should best fulfill the demands of high genius—should offer it the most advantageous field of exertion—we should unhesitatingly speak of the prose tale, as Mr. Hawthorne has here exemplified it. We allude to the short prose narrative, requiring from a half-hour to one or two hours in its perusal. The ordinary novel is objectionable, from its length, for reasons already stated in substance. As it cannot be read at one sitting, it deprives itself, of course, of the immense force derivable from *totality*.[1] Worldly interests intervening during the pauses of perusal, modify, annul, or counteract, in a greater or less degree, the impressions of the book. But simple cessation in reading, would, of itself, be sufficient to destroy the true unity. In the brief tale, however, the author is enabled to carry out the fullness of his intention, be it what it may. During the hour of perusal the soul of the reader is at

---

[1] The concentrated effect is more delightful than one which is drawn out, and so diluted. Consider the result, for example, if one were to lengthen out *Œdipus the King* into the number of lines in the *Iliad.*—ARISTOTLE's *The Art of Poetry*.

the writer's control. There are no external or extrinsic influences—resulting from weariness or interruption.

A skillful literary artist has constructed a tale. If wise, he has not fashioned his thoughts to accommodate his incidents: but having conceived, with deliberate care, a certain unique or single *effect*[1] to be wrought out, he then invents such incidents—he then combines such effects as may best aid him in establishing this preconceived effect. If his very initial sentence tend not to the outbringing of this effect, then he has failed in his first step. In the whole composition there should be no word written, of which the tendency, direct or indirect, is not to the one preestablished design. And by such means, with such care and skill, a picture is at length painted which leaves in the mind of him who contemplates it with a kindred art, a sense of the fullest satisfaction. The idea of the tale has been presented unblemished, because undisturbed; and this is an end unattainable by the novel. Undue brevity is just as exceptionable here as in the poem; but undue length is yet more to be avoided.

We have said that the tale has a point of superiority even over the poem. In fact, while the *rhythm* of this latter is an essential aid in the development of the poet's highest idea—the idea of the Beautiful—the artificialities of this rhythm are an inseparable bar to the development of all points of thought or expression which have their basis in *Truth*. But Truth is often, and in very great degree, the aim of the tale. Some of the finest tales are tales of ratiocination. Thus the field of this species of composition, if not in so elevated a region on the mountain of Mind, is a tableland of far vaster extent than the domain of the mere poem. Its products are never so rich, but infinitely more numerous, and more appreciable by the mass of mankind. The writer of the prose tale, in short, may bring to his theme a vast variety of modes or inflections of thought and expression—(the ratiocinative, for example, the sarcastic, or the humorous) which are not only antagonistical to the nature of the poem, but absolutely forbidden by one of its most peculiar and indispensable adjuncts; we allude, of course, to rhythm. It may be added here, *par parenthèse*, that the author who aims at the purely beautiful in a prose tale is laboring at great disadvantage. For Beauty can be better treated in the poem. Not so with terror, or passion, or horror, or a multitude of such other points. And here it will be seen how full of prejudice are the usual animadversions against those *tales of effect*, many fine examples of which were found in the earlier numbers of *Blackwood*. The impressions produced were wrought in a legitimate sphere of action, and

---

[1] The story should be constructed on dramatic principles: everything should turn about a single action, one that is whole, and is organically perfect—having a beginning, and a middle, and an end.—ARISTOTLE'S *The Art of Poetry*.

constituted a legitimate although sometimes an exaggerated interest.[1] They were relished by every man of genius: although there were found many men of genius who condemned them without just ground. The true critic will but demand that the design intended be accomplished, to the fullest extent, by the means most advantageously applicable.

We have very few American tales of real merit—we may say, indeed, none with the exception of *The Tales of a Traveler* of Washington Irving, and these *Twice-Told Tales* of Mr. Hawthorne. Some of the pieces of Mr. John Neal abound in vigor and originality; but in general, his compositions of this class are excessively diffuse, extravagant, and indicative of an imperfect sentiment of Art. Articles at random are, now and then, met with in our periodicals which might be advantageously compared with the best effusions of the British Magazines; but upon the whole, we are far behind our progenitors in this department of literature.

Of Mr. Hawthorne's *Tales* we would say, emphatically, that they belong to the highest region of Art—an Art subservient to genius of a very lofty order. We had supposed, with good reason for so supposing, that he had been thrust into his present position by one of the impudent *cliques* which beset our literature, and whose pretentions it is our full purpose to expose at the earliest opportunity; but we have been more agreeably mistaken. We know of few compositions which the critic can more honestly commend than these *Twice-Told Tales*. As Americans, we feel proud of the book.

Mr. Hawthorne's distinctive trait is invention, creation, imagination, originality—a trait which, in the literature of fiction, is positively worth all the rest. But the nature of originality, so far as regards its manifestation in letters, is but imperfectly understood. The inventive or original mind as frequently displays itself in novelty of *tone* as in novelty of matter. Mr. Hawthorne is original at *all* points.

VI

In the domain of the short story Poe stands for intellect, science, deliberate art, "tales of effect." In an early review of his work in *Blackwood's* a review written in the atmosphere of Poe's own day, there is this discerning word: "There is no passion in these tales, neither is there any attempt at dramatic dialogue. The bent of Mr. Poe's mind seems rather to have been toward reasoning than sentiment." In an over-sentimental age, Poe worked coldly

[1] The plot should be so constructed that, even without help from the eye one who simply hears the play recited must feel the chill of fear, and be stirred with pity, at what occurs. . . . But those who employ the means of the stage to produce what strikes us as being merely monstrous, without being terrible are absolute strangers to the art of tragedy.—ARISTOTLE'S *The Art of Poetry*.

and without sentiment; in an age grotesque with perversions of romanticism, he worked without extravagance, and weighed and analyzed, and evolved an art that is classical in its chaste proportions. He organized romanticism and codified its laws.

His art is the embodiment of simplicity. The variety of his tales is surprising, yet all have one thing in common: each sets out to accomplish a single effect, and everything is centered upon this one purpose, even at the sacrifice of truth. Nowhere is there realism. The characters are not alive; they move not at all our sympathies; we never see such people in real life. Everything is foreseen, artificial, dramatically timed. The entombed Madeline appears at precisely the right moment; the death of Usher is followed instantly by the disappearance of the house of Usher into the "tarn." The sole object of the writer was to create an impression upon his reader: every detail from the first sentence, which sets the pitch, to the final catastrophe, is added to accomplish this end. There is no attempt at localization, no attempt to portray actual human life and conditions, no hint whatever at a moral basis. In one of his letters he quoted with approval a reply of Monk Lewis, who, when asked why he had introduced black banditti into one of his plays when, in the country where the scene was laid, black people were quite unknown, made reply,

I introduced them because I truly anticipated that blacks would have more *effect* on my audience than whites—and if I had taken it into my head that, by making them sky-blue, the effect would have been greater, why sky-blue they should have been.

At many points to-day regarded as important in short-story technique Poe failed almost completely. His dialogue is bookish and unnatural; his dialect, whenever he attempts it, as in the case of the negro in "The Gold Bug," lacks in verisimilitude; his characters are abstractions without flesh and blood; his accessories and backgrounds have nowhere the sense of actuality. Not one of his tales is essentially American in any respect. He was not seeking for realism. He had no sympathy with the group that was exploiting native scenes and legends as the material for a distinctively American literature. Art to him was independent of time and place; he had no sympathy with the fundamental elements of Hawthorne's tales—their allegory and their sermonic connotation. Art to him meant beauty and moments of impression; he had no sympathy with Irving and Longfellow—he had no reverence for the past and no tendency to sentiment. In America he stood peculiarly alone. As noted in the opening chapter, romanticism—Irving and all the disciples of Scott—is retrospective: it lives in the mellow atmosphere of a vanished golden age. Hawthorne, like all the Puritans, was introspective: he saw the world within and wrestled with problems of sin. Poe alone was circumspective: like the journalist, he worked ever in the vital present; he studied and he watched his reader, intent only upon impressing him for the brief moment that was his, upon holding him and thrilling him and compelling him with no thought of past or future.

And he worked ever in a world of his own creation in materials drawn from his reading and imagining rather than from his observation. For this world he himself made the laws, and as a result it is ruled not by law, but by coincidence. Everywhere artificiality. In his detective tales we follow not nature, but a sequence of events evolved from his teeming imagination. He is a conjuror marvelous in his art, displaying with dexterity a variety of effects quite amazing, but he is little more. He leaves nothing behind save a haunting memory of a moment of sensation; an impression that depresses rather than elevates the soul. In constructive art he was superior to all his contemporaries, superior greatly to Hawthorne; but in all else he falls immeasurably below his Puritan contemporary.

His originality, a characteristic upon which he especially prided himself, proceeded from cold intellect rather than from any spontaneous improvisations of genius. His "Philosophy of Composition," in which he tells how he built his poem, "The Raven," just as an architect deliberately works out the plans for a house, undoubtedly has in it an element of truth. He thought out his art effects with calculating precision.

The method of his "tales of ratiocination," a new *genre* in fiction, he evolved with deliberation. Nothing he wrote contains more of the real Poe than those well-known four tales, the parent stock from which have come all later detective stories—"The Gold Bug," "The Murders in the Rue Morgue," "The Purloined Letter," and the "Mystery of Marie Rogêt."[1] His almost uncanny ability to decipher every variety of secret writing discloses

[1] "Poe and the Detective Story." Brander Matthews. *Scribner's Magazine.* September, 1907.

his type of mind. He was a scientist, an analyzer, an observer of microscopically minute differences. The device of the somewhat obtuse helper who serves as a foil to the Master Mind, the method of deducing the cause from a hundred obscure clues all as perfectly obvious to the Master as they are obscure to the average observer, the stupidity of the police who handle the case in the stereotyped way, and the division of the tale into two parts, the one the tale proper, and the other the explanation as given by the great detective, have become the commonplaces of the modern detective story, yet all of these devices date from Poe's four tales.[1]

His material was much of it drawn from the regions of horror and sensation, but it was the manner of the time. He did not write the horrible because there was horror in his soul: he wrote simply material that he thought would best command the market of his day. He studied the tastes of his age with the methods and the instincts of a yellow journalist. Very recently a letter has been discovered which reveals clearly his point of view. It was written to T. W. White of the *Southern Literary Messenger* April 30, 1835, during the period before Poe assumed the editorship of the magazine:

A word or two in relation to "Berenice." Your opinion of it is very just. The subject is by far too horrible, and I confess that I hesitated in sending it to you, especially as a specimen of my capabilities. The tale originated in a bet that I could produce nothing effective on a subject so singular, provided I treated it seriously. . . . You may say all this is in bad taste. I have my doubts about it. . . . To be appreciated you must be read, and these things are invariably sought after with avidity. . . . Such articles as the "MS. Found in a Madhouse" and the "Monos and Daimonos" of the *London New Monthly;* "the Confessions of an Opium Eater" and "The Man in the Bell" of *Blackwood.* The first two were written by no less a man than Bulwer; the "Confessions" universally attributed to Coleridge, although unjustly. Thus the first men in [blotted] have not thought writings of this nature unworthy of their talents. . . . In respect to "Berenice" individually I allow that it approaches the very verge of bad taste—but I will not sin quite so egregiously again.

[1] It is worthy of note that Poe's peculiar method in his detective tales had been used by Schiller in his "The Ghost Seer," and that a translation of this by Professor C. J. Hadermann, of Oxford, Georgia, appeared in *The Magnolia or Southern Magazine,* Savannah, in 1841, the year of Poe's "The Murders in the Rue Morgue."

It has been asserted often that Poe invented the American short story, that deliberately he manufactured a new *genre* and presented to the world for the first time a unique literary form. The assertion is wrong. The short story of the modern type had been evolving with definiteness for two decades. Irving had elaborated the legendary sketch and the tale of romantic incident; the Western group had brought prominently forth the romantic historical episode and at times had touched it with realism; Hawthorne had presented tales of intense moral situations and had added a symbolism all of his own; and Poe had added impressionism and "unity and totality of effect." All this had been done in an atmosphere of romance that had made for unreality and sentiment and diffuseness and vagueness. But the age of extreme romance was passing and Poe was the first to perceive it. The annuals and the magazines that had sprung up in surprising numbers to supply the new demand for sketches and tales more and more were seeking for material that within the brief space at their command would yield the maximum of effect. Poe was the first to awake to the situation, the first consciously to avail himself of a short-story technique, the first to formulate this technique into a system. In other words, the world of the short story had been discovered: Poe was the first to make an accurate chart of the new regions and to demonstrate how this chart might best be used.

BIBLIOGRAPHY

CHRONOLOGY OF POE'S TALES

1. Metzengerstein [later, in *Southern Literary Messenger*, Metzengerstein, a Tale in Imitation of the German]. *Philadelphia Saturday Courier*, Jan., 1832.
2. Duc de l'Omelette. *Philadelphia Saturday Courier*, March, 1832.
3. A Tale of Jerusalem. *Philadelphia Saturday Courier*, June, 1832.
4. Loss of Breath [originally A Decided Loss]. *Philadelphia Saturday Courier*, Nov., 1832.
5. Bon-Bon [originally The Bargain Lost]. *Philadelphia Saturday Courier*, Dec., 1832.
6. MS. Found in a Bottle. *Baltimore Saturday Visiter*, Oct., 1833.
7. The Assignation [originally The Visionary]. *Godey's Lady's Book*, Jan., 1834.
8. Berenice. *Southern Literary Messenger*, March, 1835.
9. Morella. *Southern Literary Messenger*, April, 1835.

10. Lionizing [also as Some Passages in the Life of a Lion]. *Southern Literary Messenger*, May, 1835.
11. The Unparalleled Adventure of One Hans Pfaal. *Southern Literary Messenger*, June, 1835.
12. King Pest: A Tale Containing an Allegory. *Southern Literary Messenger*, Sept., 1835.
13. Shadow: a Parable [originally Shadow. A Fable]. *Southern Literary Messenger*, Sept., 1835.
14. Four Beasts in One: The Homo-Camelopard [Originally Epimanes]. *Southern Literary Messenger*, March, 1836.
15. The Narrative of Arthur Gordon Pym [published only in part]. *Southern Literary Messenger*.
16. Silence—a Fable [originally Siope]. *The Baltimore Book*, 1839.

(Of these sixteen, 6, 10, and 7 are known to have been in the *Tales of the Folio Club* manuscript submitted for the *Visiter* prize in 1833, and there is evidence that 14 and 16 were also of the number. According to the remembrance of Latrobe, one of the judges in the contest, the sixth tale was "A Descent into the Maelstrom," but the evidence is by no means conclusive. These, together with the other ten above, with the exception of 15, doubtless made up the sixteen *Tales of the Folio Club* submitted to Carey & Lea early in 1834.)

17. Mystification [originally Von Jung, the Mystific]. *American Monthly Magazine*, June, 1837.
18. Ligeia. *American Museum*, Sept., 1838.
19. How to Write a *Blackwood* Article [originally The Psyche Zenobia]. *American Museum*, Nov., 1838.
20. A Predicament [originally The Scythe of Time]. *American Museum*, Nov., 1838.
21. The Devil in the Belfry. *Philadelphia Saturday Chronicle*, May, 1839.
22. The Man That Was Used Up. *Burton's Gentleman's Magazine*, Aug., 1839.
23. The Fall of the House of Usher. *Burton's Gentleman's Magazine*, Sept., 1839.
24. William Wilson. *The Gift*. 1840 [published before Sept. 17, 1839].
25. Conversation of Eiros and Charmion. *Burton's Gentleman's Magazine*, Dec., 1839.
26. Why the Little Frenchman Wears His Hand in a Sling. 1840.

(*Tales of the Grotesque and Arabesque*, 1840, contained the twenty-six tales above with the exception of "Arthur Gordon Pym.")

27. The Journal of Julius Rodman. *Burton's Gentleman's Magazine*, Jan., 1840.

28. The Business Man [originally Peter Pendulum, the Business Man].
    Burton's Gentleman's Magazine, Feb., 1840.
29. The Man of the Crowd, *Graham's Magazine*, Dec., 1840.
30. The Murders in the Rue Morgue, *Graham's Magazine*, April, 1841.
31. A Descent into the Maelstrom. *Graham's Magazine*, May, 1841.
32. The Island of the Fay, *Graham's Magazine*, June, 1841.
33. The Colloquy of Monos and Una. *Graham's Magazine*, Aug., 1841.
34. Never Bet the Devil Your Head: A Tale with a Moral [originally
    Never Bet Your Head: A Moral Tale]. *Graham's Magazine*,
    Sept., 1841.
35. Eleonora. *The Gift*. 1842 [out in Sept., 1841].
36. Three Sundays in a Week [originally A Succession of Sundays].
    Saturday Evening Post, Nov. 1841.
37. The Oval Portrait [originally Life in Death]. *Graham's Magazine*,
    April, 1842.
38. The Masque of the Red Death, a Fantasy. *Graham's Magazine*,
    May, 1842.
39. The Landscape Garden, *Snowden's Ladies' Companion*, Oct., 1842.
40. The Mystery of Marie Rogêt, a Sequel to the Murders in the Rue
    Morgue. *Snowden's*, Nov.-Dec., 1842; Feb., 1843.
41. The Pit and the Pendulum. *The Gift*, 1843.
42. The Tell-Tale Heart. *Pioneer*, Jan., 1843.
43. The Gold Bug, *Dollar Newspaper*, June, 1843.
44. The Black Cat. *U. S. Saturday Post*, Aug., 1843.
45. Diddling Considered as One of the Exact Sciences [originally Raising
    the Wind, or, etc.]. *Philadelphia Saturday Commercial*, Oct.,
    1843.
46. The Elk [originally Morning on the Wissahickon]. *The Opal*, 1844.
47. The Spectacles. *Dollar Newspaper*, March, 1844.
48. A Tale of the Ragged Mountains. *Godey's Lady's Book*, April, 1844.
49. The Balloon Hoax. *New York Sun*, April, 1844.
50. The Premature Burial. *Dollar Newspaper*, July, 1844.
51. Mesmeric Revelation. *Columbian Magazine*, Aug., 1844.
52. The Oblong Box. *Godey's*, Sept., 1844.
53. The Angel of the Odd. *Columbian Magazine*, Oct., 1844.
54. Thou Art the Man. *Godey's*, Nov., 1844.
55. The Literary Life of Thingum-Bob, Esq. *Southern Literary Mes-
    senger*, Dec., 1844.
56. The Purloined Letter. *The Gift*, 1845.

Tales. Edgar Allan Poe, 1845, in the following order: **43, 44, 51, 10,
23, 31, 33, 25, 30, 40, 56, 29.** Of this edition of the tales Poe wrote:
"The last selection of my tales was made from about seventy by one of
our great little cliquists and claqueurs, Wiley and Putnam's reader,

Duyckinck. He has what he thinks a taste for ratiocination, and has accordingly made up the book mostly of analytic stories. But this is not *representing* my mind in its various phases—it is not giving me fair play."

57. The Thousand and Second Tale of Scheherazade. *Godey's*, Feb., 1845.
58. Some Words with a Mummy. *American Whig Review*, April, 1845.
59. The Power of Words. *Democratic Review*, June, 1845.
60. The Imp of the Perverse. *Graham's Magazine*, July, 1845.
61. The System of Dr. Tarr and Prof. Fether. *Graham's Magazine*, Nov., 1845.
62. The Facts in the Case of M. Valdemar. *American Whig Review*, Dec., 1845.
63. The Sphynx. *Arthur's Ladies' Magazine*, Jan., 1846.
64. The Cask of Amontillado, *Godey's*, Nov., 1846.
65. The Domain of Arnheim [Combined with 39]. *Columbian Magazine*, March, 1847.
66. Mellonta Tauta. *Godey's*, Feb., 1849.
67. Hop Frog. *Flag of Our Union*, March, 1849.
68. Von Kempelen and His Discovery, *Flag of Our Union*, April, 1849.
69. X-ing a Paragrab. *Flag of Our Union*, May, 1849.
70. Landor's Cottage. *Flag of Our Union*, June, 1849.

CHAPTER VII

THE DECADE AFTER POE

I

The decade of the 'fifties that should have built consciously and artistically after Poe, and that should have deepened and broadened all its foundations after Hawthorne, stands in our literary history as the period when, with a few exceptions, the short story ceased to be distinctive, when for a time, indeed, it seemed about to disappear as a reputable literary form. The year of Poe's death closed the period that had begun with *The Sketch Book*. Seemingly it closed it at its most promising moment: Poe's "The Cask of Amontillado" had appeared in 1846, and Hawthorne's "The Great Stone Face" was to appear in 1850. But Poe's influence had been almost nothing. There is no evidence in all the critical writings of the mid-century or in any of the literary correspondence of the time that a single reader in 1842 had seen his review of Hawthorne or that anyone had profited at all from the brilliant technique of his *Tales of the Grotesque and Arabesque*. For a generation after his death his tales were mentioned only as terror-compelling things, strange exotics standing gruesomely alone and almost to be regretted among the conventional creations of American literature. New England regarded him as an unholy thing that were better forgotten. Lowell summed him up in terms of morals: he was "wholly lacking in that element of manhood which, for want of a better name, we call *character*. It is something quite distinct from genius—though all great geniuses are endowed with it." New York on the whole agreed with New England. The *Tribune*, announcing his death, added the verdict, "few will be grieved by it . . . he had few or no friends." And even Walt Whitman, a member of the Pfaff coterie of Broadway Bohemians, could discuss him in later days as a writer "almost without the first sign of moral principle, or the concrete or its heroisms, or the simple affections of the heart." While Europe was discovering him as a new master of technique

145

in poetry and in prose, the new leader of a new school, legends of his personal habits blinded America almost completely to the work of the man and the originality of his genius. Our leading master of short-story technique, he has directly influenced American short-story technique hardly at all. The tales of Hawthorne, too, exerted very little of the influence that might have been predicted of them during the decade of the 'forties, but their neglect came from reasons quite different. After *The Scarlet Letter* (1850) and *The House of the Seven Gables* (1851), the writer of *Twice-Told Tales* was swallowed up in the romancer. It was as if his earlier period of tales and sketches had been a period of apprenticeship and now he had begun upon his real work.

It is impossible to escape the conviction that the short story in 1850 as a distinct and serious literary form had won no real recognition. By most critics it was regarded as a phenomenon of the times, like the souvenirs and the lady's books, necessary, perhaps, but to be deplored. The critical press spoke of tales as "light magazine material" and offered their writers such counsel as this: "We should advise the accomplished writer to try her hand at a more elaborate and sustained effort," and this after having declared that "the most of her tales are above the average of such compositions." The more serious critical journals reviewed few collections of short stories. *The North American Review* during nearly two decades noticed prominently only two such books: Miss Prescott's *The Amber Gods* and Hale's *If, Yes, and Perhaps*.

One recognition there was, however, that must be regarded as notable, that in Griswold's *The Prose Writers of America* (1847). Undoubtedly here is one of the few places where may be detected the influence of Poe, but, whatever the source of its inspiration, the book must be counted as containing the first formal recognition of the tale as a unique literary evolution in America, and the first attempt—short and fragmentary, it is true—toward the history of the form.

Commencing with the statement that in England the unit of measure for fiction had long been the three-volume novel, Griswold gave it as his opinion that a new unit had been evolved. The Germans had started the movement. They had "gone back to the more ancient models, such as were furnished by Boccaccio and the authors of the *Gesta Romanorum*." The new form had flourished, especially in America—"Many things in our own country have tended to increase the popularity of the tale. Partly in consequence of the demand, perhaps, our productions of this sort have been exceedingly numerous, and without the imprimatur of any foreign publisher they have been read." As an art form, he had continued, the tale was worthy of being taken with all seriousness. To write it was a task peculiarly difficult: "Admitting very readily that it requires more application—more time and toil—to produce a three-volume novel, it must not be supposed that the production of the tale is a very easy business. On the contrary, there is scarcely anything more difficult, or demanding the exercise of finer genius, in the whole domain of prose and composition."

The selections that he thereupon reproduced to illustrate what had been accomplished with the new form are worthy of examination. Some are given only in part, but the excisions were made solely because of the limited space at the editor's command. According to Griswold the period produced some sixteen or eighteen writers from whose works may be selected some twenty-four representative pieces:

Washington Irving: "Rip Van Winkle"; "The Wife."
G. C. Verplanck: "Major Egerton."
R. H. Dana: "Paul Fenton"; "Edward and Mary."
James Hall: "Pete Featherton."
W. C. Bryant: "Three Nights in a Cavern."
John P. Kennedy: "A Country Gentleman"; "Old Lawyers."
Eliza Leslie: "That Gentleman."
Lydia M. Child: "The Beloved Tune."
Charles Fenno Hoffman: "Ben Blower's Story"; "The Flying Head."
Caroline M. Kirkland: "The Land Fever."
Nathaniel Hawthorne: "A Rill From the Town Pump" "David Swan"; "The Celestial Railroad."
N. P. Willis: "The Cherokee's Threat"; "Unwritten Music"; "F. Smith."
W. G. Simms: "Grayling: or, Murder Will Out."[1]

---

[1] " 'Murder Will Out' is the first and the most meritorious of the series now lying before us. We have no hesitation in calling it the best ghost story we have ever read. It is full of the richest and most vigorous imagination—is forcibly conceived—and detailed throughout with a degree of artistic skill which has no parallel among American story-tellers since the epoch of Brockden Brown."—POE.

Joseph C. Neal: "A Pretty Time of Night."
Edgar A. Poe: "The Fall of the House of Usher."
T. B. Thorpe: "Tom Owen, the Bee Hunter."

William Leggett and Mrs. Seba Smith he mentioned in high terms, but he offered no selections from their works.

In a curious way, then, one totally undreamed of by its editor, *The Prose Writers of America* stands as the first treatise on the development of the American short story, and the first collection of the typical work of the first period.

II

The reasons for the sudden close of what may be called the age of Irving and Poe and Hawthorne are many. In America the year 1850 saw the full completion of the Knickerbocker movement that had begun some thirty years before. Cooper was near the end of his career—he died in 1851; Irving was giving himself wholly to his last work, the life of Washington; Paulding had written his final novel; Miss Sedgwick was busy with new editions of her early successes; Willis was fitting new titles to new combinations of his tales of years before; and Simms was reaching the point where he was to offer nothing more that was really new. Even Hawthorne, who was not a Knickerbocker, was deserting the distinctive Knickerbocker form of sketch and tale and was applying himself to the more ambitious forms of fiction that were becoming fashionable. The old Knickerbocker impulse had expended itself and a new generation was appearing with new literary ideals.

Everywhere old fashions were passing. In its second number, February, 1853, *Putnam's Magazine* recorded the passing of the annuals: "We have never known a less prolific holiday season than that which has just passed. Have our publishers been indolent, or is the taste of the public changing? It used to be the custom to issue, when Christmas approached, an almost endless variety of 'Gifts,' 'Remembrances,' 'Gems,' 'Tokens,' 'Wreaths,' 'Irises,' 'Albums,' etc., with very bad mezzotint engravings and worse letter-press—ephemeral works destined to perish in a few weeks, but the custom appears to be rapidly passing away."

New fashions were appearing, some of them with startling suddenness. In 1854 the conservative *Putnam's* became aware of a new peril. "A most alarming avalanche of female authors has been pouring upon us the past three months," it declared, "nearly all of whom are new. The success of Uncle Tom and Fannie Fern has been the cause, doubtless, of this rapid development of female genius." And again, a few months later, appalled at the "large ingathering of novels" from the pens of "the mob of ladies who write with ease," it expressed itself with bitterness: "They have no character at all. They are stories of fashion and sentiment without much local truth or probability of incident, and incapable of lasting effect. They are written mainly by females, who now write novels, as they formerly wrote tales and verses for the newspapers. . . . Mr. Charles Dickens and Mrs. Stowe are answerable for a large number of these offenders. . . . The highest that the most of them attained is to a milk-and-water, puling, superficial, and nauseous sentimentalism. They work upon the sensibilities." *The North American Review* in Boston was also aware of the new peril. "It has become a wonderfully common piece of temerity," it announced, "for a lady to make a book." It resented the intrusion: "A female author puts much of her individuality into her work—being more prone to express emotion than ideas." And again, "We trust the appetite for bookmaking notoriety is not so alarmingly on the increase among our fair friends as from the mere number of names we might forebode."

That Hawthorne was conscious of the new feminine invasion we have decisive evidence. In a letter to Ticknor, January, 1855, he expressed himself with no uncertain words:

America is now wholly given over to a d——d mob of scribbling women. I should have no chance of success while the public taste is occupied with their trash—and should be ashamed of myself if I did succeed. What is the mystery of these innumerable editions of *The Lamplighter* and other books neither better nor worse?—worse they could not be and better they need not be, when they sell by the hundred thousand.

And again, a month later,

Generally women write like emasculated men and are only to be distinguished from male authors by greater feebleness and folly; but when they throw off the restraints of decency, and come before the public stark naked, as it were—then their books are sure to possess character and value.

Hawthorne undoubtedly had in mind Fanny Fern and the other members of the *Jane Eyre* school of fiction, though their work was mild when compared with some that was to come, and his characterization of them as a "mob of scribbling women" was, at least as to the matter of quality, but a statement of facts. A veritable flood of feminine novels was indeed to dilute the fiction of the entire period and beyond. After *Uncle Tom's Cabin*, short stories no longer satisfied the ambition of women. Short stories, moreover, were harder to write than novels. Mrs. Mary Jane Holmes, one of the most voluminous of the "Lamplighter school," declared that she had always avoided them, since she found it so "hard to bite them off." It was easier to run on and on without limit in what Poe styled the "Laura Matilda romantic manner." And this easier material could now be sold. Seemingly overnight a reading public had arisen that demanded enormous quantities of highly sugared literary pabulum, and publishers were not slow to awake to the unprecedented fact that it had become more profitable to issue this native stuff than even to pirate free of cost the best products of the English presses. This once thoroughly realized, production went swiftly to extremes. After there had appeared in 1852 the most sensationally best seller that America has ever known—*Uncle Tom's Cabin*, a book of native origin—the decade became an era of best sellers, almost all of them native products.

Considering the size of the reading public, the literary statistics of the years between 1849 and 1855 are really startling. Of *Uncle Tom's Cabin* it is needless to speak.[1] Susan Warner's *The Wide, Wide World* (1850) and *Queechy* (1852) sold 104,000 in three years; *Fern Leaves From Fanny's Portfolio* (1853), by Fanny Fern (Sarah Willis Parton), sold 80,000 the first year; the novels of Caroline Lee Hentz in three years sold 93,000; Mitchell's *Reveries of a Bachelor* (1850), sold 70,000 the first year; and *Alderbrook*, by Fanny Forrester (Mrs. Adoniram P. Judson), sold 33,000 in a few months. Figures fully as large might be quoted for the novels of Emma D. E. N. Southworth, the first of which, *Retribution*, appeared in 1849, of *Dollars and Cents* (1852) by Amy Lathrop (Anna B. Warner), of *The Lamplighter* (1854), by Maria S. Cummins; of *Ten Nights in a Bar Room* (1855), by T. S.

[1] For a contemporary study of *Uncle Tom's Cabin* and its tremendous vogue, see "Uncle Tomitudes," *Putnam's Monthly*, Vol. I., page 97.

Arthur; and of many others. By no means was this all of the
fiction demanded by the public of the period. In 1851 was started
the New York *Ledger*, devoted exclusively to popular material, and
so successful was it that its proprietor, Robert Bonner, became at
length one of the richest men in America.

It is impossible to trace the outburst to any one cause. First
of all, it was the ripening period of the tares which had been sown
during the two decades of the lady's books. A generation had
now arisen which had been nurtured upon these books, and, to
quote a critic of the period, this new generation was afflicted with
"a sickly craving from much cramming with crude, unnatural
food." But the phenomenon was wider than America. Jean
Paul's *Siebenkäs* and Lamartine's whole work had been saturated
with the emotional. A writer in *The North American Review*
could even trace the origins of American sentimentalism to what
it termed "the Eugene Sue school of fiction in France." But England was equally in the grip of the movement. A reviewer of the
work of Scribe in the early 'sixties recounted this: "Not long since,
the proprietor of one of the London penny weeklies which cir-
culated by hundreds of thousands throughout the British Islands
and furnished a considerable part of the reading matter for the
lower classes, with the view of supplying his readers with superior
mental food, dismissed his staff of sensation novelists, and commenced the serial publication of the most popular of the Waverley
Novels. But they lacked the flavor of the present, and a rapidly
diminishing subscription list warned the publisher that he must
abandon his experiment or be ruined."

In America undoubtedly the influence of English fiction had
been, especially with women, a compelling one. Higginson speaks
of "the river of tears that were shed over Bulwer's *Pilgrims of the
Rhine*." The novels *Jane Eyre* and *Wuthering Heights*, both
published in 1847, and *Shirley*, in 1849, had had a powerful effect,
especially upon the bourgeois classes. Even more influential,
perhaps, had been the work of Dickens—the Dickens of Little
Nell and Paul Dombey, and of Dickens the reformer who fought
abuses with unstinted sentimentalism. By 1849 the Dickens era
in America was in full career. His visit to this country was still
a recent sensation. The periodicals were full of his work: *Harper's Magazine*, founded in 1850, included forty-three tales and
sketches from Dickens's *Household Words* in its first six numbers,

and during its first decade it ran serially *Bleak House* and *Little Dorrit.*

The effect of the movement was everywhere cheapening and retrogressive. The feminine novelists lacked constructive art: even *Uncle Tom's Cabin* is a crude piece of workmanship; they lacked definiteness and vitality; they worked, even as they had been charged, with their emotions chiefly, in an idealized world that was true to nothing save the vagaries of their own surcharged imaginations; and sadly they degraded diction and style. The beautiful English of Irving and Hawthorne and Poe seems to have influenced them not at all. Again the inflated and rococo periods of Judge Hall and the lady's books. Never in these stories did it snow: "the earth assumed its ermine mantle"; never did the sun arise: "Aurora now flushed the eastern horizon with all her gold and glory." Everywhere intensity of epithet and excess of adjectives. Of Grace Greenwood even a reviewer of her own time could say: "If ever there should be a concordance made of her book, the repetition of the word 'gorgeous' would be startling. It occurs on almost every page and only yields now and then to such mild adjectives as 'grand,' 'superb,' and 'delicious.' . . . Sunsets, mountains, trees, churches, paintings, music, and pyrotechnics are all gorgeous."

The period between 1849 and 1860, indeed, may be termed, so far as its fiction is concerned, the gorgeous period of American literature. It was characterized chiefly by an orgy of feminine sentimentalism and emotionalism, a half-savage rioting in color and superlatives and fantastic fancies, an outburst of wild desires to reform all abuses and to bring the world swiftly to a golden age of love and beauty and feminine dreams.

III

To realize how completely the Knickerbocker tradition had faded, one needs but to read *The Knickerbocker Gallery*, a compilation made by fifty-five of the surviving contributors to the magazine as a benefit for its editor, Louis Gaylord Clark. Even in 1855, the year of its issue, its tales must have seemed antiquated. Not one of them has survived. Though contributed in the mid-'fifties, they might all of them have been written for *The Atlantic Souvenir* a generation before. Not a trace of the art of Poe or of

Hawthorne, not a trace of that new realism that soon was to make all the work of the school seem as unreal as the flamboyantly colored fashion plates of the early *Godey's*.

A small group there was, however, even of the writers of the new generation who looked back with longing to the older days. *Putnam's Monthly Magazine*, the guiding spirit of which was George William Curtis, made a gentle attempt to stay the new tide. The magazine had been established as a conservative organ to guard the best traditions of American literature, or as the New York *Evening Express* phrased it in 1856, "around this periodical are banded the best writers who can be *maintained* by our present patronage of an American literature." It strove to maintain the standard set by Irving, but it succeeded only in prolonging a period of twilight with once in a while a moment of glow that to a hopeful few seemed like the promise of a new sunrise. When *Reveries of a Bachelor* appeared in 1850 the magazine hailed its author, Donald G. Mitchell, as the founder of "a new school of littérateurs," the bringer of a fresh era of sentiment which should deal, as it phrased it, "with everyday life expressed in the form of soliloquy," the materials for it to be "reveries, musings and thinkings, memories, mysteries, shadows, and death, old times, voices from the past, stars, moonlight, night winds, old homesteads, flowing rivers, and primeval forests."

The *Reveries* and the *Dream Life* which followed it can hardly be called short stories, and yet they cannot be neglected by the student of American fiction. They must be classed as sentimental sketches—rambling essays rather than tales. They were tuned perfectly to their time, and they struck a universal chord in so far as they touched the adolescent tendency to sadness and longing and dreams. They still are republished from time to time and they still are read. They founded, however, no school. Even *Putnam's* was forced quickly to record that they had been swallowed up in a second and then a third wave of sentimentalism— the third being that wave of feminized fiction that for a time threatened to submerge all conservative landmarks. Their success, indeed, may even be reckoned as one of the many causes for this wave.

The short story struggled fitfully. *The Piazza Tales*, by Herman Melville, are peculiarly typical of the decade. They are literary rather than real, they are ornamented rather than natural. In one of them a seller of lightning rods approaches a perfect stranger, who greets him thus: "Have I the honor of a visit from that illustrious god, Jupiter Tonans? If you be he, or his viceroy, I have to thank you for this noble storm you have brewed among our mountains. Listen! That was a glorious peal"—and so on for half a page, ending with, "but condescend to be seated." The rest of the tale is in keeping. In only one piece is there anything convincing. "Benito Cereno" tells of a mutiny at sea with a mystery in it that borders on the supernatural. Despite its occasional prolixity and its sprawly ending, it is told with real power, its background is realistically sketched, and its strangeness and reality are compelling. It is a prophecy of Jack London two decades before he was born.

George William Curtis, too, is to be classed with the older school rather than with the newer forces of the period. In his earlier travel sketches his aim had been, as he had expressed it, "to represent the essentially sensuous, luxurious, languid, and sense-satisfying spirit of Eastern life," and he had done this in the manner of Irving, with abundance of ornament and an excess of all the details of sensuous romance. In his later books, in *Lotus-Eating* especially, he uses the same florid yet patrician style and the same Irving-like atmosphere, with no sharp outlines and no harsh effects. In *Potiphar Papers* there is an added note of satire, never extreme—a later *Salmagundi* manner—genteel, graceful, witty, flowing beautifully in finished periods. Then came *Prue and I*—a blend of Charles Lamb and Thackeray, with the slightest flavor of Dickens sentiment and Irving mellowness. Such an essay, if we may call it an essay, as "Chatteaux" must be ranked with the best works of the Knickerbocker school. His "Easy Chair" papers in *Harper's Magazine,* begun in 1854 and continued monthly almost without a break until his death in 1892, were of Knickerbocker texture—a series of familiar essays that in many ways has no duplicate in American literature.

The essential weakness of Curtis was pointed out early by Lowell. In a letter to Briggs, the editor of *Putnam's,* under the date of February, 1854, he classed him as essentially an essayist and not a short-story writer at all. His characters, he explained

All existing and moving in that half-ideal air which is proper to the essay, we do not demand in them so much sharpness of outline and the truth to everyday which is essential in stories of life and the world. In the essay the characters *ought* to be ideas talking—but the fault of the *Potiphar Papers* seems to me to be that in them also there are dialogizing and monologizing thoughts, but not flesh and blood enough. In Dickens, the lower part of "the World," is brought into the Police Court, as it were, and there, after cross-examination, discharged or committed, as the case may be. The characters are real and low, but they are facts. That is one way. Thackeray's is another and better. One of his books is like a Dionysius ear, through which you may hear the World talking, entirely unconscious of being overheard.

It was a call for the new realism of which Lowell was to be one of the earliest voices, one of the first symptoms that a new period was soon to come.

IV

Amid all this feminism and uncertainty one or two writers did really new and virile work, among them the most notable being Fitz-James O'Brien, a brilliant Irishman who had landed in New York in 1852 and had quickly won his way into the leading magazines. No more electric and versatile genius had ever appeared among American authors. For ten years his work in every variety and key confronted everywhere readers of the periodicals; he seemed to be growing in power and it was felt by some that he was to become a dominating figure, but as suddenly as he had come he disappeared, laid low by a bullet in the Civil War.

The biography of O'Brien is that of a soldier of fortune and literary adventurer. He had been well born, had taken his degree at Dublin University, and then, with some eight thousand pounds, his inheritance from his father's estate, had gone to London to see the world. Two years later, his fortune squandered, he had pushed on to America, and at the age of twenty-four or perhaps twenty-six—his birth date is in doubt—had settled in New York City to support himself by means of his pen. Recognition came at once. The testimony of his contemporaries is unanimous as to his winning personality, his jovial happy-go-lucky soul, and his Celtic humor and nimbleness of wit. Quickly about him gathered a group of young journalists and actors and artists and littérateurs and illustrators of comic weeklies—Frank H. Bellew, C. D. Shanly, E. G. P. Wilkins, George Arnold, Harry Clapp, N. G. Shepherd—forgotten names now, yet the nucleus of that literary Bohemian group that has brought the name of Pfaff's "dingy cellar," 647 Broadway, into the annals of American literature.

In "A Paper of All Sorts," *Harper's*, March, 1858, O'Brien defined a Bohemian as a member of "those Nomadic tribes who cultivate literature and debts, and, heedless of the necessities of life, fondly pursue the luxuries." It described his own case, and it described most of his companions. Some of the Pfaff group, however, broke away early from the Bohemian influence—men like Taylor, Whitman, Stoddard, Stedman, Aldrich, and William Winter, who had been drawn into the circle for a time by the magnetism of Arnold and O'Brien. Even Howells spent one evening with the Pfaff circle, an evening which he described most illuminatingly in later years. The Civil War put an end to the group, but not until it had made an impression upon at least one area of American literature.

The adjective best descriptive of O'Brien's work is "journalistic." He turned out in ten years an enormous amount of copy—poems of every variety; plays, two or three of which ran for surprising periods in the theaters; essays and reviews; and for *Harper's Magazine* alone some thirty short stories. He wrote also for *Putnam's Magazine*, and *Harper's Weekly*, *The Home Journal*, *The American Whig Review*, *Vanity Fair*, *The Atlantic Monthly*, and *The Saturday Press*. Yet despite his voluminous output not one of his boon companions has described him in terms of industry. According to Aldrich, his ideal life was to "sleep all day and live all night." He was regal at banquets furnished to his friends from his publishers' checks, and it was only to win such checks that he concentrated himself for intense periods of headlong composition. He wrote his long "Sewing Bird" poem at two sittings, and the tale, "What Was It?" in the odds and ends of his time during several evenings.

According to Stoddard, a little group at one time during this period headed by Taylor delighted to meet on certain ambrosial nights to dissipate in poetic composition, in deliberate burlesquings and parodyings and imitatings of the various poets with fixed time limits for the completion of an agreed-upon number of lines. O'Brien, according to Stoddard, invariably won both in quickness and in quality of product. Without a doubt it was these meetings that furnished in later years the material for Taylor's *Diversions of the Echo Club,* in which O'Brien figures as Zoilus, always the most brilliant and the first to finish.

The episode explains much. Almost all of O'Brien's tales might be used as illustrative material for a new prose *Diversions of the Echo Club.* Not that there is plagiarism in the work, or direct imitation, but the spirit and the method of each tale is such as to suggest instantly some other work. "The Bohemian," for instance, recalls "The Gold Bug"; "Baby Bloom" and "Belladonna" read like travesties of the feminine romance so fashionable during the period; "Baby Bertie's Christmas" and "A Screw Loose" and "The Child that Loved a Grave" are after the Dickens Christmas-story manner; the first part of "The Wondersmith" is also redolent of Dickens, but the rest of it reads like a translation of a Hoffman tale of "The Sand Man" variety or "Nutcracker and the King of the Mice"; "A Drawing Room Drama" and "Uncle and Nephew" are manifestly French; just as "A Nest of Nightingales" is an Irish extravaganza, and "The Dragon Fang" an echo of the Chinese manner of narration. In "Sister Anne" he has his fling at the Fanny Fern school of fiction. Sister Anne, a romantic country girl, runs away to New York to be a poetess, but is advised by a gentleman whom she meets to turn to prose. "Write some pretty country sketches," he tells her. "You can call them 'Dried Leaves' or some other vegetable title, and they will be sure to succeed." Accordingly, Sister Anne creates a sensation with a series of sketches entitled "Lichens," under the signature of "Matilda Moss," is invited to Miss Ransack's literary *soirées,* prepares to publish books, and finally marries the great literary genius, Stephen Basque, who turns out to be the gentleman who had first offered her advice.

Too often has O'Brien's name been coupled with Poe's. The two men undoubtedly were alike in one thing: both wrote tales with journalistic intent, striving always for newness and variety and telling effect upon readers, and both were quick to make use of new discoveries and new scientific theories as literary material, pressing them to their logical ends. O'Brien clearly used the methods of Poe in such scientific fantasies as "The Diamond Lens," "How I Overcame My Gravity," and "Seeing the World." Further, however, one may not go. Poe was an artist: O'Brien an amateur, groping toward art; Poe worked by deliberate intention—thinking, and analyzing, and seeing the end from the beginning: O'Brien improvised and wrought with flashes of intuition. Like all Irishmen, he could tell a moving ghost story, but his work even in this field is clumsy when compared with Poe's creations. Poe never gave the impression of hasty work, and seldom did he descend to melodrama.

Few have missed success by so narrow a margin as did O'Brien. Especially was he gifted with invention. "The Crystal Bell," had its theme been carefully wrought out, would have been a story of power; "The Diamond Lens" is a conception as original as anything of Hoffman's. The device of the ferocious manikins in his "The Wondersmith," the use made of hypnotism in "The Bohemian," the gruesome episode of "The Lost Room," and the invisible monster in "What Was It?"—a theme afterward used by Maupassant in his "La Hula," and by Bierce in "The Damned Thing"—all are decidedly ingenious, but in each there is lacking something that holds forever the tale from the domain of masterpieces. In "What Was It?" for instance, the final cast made of the thing and the statement that this cast might be viewed in the museum is a fatal defect. Neither Maupassant nor Bierce would have made such an ending. Always is it the last touch that discloses the artist.

The best tales of O'Brien from the standpoint of modern technique are his "A Drawing Room Drama," the one bit of his art that its reader does not finish with the last sentence, since it leaves him after the last sentence with a terrible and a strange surmise concerning the woman who has not been charged with guilt; "A Terrible Night," with its unusual surprise ending; "Uncle and Nephew," which is French in its lightness and vivacity of style; "The Bohemian" and "The Diamond Lens." Of this last and "The Wondersmith," published in the early numbers of *The Atlantic*, William Winter remarked that "They electrified magazine literature, and they set up a model of excellence which in this department has made it better than it ever had been, in this country, before the tales were printed." The statement is too strong, yet it cannot be denied that O'Brien's tales in the mid-'fifties, with their lightness and freshness and brilliancy of style, were a marked contrast to the lumbering and moralized fiction then all too current. There was about them an exotic atmosphere, a newness as from strange importations from over the sea, a vivacity and lightness that is only described by the adjective

"French." Undoubtedly in America their influence did far more than did the influence of Poe to take from the short story its heavy tread and its clumsy art.

And yet O'Brien is not a large figure in the history of the short story. He was an influence in a feeble decade and he brought elements that were greatly needed, but his reign was brief. He was an improviser, too headlong and excited to do work of permanence. He lacked sincerity, he lacked poise, and he lacked real taste, and taste is basically a moral quality. His weakness was the weakness of Bohemianism. To quote George E. Woodberry: "The city is a hothouse that stimulates clever youths into an unnatural activity. Resorts like Pfaff's, 'the Mermain Tavern of the town wits,' are hothouses for the development of clever lads; and literature suffered by the overproduction of small minds. When in the history of letters gregariousness begins, one may look out for mediocrity."

V

Only one other writer attracted widely the attention of the 'fifties—Harriet Elizabeth Prescott, or, as she became known to later readers, Harriet Prescott Spofford. When her tale "In a Cellar" came to *The Atlantic* office, some time during the first year of the magazine—1858 or 1859—Lowell withheld publication for several months, suspecting it of being a translation from the French. The apparent familiarity of its author with European life, her jaunty quotations and allusions, and, more than all else, her Gallicism in atmosphere and style, seemed to mark her unmistakably as an exotic like O'Brien. Decidedly was there a French flavor.

The tone, moreover, was brilliant throughout, gorgeous to the limits of Orientalism, yet nothing seemed overdone. It was like the early Hugo. Thus she described the diamond about which the story centered:

There it lay, the glowing, resplendent thing! flashing in affluence of splendor, throbbing and palpitant with life, drawing all the light from the little woman's candle, from the sparkling armor around, from the steel barbs, and the distant lantern, into its bosom. It was scarcely so large as I had expected to see it, but more brilliant than anything I could conceive of. I do not believe there is another such in the world. One saw clearly that the Oriental superstition of the sex of stones was no fable; this was essentially the female of diamonds, the queen herself, the principle of life, the rejoicing receptive force. It was not radiant, as the term literally taken implies; it seemed rather to retain its wealth—instead of emitting its glorious rays, to curl them back like the fringe of a madrepore, and lie there with redoubled quivering scintillations, a mass of white magnificence, not prismatic, but a vast milky lustre. I closed the case; on reopening it, I could scarcely believe that the beautiful sleepless eye would again flash upon me. I did not comprehend how it could afford such perpetual richness, such sheets of lustre.

Moreover, the dialogue had a distinction rare at that epoch. As one comes to the tale by way of the stories that preceded it, with their endless conversational tags of "said he," "flashed Angelina," "yawned St. Clair," "cried Eglantine," and the like, such a passage as this has a singularly modern sound:

"She has needed," I replied to the Baron, "but one thing—to be aroused, to be kindled. See, it is done! I have thought that a life of cabinets and policy might achieve this, for her talent is second not even to her beauty."
"It is unhappy that both should be wasted," said the Baron. "She, of course, will never marry."
"Why not?"
"For various reasons."
"One?"
"She is poor."
"Which will not signify to your Excellency. Another?"
"She is too beautiful. One would fall in love with her. And to love one's own wife—it is ridiculous!"
"Who should know?" I asked.
"All the world would suspect and laugh."
"Let those laugh that win."
"No—she would never do as a wife; but then as ——"
"But then in France we do not insult hospitality!"
The Baron transferred his gaze to me for a moment, then tapped his snuff box, and approached the circle round Delphine.

But the author was not at all an exotic. There was nothing French about her: she was a New England girl from an old family and she had never been out of her native region. She had been well educated for her day, first at the Putnam school at Newburyport, Massachusetts, then at Pinkerton Academy in New Hampshire, and she had read much. The total disablement of her father through a paralytic shock before her school days were barely over had thrown the support of the family upon her, and instead of turning to the cotton mills like so many country girls of her generation she had turned to her pen. For years she wrote with tireless activity, much that she produced being sold to story papers and lady's books—sensational material, doubtless, but she studied her art. She read Reade and Disraeli and Bulwer-Lytton and Elizabeth Sheppard and doubtless many of the French classics which she had learned to read at the seminary. From the first she was a romancer, extreme in her romance. She worked with care and steadily she grew in power—not, however, in constructive power. In plot always was she weak. "In a Cellar," judged as a detective story of the Poe type, is grossly defective. A detective is a scientist working with his feet always on the solid ground of facts, but the author of "In a Cellar" is a romancer: in her world anything may happen; she is not fettered by facts or even by probability. The diamond is recovered not by the skill of the detective, but through a series of mere accidents that strain more than once the credulity of the reader.

With the new realism of Dickens or Thackeray or others of the decade she had no sympathy. In a paper on her master, Charles Reade (1864), she decried with scorn those writers who "with Chinese accuracy give us gossiping drivel that reduces life to the dregs of the commonplace." She admits freely that Reade used in his work all "the true elements of modern sensational writing: there are the broad canvass, the vivid colors, the abrupt contrast, all the dramatic and startling effects that weekly fictions afford— the supernatural heroine, the more than mortal hero." But all this, she declares, is rescued by the romantic genius of the man. She reveled in it; she imitated it; she made it a part of her own soul. Like the whole school of Keats—Taylor, Stoddard, the youthful Aldrich—she rioted in color and richness and rare perfumes and the dreamy gorgeousness of the Oriental imagination. In her collected tales *The Amber Gods and Other Stories* (1863), by her allusions and her quotations she reveals to us the world of her early reading: Kinglake's *Eothen*, Keats's *Lamia*, Shelley's *The Witch of Atlas*, *The Arabian Nights*, Beckford's *Vathek*, Poe's "The Mask of the Red Death," Tennyson's "Fatima," Von Weber's *Der Freischütz*, and songs like "The Vale of Avoca."

It was a remarkable book. *The North American Review* picked it from the mass of current feminine fiction and gave it a serious review, one of the few it ever deigned to accord to a collection of mere tales, apologizing, however, as it did so, with the plea that "a writer who has at once achieved so large a popularity as Miss Prescott has already won can never be a matter of indifference to anyone who is interested in the growth of American literature." And the writer of it, be it noted, was Henry James, soon himself to be a force in American fiction. With an opening comment upon the brilliancy of the descriptions and the "passages of gorgeous magnificence, of intense interest or of startling power," he came quickly to his main object in selecting the tales for review.

A low, murky atmosphere too often hangs over them; and almost without exception they have a morbid and unhealthful tone. In four of the seven stories now before us, the dominant passion in the breast of one or more of the chief characters is illicit love. . . . A writer who makes the interest of her love stories, with a single exception, depend upon the development of an unlawful affection, commits a grave artistic fault. Illicit love in ordinary life is the exception, not the rule; and it is certainly making rather an extravagant use of the exceptional for a writer to employ it in four cases out of five in a single collection of miscellaneous stories. But it is a still more fatal objection to the too frequent use of such machinery, that the constant contemplation of a diseased side of human nature can scarcely fail to produce an unhealthy state of mind and thus to exert a dangerous influence. A writer, whose stories are so eagerly read as are those of Miss Prescott, ought not to be unmindful of the influence which she may exert on the young.

One is inclined to smile to-day at this naïve mid-Victorian solicitude. *The Amber Gods* lacks constructive art most decidedly, and it lacks sadly in reality and in knowledge of life on the part of its young author, but as we see it to-day it certainly does not lack moral basis. The tales seem actually Puritanic now in their morality. That James with his knowledge of European life and literature should have detected in them something new and dangerous—the sex motif pressed beyond the limit its generation deemed safe, is well worth noting. It was the beginning of a new element in the American short story, a new and most fascinating subject-matter for the tale, one that in time was to play an important part.

Few have made so deep an impression upon their first readers and then have disappeared so completely. Elizabeth Stuart Phelps has declared that the startling last sentence of "The Amber Gods"—"I must have died at ten minutes past one"—haunted her for years; William Dean Howells pronounced the tale "Circumstance" "still unsurpassed of its kind," and included it in his select collection of American short stories, and similar testimonials might be multiplied. But its author produced no strong later work. Perhaps in obedience to her critics she subdued her exuberant imagination. Certainly there were no more such colorful outbursts as "Desert Sands." Romance she still wrote in abundance, "the innocently prattling stories," to quote T. S. Perry's criticism in 1872, "for which *Harper's Magazine* is famous," but none of it was strong enough to demand republication. She refused to recognize—with one curious exception, her "Knitting Sale-Socks" in an early *Atlantic*—the new realism that was creeping into American fiction, and continued the old type of romance that she had begun with her novels. In her *Atlantic* tale, "The Rim," for instance, she can make the hero who has just rescued the heroine from certain death in a sudden flood and who still stands with her in a perilous position amid the plunging waters converse in this incredible fashion:

"What would you have me do? Should I have stood here, letting I dare not wait upon I would, like the cat i' the adage, while the oak caught and whirled you off to sea? Too big a broomstick for such a little witch."

Her own explanation of herself, written in later years, is worth reproducing:

You wonder why I did not continue in the vein of "The Amber Gods." I suppose because the public taste changed. With the coming of Mr. Howells as editor of the *Atlantic*, and his influence, the realistic arrived. I doubt if anything I wrote in those days would be accepted by any magazine now.

A new era indeed was opening, and those who went not along with the new tide quickly were forgotten. She must stand with those few who, when the short story was still plastic, added a single touch toward the final shaping of the form and then were seen no more.

BIBLIOGRAPHY

Leading Short Stories of the Decade

1850. *The Knickerbocker Sketch-Book*. Lewis Gaylord Clark.

1850. *Reveries of a Bachelor*. Donald G. Mitchell.

1851-3. *Clovernook Papers*. Alice Cary.

1851. *Dream Life*. Donald G. Mitchell.

1853. *Knick-Knacks From an Editor's Table*. Lewis Gaylord Clark.

1853. *The Maroon: a Legend of the Caribees and Other Tales*. William Gilmore Simms.

1853. *Wild Jack; or, the Stolen Child, and Other Stories*. Caroline Lee Hentz.

1853. *The Potiphar Papers*. (*Reprinted From "Putnam's Monthly."*) George William Curtis.

1854. *'Way Down East; or, Portraitures of Yankee Life*. By Seba Smith, the Original Major Jack Downing.
"John Wadleigh's Trial"; "Yankee Christmas"; "The Tough Yarn"; "Christopher Crotchet"; "Polly Gray and the Doctors"; "Jerry Suttridge"; "Seating the Parish"; "The Money-Diggers and Old Nick"; "Peter Punctual"; "The Speculator"; "A Dutch Wedding"; "Billy Snub"; "The Pumpkin Freshet"; "A Race for a Sweetheart"; "Old Myers, the Panther"; "Seth Woodsum's Wife."

1855. *Tales of the Marines*. Henry Augustus Wise.

1855. *The Beautiful Gate and Other Tales*. Caroline Chesebro'.

1855. *Flower Fables or Fairy Tales*. Louisa M. Alcott.

1855. *The Knickerbocker Gallery*.
"The Bride of the Ice-King," D. G. Mitchell; "Gentle Dove," F. W. Shelton; "On Lake Pepin," Epes Sargent; "Piseco," George W. Bethune; "Anteros," Donald Mac-Leod; "Rambles in the Far West," Ralph Roanoke; "Captain Nelgrave," Frederick S. Cozzens; "A Dutch Belle," P. Hamilton Myers; "The Iron Man," Henry J. Brent; "A Story of Kaskaskia," J. L. McConnel; "The Shrouded Portrait," George W. Curtis; "The Loves of Mary Jones," J. M. Legare; "The Sun-Dial of Isella," Richard B. Kimball; "A Literary Martyrdom," C. F. Briggs; "Zadoc Town," J. T. Irving.

1856. *Prue and I*. George W. Curtis.

1856. *Piazza Tales.* Herman Melville.
"The Piazza"; "Bartleby"; "Benito Cereno"; "The Lightning-rod Man"; "The Encantadas; or, Enchanted Islands"; "The Bell-tower."

1863. *The Amber Gods and Other Stories.* Harriet Elizabeth Prescott.
"The Amber Gods," *Atlantic*, Jan., Feb., 1860; "In a Cellar," *Atlantic*, Feb., 1859; "Knitting Sale-Socks," *Atlantic*, Feb., 1861; "Circumstance," *Atlantic*, May, 1860; "Desert Sands"; "Midsummer and May," *Atlantic*, Nov., Dec., 1860; "The South Breaker," *Atlantic*, May, June, 1862.

1864. *Seven Stories with Attic and Basement.* Donald G. Mitchell.
"Introduction"; "Wet Day at an Irish Inn"; "Account of a Consulate"; "The Petit Soulier"; "The Bride of the Ice-King"; "The Cabriolet"; "The Count Pesaro"; "Emile Roque"; "Under the Roof."

FITZ-JAMES O'BRIEN'S SHORT STORIES IN "HARPER'S MAGAZINE"

"Belladona," June, 1854; "The Fiddler," Sept., 1854; "My Son, Sir," Jan., 1855; "Baby Bloom," Mar., 1855; "The Beauty," July, 1855; "The Bohemian," July, 1855; "A Drawing-Room Drama," Aug., 1855; "Milly Dove," Sept., 1855; "The Duel," Oct., 1855; "The Pot of Tulips," Nov., 1855; "Sister Anne," Dec., 1855; "Baby Bertie's Christmas," Jan., 1856; "The Dragon Fang," March, 1856; "How Nellie Lee Was Pawned," Sept., 1856; "A Terrible Night," Oct., 1856; "Mary Burnie of the Mill," Nov., 1856; "The Crystal Bell," Dec., 1856; "Dora Lee," Feb., 1857; "Uncle and Nephew," March, 1857; "Seeing the World," Sept., 1857; "A Screw Loose," Oct., 1857; "The Lost Room," Sept., 1858; "What Was It? A Mystery," March, 1859; "A Nest of Nightingales," March, 1859; "Mother of Pearl," Feb., 1860; "The Child That Loved a Grave," April, 1861; "Captain Alicant," June, 1861; "Mrs. Jujube at Home," Aug., 1861; "Tommatoo," Aug., 1862; "How I Overcame My Gravity," May, 1864.

1881. *The Poems and Stories of Fitz-James O'Brien. Collected and Edited, with a Sketch of the Author,* by William Winter.
"The Diamond Lens," *Atlantic*, Jan., 1858; "The Wondersmith," *Atlantic*, Oct., 1859; "Tommatoo"; "Mother of Pearl"; "The Bohemian"; "The Lost Room"; "The Pot of Tulips"; "The Golden Ingot," *Knickerbocker's*, Aug., 1858; "My Wife's Tempter"; "What Was It? A Mystery"; "Duke Humphrey's Dinner"; "Milly Dove"; "The Dragon Fang."

CHAPTER VIII

I

The early eighteen-sixties in the annals of the short story center about *The Atlantic Monthly*. For the first time in the history of the form Boston became the distributing center, a change of base perplexing to one who has followed thus far the course of American fiction. New England literature during the mid-century had been uniformly serious. The short story, especially in the Boston atmosphere, was regarded as a magazine product, ephemeral stuff, "light reading," or at best a miniature novel that might serve as good exercise for young writers who were pluming their wings for serious flight. Collections of short stories were seldom mentioned by the reviewers, even in the lists of "books received." One may read quite through the early volumes of the New York *Nation*, which aimed to furnish a complete record of the current literary product, and be unaware that such a form existed.

One is surprised, therefore, to find the tremendously serious Boston *Atlantic Monthly*, 1857, making a specialty of short fiction. From its first issue, three short stories for each number seems to have been the policy of the magazine—in the first two volumes thirty-six pieces of fiction may fairly be rated as short stories. And by no means were they all written by New England writers. Most of the Middle States group appear in the early numbers: O'Brien, and George Arnold from the New York Bohemians, and James D. Whelpley, Bayard Taylor, Caroline Chesebro', and Rebecca Harding from a wider field. The monthly had been started at precisely the right moment. American magazines in quality had reached their lowest ebb. *The Nation*, reviewing in January, 1866, the Boston *Every Saturday*, then in charge of no less an editor than T. B. Aldrich, summed up the situation in this characteristic sentence:

As for the articles themselves, we do not find them first-rate, and, indeed, they are of the flavor of too much literature printed for the first time in our magazines—a kind of literature which is produced apparently for the perusal only of the class which writes it, which is to say, the young ladies.

So far as *Harper's* was concerned and the Philadelphia magazines, the verdict was true, and there practically were no others which had ever attempted a high standard, for *Putnam's* had died in the birth year of *The Atlantic*, and *Knickerbocker's*, which long had been senescent, had followed three years later. The new magazine from the first was able to select the best that America could produce, and from the first it kept its pages free from the sentimental and the conventional. It was the type of periodical which Poe all his life had dreamed of founding, and which every other American man of letters had dreamed of from the days of Bryant and Irving and Dana. For New England especially it came at a critical moment—at the moment, indeed, when the new generation, the sons and daughters of the Emerson-Longfellow school, was seeking an outlet—Edward Everett Hale, Theodore Winthrop, Harriet Prescott, Rose Terry, Lucretia P. Hale, Louisa M. Alcott, Elizabeth Stuart Phelps, Abigail Dodge ("Gail Hamilton"), and the others—and it not only furnished this outlet, but it held the standards high.

The directing force of the new magazine and the leader of the new literary renaissance which it created was James Russell Lowell. Never a fiction writer himself, nevertheless during the critical decade after 1857 he did more than any other person to raise the new short-story form to a place of dignity and to give it reality and substance. As the editor of the first seven volumes of *The Atlantic*, he was able to touch and mold the new literary generation at their most plastic moment. His leadership was never uncertain: he was sure of himself; he had positive literary standards and always standards in advance of his times; and he was able to speak with authority and win obedience. Distinctively was he the transition figure between two epochs: he was the youngest of the Emerson group and he was the oldest of the Harte-Twain-Howells group that followed. When the mid-century leaders had done their distinctive work and were adding to their product nothing really new, Lowell was still in the full noonday of his powers and his influence touched vitally every member of the new generation.

Though the study windows of Lowell, especially in his earlier days, were lighted largely from the east, there was within him, nevertheless, a strain distinctively and racily American, more so than in any of the others of the early New England school. He had been the first in America prominently to introduce dialect into serious literature: Hosea Biglow stands as the first of a long line of "Yankees" drawn broadly and humorously from the life. Unlike the rest of the earlier school, Lowell had been young enough to be affected by that early wave of realism which already was modifying the romanticism of Scott. Thackeray had influenced him, Thackeray with his, "I have no brain above the eyes; I describe what I see," and Dickens: not the Dickens of Little Nell (Lowell had written Briggs as early as 1853, "I do abhor sentimentality from the depth of my soul"), but the Dickens who had dared without apology to deal with lowly life as if it were the most serious thing in the world. By no means was this New Englander ever a realist, as the French Zola school or even Howells and James were realists, and yet in the first volume of *The Atlantic* he pronounced *Scenes From Clerical Life* distinctive work, since "Each story reads like a reminiscence of real life and the personages introduced show little sign of being 'rubbed down' or 'touched up and varnished for effect.'" The sentence explains the position of Lowell: he demanded real life and not dreamings about life. Of almost every one of the eighty or more short stories by some fifty writers which Lowell accepted during the three and a half years of his *Atlantic* editorship there might be echoed the judgment he had pronounced upon George Eliot. He was attracted by the genuineness and the truth to life in a tale, be it high life or low, and he rejected without hesitation the mechanically literary, the artificially romantic, and the merely sentimental. With the advent of *The Atlantic Monthly* a healthy realism for the first time decisively entered American fiction. In its second number the magazine reviewed Ludwig's *Thüringer Naturen*, one of the numerous imitations of Auerbach's *Dorf Geschichten*, in which is treated "the life of German peasants, with their simple, healthy, vigorous natures undepraved by a spurious civilization," and it ended the review with the significant remark: "It is refreshing to see that the German literary taste is becoming more realistic, pure, and natural, turning its back on the romantic school of the French." It is the first time I have found the word realistic in American criticism. A new literary perspective was everywhere opening and in America *The Atlantic Monthly* and its editor, Lowell, were leading in making it recognized and understood.

II

Just what Lowell did for the short story during the period of his editorship may best be studied, perhaps, from a volume published in 1865, entitled *Atlantic Tales: a Collection of Stories From "The Atlantic Monthly."* Though not all of the tales in the volume were chosen by him, the book is fairly his: his mark is upon every part of it. The tales number thirteen by thirteen different authors: Edward Everett Hale, Fitz-James O'Brien, Rebecca Harding, "Gail Hamilton," Robert T. S. Lowell, George Arnold, Caroline Chesebro', Charles Nordhoff, Lucretia P. Hale, Rose Terry, J. D. Whelpley, Bayard Taylor, and E. H. Appleton—seven men and six women; four who sent their manuscripts from New England addresses and nine who sent them from without the New England area. None of Miss Harriet Prescott's five stories that had appeared in *The Atlantic* was included, since already they had been republished in her volume, *The Amber Gods*.

A study of the thirteen tales reveals the fact that the quality common to the greatest number of them is what may fairly be called "Dickensonian." Emboldened by the example of the great English commoner and fortified by the example of *Uncle Tom's Cabin*, itself inspired by Dickens, the young writers of the new school now dared to do what the earlier generations, especially in New England, would have looked upon with horror. 'Dickensism," as Henry James has so brilliantly explained to us, is, after all, at basis only vulgarism.

Under Lowell's guidance, then, there entered at the moment when feminized fiction was at full tide, a new young school of writers who threw overboard the old romanticism and introduced the vulgar world of Dickens at the opposite extreme. Rose Terry, for instance, in her tale, "Miss Lucinda," could place even a pig among her major characters and introduce him to the reader through the agency of a broken-down old Yankee man-of-all-work:

I say for 't, I b'lieve that cre'tur' knows enough to be a professor in a college. Why, he talks: he re'lly doos: a leetle through his nose, maybe, but no more'n Dr. Colton allers doos,—'n' I declare he appears to have abaout as much sense. I never see the equal of him. I thought he'd 'a' larfed right out yesterday, when I gin him that mess o' corn: he got up onto his forelegs on the trough, an' he winked them knowin' eyes o' his'n, an' waggled his tail, an' then he set off an' capered round till he came bunt up ag'inst the boards. I tell *you*—that sorter sobered him; he gin a growlin' grunt, an' shook his ears, an' looked sideways at me, and then he put to an eet up that corn as sober as a judge. I swan: he does beat the Dutch!

And she could introduce her heroine Lizzy, in "Lizzy Griswold's Thanksgiving," in this unromantic fashion: "Mrs. Griswold was paring apples and Lizzy straining squash."

Largely are the characters in these *Atlantic Tales* selected from unromantic environments. Miss Appleton's "A Half Life and Half a Life" is laid in the canebrakes of the Big Sandy River in Ohio, and among the prominent characters is a "Sandy woman,"

With her lank, tall figure, round which clung those narrow skirts of "bit" calico, dingy red or dreary brown,—her feet shod in the heavy store-shoes which were brought us from Catlettburg by the returning flatboat men,—her sharp-featured face, the forehead and cheeks covered with brown, mouldy-looking spots, the eyes deep-set, with a livid dyspeptic ring around them, and the lips thin and pinched,—the whole face shaded by the eternal sun-bonnet, which never left her head from early sunrise till late bedtime.

The accompaniment of realism in fiction is inevitably dialect, and in the new *Atlantic* tales dialect quickly ran to extremes. Twenty-five years later, in the early 'eighties, *The Century Magazine* hesitated for months before it dared to publish Page's "Marse Chan" because it was written wholly in dialect, but as early as 1862 *The Atlantic* could publish a tale almost wholly in the outlandish patois of the Newfoundland natives—Robert T. S. Lowell's grippingly realistic story of a seal fisherman who, lost on the Arctic floe, drifted out to sea on an ice pan. It was made from the life by one who had spent years as a missionary among the fisher people. A passage like this is uncouth, but it rings true:

There was a cry goed up,—like the cry of a babby, 't was, an' I thowt mubbe 't was a somethun had got upon one o' they islands; but I said, agen, "How could it?" an' one John Harris said 'e thowt 't was a bird. Then another man (Moffis 'e's name was) started off wi' what they calls a gaff ('t is somethun like a short boat-hook), over the bows, an' run; an' we sid un strike, an' strike, an' we hard it go wump! wump! an' the cry

goun up so tarrible feelun, seemed as ef 'e was murderun some poor wild
Inden child 'e'd a-found (only mubbe 'c wouldn't do so bad as that:
but there 've a-been tarrible bloody, cruel work wi' Indens in my time),
an' then 'e comed back wi' a white-coat over 'e's shoulder; an' the poor
thing was n' dead, but cried an' soughed like any poor little babby.

Then in April, 1861, came a bit of realism as depressed as anything ever produced by the Russian school—Rebecca Harding's
short story, "Life in the Iron Mills," a glimpse into the hell of
the Pittsburgh roller mills in the unrecorded days. Influenced
though it may have been by Kingsley's *Alton Locke* (1850), by
Mrs. Gaskell's *Mary Barton* (1848); and by Reade's *It is Never Too
Late to Mend* (1856), the tale has a convincingness and a sharpness of outline that were its author's own and that place her
among the pioneers of American fiction. The setting of her
picture is Doré-like in its remorseless black and white:

The mills for rolling iron are simply immense tent-like roofs, covering
acres of ground, open on every side. Beneath these roofs Deborah looked
in on a city of fires, that burned hot and fiercely in the night. Fire in
every horrible form: pits of flame waving in the wind; liquid metal-
flames writhing in tortuous streams through the sand; wide caldrons
filled with boiling fire, over which bent ghastly wretches stirring the
strange brewing; and through all, crowds of half-clad men, looking like
revengeful ghosts in the red light, hurried, throwing masses of glittering
fire. It was like a street in Hell.

And over it all the smoke of Hell:

It rolls sullenly in slow folds from the great chimneys of the iron
foundries, and settles down in black, slimy pools on the muddy streets.
Smoke on the wharves, smoke on the dingy boats, on the yellow river,—
clinging in a coating of greasy soot to the house front, the two faded
poplars, the faces of the passers-by.

And under the hideous pall human figures,

Masses of men, with dull besotted faces bent to the ground, sharpened
here and there by pain or cunning; skin and muscle and flesh begrimed
with smoke and ashes; stooping all night over boiling caldrons of metal,
laired by day in dens of drunkenness and infamy; breathing from infancy
to death an air saturated with fog and grease and soot, vileness for soul
and body.

The hero and heroine, or rather the central characters, are of a
piece with this background—victims struggling in the grip of hell

and powerless. Here is the heroine, or rather the unconscious *Nemesis*, in the grim tragedy:

She untied her bonnet, which hung limp and wet over her face, and prepared to eat her supper. It was the first food that had touched her lips since morning. There was enough of it, however; there is not always. She was hungry,—one could see that easily enough,—and not drunk, as most of her companions would have been found at this hour. She did not drink, this woman,—her face told that, too,—nothing stronger than ale. Perhaps the weak, flaccid wretch had some stimulant in her pale life to keep her up,—some love or hope, it might be, or urgent need. When that stimulant was gone, she would take to whiskey. Man cannot live by work alone.

And of the hero:

He had already lost the strength and instinct vigor of a man, his muscles were thin, his nerves weak, his face (a meek, woman's face) haggard, yellow with consumption. In the mill he was known as one of the girl-men: "Molly Wolfe" was his sobriquet. He was seldom seen in the cockpit, did not own a terrier, drank but seldom; when he did, desperately. He fought sometimes, but was always thrashed, pommeled to a jelly.

At the end a crime forced upon him by the woman who thought she was helping him to escape from the grip of the Mills, desperation, horror, suicide in a prison cell with a bit of sharpened tin can, and then:

Silence deeper than the Night! Nothing that moved, save the black, nauseous stream of blood dripping slowly from the pallet to the floor.

A tale by Gogol could not be more hauntingly depressing. Shuddering realism at every point, and yet nothing too much: the reader cannot shake the effect of the thing from him for hours.

Its author, later to be known as Rebecca Harding Davis, had been born and reared in the Pittsburgh district—at Washington, Pennsylvania, and she had written the tale at Wheeling, which was then in Virginia. The success of her first venture emboldened her to enlarge her canvas; in October, 1861, *The Atlantic* began her novel, "A Story of To-day," later to be issued with the title *Margaret Howth*, and the rest of her fiction was prevailingly outside of the short-story province. A single passage, however, in her second *Atlantic* contribution may well be quoted as an indication of the way American fiction was definitely heading:

My story is very crude and homely,—only a rough sketch of one or two of those people whom you see every day, and call "dregs" sometimes— a dull bit of prose, such as you might pick for yourself out of any of these warehouses or back streets. I expect you to call it stale and plebeian, for I know the glimpses of life it pleases you best to find here: New England idyls delightfully tinted; passion-veined hearts, cut bare for curious eyes; prophetic utterances, concrete and clear; or some word of pathos or fun from the old friends who have indenizened themselves in everybody's home. You want something, in fact, to lift you out of this crowded, tobacco-stained commonplace, to kindle and chafe and glow in you. I want you to dig into this commonplace, this vulgar American life, and see what is in it. Sometimes I think it has a new and awful significance that we do not see.

The paragraph expresses what Lowell had in mind as he selected his Atlantic tales: he would "dig into this commonplace, this vulgar American life, and see what is in it." "Friend Eli's Daughter," by Bayard Taylor, is a glimpse into the soul of Quakerdom by one who was reared in a community of Quakers; "Elkanah Brewster's Temptation," by Charles Nordhoff, transports the reader into the heart of Cape Cod.

With short-story *form*, as Poe had conceived of it, however, Lowell was little concerned. That he ever looked upon the tale otherwise than as shortened fiction, or as a novel in miniature, there is no evidence. The story might begin with pages of exposition and end in a leisurely sprawl with sermonic applications; it might be loosely told with digressions and it might drag; it might extend through two or even three magazine installments— these facts were not vital to Lowell. He was concerned with matter rather than manner, with the soul of the story rather than the body. It must be true to human fundamentals; it must deal, if possible, with the actualities of American life; and it must be based upon some definite moral thesis. It is significant that the stories in the thirteen *Atlantic Tales* which come the nearest to the modern requirements as to form come from the New York group: O'Brien's "The Diamond Lens," George Arnold's "Why Thomas Was Discharged," and J. D. Whelpley's "The Denslow Palace."

III

The leading short-story contributor to *The Atlantic* during Lowell's editorship was Rose Terry, better known to-day as Rose

Terry Cooke. The first eleven numbers contain eight of her tales. Beginning with "Sally Parson's Duty" in the very first issue, and ending with "A Town and a Country Mouse" in June, 1891, she contributed to the magazine some thirty stories. To *Harper's Monthly* during the same period she contributed as many more, and to *Putnam's*, *The Independent*, *The Galaxy*, *Scribner's Monthly*, and other periodicals enough to bring her total up to nearly one hundred. Distinctively was she a magazinist: she wrote with only magazine publication in view, and the greater number of her tales still lie in the periodicals to which they were first contributed. Not until 1881, indeed, did she gather any of them into book form.

Rose Terry was born in Connecticut in 1827 and her whole life was spent within the bounds of that State, the last years of it, after her marriage in 1873, for the most part at Winsted. After this date she signed her work Rose Terry Cooke. At sixteen, having completed a course at the Hartford Female Seminary, she found employment as a teacher, but teaching was no work for her intense nature. Like Mrs. Stowe and the Cary sisters, and Harriet Prescott, she had had dreams from her childhood of literature as a profession, and she poured out her soul at first in poetry, some of it, like "The Two Villages," of more than average quality. Her first book (1860) was a book of poems. Poetry, however, brought no income, and she had set out to live by her pen. Fiction was the marketable literary commodity of the day, and short fiction gave the quickest returns and involved the smallest risk. Before she was eighteen, therefore, she had made her way into the magazines, among other early work with a long romantic story, "The Mormon's Wife," in *Graham's*. Before she was twenty she had won for herself a place on the contributing staff of *Putnam's*. The quality of this earlier work was low; not at all, indeed, above the average feminine fiction of the lady's books of the period. Such a tale, for example, as "The Assassin of Society," *Harper's*, May, 1857, is distinctively of *Charlotte Temple*-like texture. The assassin of the piece is a preternaturally beautiful but cruel young man, who deliberately strews his pathway with the hearts of maidens who have perished of love for him, among them the once joyous Esther, who now "in despair and agony" "wore out her nights in sleepless anguish and her days in delirium." Or one may note the title of another of her tales a little later in the same magazine,—"Alix

Thuriot Thorne," the maiden name of a tragic soul who, on the morning of her wedding day deserted by her husband, finds herself the victim of a diabolic plot,—she has married the deliberate murderer of her own brother.

But the touch of *The Atlantic* seemed to awake in Rose Terry new powers. There is an atmosphere of the sentimental even over much of the work that Lowell accepted, but more and more she turned now to the delineation of actual life. She dealt more and more with New England farm and village characters, with common laborers and the nondescript types found in country towns— with tight-fisted farmers and rural deacons and the women they ruled with patriarchal despotism. She was not the first to do this: Seba Smith and others had caught glimpses of the field, but she was the first fully to take possession.

The credit for first exploiting New England as a background for *genre* fiction usually has been given to Mrs. Stowe, whose *The May Flower*, a volume of sketches with Puritan settings, had appeared in 1855. But Mrs. Stowe had approached her material from a high literary level. She was dealing with the Brahmins and their neighbors and she touched them with reverence, and idealized them as one who has long been in exile idealizes the scenes of his youth. These early sketches were all of them studies of moral problems and glorifications of the old Puritan New England of her girlhood before she had left it to live in the West. Her "The Mourning Veil," for example, in the first number of *The Atlantic*, is in reality a sermon thrown into the form of a tale. There is in it no attempt to bring out coldly and without sentiment the unique qualities of New Englanders; the tale, instead, works from a text never for a moment lost sight of: "Till one has seen the world through a veil like that, one has never truly lived." Read in connection with Miss Terry's "Sally Parson's Duty" in the same number, and the contrast is evident. Here we have a tale with Eliashib Sparks, Uncle Zeke, Aunt Polly, and Long Snapps, the old Cape Cod whaler, as characters. Let us listen while the conversation turns to the fundamental New England theme of Duty:

I do'no', he's pooty stiff, that 'are feller. He's sot on duty, I see; an' that means suthin', when a man that oughter be called a man sez it. Wimmin-folks, now, don't sail on that tack. When a gal gets to talkin' about her dooty, it's allus suthin' she wants ter do and han't got no grand excuse for't. Ye never see a woman 't didn't get married for dooty yet; there a'n't narry one of 'em darst to say they wanted ter.

Late in 1858, Mrs. Stowe's *The Minister's Wooing* began its long run through *The Atlantic* and after the early installments Lowell in great satisfaction wrote this of its author:

We do not believe that there is anyone who, by birth, breeding, and natural capacity, has had the opportunity to know New England so well as she, or who has the peculiar genius so to profit by the knowledge. Already there have been scenes in *The Minister's Wooing* that, in their lowness of tone and quiet truth contrast as charmingly with the timid vagueness of the modern school of novel writers as *The Vicar of Wakefield* itself.

But this was a full year after Rose Terry's early *Atlantic* tales, which were even more remarkable for "their lowness of tone and quiet truth." The book on the whole pictures with loving sentimentalism the aristocracy of New England rather than the under classes on the Dickens level of life. The Mrs. Stowe who created Sam Lawson with his vulgar wisdom and his uncouth Yankee humor was not to come for a full decade more, and in the meantime Miss Terry had created a whole gallery of Sam Lawsons.

More, perhaps, one may not say. In short-story technique, as Poe had set it forth, the creator of "Miss Lucinda" was not strong. That the short story differed from the novel save alone in the attribute of length she seems never to have discovered. Often her tales record the whole lives of their characters with glimpses of their ancestors. Again and again in her tales the narrative is pushed ahead with "Ten years now slipped away," or "Childhood ripened at last into manhood." Often she ends the tale in the leisurely manner of the romance which accounts for the after lives of all the characters. But despite their faulty architectonics, her tales mark a distinct advance in American short-story art: they used for the first time consistently and with distinction what later was widely proclaimed as "local color," and they tempered the vulgarity of their material with humor.

This last is important. When we consider the part humor was to play in the later short story, the *genre* humor of Rose Terry Cooke becomes significant. In this she was a pioneer. She saw the quaint and laughable in her characters and she made her readers feel it. Of humor introduced as a mere humorist would introduce it, for the sole sake of the humor, she had little: hers was that subtlest of all humor, the humor that is natively inherent in the material used. In "Turkey-Tracks," for instance, her second *Atlantic* tale, even the death of the little pet turkey is made grimly humorous:

"What can we do?" asked Peggy in plaintive voice, as the feeble "week! week!" of the little turkey was gasped out, more feebly every time.

"Give it some whisky punch!" growled Peter.

"So I would" said Kate demurely.

Now if Peggy had one trait more striking than another, it was her perfect simple faith in what people said; irony was a mystery to her. She dropped a little drop into a spoon, diluted it with water, and was going to give it to the turkey in all seriousness, when Kate exclaimed,—

"Peggy, when will you learn common sense? Who ever heard of giving whisky to a turkey?"

"Why, you told me to, Kate."

"Oh, give it to the thing!" growled Peter; "it will die, of course."

"I shall give it," said Peggy resolutely. "It does *me* good, and I shall try."

In spite of kicking and choking the dose was given and the turkey marvelously revived at once; but when the family returned from tea it was found dead on the floor. Nothing could be more trivial, yet nothing could be more true to the materials in which she is working. All the crochets and homely angles of the Yankee rural stock she pictures in remorseless detail: the obstinacy and the Scotch-like penuriousness of the New England farmer one finds in such revealing pictures as "Grit" and "Too Late," which reads like a tale from the pen of the later Miss Wilkins; the Puritan religious strictness of New England, run in later days to narrowness and bigotry, appears in such tales as "The Deacon's Week" and "Cal Culver and the Devil." Cal in the village store relates a modern instance:

"You know it hain't ben real fust-rate sugarin' weather: it hain't threw days, though it's friz considerable night-times. But it's kinder late for tappin', any way, 'cordin' to the year: so parson he reckoned he'd be amazin' forehanded this year, and git his holes bored, and spouts drove in, and buckets set, so's to be on hand, ye see. Now them trees never dripped a drop a Thursday, nor a Friday, nor a Saturday: three days the buckets hung right there and was empty; but Sabba'-day it come round real warm, the sun shone powerful, and, when he went to the bush Monday mornin', the sap troughs and buckets was brimmin' over full, as sure as you're born. What does parson do but take an' tip 'em all up; and Jim Beebe, he was behind him—heard him say, 'I know thy works Satan, temptin' me with Lord's day sap. Get thee behind me!'' And he up and tipped over every drop onto the ground, and went off.''

IV

Equally deserving of mention is the work of another pioneer in New England *genre* fiction. Elizabeth Stuart Phelps, later to be known as Mrs. Ward, who, although her first widely recognized short story, "The Tenth of January," did not appear until 1868, began to contribute to *The Atlantic* almost as early as did Rose Terry. She was one of the first of American story writers to localize her fiction with especially collected material, to write, indeed, as a special correspondent writes from notes taken deliberately on the spot. Not consciously was she a realist, however, and not intentionally was she an innovator: her methods and her point of view came spontaneously as a result of her home training and her temperament. To quote her own words:

I had heard nothing in those days about "material," and conscience in the use of it, and little enough about art. We did not talk about realism then. Of critical phraseology I knew nothing; and of critical standards only what I had observed by reading the best fiction. Poor novels and stories I did not read. I do not remember being forbidden them; but, by that parental art finer than denial, they were absent from my convenience.

I needed no instruction in the canons of art, however, to teach me that to do a good thing one must work hard for it. So I gave the best part of a month to the study of the Pemberton mill tragedy, driving to Lawrence and investigating every possible avenue of information left at that too long remove of time which might give the data. I revisited the rebuilt mills, and studied the machinery. I consulted engineers and officials and physicians, newspaper men, and persons who had been in the mill at the time of its fall. I scoured the files of old local papers, and from these I took certain portions of names, actually involved in the catastrophe; though, of course, fictitiously used. When there was nothing left for me to learn upon the subject, I came home and wrote a little story called "The Tenth of January" and sent it to *The Atlantic Monthly*, where it appeared in due form.[1]

[1] *Chapters From a Life*, page 91.

The daughter of a Brahmin household and reared among books and literary materials, Miss Phelps had begun to write even in her childhood; and while yet a schoolgirl was publishing books. At sixteen she was contributing to *The Atlantic*, "'Tenty Scran," first of all, a tale remarkable even when considered apart from the age of its author. Of art and of all that to-day is known as short-story technique the tale is guiltless enough—even a sophomore might point out its inherent weaknesses of structure, but its excellencies overbalance everything that may be said against it. The story is alive; one feels that the author is writing not from her knowledge alone, but from her actual experience as well, that she is writing, indeed, with intensity and conviction. And the tale is true: it is redolent of New England rural life, a bit of somber realism that seems remarkable, considering its date—Harriet Prescott's "Midsummer and May" appeared in the same number of the magazine—and considering the youth of its author. There is no straining for unusual effects, no heightening of materials: everything is drab and gray.

There is but little incident in a New England village of the Deerfield style and size—full of commonplace people, who live commonplace lives, in the same white and brown and red houses they were born in, and die respectably in their beds, and are quietly buried among the mulleins and dewberry vines in the hillside graveyard. Mary Scarton's life and death, though they possessed the elements of a tragedy, were divested of their tragic interest by this calm and pensive New-England atmosphere. Nothing so romantic had happened there for many years, nor did occur again for more; yet nobody knew a romance had come and gone. People in Deerfield lived their lives with a view of this world and the next, after the old Puritanic fashion somewhat modified, and so preserved the equilibrium.

With her, romance was not a thing to be placed in an elevated world by itself and treated only in high poetic terms. There was romance everywhere even in the most common and lowly of places. Poets might sing and painters might paint the romance of a Theseus and an Ariadne—

I myself never for a moment believed that Ariadne was a particle more unhappy or pitiable than Nancy Bunker, our seamstress, was, when Hiram Fenn went West to peddle essences, and married a female Hoosier whose father owned half a prairie. They would by no means make as lovely a picture; for Nancy's upper jaw projects, and she has a wart on her nose, very stiff black hair, and a shingle figure, none of which adds grace to a scene; and Hiram went off in the Slabtown stage, with a tin box on his knees, instead of in a shell-shaped boat with silken sails; but I know Nancy reads love stories with great zest, and I know she had a slow fever after Hiram was married.

And another of her early stories, "Calico," she opens with this unromantic note:

It was about time for the four-o'clock train.

After all, I wonder if it is worth telling—such a simple, plotless record of a young girl's life, made up of Mondays and Tuesdays and Wednesdays, like yours or mine. Sharley was so exactly like other people! How can it be helped that nothing remarkable happened to her?

Beginning early in 1864, the element of the emotional began to dominate Miss Phelps's tales. "A Sacrifice Consumed" in the January number of *Harper's* tells of a lover shot at Antietam and of the effect upon her whom he had loved. It was a record of her own actual experience: it was autobiography. Other tales of the period deal with the same subject, like "My Refugees," and "Margarte Bronson," which begins with the familiar sentiment: "I know you are tired enough of tales of the war, and that your own dark memories of the sealed record of the nation's bloody baptism need no fresh reminders." But she was powerless to avoid the subject. She was writing now in the tragic materials of her own life; from now on the somber, the emotional, the sympathetically human ruled her fiction, culminating in her intense novel, *Gates Ajar*. The story, "Tiny," sets forth with agonizing vividness the vivisection of a pet dog—one feels that it was her own dog. Before she wrote, she must, like Byron, have projected herself into the tragedy she was to record and have become in a way her own materials. Before telling of the fall of the Pemberton mill she must live for weeks in the environment of the mill and be present in imagination at the moment of the catastrophe. It was necessary for her to work in the concrete, and to be in every tale her own chief character. She herself was the victim; she herself was Asenath, her face smashed to ghastly horror by the broken jug in the hands of her drunken mother; she herself it was who was now slave to the looms in the Pemberton mill:

She was tired. Her reels had troubled her all the afternoon; the overseer was cross; the day was hot and long. Somebody on the way home had said in passing her: "Look at that girl! I'd kill myself if I looked like that": it was in a whisper, but she heard it. All life looked hot and long; the reels would always be out of order; the overseer would never be kind. Her temples would always throb, and her back would ache. People would always say, "Look at that girl!"

The tale ends in a climax of emotionalism. The old father finds his daughter pinned down by a beam, unable to be rescued, and the flames approaching. Beside her he finds a frightened little girl also beyond help. As the flames approach them the two begin feebly to sing:

"We're going home to die no more."

No detail of emotion is neglected, for she has studied the tragedy with the thoroughness of a historian, and now she herself is the victim and the father her own father. No ending could be more dramatic:

"Senath!" cried the old man out upon the burning bricks; he was scorched now, from his gray hair to his patched boots.
The answer came triumphantly—
"To die no more, no more, no more!"
"Sene! little Sene!"
But some one pulled him back.

No other woman of the period may be compared with Miss Phelps for sheer literary power—the power that feels a situation and makes the reader feel. She was a realist because of the limitations of her imagination: she projected her sympathies into the concrete case and made it seem real. In later years, commenting upon the tales that had influenced her in this early period, she mentioned as heading the list "The Amber Gods" because of its startlingly original final sentence, and "Life in the Iron Mills," because of its "scorching vividness": "Rebecca Harding may have been too terribly in earnest. Her intensity was essentially feminine, but her grip was like that of a masculine hand. Her men and women breathed and suffered, loved and missed of love, won life or wasted it with an ardor that was human and a power that was art." And then she summed up her own theory of what a short story must be if it is to survive its own generation:

What are the sources of power in the tale that one finds it impossible to escape? I think these will be found to be chiefly four: originality, humanity, force, and finish. In most of the passing stories that have selected me for their captive, there would, I think, be found surprise or shock of novelty; some heaven or hell of human feeling; or some grip of absolute strength. The literary quality, the ineffable touch which we call style, will sustain these other qualities; but, without them, it will not go on living.[1]

This criticism, written with the perspective of thirty years after her first youthful work, illuminates her own tales. In her later years she wrote with less abandon and more art, and, in the opinion at least of Dr. Holmes, produced tales, like "Jack the Fisherman" and "The Bell of St. Basil," that rank with the best short stories of her century.[2]

V

More broadly realistic was the work of another contributor to the *Atlantic*, Mr. John T. Trowbridge, who, beginning in 1865 with his long short story, *Coupon Bonds*, wrote a series of tales in which the Yankee character was laid bare without sentiment and without reverence. The New York *Nation* as late as 1869 could even rate him as the only author "of any ability and prominence who had written of New Englanders as if he had not been 'retained for the defense.'" "Mr. Trowbridge," it declared, "in virtue of his vivid delineations of the utterly materialistic, grippingly mean, and cunningly rascally side of the Yankee nature, ought almost to go unopposed to Congress from Kentucky or the Blue Grass region of Tennessee. As yet he is alone, so far as we recollect."

The widespread popularity of *Coupon Bonds* gave to Trowbridge an advantage that Miss Terry never possessed. He was fortunate in his theme and fortunate in his period. Using the Dickens method and the Dickens humor, he found a subject universally attractive in the days after the War: the trials and final discomfiture of a profiteering old couple who had enriched themselves at home while their neighbors fought at the front. The humor is broader and more abundant than in Miss Terry's tales, and one element of it was new, the element of the mischievous

---

[1] "Stories That Stay," Elizabeth Stuart Phelps, *Century Magazine*, November, 1910. See also *The Independent*, November 3, 1892.
[2] *Life and Letters of Oliver Wendell Holmes*, Morse, Vol. II, p. 264.

country small boy who becomes the *diabolus ex machina* of the plot. Beyond the touches which make alive the small boy Taddy the commonplace may not go. Note the episode of Taddy sent to bed, and "behind the stairway door, kicking off a very small pair of trousers":

"Say, ma, need I go to bed now!" he exclaimed rather than inquired, starting to pull on the trousers again after he had got one leg free. "He'll want me to hold the lantern for him to take care of the hoss."

"No, no, Taddy, you'll only be in the way, if you set up. Besides, I want to mend your pants."

"You're always wantin' to mend my pants!" complained the youngster. "I wish there wasn't such a thing as pants in the world."

It's humor alone saves it from the commonplace level of vulgarity. The point is a vital one: the element of humor found in materials that are essentially lowly, even vulgar, is a distinguishing characteristic of one area of the later American short story. That Trowbridge was a pioneer in this field one may show by quoting merely the title of one of his early *Atlantic* tales; "The Man Who Stole a Meeting House." Surely nothing could be more American than that.

VI

With the addition of Edward Everett Hale the group of the early *Atlantic* realists stands complete. Hale was peculiarly the Boston member of the school, the first prominent short-story writer, indeed, that Boston had produced. Everything about him was of the Boston quality: ancestry, training, point of view. He was literary from his cradle. "All of us," he records, "were born into a home crammed with newspapers and books, perfectly familiar with types and paper and proof sheets and manuscripts." His father was editor of *The Daily Advertiser*, and a publisher of books, and to him came copies of everything new issued in America and even beyond the sea. His mother was a writer of books, one of the most cultured women of her generation. "My mother was the only woman in Boston who could read German when I was a boy, and from the day of her marriage to the time of her death her translations from the French and German appeared in the newspaper."

Reared in such a home, the boy became early a reader and a

writer with literary ambitions. In a peculiarly un-Puritanical way his reading inclined in the direction of fiction, a tendency not discouraged by his parents. Before he entered Harvard at the age of thirteen he was, as a subscriber to a circulating library, entitled, if he cared to draw them, to eight volumes a week, but he naïvely records in his autobiography, "I doubt if I averaged more than four volumes a week of fiction," a surprising admission for a Boston lad of the period.

Jane Austen was his favorite novelist—"I knew Miss Austen by heart"—and he read also all of Scott and G. P. R. James. The work, too, of Bulwer, Disraeli, and Dickens came to him with vital appeal, much of it as new material just off the English presses.

When he was twenty and in doubt as to his future profession, his brother, Nathan Hale, started the *Boston Miscellany*, and, to quote the author's own words, "It gave a very happy escape-pipe for the high spirits of some of us who had just left college, and, through my brother's kindness, I was sometimes permitted to contribute to the journal." Three of the contributions were tales: "Tale of a Salamander," "Love by the Way," and "The South American Editor"—three remarkable pieces of work, considering the youth of their author and the time at which they were produced. "If the *Boston Miscellany* had been successful," observes Edward Everett Hale, Jr., in his biography of his father, "perhaps he would have become a story writer twenty years before he did."

Many things are notable about these early tales. Their style is remarkably simple and natural when compared with the over-literary and artificial vogue of their day. Part of it had resulted from the writer's training. As a mere boy his father had given him to review the first number of *Graham's Magazine*, but before printing the review had compelled the boy to strike all the "verys" from his manuscript. The rest of it had come from the fact that literary composition had been from childhood as much a part of his daily life as his meals or his exercise. *The North American Review*, commenting in later years on Hale's first collection of tales, dwelt upon this naturalness and simplicity of style: "He has the rare gift of a light touch, and does not, like so many of our writers, betray a want of training, by bearing on too hard, and making all his strokes of the same laborious thickness."

Moreover, in these early tales there are hints of several modern methods of short-story technique. "Love by the Way," for instance, is the light and vivacious narrative of a young man who on a stagecoach journey flirted and talked incessantly with an attractive girl, only to find at the end of the day that she was deaf and dumb—a tale of the "Marjorie Daw," O. Henry type years before the Civil War.

Hale's fame to-day, however, rests on two tales in the early *Atlantic*, "My Double and How He Undid Me" and "The Man Without a Country." He wrote many short stories after these two masterpieces—enough, indeed, for half a dozen volumes—but little save these two is remembered to-day. The tremendous popularity of the second of these came not, first of all, from its technique, for in technique it is open to criticism, nor from its style, though its style is distinctive; it came from the fact that, like "Coupon Bonds," it voiced a war theme that for the moment was universal. It was an appeal for loyalty in the critical year of the Civil War. It was the publicity given this tale that brought all of Hale's work into prominence and made of him an influence upon the fiction of his period.

The influence of Hale, indeed, overbalances the real value of his work. He came to the American short story at a critical moment, and the emphasis that he received was emphasis upon several things much needed by American fiction.

He stood for realism, but it was a far different realism than that presented by Miss Harding, Miss Terry, and Trowbridge. He made use of what may be called realistic extravagance; not mere wild fancy such as O'Brien had used, but extravaganza touched with specific realism. *The North American Review*, October, 1868, recognized it as a new method and described it thus: "He has so easy a way of making a story seem natural by little matter-of-fact touches that a justly outraged religious public has actually turned upon him for doing his business too well—as if it were not a story-teller's duty to take us in, if he can." This multitude of "little matter-of-fact touches" conceals not only the utter impossibility of the central situation, but it conceals as well the faulty structural technique of the tale, for by modern standards at least it is all but fatally weak—it begins with leisurely exposition, it rambles until it may be called a mere jotting down of episodes, and it ends with no culminating stroke. Its unity is the unity of a situation made single and impressive by a multitude of realistic touches—unity of impression rather than unity of materials. Yet in all of Hale's short stories the reader, however he may have rambled, has borne in upon him at the end one single impressive situation that is beyond his power of forgetting.

Hale was the originator of that peculiar short-story manner which in later years acquired the name "Stocktonesque." It is impossible to read some of the more whimsical of his stories like "Round the World in a Hack," "Crusoe in New York," and "The Children of the Public," for instance, without thinking often of the author of "The Casting Away of Mrs. Lecks and Mrs. Aleshine" and "Rudder Grange." The same flimsy material, the same impossibilities of character and incident made plausible by serious treatment and a multiplicity of trivial details, the same preposterous humor, the same gossipy, ingratiating style that captures the reader at length and holds him to the end, however completely he may have been on his guard.

Another element that Hale added prominently to the short story of his day, in addition to realistic extravaganza and humor, was lightness of touch, vivacity, mere entertainment—the qualities that N. P. Willis had sought to impart to the form and had failed to make popular because of insurmountable handicaps both subjective and objective. *The North American Review*, commenting upon *If, Yes, and Perhaps* (1868), made this happy comparison: "We should say that his stories compared with others as good *vers de société* with more serious verse—less solemn, but more clever— *better to take*, as they say." That the ponderous old Boston *Review* could commend thus heartily such a collection of extravaganzas and brief tales, told for the most part for entertainment only, and that it could do so in a style so human and so unliterary, indicated clearly that a new spirit was coming into American literature.

The *Review*, indeed, had surrendered to the new form seven years before. When in 1861 the Boston that had expelled Willis and killed, as it supposed, Poe started the first magazine published in America devoted exclusively to the short story, *Tales of the Day, Original and Selected*, the May, June, and August numbers issued as a volume the same year, together with an abbreviated volume, *Short Stories for Leisure Hours. Selected from "Tales of the Day,"* the *Review* had felt itself compelled to take notice:

We are interested. The question is not whether tales shall be extensively read. A large and increasing public has answered this question in the affirmative. Those whose pursuits are of the very gravest character are not unwilling thus to occupy their weary hours, their vacation seasons, and their journeyings; while for the many who will read little else it is certainly of great consequence that their appetite should be catered for without detriment, and if possible with benefit to principle and character.

As long as tales are "high toned in their moral character" they may be endured and even commended—this was the trend of the review.

Thus the short story made its entrance into New England.

BIBLIOGRAPHY

1861.   *Tales of the Day, Original and Selected.*   Vol. I.

1861.   *Short Stories for Leisure Hours.   Selected from " Tales of the Day."*

1863.   *The Sparrow's Fall; or, Under the Willow; and Other Stories.*
Caroline Chesebro'.

1863.   *Hospital Sketches; and Camp and Fireside Stories.*   Louisa M.
Alcott.

1864.   *Georgia Sketches, by an Old Man.*   Richard Malcolm Johnston.

1864.   *Centeola, and Other Tales.*   Daniel Pierce Thompson.

1865.   *Atlantic Tales; Stories from " The Atlantic Monthly."*
"My Double and How He Undid Me," Edward Everett
Hale, Sept., 1859; "The Diamond Lens," Fitz-James O'Brien,
Jan., 1858; "Life in the Iron Mills," Miss R. B. Harding,
April, 1861; "The Pursuit of Knowledge Under Difficulties,"
Gail Hamilton, March, 1860; "A Raft That No Man Made,"
Robert T. S. Lowell, March, 1862; "Why Thomas Was
Discharged," George Arnold, June, 1863; "Victor and Jacqueline," Miss Caroline Chesebro', Aug., 1860; "Elkanah
Brewster's Temptation," Charles Nordhoff, Dec., 1859;
"The Queen of the Red Chessmen," Miss Lucretia P. Hale,
Feb., 1858; "Miss Lucinda," Miss Rose Terry, Aug., 1861;
"The Denslow Palace," J. D. Whelpley, July, 1858; "Friend
Eli's Daughter," Bayard Taylor, July, 1862; "A Half Life
and Half a Life," Miss E. H. Appleton, Feb., 1864.

1867.   *Little Brother, and Other Genre Pictures.*   Fitz-Hugh Ludlow.

1867.   *The Celebrated Jumping Frog of Calaveras County, and Other
Sketches.*   Mark Twain.

1868. *If, Yes, and Perhaps. Four Possibilities and Six Exaggerations, with Some Bits of Fact.* Edward Everett Hale.

"The Children of the Public," *Frank Leslie's*, Jan., 1863; "A Piece of Possible History," *Monthly Religious Magazine*, Oct., 1851; "The South American Editor," *Boston Miscellany*, 1842; "The Old and the New, Face to Face," *Sartain's Magazine*, 1852; "The Dot and Line Alphabet," *Atlantic*, Oct., 1858; "The Last Voyage of the *Resolute*," Boston *Daily Advertiser*, June, 1856; "My Double and How He Undid Me," *Atlantic*, Sept., 1859; "The Man Without a Country," *Atlantic*, Dec., 1863; "The Last of the Florida," *Boatswain's Whistle*, Nov., 1864; "The Skeleton in the Closet," *The Galaxy*, 1866; "Christmas Waits in Boston," *Daily Advertiser*, 1867.

1869. *The Ingham Papers; Some Memorials of the Life of Capt. Frederic Ingham, U. S. M., Sometime Pastor of the First Sandemanian Church of Nahuadavick and Major General by Brevet in the Patriot Service in Italy.* Edward Everett Hale.

"The Good-Natured Pendulum," *Atlantic*, Jan., 1869; "Paul Jones and Denis Duval," *Atlantic*, Oct., 1864; "Round the World in a Hack," *Atlantic Almanac*, 1869; "The Friend's Meeting," *The Rosary*, 1848; "Did He Take the Prince to Ride?" *Atlantic*, May, 1868; "How Mr. Frye Would Have Preached It," *Atlantic*, Feb., 1867; "The Rag-Man and the Rag-Woman," *Atlantic Almanac*, First Number; "Dinner Speaking," *Atlantic*, Oct., 1867; "Good Society," New York *Ledger*, Oct., 1868; "Daily Bread," *Daily Advertiser*, Dec., 1869.

1869. *Short Stories for Spare Moments. Selected from "Lippincott's Magazine."* 1869.

"Alas, Poor Ghost!" Leonard Kip; "Lady Haughton's Mistake," Annie Thomas; "To Please Aunt Martha," Margaret Hosmer; "Ranlock Branch," J. T. McKay; "The Forget-me-not," Gustav zu Putlitz; "A Wreck Upon the Shore," L. Clarke Davis; "The Strange Passengers," Harriet Prescott Spofford; "Love and Ghosts," D. B. Dorsey; "Loyal en Tout," Kate P. Kereven; "The Legend of Ball's Lake," Rev. R. Wilson; "Vox Humana," Anne Brewster; "Willie's Wife," Rosamond Dale Owen; "Made Whole," Maria L. Pool; "Love on the Ohio," D. B. Dorsey.

Short Stories for Spare Moments. Second Series. 1869.

"The Record of Dorcas Bently," Caroline Chesebro'; "The Blue Cabinet," Lucy Hamilton Hooper; "Golden Dreams,"

Albert Fabre; "The Pearl of Great Price," Rebecca Harding Davis; "Nor Dead, nor Living," Jane G. Austen; "Doctor Aar," Kate P. Kereven; "The Mannerings, "Louise S. Dorr; "Mahala's Drive," F. R. Stockton; "The Photographer's Story," Lucy H. Hooper; "Who Shall Separate Us?" Mary W. Janvrin; "The Young Priest," W. Maud Evelyn; "Ricardo Il Falcone," Robert Boggs.

Short Stories for Spare Moments. Third Series. 1870.
"Rougegorge," Harriet Prescott Spofford; "Sam's Sermon," S. Watkins Tuttle; "The Shadow of Fate," Riter Fitzgerald; "The Prince's Surprise"; "My Grandmother— That Might Have Been," Alice Cary; "Snow Upon the Waters," Lucy H. Hooper; "That Man"; "Harneyhow's Hummock," Jane G. Austen; "Myra's Mirror," James Franklin Fitts; "Dick Libby," George Jones; "Dick Lyle's Fee," L. Clarke Davis; "Peter Crisp's Spectacles," Solomon Soberside; "Only No Love," Translated by Mrs. A. L. Wister; "The Price of a Dream," Frank Lee Benedict.

1869. *Men, Women, and Ghosts.* Elizabeth Stuart Phelps.
"No News," *Atlantic*, Sept., 1868; "The Tenth of January," *Atlantic*, March, 1868; "Night Watches," *Harper's*, May, 1866 [as "Voices of the Night"]; "The Day of My Death," *Harper's*, Oct., 1868; "Little Tommy Tucker, *Watchman and Reflector;* "One of the Elect," *Hours at Home* [as "Magdalene"]; "What Was the Matter?" *Atlanti*, Aug., 1866 [as "What Did She See With?"]; "In the Gray Goth," *Atlantic*, Nov., 1867; "Calico," *Harper's*, Nov., 1867; "Kentucky's Ghost," *Atlantic*, Nov., 1868.

1872. *His Level Best and Other Stories.* Edward Everett Hale.
"His Level Best"; "The Brick Moon"; "Water Talk"; "Mouse and Lion"; "The Modern Sindbad"; "A Tale of a Salamander"; "The Queen of California"; "Confidence."

1872. *Beauty and the Beast: and Tales of Home.* Bayard Taylor.
"Beauty and the Beast," *Atlantic*, Jan., 1866; "The Strange Friend," *Atlantic*, Jan., 1867; "Jacob Flint's Journey," *Atlantic*, Sept., 1869; "Can a Life Hide Itself?" *Atlantic*, May, 1869; "Twin Love," *Atlantic*, Sept., 1871; "The Experiences of the A C," *Atlantic*, Feb., 1862; "Friend Eli's Daughter," *Atlantic*, July, 1862; "Miss Bartram's Trouble"; "Mrs. Stronggitharm's Report."

1872. *Christmas Eve and Christmas Day.* Edward Everett Hale.

1877. *Tales From Two Hemispheres.* Hjalmar Hjorth Boyesen.
"The Man Who Lost His Name"; "The Story of an Out-

cast"; "The Good-for-nothing"; "A Scientific Vagabond"; "Truls, the Nameless"; "Asathor's Vengeance."

1879. *Sealed Orders*. Elizabeth Stuart Phelps.

"Sealed Orders"; "Old Mother Goose"; "The Lady of Shalott"; "The True Story of Guenever"; "Doherty"; "The Voyage of the *America*"; "Wrecked in Port"; "Running the Risk"; "Long, Long Ago"; "Since I Died"; "A Woman's Pulpit"; "Number 13"; "Two Hundred and Two"; "Cloth of Gold"; "Saint Caligula"; "Miss Mildred's Friend"; "Neblitt."

1880. *Crusoe in New York, and Other Tales*. Edward Everett Hale.

1881. *Somebody's Neighbors*. Rose Terry Cooke.

"Eben Jackson," *Atlantic*, March, 1858; "Miss Lucinda," *Atlantic*, Aug., 1861; "Dely's Cow," *Atlantic*, June, 1865; "Squire Paine's Conversion," *Harper's*, March, 1878; "Miss Beula's Bonnet," *Harper's*, March, 1880; "Cal Culver and the Devil," *Harper's*, Sept., 1878; "Amandar," *Harper's*, Sept., 1880; "Polly Marner, Tailoress"; "Uncle Josh"; "Polly Jenning's Hair"; "Freedom Wheeler's Controversy With Providence," *Atlantic*, Aug., 1877; "Mrs. Flint's Married Experience," *Harper's*, Dec., 1880.

1884. *Christmas in Narragansett*. Edward Everett Hale.

1885. *Root Bound*. Rose Terry Cooke.

1886. *The Sphynx's Children*. Rose Terry Cooke.

1891. *Huckleberries Gathered From New England Hills*. Rose Terry Cooke.

"Grit," *Harper's*, Jan., 1877; "Mary Ann's Mind," *Galaxy*, 24: 241; "Love"; "Odd Miss Todd," *Harper's*, Oct., 1882; "An Old-Fashioned Thanksgiving," "Hobson's Choice," *Harper's*, Sept., 1884; "Clary's Trial," *Atlantic*, 45:645; "A Double Thanksgiving"; "Home Again"; "How Celia Changed Her Mind"; "A Town Mouse and a Country Mouse," *Atlantic*, June, 1891.

1897. *Susan's Escort, and Others*. Edward Everett Hale.

CHAPTER IX

I

The first literary result of the Civil War was a sudden growth of new periodicals, which sprang up everywhere like poppies from a battlefield. Many were mere ephemeral growths which quickly gave place to others just as ephemeral; many persisted vigorously, but with little to commend them save their popularity; others became dominating influences in the new period. Of these last the New York *Nation* is the best example, founded in 1866, to quote `rom its salutatory, "to promote and develop a higher standard of criticism." The work of this influential journal really opened a new period in every branch of American literature. In its literary department it stood from the first for fixed standards, for seriousness, for careful workmanship. Criticism in America, it declared, had passed through its first "chaotic or embryonic period, when the whole energy of the people is employed in overcoming physical obstacles" and "when literature is an exotic"; it had almost emerged from its second stage, "the childish stage, or that of promiscuous and often silly admiration or indiscriminate censure"; and now it was entering upon its final stage, "orderly and scientific criticism without personal animosity or bias." For this last variety of criticism it proposed to be in America the leading organ, and for two or three decades at least it realized its ambition.

Viewing the literary field in 1866, *The Nation* found the new magazine situation on the whole a hopeful symptom:

The fact noticed by some old writer—Pliny, we believe—that literature flourishes immediately after great civil convulsions, is repeating itself here since the suppression of the rebellion—a brief period which has witnessed the commencement and projection of more newspapers and periodicals than the ten preceding years.

A new flourishing of literature, it declared, was certainly needed in America, since "the reading matter of this country is almost entirely foreign," but there was a tremendous handicap to be overcome. The weak point in American literature was its fiction. To found a popular magazine was easy enough, but after that came the necessity "to find a corps of writers, which is no easy task, and to get good 'copy' from them, which is not much easier." "Good 'copy'" meant fiction.

A first-class serial novel is necessary for success, and this is just what cannot be had at any price, the prose writers of America not being novelists, or at best but indifferent ones. . . . *The Atlantic Monthly* is fain to take up with Mr. Charles Reade, as *Harper's* is with Dickens, Mr. Wilkie Collins, or Mr. Anybodyelse who happens to be popular in England. Lacking the serial novel, there remain the tale and the essay, in which our writers, though certainly meritorious, are not up to the English standard of excellence.

A dismal outlook surely, but ten years later, February, 1875, *The Galaxy*, another of the new magazines, drew a picture even darker. Apologizing for beginning a serial by Justin McCarthy, the editor declared that

The faculty of story-telling seems to have died out of us. . . . We read novels chiefly written by British authors. . . . The narrative faculty is notably lacking among us. Our public has no notion whatever of the poor quality of almost all the writing in this department of literature that is submitted to publishers and editors.

Scribner's Monthly, founded in 1870 primarily for the purpose of encouraging American writers, was forced to run during its first year a novel by George MacDonald, and in all its later advertising it emphasized heavily its English contributors.

The weakness, however, was almost wholly in the longer forms of fiction. The richness and quantity of the British novel of social life all through the later nineteenth century discouraged American writers. America, for one thing, had no material for such work: our social system as yet was primitive. It would have been impossible to compete with the British product even had there been an inflexible copyright agreement between the two nations. But the increasingly growing numbers of new magazines afforded another market for literary wares that was not so easily supplied from foreign sources. Short stories and sketches and single-number magazine material of all varieties began to be called for in quantities unprecedented, and prices began to be paid that in earlier years would have been deemed impossible, for this shorter variety of fiction. American material, attenuated though it might be for prolonged studies, was even better than the English. The result was that American authors more and more devoted their energies to the production of what they could do and what they could sell. More short stories were produced during the decade after 1865 than during any two preceding decades, and the quality increased steadily with the quantity. Moreover, the spirit of the age was demanding shortened work. The war had rendered America restless; it had set in motion enormous activities which absorbed men and even women, and made reading, if it were to be done at all, a thing for intense moments rather than for leisurely hours and days. The serial after a time began to lose its hold: by 1888 *Harper's Monthly* could announce as one of its attractions: "No continued stories."

A new fastidiousness, too, had begun to affect the readers of short stories in the multitudinous magazines. The crude and sprawly work that had satisfied the mid-century no longer was tolerated, the word "technique" began increasingly to appear in American criticism. War exalts efficiency: it is impatient of the inaccurate and the haphazard. Science had become a dominating word, and science means Truth, accuracy of method, a body of laws. Lowell during his editorship had admitted much native and realistically treated material into the volumes of *The Atlantic*— a real advance—but it was lawless in structure, abounding in surplusage, and, to the fastidious, at least, it was, much of it, barbarous in material and low in effect. Lowell himself had realized the danger always attendant upon the use of such material. To Thomas Hughes he wrote, "Is Democracy doomed by its very nature to a dead level of commonplace?" and to Howells in 1865:

The danger of our literature (with plenty of talent) seems to me to be carelessness and want of scholarly refinement. That is the rock I see ahead just now, and I fear we may go to pieces on it if we don't look sharp. Perhaps you will be inclined to send back a stone at the glass house of the *Biglow Papers*—but it was for this very reason that I made a balance for Hosea in the pedantic parson.

The new period was led not by Hosea, but by the pedantic parson. It was critical; it followed *The Nation*. It centered about a remarkable group of young men—James, Howells, Aldrich, and others—men cosmopolitan where the earlier leaders had been provincial, cultured, and traveled men who were thoroughly awake to the new movements in England and France and Italy. Under their leadership the short story became an art form in a new sense. They purged it of the coarseness that had been given it by the pioneer realists, they removed from it the theatricality and artificial machinery that had been put upon it by Poe, and they made it obedient to Truth, but always with a realism chastened and held firmly in leash. They stood for workmanship at any cost, for style, for artistry over all. With them began the age of criticism, the age of literature as a deliberate science, of literature as a conscious art.

II

The leader of the group, if the most consistent member and the most distinctive writer may be called its leader, was Henry James, Jr., whose critical papers became influential from 1864, and whose earliest tale, "The Story of a Year," appeared in *The Atlantic* a year later. Never a leader in the popular sense of the word, scorning ever the multitude and working ever on the highest plane of his own ideals though all his readers might leave him, nevertheless, as viewed to-day in full circle, he emerges as the dominant figure in a literary movement which was little short of a revolution. He took his stand deliberately and never for a moment wavered or compromised. From his earliest critical dictum published in *The North American Review* when he was twenty-one, through a series of reviews, some thirty in number in the next three years, during forty years devoted almost wholly to fiction, he stood both in theory and practice for positive standards of art, for work based on Truth and reflection, for conscientious workmanship and distinction in style. He brought a cosmopolitan air into American fiction. He was the earliest to explain with clearness the work of the French school led by Balzac and Flaubert, and to bring the artistic fundamentals of this school to practical bearing upon American fiction.

To trace the evolution of James through his inheritances and his environments and his training is a task that only a Henry James might accomplish. His "education," in the Henry Adams sense of the term, was unique. His father, Henry James, Sr., had been a product of that intense epoch which had produced the New England prophets—the Bronson Alcotts and the Emersons and the Thoreaus. Unlike his fellow philosophers, however, he had inherited wealth, and, freed from the necessity of a profession, had lived as a philosopher at large a life detached, devoted wholly to the metaphysical. His bent everywhere was toward the esoteric. He was a reformer with theories, an interpreter of Swedenborg, a critic in advance of his generation who wrote and published voluminously in a style peculiarly trenchant and distinctive. Fastidiously sensitive, he shrank from commonness as from the physically unclean. His children he reared on high planes of theory, guarding them from all contacts that might mar their manners or render commonplace their ideals, keeping them carefully from the streets and the public schools, supplying them with tutors who imparted a chaste though desultory training, withholding from them with strictness all books and publications American lest they become provincial and vulgar, and feeding them always with the best to be procured from the English and Parisian presses. Always about them was kept golden an atmosphere of overseas culture—a refinement of civilization, it was ever borne in upon them—from which somehow they had been defrauded as from a birthright.

Thus the imaginative youth, though physically residing in his native New York City until he was twelve, really lived in a land the very antipodes of New York, a land created by his youthful imagination from the materials of his reading and from the glowing pictures drawn by his parents, who seemed to him like exiles in a land essentially barbarous. Then at twelve had come the first sojourn abroad, a move planned carefully to counteract all tendencies toward attachment to locality. In the years of European education that followed, the father allowed the sons no time for sending roots into any soil. He would develop them into men cosmopolitan, men utterly free from bias and the narrowness of provincialism. For a few months they were at Geneva, then at London, at Paris, at Boulogne-sur-Mer. Back again in America, the young student spent a year at Newport, after which followed a year again at Geneva, and short periods at Newport and Cambridge.

His schooling was as desultory as his travels. Sometimes he worked with private tutors, sometimes in select private schools, but always he was permitted to study only what appealed to his fancy—never mathematics, never anything that ran counter to his enthusiasms. Once he chose art as a life work and for a time studied it with intensity. He became proficient in languages, especially in the French, which he mastered to the degree of being able in later years to contribute translations of his own work to the *Revue de Deux Mondes*. But early he settled upon literature as his profession. Before he wrote a word he set about mastering it as one masters painting or music. He read Balzac, George Eliot, Trollope, the later French novelists, and he read pencil in hand, taking notes, observant of technique.

At nineteen he was at Harvard, attending in desultory way lectures in the law school, but his heart was not in the law: he was reading fiction. The Civil War, which was affecting so tremendously the young men of his generation, touched him not at all, or at most only to reveal to him his unfitness for practical life and to put him still more out of step with the great average of his countrymen. Everything had tended to render him a man solitary and detached. The family means made life, even in the circles which alone he knew, entirely possible without even the formality of a profession, and he sat down, as Hawthorne had done, to work out alone his problem of life. But Hawthorne, despite his solitude and his detachment, was a man with foundations. He was permeated, despite himself, with the New England provincialism and the New England Puritanism that even prenatally had environed his life. But James had been reared deliberately for detachment; he was as free from religious bias as a scientist, and he was free from patriotic narrowness to the extent even of being for the most of his life a man without a country. Everything had fitted him for an impartial observer, a philosopher without preconceptions, a social scientist in a laboratory.

Such a personality entering the literary life will enter it deliberately, and not, as with the men of emotion and turbulent genius, with fire and smoke and irruptive force. For James the creation of masterpieces must be preceded by a deliberate mastery of the science underlying the art of creating masterpieces. In 1864 there was no formulated science of fiction—perhaps there is none today—but certainly there was an abundance of fiction in English, much of it phenomenally successful, and a careful study of it should reveal the laws. And accordingly he read as a scientist makes a dissection. For much that was popular he could find no logical reason for popularity. He read Dickens, and in a paper for *The Nation* set forth at length "the limitations of Dickens"; Trollope he read extensively and he summed him up as the patient chronicler of vulgarity; Mrs. Braddon and the feminine school filled him with wrath.

In American fiction he found nothing to praise except Hawthorne. Short stories and novels based upon materials drawn from American life and manners he counted not literature at all, for art, as he had begun to define art, is the product of achieved civilization and its materials never are to be drawn from the barbarous and the squalid. The American feminine writers of the "*Azarian* school—for, alas! there is a school"—worked, he declared, totally without technique, and that in a period when technique was becoming imperative:

> The public taste has been educated to a spirit of the finest discernment, the sternest exaction. . . . The secrets of the novelist's craft have been laid bare, new contrivances have been invented; and as fast as the old machinery wears out, it is repaired by the clever artisans of the day.

Thereupon he proceeded to set forth for the benefit of the author of *Azarian* and her school "the secrets of the novelist's craft" as he had learned them before he himself had written a word of fiction. His first principles he enunciated in *The North American Review* in 1865. The primitive canon of Art, he declared, is Truth:

> When once a work of fiction may be classed as a novel, its foremost claim to merit, is its *Truth*—its truth to something, however questionable that thing may be in point of morals or of taste.

And the second is like it:

> The only lasting fictions are those which have spoken to the reader's heart, and not to his eye.

Fiction, however, is a science as well as an art. It is ruled by cold laws and is not a thing of haphazard and impulse. The writings of the French realists he cited as an example:

> Balzac's work was clearly done because it was scientifically done. That word resumes our lesson. He set down things in black and white,

not, as Miss Prescott seems vaguely to aim at doing, in red, blue, and green—in prose, scientifically as they stood. He aimed at local color; that is, at giving the facts of things.

Another imperative requisite of the fiction writer, he maintained, is style, accuracy of diction, inevitableness of word and phrase, utter Truth in epithet and adjective, clearness as the work of the French school possessed clearness, and avoidance at every point of intensity and surplusage—that "fatal gift of fluency" possessed by "the majority of feminine writers—Mrs. Browning, George Sand, Gail Hamilton, Mrs. Stowe." Especially was this needed by American writers. The curse of American fiction from the first had been fine writing, intensity, overornamentation even to tawdriness:

The fine writing in which *Azarian* abounds is the cheapest writing of the day. Every magazine story bears traces of it. It is so widely adopted, because to a person of clever fancy there is no kind of writing that is so easy—so easy, we mean, considering the effect produced. Of course, it is much easier to write in a style which necessitates no looking out for words: but such a style makes comparatively little impression. The manner in question is easy because the writer recognizes no standard of truth or accuracy by which his performances may be measured. He does not transcribe facts—facts must be counted, measured, weighed, which takes far too much trouble. He does not patiently study the nature and appearance of a thing until he has won from it the confession of that absolute appreciable quality, the correct statement of which is alone true description; he does not commit himself to statements, for these are dangerous things; he does not, in short, extract; he affixes.

Thus Henry James at twenty-two—a craftsman, a technician who approached his art with labor and with seriousness, a critic who during the first three years of his apprenticeship wrote what has been collected into a distinctive volume of criticism. Whatever he did he did with thoroughness, deliberately, with knowledge not only of his materials, but of the rules of his art. His conscientious thoroughness one may illustrate from an incident in his later years. For a period he turned to the drama as his form of expression, but before he wrote a word he labored over dramatic technique like a veritable apprentice:

I have worked like a horse—far harder than anyone will ever know—over the whole stiff mystery of "technique"—I have run it to earth, and

I don't in the least hesitate to say that, for the comparatively poor and meager, the piteously simplified, purposes of the English stage, I have made it absolutely my own, put it into my pocket.

Whatever else James may have given to American fiction, he gave conscientious workmanship, thought, seriousness, and, if one uses the word in the sense of attempted truthfulness in the use of materials, Realism, a word destined greatly to disturb the coming decades.

III

During the years of his apprenticeship James worked almost exclusively with the short-story form, producing before 1875 upward of thirty pieces, the most of them of single-magazine-issue length. He had settled upon the shorter form not accidentally and not because of compulsion. Deliberately he had decided to make it his sole form of expression. To Norton he wrote in 1871, "To write a series of good little tales I deem ample work for a lifetime." But he had not yet completely found himself. Hawthorne had greatly influenced him at first. He had even written for a time in the Hawthorne manner with Hawthorne materials, as in "The Romance of Certain Old Clothes" and "De Grey: a Romance," but not for long. Hawthorne might chord with a mood of adolescent years when romance and realism are synonymous terms, but in his later period he could say with honesty, "I hate old New England stories—which are lean and pale and poor and ugly." Hawthorne, too, with his problems of New England Puritanism and his constant dwelling upon the deeper currents of the moral and the religious, had little in common with the later James. Not all at once, however, did he become a scientist. For a period another field of romance attracted him: he had made in 1869 a "passionate pilgrimage" to Europe, had discovered with emotion Italy and France and England, and, like Irving and Willis and Longfellow, had found over them a golden atmosphere which he attempted to reproduce in a series of tales like "At Isella," "Travelling Companions," and "A Passionate Pilgrim."

In "Benvolio," which in all save its final details is autobiography, he has told of the struggles of this early period from which he finally emerged as the Henry James we know to-day. His native bent was critical and scientific; his early environment and his training had made him romantic. *He* was Benvolio:

At home he lived in two chambers. One was an immense room hung with pictures, lined with books, draped with rugs and tapestries, decorated with a multitude of ingenious devices (for all of these things he was very fond); the other, his sleeping room, was almost as bare as a monastic cell. It had a meager little strip of carpet on the floor, and a dozen well-thumbed volumes of classic poets and sages on the mantelshelf. On the wall hung three or four coarsely engraved portraits of the most exemplary of these worthies; these were the only ornaments. But the room had the charm of a great window, in a deep embrasure, looking out upon a tangled, silent, moss-grown garden, and in the embrasure stood the ink-blotted table at which Benvolio did most of his poetic scribbling. The windows of his sumptuous sitting room commanded a wide public square, where people were always passing and lounging, where military music used to play on vernal nights, and half the life of the great town went forward. At the risk of your thinking our hero a sad idler, I will say that he spent an inordinate amount of time in gazing out of these windows (on either side) with his elbows on the sill.

It is allegory and it savors of Hawthorne, but it reveals the soul of Henry James. More and more as he mastered his art he turned from the garden of romance and centered his attention upon the public square—upon real life, real men and women living their real lives, but always was it a perfectly civilized public square, and always, Hawthorne-like, he viewed it from his solitary window, from his "room hung with pictures, lined with books, draped with rugs and tapestries." He studied life without contacts with life and he recorded what he saw, himself as totally detached from his material as if it were a laboratory record. He was Henry Adams: "he never got to the point of playing the game at all; he lost himself in the study of it, watching the errors of the players." He was Montaigne: "Others form man, I report him."

And his methods of record at every step were scientific. He worked never by impulse and seldom with emotion: always he proceeded coldly and accurately with full knowledge of all the laws. And only limitedly were these laws the canons held fundamental by Poe. Life as he saw it lived about him was not a series of complete dramas with culminating climaxes and theatrical final curtains. It was not a thing of single color tones and rigidly unified impressions, of swift movement and constant happenings. To Henry James art, even the art of the short story, dealt with the ordinary areas of life, areas that blended almost imperceptibly into other areas, and then still other areas. As he recorded life, the web moves slowly on and on, the pattern grows, but not by startling jumps: nothing, save at rarest intervals, really happens. To throw the spot light upon one single figure in the pattern, as did Poe, and then to hold it there for an intense moment made only for sensation and untruth. Poe's dramatic dénouement he considered artificial and false to life. Even in his dramas, written with the utmost attention to technique, he made no attempt to gather at the end all the threads of the action into a culminating curtain effect, but left them loose and unexplained as for the most part they lie in actual life.

To him the imperative thing was Truth—accurate characterization, accurate reporting of dialogue, accurate picturization, accurate determination of motive and of mental reactions. His fictions, whether they be denominated short stories or novels, deal each of them with an episode, a period of time in which men and women meet, have experiences, and part. The whole leaves, when one has completed it, a definite impression upon the reader, single and often vivid. There has been analysis, at times seemingly interminable, and often oversubtle, it would seem, but as one views the piece in retrospect one is surprised to find there has been no surplusage. Of "Daisy Miller," for example, written in the fullness of the mid-Henry James manner, Howells, by no means given to superlatives, could say: "The perfection of the workmanship could not be represented without apparent exaggeration. If no word could be spared without in some degree spoiling it, none could be added without cumbering its beauty with a vain decoration."

With such a conception of fiction, it was but natural that James should be tempted constantly to enlarge his area of observation and present his reports in greater length. His tales began to extend to two magazine installments, then to three, then in *Watch and Ward* to six, and then in *Roderick Hudson* to twelve. After 1875 his single installment tales were few. More and more he made use of European material for his work, using the American scene or American characters as a contrast or foil. From his viewpoint anything else were impossible. To analyze with minuteness social conditions and manners and the actions and reactions of men and women under highly civilized conditions—to deal with uncivilized conditions, he believed, was to degrade art—demanded material, almost wholly lacking in America, even in Boston. It was an old idea in Britain, old as the beginnings of American literature. The Dublin *University Magazine*, for instance, had settled the matter in 1850 in words that might have been written by James himself.

Where every kind of social rank is obliterated, the field of observation, which is the province of fiction, becomes proportionally narrow; and although human nature must be the same under every form of government, the liberty of a thorough democracy by no means compensates for its vulgarity.

With such a conception of literature and of life it was inevitable that at last he should have taken up his permanent residence abroad. When in 1875 he left America to return only as a rare visitant he was but following his material and the call of his affinities. Five years later he wrote to Howells:

I sympathise even less with your protest against the idea that it takes an old civilization to set a novelist in motion—a proposition that seems to me so true as to be a truism. It is on manners, customs, usages, habits, forms, upon all these things matured and established, that a novelist lives— they are the very stuff his work is made of; and in saying that in the absence of those "dreary and worn-out paraphernalia" which I enumerate as being wanting in American society, "we have simply the whole of human life left," you beg (to my sense) the question.

The deliberate training of his father was bearing its perfect fruit. Not only was he not a man provincial; he was not even national. In 1888 he could write:

I can't look at the English-American world, or feel about them, any more, save as a big Anglo-Saxon total, destined to such an amount of melting together that an insistence on their differences becomes more and more idle and pedantic. . . . I have not the least hesitation in saying that I aspire to write in such a way that it would be impossible to an outsider to say whether I am at a given moment an American writing about England or an Englishman writing about America (dealing as I do with both countries) and so far from being ashamed of such an ambiguity I should be highly proud of it, for it would be highly civilized.

More often than anything else James has been called an international novelist, but the term seems narrow and provincial after reading a passage like this. He could contrast English and

American manners and English and American men and women
to the clarifying of both, but his real field, as he conceived of it,
was the Anglo-Saxon world: he would picture for posterity the
English-speaking race.

IV

Beginning his literary career with intent to produce only brief
tales, James ended it pre-eminently as a novelist. The work which
he selected for the definitive edition of his writings is almost
wholly made up of novels, some of them, like *The Golden Bowl*,
exceedingly long.   Of the thirty short stories which he wrote
before *Roderick Hudson* he retained only one; the most of them
he never republished from the magazines. The novel, as he defined
the novel, gave scope in perfection to his peculiar powers. It
gave him freedom, it enabled him to use with fullest effect his
multitudinous materials, and it permitted analysis and subtle
character development in extenso.   "The breath of the novelist's
being is his liberty," he wrote to Stevenson, "and the incompa-
rable virtue of the form he uses is that it lends itself to views innumerable and diverse, to every variety of illustration.   There is
certainly no other mold of so large capacity."

To attempt a hard and fast classification of his writings, however, and to separate them into novels and novelettes and short
stories, is a task that is hopeless. There are no inflexible standards
of measurement. In all but mere length some of his acknowledged
novels are of short-story texture: they deal with an episode, they
make use of a minimum of characters, they move with a single line
of action, and, for the most part, they trace no character development. Length he seemed never to have considered a determining
element: he stopped when he had made clear in his own way all
the materials which had entered into the episode under study.
Howells was inclined to classify the stories by mere application
of the yardstick:

We may realize them physically if we adopt the magazine parlance
and speak of the novella as a one-number story, of the novel as a serial,
and of the novelette as a two-number or a three-number story; if it
passes the three-number limit it seems to have become a novel.

Measured by this rule, James, after his period of apprenticeship,
wrote few "novellas" or short stories.   The most distinctive of

his shorter fictions, like "Daisy Miller" and "The Turn of the Screw," would be classed as novelettes. Indeed, the one-number tales among his writings are almost a negligible quantity. And there is little doubt that James himself measured with Howells's rule. That the short story, be it a one-number or a three-number product, was to follow a set of rules distinct from those which governed the so-called novel there is nothing in his writings to indicate. The single-number story, to be sure, would require greater economy with materials to make it fit the narrower bounds, and there would be, per force, fewer characters and less leisurely dialogue for character and situation development, but otherwise the texture of the two forms would be the same. And almost the same thing might be said of the short story, as James conceived of it, when compared even with the novel. Howells, who of all critics has best interpreted James, has expressed it thus, explaining his own position as well as that of his fellow novelist:

A big book is necessarily a group of episodes more or less loosely connected by a thread of narrative, and there seems no reason why this thread must always be supplied. Each episode may be quite distinct or it may be one of a connected group; the final effect will be from the truth of each episode, not from the size of the group.

Or to put it in the form of a definition: a novel is a collection of episodes; a short story is a detached episode treated either briefly or at length. The shorter form became irksome to James for the simple reason that it kept him constantly centered upon metes and bounds. Freedom was "the breath of his life"; he would follow his analyses to their subtle ends with no thought of omitting for mere space reasons illuminating details. His five years of struggle with the drama, a form as tyrannical in its bounds and its cameo-like technique as the short story, ended in complete failure. In exasperation he threw it from him and all other forms that would concentrate his powers upon his methods and his bounds rather than upon his materials. "The rebound," says Gosse in his brilliant study of James, "was extreme. I recall his saying to me, after the fiasco of 'Guy Domvile': 'at all events, I have escaped forever from the foul fiend Excision.'"

And yet it is in his shorter pieces rather than in his novels that his most valuable work is to be found. One can but quote Howells:

In his short stories—one is obliged to call them stories for want of a more fitting word,—rather than his more extended fictions are the heroes and heroines we know him best by. He has the art of so environing the slightest presentment of female motive that it shows life size in the narrow space of a sketch or study.

There were periods when he turned almost exclusively to the shorter form, the three-number limit being at such times his favorite measure. It permitted him, he believed at such times, to cover more ground and to present a more varied area of human life. The novel, despite all its varied episodes, was, nevertheless, a single canvas restricted to a single group of characters, but a series of short stories was a collection of canvases which allowed the depicting of a multitude of different characters and environments and diverse situations. To Stevenson he wrote in 1888:

I propose, for a longish period, to do nothing but short lengths. I want to leave a multitude of pictures of my time, projecting my small circular frame upon as many different spots as possible and going in for number as well as quality, so that the number may constitute a total having a certain value as observation and testimony.

This passage also is a definition: To James the short story was a short-length fiction. It was conceived as a picture, and its purpose was fundamentally historical: it was to preserve for the future its author's observations upon the life and character and manners of his epoch.

V

The high seriousness with which James approached his art made his fiction an advance in quality upon anything that previously had been produced in America except by Hawthorne. With him for the first time came the fiction of a new and refined age. The earlier periods had relied upon plot and its concomitants, but now, the incidents of invention exhausted, the novelist was forced to turn to character dissection, to studies of the subtleties of conduct, to analysis unsupported by incident, or else to turn to the other alternative—journalism. But journalism was to James anathema. To Howells he wrote in 1902:

The *faculty of attention* has utterly vanished from the general Anglo-Saxon mind, extinguished at its source by the big blatant *Bayadére* of Journalism, of the newspaper and the *picture* (above all) magazine; who keeps screaming: "Look at me! *I* am the thing, and I only, the thing that will keep you in relation with me *all the time* without your having to attend *one minute of the time*."

A voice in the wilderness it was, heard doubtless by few and heeded by none, yet a voice like a Sabbath bell calling ever to the highest and the best. Uncompromisingly he stood for fiction with intellectual fiber, carefully wrought, that was to be a product of positive and permanent value to humanity, but in taking this position he became to the general "a highbrow," a weaver of subtleties too abstruse to penetrate, a laughter and a byword among those who could appreciate, as James himself expressed it, only "the vulgarity of popular acclaim." In his estimation popularity could be won only by using the trumpet and the bass drum, and by trampling upon all the finer things of art.

Poe a whole generation earlier had expressed the same criticism of the American public. Writers were not writing literature, he complained in 1836: they were simply seeking to please "that great, overgrown, majestical gander, the critical and bibliographical rabble." Instead of envying Kipling his first great ovation of applause world-wide, James could only sigh: He possesses "almost nothing of the complicated soul or of the feminine form or any question of *shades*—which latter constitute, to my sense, the real formative literary discipline."

Never did he work from his emotions: always he viewed life objectively, coldly, accurately, recording only what he saw within the area he thought worthy of study. Never after his earlier period could he be swept away by his imagination or his feelings. "The Turn of the Screw," for instance, one of his most telling creations, illustrates perfectly the point. The story when he first heard it had appealed to him strongly on the side of the emotional and the romantic, and by an impulse rare with him he had done his best, as he has told us in one of his letters, to record it in the atmosphere of his original emotions. He had sought with all his art, as he has expressed it, "to give the impression of the communication to the children of the most infernal imaginable evil and danger. . . . I evoked the worst I could." Yet so fundamental was his scientific habit, his recording only that which had come within the range

of his material experience, that the story may be read not as a
ghost story at all, but as the record of a clinic: the study of the
growth of a suggested infernal *cliché* in the brain of the nurse who
alone sees the ghosts, of her final dementia which is pressed to a
focus that overwhelms in her mind every other idea, and makes of
the children her innocent victims.   As such it becomes a record
unspeakably pathetic.   The boy becomes a brave little martyr.
It is the triumph of science over romance.

And it is just at this point that James has been most severely
criticized.   He has been called a mere craftsman, a scientist only,
lacking the fervor and the imagination of genius.   His men, it is
said, stand and analyze rather than rush at the call of their emotions, his dialogue is overintellectual—people even in the most
cultured of environments do not talk always in epigrams and in
half sentences finished by intuition on the part of the hearer.
And the criticisms are just.   It is true that he fails in the main to
move his readers strongly, and it is true that he appeals to a cultured few rather than to the common average of readers.   One
might go on—it is easy to criticize Henry James.   But the critic
having done all, Henry James still stands.   Of not many American
writers may it be said that from first to last he stood for the dignity
of literature, and that he never for a moment lowered his standard
though most of the world forsook him.   As a master of technique
he has been surpassed by no one in America.   In his critical
essays and in the critical introductions to his final edition he has
given the most comprehensive and enlightening treatise on the
nature and technique of fiction that is to be found in English.
Moreover, it must not be forgotten that the field he took to de-
lineate was the entire Anglo-Saxon world—no mean ambition—
and that his studies of it cannot fail to grow more valuable as the
years go by.   Finally, let it be added, he gave new richness to
the English tongue; in style and diction he takes us back to
the unhurried ages when literature had distinction and words
were weighed like ingots of gold.   Howells reviewing in 1875
A Passionate Pilgrim spoke first of all of its author's perfect
style:

Something of an old-time stateliness distinguishes his style, and in a
certain weight of manner he is like the writers of an age when literature
was a far politer thing than it is now.   In a reverent ideal of work, too, he
is to be rated with the first.   His aim is high; he respects his material;

he is full of his theme; the latter-day sins of flippancy, slovenliness, and insincerity are immeasurably far from him.

One need say no more.

VI

A more immediate influence in the new period undoubtedly was William Dean Howells, whose name, in popular circles at least, was for a time more frequently mentioned than any others in connection with the realistic movement which gathered momentum in the 'seventies and 'eighties. His position as assistant editor of *The Atlantic* from 1866 until 1872 gave him at a formative moment a peculiar advantage. He reviewed all the American books during a critical decade, and his reviews, backed by the prestige of *The Atlantic*, were widely influential. Moreover, his influence was potent in directing the policy of the magazine. He was able to be the first to give encouragement and publication to Henry James, and later, as editor of the magazine until 1882, to introduce to the New England literary dictators the early work of Harte and Mark Twain and Charles Egbert Craddock and many others who were to be influential in shaping the new fiction.

In his theories of art Howells stood in the main with James. He stood for definite standards, for workmanship, for adherence to the realities—for "Truth." He was more poetic than James— in his earlier years he had dreamed of a poetical career like Longfellow's; he was more democratic than James—he had spent his boyhood and youth in a small Ohio village and had been educated in the most democratic of all schools, a rural newspaper office. Like James, too, he had been self-taught with literature as his major, almost his only, enthusiasm. From his boyhood he had had literary "passions" and always had he read as a student of literature, learning the art of it painfully and with infinite study. He was an author even from infancy. At seven he was composing an essay and printing it with his own hands; a little later he was serializing in his father's newspaper a romance, putting it into type at the case as he composed it without the medium of manuscript.

His Western birth and rearing made it natural that he should locate the culture for which his soul hungered in the East, in New England, the home of Lowell, the editor of *The Atlantic*, the home

of Longfellow and Emerson and Hawthorne. At the age when
James was making his passionate pilgrimage to the Italy of his
dreams, Howells made reverent pilgrimage to the literary shrines of
Boston and old Concord, and he was not disillusioned. A year
later, at twenty-four, he, too, was in Italy, consul at Venice, and
for the next four years he was an eager student of Italian literature
and language and art. His official duties were nominal merely:
he was enabled to visit the shrines of Italy; he read among a
multitude of other writers Goldoni, termed later by him "the
first of the realists," and he caught with distinctness the new tones
that were coming everywhere into European literature. Then,
like all Americans in Europe before his day—Irving, Willis,
Longfellow, Taylor, and the rest—he wrote sketches of European
travel, later to be gathered into Italian sketch-books—*Venetian
Life* and *Italian Journeys*.

Then had come the miracle of *The Atlantic* assistant editorship—
a native Westerner in the seat of the Brahmins—and then the
Cambridge sketch-book, *Suburban Sketches*. Had he died at this
point, every critical conjecture would have labeled him as a latter-
day Irving—a writer of graceful, romantically tinted travel
sketches, as a humorist, and a chatty sketch writer. *The Nation*,
reviewing *Suburban Sketches*, classed its author as pre-eminently a
man with "the humoristic spirit." In him, it declared, "we possess
a humorist who, in virtue of the genuineness of his gift, would be
admitted by their own suffrages to a secure place among the best
humorists who have at any time written in our tongue." And
compared with the great mass of humorous writing of that time
his humor is remarkable for its refinement. There is about it no
element of the coarse and the uncouth: "of their remarkable
fineness of quality," continued *The Nation*, "there can be no intelligent doubt. He is, in fact, all but unique in unadulterated fineness of quality."

The book stands midway between the travel sketch as found in
Venetian Life and the novel of the type of *Their Wedding Journey*.
One of its sketches, "A Day's Outing," may be reckoned as a
short story, but a short story after the canon of James rather than
that of Poe. It is a mere episode without plot or culmination save
as a picnic outing has culmination, and it deals with the tribu-
lations and even the inanities of a common day. Already had he
ranged himself in the ranks of revolt alongside James, though as

yet not unreservedly. At points he differed from his fellow craftsman in the very fundamentals. To Howells nothing clean and wholesome was unfit for literary use, even the very trivialities of common American life—even of rural life. New England manners, even the manners of a country boarding house, furnished for him timber as legitimate for fiction as if they were the manners of English drawing-rooms or ducal palaces. His early reverence for everything New England, perhaps, may explain this in part, but the deeper reason lay in the man himself. He was by nature more democratic than James, more sympathetic, more richly endowed with humor, more essentially human. In the opinion of James the use by Howells of almost exclusively American materials was a serious defect. "Howells," he once declared, "seems to have resolved himself into one who can write solely of what his fleshly eyes have seen, and for this reason I wish he were 'located' where they would rest upon richer and fairer things than this immediate landscape." "This immediate landscape"—America in general— James in later years was to characterize as "Oh of such an unimagined dreariness of ugliness"! and of American society, at least in its best Western aspects, he was to say that "the sense of the shining social and human inane is utter."

Otherwise the two may be classed as congenial workers in the new school, that school which has been so admirably characterized by Howells:

The new school derives from Hawthorne and George Eliot rather than any others; but it studies human nature much more in its wonted aspects, and finds its ethical and dramatic examples in the operation of lighter but not really less vital motives. The moving accident is certainly not its trade; and it prefers to avoid all manner of dire catastrophe. It is largely influenced by French fiction in form; but it is the realism of Daudet rather than the realism of Zola that prevails with it.

That Howells did not, as could have been predicted after *Suburban Sketches*, surrender himself to the humorous sketch and short story, came perhaps from the position he occupied and his reverence for the traditions of *The Atlantic*. Doubts as to the marketability of his product—doubts that drove so many beginners of his generation into a preliminary course of short-story writing—never assailed him. He wrote precisely as he desired: the columns of *The Atlantic* were always open for him and he

responded with the dignity of serials. Like James, he considered
the short-story form simply a "short length," a one-number piece
of fiction, and that it had laws that differed radically from those
governing the novel seems never in his earlier period to have
occurred to him. In all his early reviews in *The Atlantic* there is
not a sentence to indicate that he considered the short story an
independent form with laws of its own. In later years, after the
short story had completely established itself, he wrote much about
it, and, as in *Questionable Shapes* (1903) and *Between the Dark
and the Daylight* (1907), added his quota of exceedingly well-done
pieces in the approved form of the period, but he did no pioneer
work.

He must be reckoned as distinctively a novelist, and whatever
influence he exerted upon the evolution of the short-story form—
and it was not a small one—came from his influence as director of
The Atlantic, his adherence to American materials, and his far-
flung theories as to the fundamentals of literary art.

VII

Closely associated with Howells was Thomas Bailey Aldrich,
who was "imported," to use his own word, for the editorship of
Every Saturday the same year the Westerner was brought to
Boston for the assistant editorship of *The Atlantic Monthly*, issued
by the same firm. Unlike his colleague, however, he was no exotic
in the New England environment. He was a native of Portsmouth, New Hampshire, and, despite years of absence with his
family at two different periods in New York and New Orleans,
had received there that education so delightfully described in
The Story of a Bad Boy. At sixteen he had lost his father, a
calamity indeed: it had rendered impossible the Harvard course
for which he was preparing and had compelled him, because of the
condition of the family finances, at once to find means of support.
A clerkship in his uncle's countinghouse in New York solved the
problem of support, but his dreams were far from countingrooms
and business. Literature had laid its hand upon him. He read
poetry and dreamed of poetry over his daybooks and ledgers, and
he wrote poetry voluminously, showering it upon the magazines.
At nineteen he was emboldened to issue a volume of lyrics and to
follow it with a ballad—"The Ballad of Babie Bell." The book

fell unnoticed, but the ballad struck a popular chord and was copied everywhere, even in England and on the Continent. For a moment it turned the head of the young poet: he resigned his clerkship to devote himself wholly to poetry, but before he could realize the precariousness of such a profession he was discovered by Willis and made "junior literary critic" of *The Evening Mirror*. Then quickly had come the second wonder: James Parton, subeditor of the magazine, quarreled with Willis and resigned, and the subeditorship was thereupon given to Aldrich, a remarkable advancement for one so young and so limited in literary experience. The responsibility developed the powers of the boy and gave him literary perspective: it was a practical course in the sternest of universities.

From this moment letters became his profession. For ten years he lived his life in the heart of literary New York, a member of that Bohemian circle which had gathered about Fitz-James O'Brien. Unconsciously was he shaped by the contacts of this period—by the art ideals of O'Brien, by the cosmopolitan canons so windily discussed at Pfaff's that minor Mermaid Inn of the period, and put into practice by the Bohemian *Saturday Press*, of which he became an editor, but most of all was he influenced by Willis. His years upon the *Mirror* and *The Home Journal* had stimulated his youthful romanticism and had inclined it to sentimentalism and often extravagance. The poetry in the seven volumes which he issued during these formative years was the poetry of soft sensuousness and dreamy beauty, such as the early Tennyson wrote and the youthful Taylor and Stoddard. At times he could go to such extremes as "Mabel, Little Mabel" in perfect chord with the annuals and the lady's books, but always was there a voice within him that cried out against this early self, like a second personality. He was Willis, but he was also Henry James, and the James that at first was secondary in his life, the artisan and the critic, came more and more into control as he receded from his exuberant boyhood. His sense of humor was a saving element, as was also a certain inherited fineness of intellectual fiber, that patrician soul, as in the case of James, which led him at last to extremes of fastidiousness, to a chaste artistry indeed that, within its cameo-like compass, is well-nigh perfect. The two forces contending within him during this early period can nowhere be better illustrated than by his first prose work, *Daisy's*

Necklace, 1857, a gorgeous mélange written manifestly in all seriousness and then at the last moment in a wholly needless Prologue and Epilogue, apologized for with the explanation that it was all a *jeu d'esprit,* a mere burlesque upon feminine fiction.

Living constantly in the atmosphere of the Willis journals and of O'Brien's excited creations, it was but natural that early he should have experimented with the short-story form. The first tale, however, known to be his is one that appeared in *Knickerbocker's* in 1857, "What Jed Pallfry Found in the Coffin," an O'Brien-like product, never since reprinted, and the second a more ambitious effort followed a year later in the same magazine, "Out of His Head," a novelette, characterized by its author as a romance. Again the O'Brien influence, the attempt at Poe-like effects, again the Willis-like jauntiness and vivacity, and in addition to all this an affectation of French form *à la mode.* The paragraphing reminds one of a Bret Harte travesty:

For two years I lost all trace of him. Then he abruptly turned up in Panama, on the way to California.

Then I heard of him in a small town on the coast of South America.

Then in India.

Then in Switzerland.

Afterward in Egypt and Syria.

Always wandering.

In plot and motif, however, the tale was influenced by Hawthorne. It is the story of an ancestral curse. The hero is a madman who believed himself to be the reincarnation after a century and a half of an innocent victim of Puritan injustice and who at every step of his career sees the vengeance of Heaven completed upon the descendants of his persecutors. The explanatory tale near the close of the story, entitled, "Matthew Lynde's Legend of the Jocelyn House," might be mistaken for a newly discovered legend of the Province House.

In 1862 Aldrich issued his first short-story collection, six tales with the title, *Out of His Head, a Romance.* With the exception of an abbreviated version of "Père Antoine's Date-Palm," none of them has since been republished. The later Aldrich considered them, like the most of his early lyrics, immaturities to be forgotten, yet, full of defects as indeed they are, they must be read by one who would follow the evolution of the American short story. In them one may find traces at least of all the elements which Aldrich was to add to the form. The "Père Antoine's Date-Palm" has the restraint, the studied simplicity, the human appeal that are the very fundamentals of art; "A Word for the Town" has over it that subdued Ik Marvel atmosphere and that Irving-like refinement of sentiment which link all of Aldrich's work with the romantic rather than the realistic; and the two tales, "Miss Hebzibah's Lover" and "The Lady with the Balmoral," with their sprightliness, their innuendo, their sparkling humor, their surprise endings, reveal that already their author was mastering that artistry in which later he was so brilliantly to excel. The first of these tales is particularly well done. In the dénouement it is revealed as a surprise that the lover of the venerable old maid, Miss Hepzibah, is a somnambulist who is wooing her in his sleep. Suddenly awakened by his father, the man is aghast at the position in which he finds himself and flees. His real fiancée, hearing of the episode, refuses him:

"I am sure I can't think of marrying a man who doesn't know when he is asleep!"
"But she did."

And then follows the final sentence, which is pure Aldrich; it contains the essence of what he was to add to the short-story form: lightness of touch, wit, epigrammatic compression, and then a flash of suggestion that makes the end not an end at all, but a beginning—in a word, art. Miss Hepzibah spent the rest of her life dreaming of her lover.

"*She* thinks he was not so fast asleep as he appeared to be!"

When Field, Osgood & Co. invited Aldrich from New York to Boston they invited the spirit of N. P. Willis, who a generation before had shaken the dust of Boston from his feet because they had despised his lightness and his lack of message. A subdued Willis it was, to be sure, and the master of an art which the earlier penciler never knew, but, nevertheless, it was Willis. And they invited, moreover, the spirit of Poe, whom Boston also had consigned to the limbo of the un-Boston-like. Never was there resurgence more striking. Poe, flouted by his own countrymen, had been discovered by France, by Baudelaire first of all, and had been made the master of a virile school of young writers. And this school was reacting now upon America. The canons of Poe dressed in strange French fashions were now hailed as something new and compelling in literary art. The second collection of Aldrich's tales in 1873 was received everywhere as an example of French influence. *Scribner's Monthly* considered them a striking example of "how readily America assimilates the best flavor of every foreign method, for they are strikingly marked by the grace, epigrammatic point, and aërial lightness of touch, which combine to render the stories of the modern French school unquestionable works of art." They are based upon the art principles of Poe, not directly, but upon those principles refined and elaborated by a dominating school of French artists. One may search long for a more striking vindication of the genius of a master.

In Boston Aldrich became the editor of *Every Saturday,* an eclectic magazine that aimed to reproduce for American readers the best pieces in the foreign periodicals. More than ever the field of his interest became cosmopolitan. It was now his profession to study new movements in literature abroad and to single out the most distinctive. The effect upon one so alert and sensitive was inevitable. After a year in Boston he launched out again with the short-story form, but with more art now, more sense of form. One feels, as one reads "A Struggle for Life," the first fruit of this second period, that the story had appealed to him first of all in terms of structure. Everything in the tale is shaped for the culminating surprise stroke at the end. This given, the story is properly ended, but not yet is it completely finished. There is added a second surprise that can be described only as pure Aldrich: by a swift touch the whole tragedy is transformed into farce. It is the work of that second personality which had added the Prologue and Epilogue to *Daisy's Necklace.* The tragic mask is suddenly lifted to reveal the incorrigible joker and humorist who all the time has been hiding behind it. Undoubtedly this was the new element Aldrich believed he had added to the short-story form. Alluding to his tale, "Quite So," he had written Taylor in April, 1872: "The story is the second chunk of metal from my new mine (not a lead mine, I hope) . . . I intend to become a 'subtle humorist' while you are abroad."

And then had come the tale which all in a moment had placed him in the forefront of American story-tellers. Few American short stories, not even "The Luck of Roaring Camp" and "The Lady or the Tiger?" have received a more tremendous ovation than was accorded "Marjorie Daw" when it first appeared in *The Atlantic* in 1873. The methods of the author were discussed now in every literary circle as if they were something completely new, and the technique of story-telling was brought to the attention of writers and readers as never before in the history of American fiction.

The effect was salutary. *Marjorie Daw* became a type. It stood for artistry, for the art that is artless: the narrative is so unlabored and so limpidly easy of flow that it seems to move without effort, as if the piece had been a careless improvisation. It stood, moreover, for a whimsical wit never intended for explosions of laughter, but pervasive like an atmosphere, for a Daudet-like grace and brilliance, for a patrician touch never commonplace or hackneyed, and finally for an incongruous dénouement totally unexpected, that sends the reader swiftly back over the main threads of the story and then as swiftly forward, far away beyond the story into the regions of chuckling conjecture.

Like most short-story writers of the period Aldrich no sooner had succeeded with the shorter form than he became ambitious to write a novel. "For years," writes his biographer, "the newspaper reviews had been advising him to try a novel of New England life"—as if the short story were a form for apprentice hands, to be abandoned as soon as possible. Scarce a year after "Marjorie Daw," therefore—in January, 1874—he began the serial publication of his *Prudence Palfrey* in *The Atlantic*, and from this time on only occasionally did he lapse into the shorter form. The 1873 collection, *Marjorie Daw and Other People*, contains unquestionably his best work.

The bulk of his short-story product is small. In the collections upon which he finally set his approval there are but twenty-six titles, but all are distinctive. Like Poe and Maupassant, he had nothing important to say to the world, but he was a peerless entertainer, faultless in workmanship. His short stories are to American fiction what his lyrics are to American poetry, trivial things, but wrought with a perfection of art that renders them gems that are imperishable.

BIBLIOGRAPHY

I. HENRY JAMES

A. COLLECTIONS OF STORIES WHICH WERE WRITTEN BEFORE 1875:
1. *A Passionate Pilgrim*, 1875.
2. *Stories Revived*, 3 vol., London, 1885.
3. *Travelling Companions*, 1919.
4. *A Landscape Painter*, 1919.
5. *Master Eustace*, 1920.

B. STORIES WRITTEN BEFORE 1875:
"The Story of a Year," *Atlantic*, March, 1865.
4. "A Landscape Painter," *Atlantic*, Feb., 1866.
2, 4. "A Day of Days," *Galaxy*, June, 1866.
"My Friend Bingham," *Atlantic*, March, 1867.
2, 4. "Poor Richard," *Atlantic*, June-Aug., 1867.
"The Story of a Masterpiece," *Galaxy*, Jan.-Feb., 1868.
1, 2. "The Romance of Certain Old Clothes," *Atlantic*, 1868.
2, 4. "A Most Extraordinary Case," *Atlantic*, April, 1868.
"A Problem," *Galaxy*, June, 1868.
3. "De Gray: A Romance," *Atlantic*, July, 1868.
"Osborne's Revenge," *Galaxy*, July, 1868.
"Pyramus and Thisbe," a Comedietta, *Galaxy*, July, 1869.
2, 5. "A Light Man," *Galaxy*, July, 1869.
"Gabrielle de Bergerac," *Atlantic*, Sept., 1869.
3. "Travelling Companions," *Atlantic*, Nov.-Dec., 1870.
1, 2. "A Passionate Pilgrim," *Atlantic*, March-April, 1871.
"Still Waters," *Balloon Post*, April, 1871.
3. "St. Isella," *Galaxy*, Aug., 1871.
2, 5. "Master Eustace," *Galaxy*, Nov., 1871.
"A Change of Heart," A Comedietta, *Atlantic*, Jan., 1872.
3. "Guest's Confession," *Atlantic*, Oct., 1872.
1. "The Madonna of the Future," *Atlantic*, Mar., 1873.
3. "The Sweetheart of M. Briseux," *Galaxy*, June, 1873.
1, 2. "The Last of the Valerii," *Atlantic*, Jan., 1874.
1. "Madame de Mauves," *Galaxy*, Feb.-March, 1874.
3. "Adina," *Scribner's Monthly*, June-July, 1874.
3. "Professor Fargo," *Galaxy*, Aug., 1874.
1. "Eugene Pickering," *Atlantic*, Oct.-Nov., 1874.
5. "Benvolio," *Galaxy*, Aug., 1875.

C. LATER COLLECTIONS.
The Madonna of the Future, 1879.
1. "The Madonna of the Future"; "A Bundle of Letters"; "The Diary of a Man of 50"; "Eugene Pickering."

The Siege of London, 1883.
"The Siege of London"; "The Pension Beaurepas"; "The Point of View."

Tales of Three Cities, 1884.
"The Impressions of a Cousin"; "Lady Barbarina"; "A New England Winter."

The Author of Beltraffio, 1885.
"The Author of Beltraffio"; "Pandora"; "Georgina's Reasons"; "The Path of Duty"; "Four Meetings."

The Aspern Papers, 1888.
"The Aspern Papers"; "Louisa Pallant"; "The Modern Warning."

A London Life, 1889.
"A London Life"; "The Patagonian"; "The Liar"; "Mrs. Temperly."

The Lesson of the Master, 1892.
"The Lesson of the Master"; "The Marriages"; "The Pupil"; "Brooksmith"; "Sir Edward Orme."

The Private Life, 1892.
"The Private Life"; "The Visits"; "Lord Beaupré."

The Wheel of Time, 1892.
"The Wheel of Time"; "Collaboration"; "Owen Wingrave."

The Real Thing and Other Tales, 1892.
"The Real Thing"; "Sir Dominick Fairand"; "Nona Vincent"; "The Chaperon"; "Greville Fane."

Terminations, 1895.
"The Death of the Lion"; "The Coxon Fund"; "The Middle Years"; "The Altar of the Dead."

Embarrassments, 1896.
"The Figure in the Carpet"; "Glasses"; "The Next Time"; "The Way It Came."

The Two Magics, 1898.
"The Turn of the Screw"; "Covering End."

The Soft Side, 1900.
"The Great Good Place"; "Europe"; "Caste"; "The Real Right Thing"; "The Great Condition"; "The Tree of Knowledge"; "The Abasement of the Northmass"; "The Given Case"; "John Delavoy"; "The Third Person"; "Maud-Evelyn"; "Mrs. Sunton of Poughkeepsie."

The Better Sort, 1903.
"Broken Wings"; "The Beldonald Holbein"; "The Two Faces";

"The Tone of Time"; "The Special Type"; "Mrs. Medwin";
"Flickerbudge"; "The Story in It"; "The Beast in the Jungle";
"The Birthplace"; "The Papers."

II. THOMAS BAILEY ALDRICH

A. COLLECTIONS:
1. *Out of His Head, a Romance,* 1862.
2. *Marjorie Daw and Other People,* 1873.
3. *A Midnight Fantasy and The Little Violinist,* 1877.
4. *Marjorie Daw and Other Stories,* 1885.
5. *Two Bites at a Cherry with Other Tales,* 1893.
6. *A Sea Turn and Other Matters,* 1902.

B. TALES IN CHRONOLOGICAL ORDER:
1. "Out of His Head," *Knickerbocker's,* Oct., 1858.
1. "The Lady With the Balmoral," *Harper's,* June, 1859.
1. "A Word for the Town."
1. "The Cup and the Lip."
1. "Miss Hepzibah's Lover."
1, 2, 4. "Père Antoine's Date-Palm," *Atlantic,* June, 1862.
2, 4. "A Struggle for Life," *Atlantic,* July, 1867.
2, 4. "A Young Desperado," *Atlantic,* Dec., 1867.
2. "The Friend of My Youth," *Atlantic,* Feb., 1871.
2, 4. "Quite So." *Atlantic,* April, 1872.
2, 4. "A Rivermouth Romance," *Atlantic,* Aug., 1872.
2, 4. "Marjorie Daw," *Atlantic,* April, 1873.
2, 4. "Miss Mehetabel's Son," *Atlantic,* June, 1873.
2, 4. "Mademoiselle Olympe Zabriski," *Atlantic,* Oct., 1873.
3, 4. "A Midnight Fantasy," *Atlantic,* April, 1875.
3, 4. "The Little Violinist."
4. "Our New Neighbors at Ponkapog."
5. "Two Bites at a Cherry," *Atlantic,* Jan., 1886.
5. "My Cousin the Colonel," *Harper's,* Dec., 1891.
5. "A Christmas Fantasy," *Century,* Dec., 1891.
5. "For Bravery on the Field of Battle," *Century,* 1892.
5. "Goliath," *Century,* Feb., 1893.
5. "The Chevalier Resseguier," *Century,* May, 1893.
5. "Her Dying Words," *Scribner's,* Aug., 1893.
6. "His Grace the Duke," *Century,* May, 1898.
6. "Shaw's Folly," *Harper's,* Dec., 1900.
6. "An Untold Story," *Scribner's,* Dec., 1900.
6. "A Sea Turn," *Harper's,* June, 1901.
6. "The Case of Thomas Phipps," *Harper's,* Sept., 1901.
6. "The White Feather," *Harper's,* Sept., 1902.
 "Tom Folio," *Scribner's,* Sept., 1903.

CHAPTER X

I

At this point—at the moment when James and Howells and Aldrich and others seemed to be succeeding in their attempt to standardize the short story and to bring it to a basis of truth, with the technique that Poe had dreamed of and that his French disciples had accomplished—suddenly occurred an incident that stampeded the new form and turned it for a generation at least into new directions. The Pacific railroad had finally been driven across the Sierras in 1868, and one of the first products it bore back to the East was a new California magazine, *The Overland Monthly*, designed in all seriousness to be *The Atlantic Monthly* of the gold coast. Its first number provoked no comment, but in the second number was a "sketch," to use its author's designation, that attracted the attention of the East—"The Luck of Roaring Camp," by one Francis Bret Harte, editor of the magazine. Six months later came another still better, "The Outcasts of Poker Flat," and then "Tennessee's Partner," best of all—the unknown writer was gaining in power. Then had come the second startling event: the young editor contributed to his magazine a humorous poem—a mere "squib," indeed—which swept over America like the gold news of '49—"Plain Language From Truthful James," or, as it became better known, "The Heathen Chinee." It was printed in every newspaper and quoted on every tongue, in England as well as in America. Hard upon this sensation had come another: the new author was abandoning California; he was moving eastward; in Chicago he had refused the editorship of a great mid-Western magazine that was to be endowed with true Western lavishness. Following it hard had come the news that he was in Boston fêted by the Brahmins of the Saturday Club, then that he had been made a contributing editor of *The Atlantic* with a salary of $10,000 for whatever he might deign to write for the magazine during a year. Never before, even in the days of Irving and the

Sketch Book, had the fierce light of success and publicity so beat upon the American short story, never before in America had a literary form been so widely and so excitedly advertised. Everywhere now was it studied by aspiring authors eager to detect the constituent elements of a success so amazing.

II

By inheritance and by early associations Bret Harte—he dropped the "Francis" after his first success—was a New Yorker, totally untouched by New England. The cosmopolitanism of his native state was his birthright: his paternal grandfather, Bernard Hart, was pure Hebrew; his paternal grandmother, Catherine Brett, was pure English; his mother, Elizabeth Ostrander, was pure Dutch. His father, Henry Harte—temperamental, restless, a Colonel Sellers type—had been educated at Union College, and had spent his life as a teacher of languages in various schools. He had died at the age of forty-five of chagrin, it is said, at the outcome of the Henry Clay presidential campaign—it reveals to us the intensity of the man. From him it was that the boy, Francis Bret, nine years old when the father died, had inherited his temperament, his restlessness, his lack of fixed convictions moral or social—offspring, perhaps, of his mixed racial inheritance. From him also had come his artistic bent and his early leanings toward literature as a profession. He had been reared among books: the family library, despite its peregrinations, was unusually large, well varied in content, and the imaginative boy discovered it early and read it all. At six he was poring over Shakespeare and Froissart; at seven he had discovered Dickens. His schooling, desultory at best because of his physical frailty, ended when he was thirteen, and then for a year he found employment in a lawyer's office, leaving it to enter a countingroom, where he remained until he was eighteen. Like Irving, in whom he delighted, he picked his reading from the eighteenth century—Fielding, Defoe, Smollett, Goldsmith—varying it at times with Cervantes and the French romancers. The world he later depicted, even after his California experiences, had over it a curious eighteenth-century atmosphere: the manners and the conversation of his characters, when they endeavor to show their manners and be correct in their language, are certainly not of their own period and certainly not American. They are drawn from a knowledge of books rather than from a knowledge of life. From early boyhood until he was eighteen his home was New York City: it gave him the urban viewpoint, it developed cleverness, fastidiousness in the externals of dress and manners, a taste for the artificial and the theatric. It developed, too, an abnormal precocity: at four he was writing a burlesque of his primer; at eleven his poetry had appeared in a New York magazine.

Such a temperament, one might think, would be attracted naturally to the adventure and romance of the new Eldorado in the West. On the contrary, he went unwillingly to California, and during all the seventeen years of his residence there he regarded himself as an exile. Essentially was he a creature of civilization: he longed for refined society, for art, for literary atmosphere, for the world of books and theaters and music. His elder brother, however, had settled in California out of pure joy of adventure, and it was to be with him that the mother in 1853 had ventured across the continent after arranging for her two younger children to join her some months later. Her marriage to a college friend of her first husband's had followed almost immediately upon her arrival, and it was in her new home that the boy spent the next two years.

Faced now with the problem of a life work, he thought first of all of literature. He began with poetry of the Longfellow order, but the whole continent lay between him and any profitable outlet for his wares. The idea of creating a California market, with Californian writers and publishers and readers, had occurred to no one. The literary profession seemed impossible under such circumstances, and at twenty, in desperation, he left the city for the wilder regions of the state to enter upon any career that might open before him. The next two years are the legendary period in Bret Harte annals. His biographers are hazy here and conflicting. He went, we know, north into the San Ramon Valley, and for a period, we know, he taught school; there is shadowy evidence that he was for a time an express messenger; by his own account he found employment in the mines, but during the greater part of the two years, as an abundance of evidence makes clear, he was a compositor upon *The Northern Californian*, a small sheet issued at Eureka, a seacoast town in Humboldt County.

Returning to San Francisco in 1857, he found employment upon *The Golden Era* newspaper as a typesetter, and the story of the next fourteen years is the story of his literary apprenticeship. To *The Golden Era* he contributed his first essays and poems that have been preserved for us, *The Bohemian Sketches*, the *Condensed Novels*, and the other papers that have since been collected from its columns. Soon he was advanced to the editorial department, and it was not long before he was regarded in San Francisco as one of the leading literary men of the Pacific coast. When the rewritten "M'liss" in 1863 was advertised to appear as a serial in *The Golden Era*, it was "by 'Bret,' one of the best writers of romance in America." A year later came *The Californian*, edited at first by the versatile Charles Henry Webb, and then by Harte. There were other ventures in editorship. Assured of an income after 1864 because of his appointment as secretary of the California Mint, a sinecure that interfered not at all with his editorial and literary labors, he wrote almost continuously. In 1867 he issued a book of poems, *The Lost Galleon and Other Tales*, and the same year a collection of his fugitive sketches, *Condensed Novels and Other Papers*. A year later had come *The Overland Monthly* editorship and the happy strike that all in a moment had made him a national figure. Though he had been writing steadily for more than fourteen years, it was not until the appearance of "The Luck of Roaring Camp," when he was thirty-two, that he became at all known outside of California. During the period he had written a surprising amount of good material—poems, essays, sketches, tales, editorials, parodies, paragraphs—the most of which he never reissued. It is good 'prentice material, unusually good. It is all of it the work of a serious artist who is experimenting in many manners and many materials and who finds himself after years of effort; it is the work of one who, like James and Aldrich, perfected his art by patient study of many models. That so little of it was republished from the magazines was in the end to Harte's great advantage. "The Luck of Roaring Camp" came to the East in 1868 as the initial creation of a young genius just entering the literary field—marvelous! What might not be expected from such an amazing first attempt? It helped advertise the new writer. As we know it now, however, the tale was an end rather than a beginning: it was the final journeyman product of one who by the hardest of toil for years continued had completely mastered his art.

III

The first observation to be made upon Harte as a writer concerns his profession: he had been trained as an editor; he had begun at the type case and had worked up through all the departments to the editor's chair. Such education leaves inevitably its mark upon a writer. As gained in the environment that Harte knew, it was uniquely American and wholly democratic. Moreover, it tended to cultivate, as it did in Poe, what may be termed the editorial instinct—that sixth sense that is intuitive of the likes and dislikes of its readers, that is alert for the new and the original, that thinks in terms of columns and limited space and literary form. From the California newspaper standpoint a story to be acceptable to readers had to be short and pithy and condensed to lowest terms. "Brevity especially," as Harte himself expressed it, "is the soul of California Wit. The sagacious modern editor is well aware of the fact that it is a much easier and neater thing to stiletto a man with a line of solid minion than to knock him down with a column of leaded long primer." Then, too, in the California atmosphere of the 'fifties and 'sixties newspaper literature to appeal must needs possess humor and vivacity and modernness. The air was electric with youth and energy unbounded. Nothing slow or dull or long drawn-out appealed to that headlong generation. The journals of San Francisco during the period were the training ground of a new American school of humorists— Mark Twain, Artemus Ward, John Paul, Orpheus C. Kerr, and others less known to-day. The apprenticeship of Bret Harte is the story of a gradual evolution from his early Irving-Hawthorne-Longfellow-Dickens prepossessions, step by step by means of magazine and newspaper training in the electric California environment, to his final literary form, which is a dramatic blend of romance, of Hugo intensity and melodrama, of California humor, of Dickens sentiment, and of Harte originality.

His first master unquestionably was Irving. The earliest bit of his prose that has been preserved for us, "A Trip Up the Coast," in *The Golden Era* of 1857, has over it the romantic atmosphere of the Hudson:

It was one of those glorious, smoky, hazy days so rare to these bright, blue skies, resembling the Indian Summer of the Northern States, and carrying me back to the fairy hills, dreamy uplands, and pleasant valleys of the Catskills. It was a Sabbath, so like those doubly-blessed ones, years past, that in my fancy I could hear the church bells ringing lazily out of the soft valleys and swelling into a subdued and dreamy music, all in harmony with the drowsy landscape: One of those days, when a child, I no longer doubted or wondered that on such had Rip Van Winkle closed his eyes and never cared to wake.

It was through Irving, too, that he took the first step toward his final literary field. Irving had done for the Hudson what Scott had done for the Scottish Highlands: why could not the same thing be done for California, every whit as romantic and picturesque as Knickerbocker New York? Reared as he had been in the atmosphere of Scott's romance, he was not stirred at all in his imagination by the realities about him, picturesque in the extreme though undoubtedly they were. As with Longfellow and Irving and all the romantics, the realm of literature lay for him in the old and the forgotten and the far-off, rather than in the garish here and now. One of his earliest ambitions, so he has told us, had been "to become the founder of a characteristic western literature," but for years his conception of such a *genre* differed very little from that held by Hall and Pike and the other Western historical romancers of the mid-century. He would make himself the Washington Irving of the Pacific coast and weave in the beautiful Irving manner rich legends of Father Junipero and the Spanish era of California. In 1863, after ten years on the gold coast and after the state had thrilled with more than a decade of its most picturesque mining adventure, he sent to *The Atlantic Monthly* his sketch, "The Legend of Monte del Diablo," wholly in the manner of Washington Irving, and for months he applied himself diligently to similar *Sketch Book*-like work—"The Adventure of Padre Vincentio," "The Devil and the Broker," and others, half a dozen in all, beautifully finished, golden of atmosphere, romantic in the Spanish sense but work really to be classed with the rest of his "Condensed Novels." There was nothing new about them save the materials, and these were so shadowy and so unreal of texture that to readers they seemed not like glimpses of the actual California, but like the fabric of Irving's dreamings in the old Spanish atmosphere of the early missions.

To read in sequence all of Harte's abundant prose written during these years of apprenticeship is to be impressed precisely as one is impressed by this Irvingesque area of them: there is nothing about them strongly original, nothing peculiarly the author's own in style or method. He was not an inspired creator working because he must, and, despite the claims of his uncritical admirers, he was not an innovator with a totally original *genre* and method. He learned his art by long and patient effort; he was a conscious artist who after seventeen years of almost continuous reading and continuous writing found at last an art combination that captured the reading public of his day.

How carefully he studied his art is revealed by his series of parodies and travesties and distillations which he called *Condensed Novels*. Primarily was he interested in the artistry of masterpieces, that atmosphere all his own which a writer throws over his work: his unconscious mannerisms, his deliberate tricks of style, his totality of viewpoint—to all these was he peculiarly sensitive, and he had a power little short of genius to catch and to hold these individualities which together make up the soul of a book and to present them in a compass amazingly small. These condensations, the first of which, "Fantine," a travesty of *Les Misérables*, appeared in *The Golden Era* in 1862, and the whole series of which were issued in book form the year before the appearance of "The Luck of Roaring Camp," may be taken from all his writings as the *genre* that is most completely his. The power to excel in such an art has its dangers; exercised too often and too long it creates a habit—a habit, to be sure, that makes for artistry, but one at the same time that tends to destroy originality and to give macaronic qualities to creations that should be compellingly individual. The work of Harte's early period unquestionably is a *mélange* of material that suggests older writers. Sketches like "The Mission Dolores" are pure Irving; others, like "From a Balcony," are pure Hawthorne; still others, like "The Surprising Adventure of Master Charles Summerton," are pure Dickens; and one, "The Countess," a brilliant bit of artistry, light as a feather, surprisingly ended, is pure Willis. One might add other examples. Nor are his later writings exempt from this characteristic. "A Knight Errant of the Foot-hills," for instance, is a "Condensed Novel," a miniature Don Quixote with no essential character omitted. Everywhere there is the macaronic quality:

here the style is like Dickens, here it is like Hugo, here it is like Irving or Hawthorne. One who is too brilliant in catching the soul of the work of others sometimes loses thereby his own.

For the student of Harte, *Condensed Novels* has a value altogether out of proportion to its own worth. It is the leading document for one who would trace all the elements in the evolution of the Bret Harte short story. The Scandinavian critic, H. H. Boyesen, for instance, in a review of one of the earlier collections of Harte's tales, found the sources of their individuality in Hugo:

> The ancestry of his noble villains, the magnanimous gamblers with seraphic tenor voices, the chivalrous murderers, the generous strumpets, may be traced to that high priest of romanticism, Victor Hugo, who delighted in the same violent antithesis, defying probability and straining our credulity beyond endurance.

This is good criticism. Turning to *Condensed Novels*, we find that as early as 1862 Harte had mastered the art of Hugo and had emphasized as his leading characteristics those very qualities which Boyesen had so discerningly noted. We find, too, that he had caught the manner of Dumas, of Michelet, of the whole school of French paragraphists, and in travestying them had learned the secrets of paradox, of antithesis, of lightness of touch, of vivacious dialogue, of that syncopated style that dares to omit even the verbs and nouns from its sentences. Moreover, he had learned the value of finesse and of the startling or the epigrammatic ending. All of his chapters c ose with a snap. The last chapter in *La Femme* is headed, "Her Old Age," and the chapter contains but this single sentence: "A Frenchwoman never grows old." Consciously or unconsciously to Harte, all this entered into his own later style. The clumsiness and heaviness and lack of artistry which had characterized so much of the American fiction of the period became impossibilities after such work as this:

> Fantine was one of those women who do wrong in the most virtuous and touching manner. This is a peculiarity of French grisettes.
>
> You are an Englishman, and you don't understand. Learn, my friend, learn. Come to Paris and improve your morals.
>
> Fantine was the soul of modesty. She always wore high-neck dresses. High-neck dresses are a sign of modesty.
>
> Fantine loved Tholmoyes. Why? My God! What are you to do?

It was the fault of her parents, and she hadn't any. How shall you teach her? You must teach the parent if you wish to educate the child. How would you become virtuous?

Teach your grandmother!

Or as this travesty of Michelet:

THE WIFE

She is tired of loving and she marries.

Her mother thinks it, on the whole, the best thing. As the day approaches, she is found frequently in tears. Her mother will not permit the affianced one to see her, and he makes several attempts to commit suicide.

But something happens. Perhaps it is winter, and the water is cold. Perhaps there are not enough people present to witness his heroism.

In this way her future husband is spared to her. The ways of Providence are indeed mysterious. At this time her mother will talk with her. She will offer philosophy. She will tell her she was married herself.

But what is this new and ravishing light that breaks upon her? The toilet and wedding clothes! She is in a new sphere.

She makes out her list in her own charming writing. Here it is. Let every mother heed it. . . . (The delicate reader will appreciate the omission of certain articles for which English synonymes are forbidden). . . .

She is married. On the day after, she meets her old lover, Hippolyte. He is again transported.

But the best of all in *Condensed Novels* is his distillate of Dickens which he entitled "The Haunted Man." No travesty here: it is interpretation, it is appreciation, it is admiration undisguised. Within it lies the whole essence of Dickens: his myth-making genius that could breathe life into gargoyles and caricatures, his moving sentiment, his theatric art, his melodrama, his enormous vivacity and zest in life, his humor. Other writers schooled Harte: Dickens molded and made him.

One might go on. *Condensed Novels* is an illuminating book: it admits us into the workshop of an artist during the molding period which made him what he was to be.

IV

In July, 1867, Harte collected all that he deemed valuable of his parodies and sketches and legends and tales and issued them with the title, *Condensed Novels and Other Papers*. It was to be primarily a humorous publication: both the New York firm that accepted it and the readers who bought it classed it with Mark Twain's *The Jumping Frog and Other Sketches* which appeared at almost the same moment—the new California humor. But it was only the condensations that were humorous: the "Other Papers," the most of them solid and serious, were to be floated by the lightness of these vivacious parodies: "their introduction here," he was careful to assure his readers, "must rest solely upon the assumed popularity of the 'Condensed Novels.'" He did not claim for them any California characteristics, not even for the legends: he had intended them as serious literary exercises independent of time or place. "Though based upon local scenery and local subjects, no one is better aware than their author of their deficiency in local coloring, a deficiency which he nevertheless believes is made up by such general interest and abstract fidelity as may make them applicable to any locality."

That Harte almost up to the date of "The Luck of Roaring Camp" deemed local-color studies inferior to Hawthorne-like sketches is forced upon anyone who reads straight through his early writings. That, however, he was early capable of such "local coloring" we have the best of evidence. As one toils through his early travesties, his conventional sketches and poems, his Irving-like legends, one stumbles all at once upon a discovery as thrilling as the finding of a nugget in a bank of clay. Once, for just a moment, it would seem, he forgot to be literary, forgot his traditions and his models and his proprieties, and let himself go. In the December, 1860, number of the *Era* appeared his sketch, "The Work on Red Mountain"—the first arresting title he had used. As one reads it, its conventional Irving-like opening, its introduction of its characters with their Dickens-like names— McSnagley, Kerg, Clytemnestra Morpher, Cellerstina Montmoressy—and its gargoyle-like characterization, suddenly one sits erect. The leading character has entered:

"My name's M'liss—M'liss Smith! You can bet your life on that. My father's old Smith—old Bummer Smith—that's what's the matter with him. M'liss Smith—and I'm coming to school!"

It is a landmark. At this moment something new came into American fiction. Oliver Twist in an earlier period had confronted another schoolmaster, but there was nothing in the episode to compare with this. One was a cringing pauper in a civilization one large part of which fawned upon the other, and the demand of Oliver was but a spurt of audacity: the other was the incarnation of the wild lawlessness of a whole area, that primitive passion unchecked by convention or precedent, that irreverence and imperious self-assertion which had been born of the frontier and had culminated in the California of the gold-rush decade. Dickens never could have created M'liss; no European, no New Englander even, could have created her. She was uniquely Californian. She had grown up untutored in the wild gulches of "Smith's Pocket" with men elemental in their hates and loves and appetites and ideals of freedom. She was as unconventional as a coyote, and when crossed she was as fiercely alive. Told that Joshua once made the sun stand still, she burst out even in the awful presence of the school committee:

"It's a damned lie. I don't believe it."

Wherever she appears the story is alive and compelling. It ends grippingly as a short story should end:

"If you lock me up in jail," said M'liss, fiercely, "to keep me from the play-actors, I'll poison myself. Father killed himself—why shouldn't I? You said a mouthful of that root would kill me, and I always carry it here," and she struck her breast with her clenched fist. . . .
"Lissy, will you go with me?"
The child put her arms around his neck, and said, joyfully, "Yes."
"But now—to-night?"
"To-night" . . .
The stars glittered brightly above them. For good or ill the lesson had been learned, and behind them the schoolhouse of Red Mountain closed upon them forever.

Unlike the rest of Harte's early work, the story struck fire. Californians recognized M'liss as one of themselves and asked for more. Harte humored them with a serial in the *Era* beginning September, 1863, an expansion of the earlier short story into a novel with proportions commensurate with their expectations. The result was a failure so complete that it may be described as a debacle. The vein of gold accidentally opened in his earlier tale he turned his back upon, and elaborately he sought to please his California readers with what he considered they would most enjoy, with strongly localized sensation. M'liss's letter to the schoolmaster proved to be a leaf torn from Bummer Smith's account book, and a jotting on the back gave the location of a new mine fabulously rich. It began to be whispered that the man had not committed suicide, but had been murdered on account of his secret—perhaps by M'liss. Immediately the plot spread out sensationally in all directions in dime novel fashion, until in the eighth installment it mastered its creator. A whole chapter he devotes to an explanation of his dilemma, closing it by begging his readers to send him letters suggesting ways out. Evidently none came, for, after floundering on for two installments more, the hodgepodge ends in chaos. It is like a "Condensed Novel" travesty of Nick Carter. Strange that the hand which had created "M'liss" should have produced nothing more like it for eight years, strange that he did not deem it worthy of inclusion in his 1867 volume, yet we of to-day can hardly realize how savage a thing "M'liss" seemed in 1860, how uncouth and how unliterary. Young Harte was not then seeking to be an innovator: he was seeking to learn the art of producing polite literature as the world in general defined such literature. Even after his great success, when he had settled in the East and knew fully the worth of the field he had discovered, he turned from it again and again to do work for which his soul longed in areas the very antipodes from those he felt himself condemned to cultivate.

But one could not live long in San Francisco during the decade of the 'sixties without unconsciously revising one's literary ideals. In 1863 Artemus Ward visited the Coast and did much toward precipitating in literary form the crude native humor of the region. In an editorial in the *Era*, December, 1863, Harte summed up the essence of his humor with comprehension and clearness. "It is," he said,

The humor of audacious exaggeration—of perfect lawlessness; a humor that belongs to the country of boundless prairies, limitless rivers, and stupendous cataracts. In this respect Mr. Ward is the American humorist, *par excellence*, and "his book" is the essence of that fun which overlies the surface of our national life, which is met in the stage, rail car, canal and flatboat, which bursts out over campfires and around barroom stoves—a humor that has more or less local coloring, that takes kindly to, and half elevates, slang, that is of to-day and full of present application. The showman has no purpose to subserve beyond the present laugh.

There had come to California Mark Twain and Prentice Mulford and Charles Henry Webb and Orpheus C. Kerr—a whole school of new writers. The "M'liss" atmosphere lay everywhere over the new literary product, the most of it written in sublime contempt for the "effete Eastern" standards. Originality reigned supreme. Mark Twain, for instance, reports for the *Era* the notable painting "Delilah," then on exhibition in San Francisco, and his critique centers not on the real magnificence of the masterpiece, but on the scissors at the feet of the woman:

"Them scissors is too modern; thar warn't no scissors like them in them days—by a d——d sight."

The new humor which had been on the lips of men in mines and camps, coach lines and flatboats, appeared more and more in printed form in newspaper and periodical—farcical paragraphs and anecdotes and grotesque sketches like "The Jumping Frog of Calaveras County." This element of humor was the last ingredient Harte was to add to his literary mixture, and of all it was by far the most important. Without it he would have been but a San Francisco Irving, a California Dickens unheard of beyond the Sierras.

Harte in later years could contend that humor had been the parent of his art, as it had been indeed the parent of the American short story. In his "The Rise of the American Short Story"[1] article he said:

But while the American literary imagination was still under the influence of English tradition, an unexpected factor was developing to diminish its power. It was *humor*, of a quality as distinct and original as the country and civilization in which it was developed. It was at first noticeable in the anecdote or "story," and, after the fashion of such beginnings, was orally transmitted. It was common in the bar-rooms, the gatherings in the country store, and finally at public meetings in the mouths of "stump orators." Arguments were clinched and political principles illustrated by a "funny story." It invaded even the camp meeting and pulpit. It at last received the currency of the public press. But wherever met it was so distinctively original and novel, so individual and characteristic, that it was at once known and appreciated abroad as an American story. Crude at first, it received a literary polish in the press, but its dominant quality remained. It was concise and condensed, yet suggestive. It was

[1] *The Cornhill Magazine*, July, 1899.

delightfully extravagant, or a miracle of understatement. It voiced not only the dialect, but the habits of thought of a people or locality. It gave a new interest to slang. From a paragraph of a dozen lines it grew into half a column, but always retaining its conciseness and felicity of statement. It was a foe to prolixity of any kind; it admitted no fine writing nor affectation of style. It went directly to the point. It was burdened by no conscientiousness; it was often irreverent; it was devoid of all moral responsibility, but it was original. By degrees it developed character with its incident, often, in a few lines, gave a striking photograph of a community or a section, but always reached its conclusion without an unnecessary word. It became—and still exists as—an essential feature of newspaper literature. It was the parent of the American "short story."

In "M'liss" Harte had sprinkled only here and there the wild California flavors, in "The Luck of Roaring Camp" he made them the predominating characteristic. *The Overland Monthly* had been established to promote things Californian, but after the first issue, to quote Harte's own words, "its editor called the publisher's attention to the lack of any distinctive Californian romance in its pages and averred that, should no other come in, he himself would supply the omission in the next number." The result was "The Luck of Roaring Camp," written deliberately to furnish a peculiarly Californian magazine with a peculiarly Californian tale. Its author had learned his art: the story would have satisfied Poe in the externals of technique, but it was not its art that gave it all in a moment its overwhelming vogue. It was its newness of atmosphere and background, its fresh wild humor, and, moreover, its *risqué* theme, for in 1868 the theme was indeed deemed upon the borders of propriety. The first proof reader upon it prudishly refused to proceed with such material. It insulted her. Then, too, its atmosphere of paradox, whether caught from Hugo or not, seemed new and startling.

Harte had found his formula: the voice of the East assured him so in no uncertain words, and, inspired by the new joys of recognition, he began to write with confidence. In half a dozen stories he reached remarkable levels. He was at his best: in all his later voluminous output there is nothing to compare in freshness and zest and artistry with this work poured out when the new wine of his first enthusiasm flowed clear. Various were the causes for his gradual failure, but the chief among them undoubtedly was the fact—to change the figure—that the mine he had discovered was a pocket and not a lode. Whatever might be his enthusiasm, he was fated to see diminishing returns. He who would confine himself to the social régime of a fleeting and squalid community in the wilds must soon run out of materials, or else repeat himself, especially if he work with that most material-exhausting of all literary forms, the short story. In later years Harte could only repeat in varied combinations his old characters and backgrounds and motifs, and always it was with a growing mechanicalness and loss of original freshness and charm.

V

Harte did perhaps six distinctive things for the short-story form. First, he threw over his stories, especially over his early masterpieces, a peculiar atmosphere of locality, one that to the readers of his day was startlingly new. He did for California what Dickens had done for London: he romanticized it; he gave it a mythology with a background perfectly in keeping. His methods of securing his localizing effect were unusual. Seemingly he made little of his setting: one may glance through one of his tales and be surprised to find only here and there a sentence touching upon landscape or surroundings, and yet one carries away from it local coloring as the dominating impression. Never does Harte, in notable contrast with many of his disciples, describe the landscape setting simply because it is unusual or unique. Always is it introduced as background, as scenery for his little theater, and, like all scenery, it is painted splashingly with swift impressionistic strokes. The tragedy of "The Outcasts of Poker Flat" is played before this drop curtain:

The spot was singularly wild and impressive. A wooded amphitheatre surrounded on three sides by precipitous cliffs of naked granite, sloped gently toward the crest of another precipice that overlooked the valley.

"The Luck of Roaring Camp" opens with this setting:

The camp lay in a triangular valley, between two hills and a river. The only outlet was a steep trail over the summit of a hill that faced the cabin, now illuminated by the rising moon.

It is like directions to a scene painter. Always is the scenery in accord or in contrast with the tragedy or the comedy enacting in the foreground. Tennessee is being tried for what the camp considers a capital crime, and the elements are in sympathy.

The little cañon was stifling with heated resinous odors, and the decaying driftwood on the bar sent forth faint, sickening exhalations. The feverishness of the day, and its fierce passions, still filled the camp.

But

Above all this, etched on the dark firmament, rose the Sierra, remote and passionless, crowned with remoter passionless stars.

Sometimes, not often, the background becomes a character in the plot and dominates the tale like a personality. The opening of the tale, "Highwater Mark," reminds one strongly of the opening chapter of Hardy's *Return of the Native*, written years later:

But if Dedlow Marsh was cheerless at the slack of the low tide, you should have seen it when the tide was strong and full. When the damp air blew chilly over the cold, glittering expanse, and came to the faces of those who looked seaward like another tide: when a steel-like glint marked the low hollows and the sinuous line of slough; when the great shell-incrusted trunks of fallen trees arose again, and went forth on their dreary, purposeless wanderings, drifting hither and thither, but getting no farther toward any goal at the falling tide or the day's decline than the cursed Hebrew in the legend; when the glossy ducks swung silently, making neither ripple nor furrow on the shimmering surface; when the fog came in with the tide and shut out the blue above, even as the green below had been obliterated; when boatmen, lost in that fog, paddling about in a hopeless way, started at what seemed the brushing of mermen's fingers on the boat's keel, or shrank from the tufts of grass spreading around like the floating hair of a corpse, and knew by these signs that they were lost upon Dedlow Marsh, and must make a night of it, and a gloomy one at that,—then you might know something of Dedlow Marsh at high water.

The second element emphasized by Harte was a saving dash of the new Western humor. In "Tennessee's Partner" he has recorded that in the gulches and the bar-rooms of early California "all sentiment was modified by a strong sense of humor." The statement is illuminating: without this peculiar quality in his work, which often is an atmosphere rather than a quotable entity, Harte would have been as sentimentally extreme as Dickens, his master. The funeral scene in "Tennessee's Partner" would have been mere gush. Even as it is, the last paragraph is mawkish sentimentality: the faithful partner dies of a broken heart and the two meet in heaven. And it is only this same atmosphere of humor that saves his melodrama from ridiculousness, for melodrama is everywhere present in his work. At times, as in "The Rose of Tuolumne," it rises to all the shrillness of the Bowery villain play:

Look! Do you see? This is his blood—my darling boy's blood!—one drop of which, dead and faded as it is, is more precious to me than the whole living pulse of any other man. Look! I come to you to-night, christened with his blood, and dare you to strike—dare you to strike him again through me, and mingle my blood with his. Strike, I implore you! Strike! if you have any pity on me, for God's sake! Strike! if you are a man! Look! Here lay his head on my shoulder; here I held him to my breast, where never—so help me my God—another man—Ah!—

The story is saved only by Mr. McClosky, a pure Bret Harte creation, and by its constant grim humor such as that which accounted for the deadly assault upon Dent by the explanation "that his misfortune was the result of the defective moral quality of his being a stranger, and was, in a vague sort of way, a warning to others, and a lesson to him."

The third characteristic was his startling use of paradox and antithesis. The world he presents is topsy-turvy. Of the dwellers in Roaring Camp he notes that

The greatest scamp had a Raphael face, with a profusion of blonde hair; Oakhurst, a gambler, had the melancholy air and intellectual abstraction of a Hamlet; the coolest and most courageous man was scarcely over five feet in height, with a soft voice and an embarrassed, timid manner. . . . The strongest man had but three fingers on his right hand; the best shot had but one eye.

This became a mannerism with Harte. His heroes are men whom the world usually brands as villains. "A Passage in the Life of Mr. John Oakhurst" illustrates his method perfectly. There are two sets of characters, represented by Mrs. Decker, a pathetic invalid and a saintly soul, on the one hand, and by John Oakhurst, a notorious gambler, on the other. The two elements meet and the result furnishes the motif of the story. Oakhurst is everywhere regarded as a villain of melodramatic dye. Once, to be near the devout Mrs. Decker, he attended her church, and his

appearance was considered by all the church members as an
impertinence:

One or two thought that the sexton was exceeding remiss in not turning
him out after discovering who he was; and a prominent pewholder
remarked, that if he couldn't take his wife and daughters to that church,
without exposing them to such an influence, he would try to find some
church where he could.   Another traced Mr. Oakhurst's presence to
certain broad Church radical tendencies, which he regretted to say he had
lately noted in their pastor, Deacon Sawyer, whose delicately organized
sickly wife had already borne him eleven children, and died in an ambitious attempt to complete the dozen, avowed that the presence of Mr.
Oakhurst's various and indiscriminate gallantries was an insult to the
memory of the deceased, that, as a man, he could not brook.

But Oakhurst proves to be the only *man* in the story and the only
character that is in the least admirable.   Whenever he appears, he
satisfies our ideals of what a hero should be.

However Mr. Oakhurst might hide his shapely limbs in homespun and
home-made garments, there was something in his carriage, something in
the pose of his beautiful head, something in the strong and fine manliness
of his presence, something in the perfect and utter discipline and control
of his muscles, something in the high repose of his nature—a repose not
so much a matter of intellectual ruling as of his very nature—that, go
where he would, and with whom, he was always a notable man in ten
thousand.

But this is not enough: like his namesake in "The Outcasts of
Poker Flat," despite the fact that he is a beast of prey living richly
upon his winnings, he is a saint: he sacrifices himself in the end
for the sake of a principle.   And the woman whom her husband
worshiped as a saint proved to be as black inwardly as Oakhurst
was black outwardly.   She is the deliberate ruiner of at least two
men; she has been all the time false to her husband, but when she
meets the deluded man after she has learned the outcome of the
tragedy, she is like an innocent child.   He is bursting with the
awful news concerning Oakhurst and Hamilton, but she sweetly
begs him not to annoy her: She has a headache.

Mr. Decker could not resist the petitionary grace of those white hands
and that sensitive mouth, and took her in his arms. Suddenly he said,
"What's that?"

He was pointing to the bosom of her white dress. Where Mr. Oakhurst had touched her, there was a spot of blood.

It was nothing; she had slightly cut her hand in closing the window; it shut so hard! If Mr. Decker had remembered to close and bolt the shutter before he went out, he might have saved her this. There was such a genuine irritability and force in this remark that Mr. Decker was quite overcome with remorse. But Mrs. Decker forgave him with that graciousness which I have before pointed out in these pages. And with the halo of that forgiveness and matrimonial confidence still lingering above the pair, with the reader's permission we will leave them.

Everywhere it is the same: it is a mannerism. Trappington in "A Secret of Telegraph Hill" became a criminal because his mother took him so frequently to church when he was young. In the tale "In the Carquinez Woods" it is the courtesan Teresa who proves to be an angel in the hour of fire, and it is the eminently proper parson's daughter, whom the reader had supposed was to be the heroine, that is cursed by her dying lover as the veritable "daughter of hell." A moment of brightness in a life supposed by all to be unrelievably black; a deed of sacrifice that atones for a life of wickedness: that is the typical motif in the Bret Harte short story.

His fourth characteristic concerns his methods of characterization. He peopled his stories with highly individualized types, with picturesque extremes in an abnormal social régime. They are not photographs, they are not actual individuals, they are composites made up by fusing the unique qualities of many actual men or women into a single personality. Yuba Bill is the dream of a romancer who has known or has read about many California stage drivers. Colonel Starbottle is redolent of the make-up box: he changes from story to story. He is a gargoyle, and yet for all that he is alive, for Harte had learned from his master, Dickens, that art of creating what in reality is a realm of Munchausen, and then, miracle of miracles, of actually breathing into it the breath of life.

The fifth distinctive element in his work is a splashy type of impressionism. His treatment of background we have noted: he painted with broad strokes and strong colors, and he applied the method to his characters. Usually he works with extremes, with incarnated peculiarities, sharply emphasized. From him it was that Kipling learned the secret of the colorful impressionistic epithet, of the telling comparison, the single adjective that flashes a vivid picture.   Harte describes a certain squaw as "a berry-eyed old woman with the complexion of dried salmon."   Her daughter he describes as having also "berry eyes, and a face that seemed made of a moist laugh."   Another character he pictures as "a stout, middle-aged woman of ungirt waist and beshawled head and shoulders."

Finally, like James and Aldrich, who were contemporaneous workers, he emphasized the technique of his art.   He, too, had found Poe by way of France, he, too, was a conscious workman who knew the rules.   Like Poe, too, he brought to the short story the training of the experienced magazine editor, and it was a training that kept him so long upon short, single-issue effects that he grew powerless to work effectively with the longer units.   Again and again after the period of the serialized "M'liss" he tried to enter what was then considered the more serious field of fictional endeavor, the extended romance.   One novel, *Gabriel Conroy*, he wrote, and at least sixteen novelettes which were issued as separate volumes,[1] but not one of them is to be found in a list of his best writings.   He was brilliant in short dashes, but he had not the patience to hold himself to a long and leisurely plot and to slow character development.   There were other reasons for his failure: Harte lacked moral basis; he was superficial; he was theatric. He was temperamental, too, like Irving, and worked by impulse. Moreover, he dealt with materials impossible to be prolongated to novel length.   If one is to make John Oakhurst or Mother Shipton heroic, one must deal with episodes: must make impressionistic sketches of vivid moments: to go farther would be to relate mere picaresque miscellany.   It was only within narrow limits with single situations and highly colored materials that he could work at all effectively or artistically.

VI

Unquestionably the influence of Harte upon the American short story has been greater than that exerted by any other American

---

[1] *Gabriel Conroy*, 1876; *Thankful Blossom: a Romance of the Jerseys*, 1877; *The Story of a Mine*, 1877; *In the Carquinez Woods*, 1883; *Maruja*, 1855; *Snow-Bound at Eagle's*, 1886; *A Millionaire of Rough and Ready*, 1887; *The Argonauts of North Liberty*, 1888; *Cressy*, 1889; *A Ward of the Golden Gate*, 1890; *A First Family of Tasajara*, 1891; *Susy: a Story of the Plains*, 1893; *A Waif of the Plains*, 1894; *Clarence: a Novel*, 1895; *In a Hollow of the Hills*, 1895; *Three Partners*, 1897; *Salomy Jane*, 1910.

author, always excepting Irving. His influence was far greater than the quality of his work entitled him to exert. He was peculiarly fortunate: everything for a time conspired to give him the center of the stage. The imagination of the whole world had been fired by the California gold era and the field had been untouched by romancers: his material was timely to the moment. Dickens had just visited America and the fame of him and his work had penetrated every household; then had come the news of his death, and enormous space had been given to him in all the journals of the world and new editions had crowded upon one another, until everyone had his Dickens:—the reading public had been educated to appreciate the type of work that Harte was to give them. Moreover, he came at the moment when better art was demanded, when the feminized fiction of the mid-century was no longer satisfying the majority of the readers, and he gave them his work in a form that seemed to them to be peculiarly adequate. In him may be found all the elements that had characterized the popular fiction of the earlier period, and yet his fresh, wild materials, his new Western humor, and his peculiarly effective technique made him appear like the inspired creator of a new *genre*.

Great as has been his influence, however, he can never be a permanently commanding figure in American fiction. He lacked sincerity. One of his earliest reviewers characterized "Mrs. Skagg's Husbands" as a tale showing the "uncertain touch of a hand which has no sympathy with its work." It was a drastic arraignment, but, viewed in the calmness and perspective of to-day, it is seen to have been deserved. His work is not truth, it is extravaganza, and it is an extravaganza which touches not alone California manners and men, but all Americans generally as they have come from the mold of democracy, and it is not true. He wrote only to entertain. He would not report California; he would deliberately manufacture a California that would fill his reader with wonder. Nowhere is there realism; nowhere is there attempt to paint things as they are. Imagine reporting the robustly masculine Yuba Bill as saying not "damn," but "d——n." Imagine him "dancing about in an excess of fury" and giving vent to his feelings with: "Be a man, Miggles: Don't hide in the dark; I wouldn't if I were you, Miggles," and imagine a sane man talking this variety of talk to an ignorant street Arab of seven years:

Melons, this is all irrelevant and impertinent to the case. *You* took those bananas. Your proposition regarding Carrots, even if I were inclined to accept it as credible information, does not alter the material issue. You took those bananas. The offense under the statutes of California is felony. How far Carrots may have been accessory to the fact either before or after, is not my intention at present to discuss. The act is complete. Your present conduct shows the *animo furandi* to have been equally clear.

It is vaudeville; it is posturing; it is mere smartness. In all of his work there is no experience, no genuine feeling, no sympathy of comprehension; it is the theater and not life. Moreover, the moral perspective of it is wrong. Men do not at will put on a new suit of morals as they put on a new suit of clothes. Ruled by emotion and not by principle, by the desire to create wonder and sensation in his reader rather than to interpret for him life, he tells not the truth, and the ultimate basis of all great fiction, be it long or be it short, is the Truth.

BIBLIOGRAPHY

HARTE'S LEADING SKETCHES AND STORIES

1867. *Condensed Novels and Other Papers,* with comic illustrations, by Frank Bellew.

I. Condensed Novels: "Muck a Muck. An Indian novel, after Cooper"; "Terence Denville, by Ch—ls L—v—r"; "Selina Sedilia, by Miss B—dd—n and Mrs. H—y W—d"; "Ninety-Nine Guardsmen, by Al—x—ndr D—m—s"; "The Dweller of the Threshold, by Sir Ed—d L—tt—n B—lw—r"; "The Haunted Man, by Ch—l—s D—k—ns"; "Miss Mix, by Ch—l—tte Br—nte"; "Guy Heavystone. By Author of Sword and Gun;" "Mr. Midshipman Breezy, by Capt. M—ry—t"; "John Jenkins, by T. S. A—rth—r"; "No Title, by W—lk—e C—ll—ns"; "N. N. A French Paragraphic Novel"; "Fantine, *after* the French of Victor Hugo"; "La Femme, *after* the French of M. Michelet"; "Mary McGillup, a Southern Novel." II. Civic Sketches: "A Venerable Imposter"; "From a Balcony"; "Melons"; "Surprising Adventures of Mr. Chas. Summerton"; "Sidewalkings"; "A Boy's Dog"; "Charitable Reminiscences"; "Seeing the Steamer Off"; "Neighborhoods I Have Moved From"; "My Suburban Residence"; "A Vulgar Little Boy";

"Waiting for the Ship." III. Legends and Tales: "The Legend of Monte del Diablo"; "Adventure of Padre Vincentio"; "The Legend of Devil's Point"; "The Devil and the Broker"; "The Ogress of Silver Land"; "Ruins of San Francisco"; "Night at Wingdam."

1870. *The Luck of Roaring Camp and Other Sketches.*
"The Luck of Roaring Camp," *Overland,* Aug., 1868; "The Outcasts of Poker Flat," *Overland,* Jan., 1869; "Miggles," *Overland,* June, 1869; "Tennessee's Partner," *Overland,* Oct., 1869; "The Idyl of Red Gulch," *Overland,* Dec., 1869; "Brown of Calaveras"; "High-water Mark"; "A Lonely Ride"; "M'liss"; "The Right Eye of the Commander"; "Notes by Flood and Field"; "The Mission Dolores"; "John Chinaman"; "From a Back Window"; "Boonder."

1873. *Mrs. Skagg's Husbands and Other Sketches.*
"Mrs. Skagg's Husbands"; "How Santa Claus Came to Simpson's Bar,"; "The Princess Bob and Her Friends"; "The Iliad of Sandy Bar"; "Mr. Thompson's Prodigal"; "The Romance of Madrono Hollow"; [Sections II and III of *Condensed Novels,* as above, repeated]; "The Poet of Sierra Flat"; "The Christmas Gift That Came to Rupert."

1875. *Tales of the Argonauts and Other Sketches.*
"The Rose of Tuolumne"; "A Passage in the Life of Mr. John Oakhurst"; "Wan Lee, the Pagan"; "How Old Man Plunkett Went Home"; "The Fool of Five Forks"; "Baby Sylvester"; "An Episode of Fiddletown"; "A Jersey Centenarian."

1878. *Drift From Two Shores.*
"The Man on the Beach"; "Two Saints of the Foot-hills"; "Jinny"; "Roger Catron's Friend"; "Who Was My Quiet Friend?"; "A Ghost of the Sierras"; "The Hoodlum Band (a Condensed Novel)"; "The Man Whose Yoke Was Not Easy"; "My Friend, the Tramp"; "The Man from Solano"; "The Office Seeker"; "A Sleeping-car Experience"; "Five O'Clock in the Morning"; "With the Entrées."

1879. *Twins of Table Mountain and Other Stories.*
"The Twins of Table Mountain"; "Legend of Sammstadt"; "The House of Red Dog"; "The Great Deadhead Mystery."

1882. *Flip, and Found at Blazing Star.*

1884. *On the Frontier.*
"At the Mission of Dan Carmel"; "A Blue Grass Penelope"; "Left Out on Lone Star Mountain."

1885. *By Shore and Sedge.*
"An Apostle of the Tules"; "Sarah Walker"; "A Ship of '49."

1889. *The Heritage of Dedlow Marsh and Other Stories.*
"The Heritage of Deadlow Marsh"; "A Knight Errant of the Foot-Hills"; "A Secret of Telegraph Hill"; "Captain Jim's Friend."

1891. *A Sappho of Green Springs and Other Stories.*
"A Sappho of Green Springs"; "The Chatelaine of Burnt Ridge"; "Through the Santa Clara Wheat"; "A Mæcenas fo the Pacific Slope."

1892. *Colonel Starbottle's Client and Some Other People.*
"Colonel Starbottle's Client"; "The Postmistress of Laurel Run"; "A Night at Hays"; "Johnson's 'Old Woman'"; "The New Assistant at Pine Clearing School"; "On a Pioneer Restaurant"; "A Treasure of the Galleon"; "Out of a Pioneer's Trunk"; "The Ghosts of Stukeley Castle."

1893. *Sally Dows and Other Stories.*
"Sally Dows"; "The Conspiracy of Mrs. Bunker"; "Their Uncle From California"; "Transformation of Buckeye Camp."

1894. *A Protégée of Jack Hamlin's and Other Stories.*
"A Protégée of Jack Hamlin's"; "An Ingénue of the Sierras"; "The Reformation of James Reddy"; "The Heir of the McHulishes"; "An Episode of West Woodlands"; "The Home-coming of Jim Wilkes."

1894. *The Bell Ringer of Angels and Other Stories.*
"The Bell Ringer of Angels'; "Johnny Boy"; "Young Robin Gray"; "The Sheriff of Siskyou"; "The Rose of Glenbogie"; "The Mystery of the Hacienda"; "Chu Chu"; "My Fast Book."

1896. *Barker's Luck and Other Stories.*
"Barker's Luck"; "A Yellow Dog"; "A Mother of Five"; "Bridger's Reputation"; "In the Tules"; "A Convert of the Mission"; "The Indiscretion of Elizabeth"; "The Devotion of Enriquez."

1898. *Stories in Light and Shadow.*
"Unser Karl"; "Uncle Jim and Uncle Billy"; "Su Yup"; "The Desborough Connections"; "Salomy Jane's Kiss"; "The Man of the Mountain"; "The Passing of Enriquez."

1898. *Tales of Travel and Town.*
"The Ancestors of Peter Atherly"; "Two Americans"; "The

Judgment of Bolinas Plain"; "The Strange Experience of Alkali Dick"; "A Night on the Divide"; "The Youngest Prospector in Calaveras"; "A Tale of Three Truants."

1899. *Mr. Jack Hamlin's Meditation and Other Stories.*
"Mr. Jack Hamlin's Meditation"; "The Man at the Semaphore"; "An Esmeralda of Rocky Cañon"; "Dick Spindler's Family Christmas"; "When the Waters Were Up at 'Jules'"; "The Boom in the Calaveras 'Clarion'"; "The Secret of Sobriente's Well"; "Liberty Jones's Discovery."

1900. *From Sand-hill to Pine.*
"A Niece of Snapshot Harry's"; "A Treasure of the Redwoods"; "A Belle of Canada City"; "What Happened at Tonda"; "A Jack and Jill of the Sierras"; "Mr. Bilson's Housekeeper."

1901. *Under the Redwoods.*
"Jimmy's Big Brother From California"; "The Youngest Miss Piper"; "A Widow of the Santa Ana Valley"; "The Mermaid of Lighthouse Point"; "Under the Eaves"; "How Reuben Allen 'Saw Life' in San Francisco"; "Three Vagabonds of Trinidad"; "A Vision of the Fountain"; "A Romance of the Line"; "Bohemian Days in San Francisco."

1902. *Openings in the Old Trail.*
"A Mercury of the Foot-hills"; "Colonel Starbottle for the Plaintiff"; "The Landlord of the Big Flume Hotel"; "A Buckeye Hollow Inheritance"; "The Reincarnation of Smith"; "Lanty Foster's Mistake"; "An Ali Baba of the Sierras"; "Miss Peggy's Protégées"; "The Goddess of Excelsior."

1902. *Condensed Novels.*
"Rupert the Resembler, by A—th—y H—pe"; "The Stolen Cigar Case, by A. C—n—n D—le"; "Golly and the Christian: or The Minx and the Manxman, by H—ll C—ne"; "The Adventures of John Longbowe, Yeoman, compiled from Several Eminent Sources"; "Dan'l Borem, by E. N—s W—t—t"; "Stories Three—For Single Reasons—A Private's Honour—Jungle Folk, by R—dy—d K—pl—g"; "Zut-ski. By M—r—e C—r—ll."

1903. *Trent's Trust and Other Stories.*
"Trent's Trust"; "Mr. MacGlowrie's Widow"; "A Ward of Colonel Starbottle's"; "Prosper's 'Old Mother'"; "The Convalescence of Jack Hamlin"; "A Pupil of Chestnut Ridge"; "Dick Broyle's Business Card."

CHAPTER XI

In 1870 America, so far as fiction was concerned, was divided into two camps: the first, the conservative group that clung to the traditions of the mid-century; the second, the element which a reviewer of the period denominated "the invading Goths from over the mountains." As early as 1873 *The Atlantic* could speak of these "Goths" as a "school," and deem it worthy of record that almost to a man the writers were now in the East. Their increasing popularity was filling the old New England group with alarm. Readers everywhere were discussing the sudden rise of Bret Harte. Book agents were entering every home in America with *Innocents Abroad*, a book that made light of the whole serious alcove of American travel literature, that exhibited the sacred shrines of Europe humorously and with no more reverence than if they were mining camps in the Sierras. Even the poetic John Hay, just back from Spain with a new Spanish sketch-book, *Castilian Days*, had gone over to the Goths and was writing ballads that out-Piked the work of even the "Dow's Flat" school. Eggleston was making use of the wild Hoosiers as if they were legitimate material for romance. Mark Twain had been added to the contributing staff of *The Galaxy* and very soon was to run in *The Atlantic* his southwestern serial, *Old Times on the Mississippi*. Most decidedly were the Goths taking possession of the East.

The new product was accepted at first as a passing phenomenon, to be explained by the fact that the multitude loved the humorous, and in everything save the word "passing" the judgment was right. The California writers were nothing if not humorous. *The Atlantic* tried to explain the entire literary situation in terms of humor:

Their humor [that of the California school] broad or fine, has the same general character, as if in each of them it came from a sense of their own anomaly, as men of the literary temperament and ambition in a world of rude adventure, rapacious money getting and barbarous profusion.

The state of things in which they found themselves must have affected them as immensely droll; in it, but not of it, they must have felt themselves rather more comic than anything about them; and this sense of one's grotesqueness is Humor, with the large H, which we have been gradually coming at. All literary men, we suppose, feel their want of relevance to surrounding conditions at times and in some degree; and the conditions being exaggerated in the case of the Californian *littérateurs*, we can readily account for the greater irreverence and abandon of their humor, which has now become the type of American humor, so that no merry person can hope to please the public unless he approaches with it.

Whatever one may think of this explanation, one cannot escape the conviction that it was the humor of the new school that chiefly gave it its early vogue. Harte entered the East as a humorist as certainly as did Mark Twain. The strangeness of his material was of secondary interest. *Appleton's* summary of literary conditions for the year 1870 listed *The Luck of Roaring Camp* volume not among the fiction, but among the humorous and unclassified publications. Harte's "instantaneous and widespread popularity," it declared, was simply "one of the caprices of literary taste—a fashion of the time." It is noteworthy that both *The Atlantic* and the New York *Nation* could classify a book as poetic and as seriously romantic as even Stoddard's *South Sea Idylls* as primarily a humorous product. What else *could* it be? Did its author not belong to the California school? "We have found the book, with all the drawbacks we have enumerated," declared *The Nation*, "amusing with a dreamy sort of amusement, which we suppose is the proper color for California humor to take upon itself in the tropics." Howells in later years could speak of the sketches—for they are sketches and not short stories at all— as "the lightest, sweetest, wildest, freshest things that ever were written about the life of that summer ocean. . . . I remember very well my joy in 'A Prodigal in Tahiti,' when I accepted it for *The Atlantic Monthly*, and I think now that there are few such delicious bits of literature in the language." But to the old school in the East in 1873 it was a collection of exaggerated California sailor yarns to be tolerated only because of its humor.

This toleration of the new type of prose had a wider application. Much of the growing realism that has been noted in *The Atlantic* fiction of the 'sixties had been regarded by the conservative as also an episode in American facetiousness. *The Atlantic* in 1871 could classify Howells's *Suburban Sketches* as primarily a humorous work. A writer, it seemed to imply, who "finds as much of travel in a horse-car ride through Cambridgeport as in the voyage to Venice and the gondolas," surely cannot be taken as a producer of serious literature. Unquestionably the localized sketch and short story entered the 'seventies under the caption of *humor*.

And, contrary to the general impression, the new short story of the decade was not realistic. Rebecca Harding Davis with her grim tale, "Life in the Iron Mills," and Rose Terry Cooke and Hale and the others, had created no school of realists, as one in the early 'sixties might have prophesied they were to do. Their realism was stopped short. The war had given the reading public tragedy enough: they wanted to laugh; it had given them reality in tragic abundance: they wanted to read themselves into regions beyond those they actually inhabited. Thousands of them turned to the New York *Ledger*, which entered again upon a golden era. Then had come Harte and Eggleston and the stampede toward localized romance with Dickens-like characters. Even the judicious who realized the inanity of the *Ledger* fiction could read this. This was entertaining and at the same time it read as if it were true. Utterly ignorant of the actual California, they accepted Harte's pictures of the mines and the gulches as photographic in their realism. Was it not the Truth stranger than romance? they asked. We to-day say, *No;* it was romance that was holding them, romance tempered with humor and given verisimilitude by carefully chosen details. America was not ready for naked realism as we to-day define realism. Fiction should deal with a refined and idealized society: that was the unwritten law of the 'seventies. *The Nation* in 1872 was doubtful concerning the future of *The Hoosier Schoolmaster*, because "the faithfulness of its transcript of the life it depicts will alone make it to many a repulsive book." Even Howells was not a realist during the romantic 'seventies. It is noteworthy, too, that neither Rebecca Harding Davis nor Rose Terry Cooke was able to republish from the early *Atlantic* in book form their realistic tales for at least two decades.

But while still holding to romance, America was more and more demanding native materials. The war had created a great wave of patriotism. It had broken down the provincial barriers. In 1870 T. W. Higginson in *The Atlantic* declared the time ripe for an American literature that should include *every* part of the whole nation. "We must look beyond our little Boston or New York or Chicago or San Francisco and be willing citizens of the great republic." Everything was conspiring to bring a national era with a literature unprovincial and wholly American. The tremendous forces and resources that had been wholly employed in the making of war were now turned to the development of the country. A great wave of settlers now poured into the West, a railroad was pushed through to the Pacific, great transportation systems penetrated everywhere, telegraphs began to cover the land with an ever-broadening network, newspapers sprang up in a profusion that exceeds belief—soon all the remote places of the whole land were exposed to full view. And some of them were startling in their strangeness. People began to read about their own United States, especially about its picturesque regions, now seemingly for the first time brought to the light. There came a revival of the forgotten localized sketches of the early Western period. The Harpers in 1867 issued a new edition of Longstreet's *Georgia Scenes;* in 1872 came a reissue of Thompson's *Major Jones's Courtship*, a book seemingly dead for twenty-seven years. America became interested in America.

The emphasis first was upon the characterization of unique personalities exaggerated after the Dickens fashion—the story with dominating background was to come later. After Harte, Mrs. Stowe was the earliest to enter this field. In 1870 she began in *The Atlantic* her *Oldtown Fireside Stories*, careful sketches accurate as to dialect and details, but wholly romantic in atmosphere and setting, since they deal with the New England of the early years of the century and since over this vanished era they throw the golden light that realism never knows. They are valuable now chiefly because they make tremendously alive Sam Lawson, a Yankee Uncle Remus, who told not folklore, but legends. As short stories, however, they failed so lamentably that their author felt an apology was due her readers:

Sam's method of telling a story was as leisurely as that of some modern novel writers. He would take his time for it and proceed by easy stages. It was like the course of a dreamy, slow-moving river through a tangled meadow flat—not a rush nor a bush but was repeated in it; in short, Sam gave his philosophy of matters and things in general as he went along, and was especially careful to impress an edifying moral.

Opposed to all this, oblivious in a large degree of it all, was the other current. Side by side with the struggling realism of James and the careful art of Aldrich and all the new work of the Californians, there was running, just as in the 'fifties and the 'sixties, the strong current of the older type of romanticism, the lady's book type of sentimentalized fiction, revised, it may be, and given modern elements of appeal, but still true to type. A nation at work with the plow on millions of acres newly wrested from nature demands, if it reads at all, rather primitive themes and rather primitive methods. To realize what the majority in America in the 'seventies really demanded, one may read the three volumes of *Short Stories for Spare Moments*—forty tales gathered from the first eighteen numbers of the new *Lippincott's Magazine* (1869-70). Choose one at random—"Love on the Ohio," D. P. Dorsey. The hero on a steamboat deck catches sight of a woman in the crowd, an utter stranger, and instantly bursts forth into this: "Hebe, what a face! O Terpsichore, what a form!" Then breathlessly "he quotes one of Horace's most amatory passages." "He had in those few minutes become a votary of Venus. Cupid had shot a quiverful of arrows into his heart." We read no further. All the others are in the same *Godey's Lady's Book* key. The novelist for this uncritical school was E. P. Roe; their most-talked-about short-story writer was "Saxe Holm." The series which became known as "the Saxe Holm's Stories" began in *Scribner's Monthly* in September, 1871, and for a decade the work of their mysterious author, who seemed to have the name of a man and the literary style of a woman, furnished material for speculation. The problem became even a subject for newspaper controversy, many claiming with vehemence their authorship, and the real author at one time publishing a notice in a New York daily denying with equal emphasis that she had written a word of them. Curiosity on the part of the reading public undoubtedly explains something of their vogue—they were well advertised—but it cannot be denied that there were other contributing elements; they were vivacious, they were poetic at times even to distinction, they were sentimental, they were many of them really original in material and manner. The reading class that was demanding edition after edition of *Barriers Burned Away* found such stories as "Whose Wife Was She?" and "How One Woman Kept Her Husband" peculiarly satisfying. The tales seemed to thrive upon prosperity;

they grew in length with every added number; quickly they became novelettes, then complete novels in the No Name Series. Undoubtedly they were unplanned by this author both as to form and as to conclusion, and, after the first two tales, undoubtedly they were unrestricted in any way. They ramble on and on. Of short-story art, as James and Aldrich and Harte were conceiving of it, she was as guiltless as was the creator of Sam Lawson. The stories have other blemishes: they are over-intense, they are at times morbidly sentimental, their author, as one contemporary reviewer happily expressed it, had "constantly a tendency to flat." They have disappeared; they have never been reprinted from their first editions, their author, Helen Hunt Jackson, is remembered now only because of her localized romance *Ramona*, and yet for a time these sentimental creations vied in popularity even with the contemporary stories of Bret Harte. That she numbered even more readers than he would seem to be the implication of her contemporary, Constance Fenimore Woolson. In her sketch, "Misery Landing" (1874), she wrote:

I read aloud last evening. George [a boy of the Lakes, abysmally ignorant] did not seem much interested in Bret Harte, but was captivated with the pageantry of "Ivanhoe." Strange that it should be so, but everywhere it is the cultivated people only who are taken with Bret. But they must be imaginative as well as cultivated; routine people, whether in life or in literature, dislike anything unconventional or new.

II

Miss Woolson herself had taken position with Harte rather than with E. P. Roe. During the 'seventies undoubtedly she was the most "unconventional" feminine writer that had yet appeared in America. Her antecedents and her training had been unusual. She was a grandniece of Cooper, a fact of real importance when one considers the influence that the Cooper and Cooperstown tradition exerted upon her imaginative childhood. She, too, became a lover of the vast lonely places. She, too, like her cousin Susan Fenimore Cooper, lived long "near to Nature's heart." Her education had been ideally balanced. Born in the East, she had gone early with her family to the Middle West and had become a part of it. No other writer until later years knew so intimately what then was called "the West":

I have walked to the shores of Lake Erie, driven all through the "coal country" and the "corn country" with my father; I know all the hills and dales and rivers; I have sailed up and down the Ohio; I have been to the harvest fields and even helped; have gathered the apples and been to state fairs.

She knew the northern regions, too. Her family spent their summers on the island of Mackinac in the straits connecting Huron and Michigan, and here among the descendants of the *voyageurs* and the *coureurs de bois* she learned the local French patois, and from the priests—remarkable men wherever they appear in her volumes—caught glimpses of the earlier and more romantic years of the Lake lands and the St. Lawrence.

And now for the second time had her education been balanced. Like the daughter of the Lakes in her novel, *Anne*, she, too, was sent to the East, to New York City, to the French school of Madame Chegary, where, to quote from the novel, "the extreme of everything called 'accomplishment' was taught." Here she perfected her French, read in the original George Sand and the later realists, dreamed over Charlotte Brontë, and awoke to the meaning of George Eliot. Then had come the powerful influence of Bret Harte: why not do for her wild Lakes and her obscure Ohio valleys what he had done for California?

Her first sketch, "The Happy Valley," dealing with a peculiar settlement on the "Tuscarawas River" in Ohio, appeared in *Harper's Monthly* in July, 1873. She chose the subject we feel only because of its strangeness: she could present an American environment with characters just as startlingly new as Harte's. In a later sketch she described a community of "Zoarites." Other stories and travel sketches, some of them illustrated, swiftly followed, and then a series of tales dealing with the wild and winter-swept islands of the upper Superior.

Her relationship to Cooper, skillfully played up by the publishers, brought immediate results. They used her full name—Constance Fenimore Woolson, and the early reviewers hailed her as the natural inheritor of the Cooper tradition. It enabled her, like Harte, to start her literary career with momentum, more momentum, perhaps, than the quality of her early work deserved; it enabled her, moreover, to introduce to readers a second strange region for literary exploitation—the wild upper northwest with its unique population of mixed French and Indian and its backgrounds dimly shadowing a romantic *ancien régime*. She became thus the second strong influence that during the decade was to create what was to be known as the new "local-color school."

The influence of Harte upon her work was at first considerable. In the story, "Castle Nowhere," old Fog, a New York criminal fleeing for his life, builds a "castle" in the inner tangle of the marshes, and for years lives on the wreckage of vessels he has lured to death with his false lights; but at the end he dies like a hero and a saint, all his crimes blotted out because he had done his murders to keep alive an innocent and adopted girl and because for her in his last hours he does a real deed of sacrifice. Again, in "The Lady of Little Fishing," by many considered her best short story, there is "The Luck of Roaring Camp" motif: a wild trapping camp peopled with thirty of the dregs of men tamed and made a paradise by a single beautiful woman.

Like Harte, she posed as a realist—"All I write is founded, and intended to be founded, upon actual realities. I have no interest in anything else"—but despite her knowledge of her materials and her sympathy with her people she can hardly be classed in the school of Howells and James. She was a poet; she worked always with selected materials; she demanded heavy lights and shadows—"a glamour" over it all, Henry James termed it. She had unusual power to create a local tone, but it was always poeticized and idealized and purged of all grossness of reality. Henry Mills Alden, who accepted for *Harper's* her first sketch, has given it this expression: "These shifting sojourns (on the Lakes and in the South) gave her the material for all her novels and for nearly all her short stories—material, however, so transformed in the alembic of her imagination, so transfused in its association with the living world of her creation, that anyone attempting to trace in her literary landmarks would find them, perhaps, in sea and sky and in local color, but for the most part they would elude him, escaping definition."

Her power lay first of all in her Cooper-like imagination, which awoke always in the presence of vast wildness and desolation. In sketches like "Castle Nowhere" she catches and holds the very spirit of the Great Lakes; in "The South Devil" she makes us realize all the horrors and the beauties of the Southern swamps; in "Up in the Blue Ridge" she shows the desolate barrens of the Appalachians—"as purple-black, wild, and pathless, some of them, as the peaks of the Western Sierras." Given material like this, she could create a local impressionism, vivid, vibrant with color, alive—all her own. The second element of her strength lay in her power to make her reader realize certain forlorn human types. "She is fond of irretrievable personal failures," says James. "She is interested in general in secret histories, in the 'inner life' of the weak, the superfluous, the disappointed, the bereaved, the unmarried." Only when her sympathies were fully aroused and her imagination was able to throw over her subject the pathos of a forever-vanished glory was she at her best. A character to kindle her pen must stand in the fading light of an old régime—an aged priest who can tell of the day when France ruled the St. Lawrence and the Lakes, a soldier of Napoleon spending his last years in the deserted agency and glorious in his memories, a wounded Confederate soldier who has come home to find his plantation ruined and his fortune gone, but who dies unconquered, a man of the Old South. They are sketched with actual material pigments carefully chosen, but fundamentally they are all of them of the world of romance—they cast shadows, single and impressive, such as realism with its thousand angles and its myriad lights can never know.

The second period in her literary life began in 1873, when, with her mother, who was in feeble health, she removed to Florida to spend there and in the mountains of Georgia and North Carolina the next five years. Just as in her earlier days she had explored her mid-Western country, she now acquainted herself with the South which lay voiceless amid the wreckage of the war. What she found is recorded first in her volume of short stories, *Rodman the Keeper*, and later in a notable series of novels. Her sketches, done with sympathy and with impartial honesty, were the first pictures of the after-the-war South to attract Northern attention. They were pioneer work, even more so than had been her Lake-country sketches. Here was material that aroused her sympathies to the full and here was a background of wild mountains and tropic swamps to stir to the deeps her imagination. The volume, *Rodman the Keeper*, contains the best of her short-story work. She had broken now from Harte and was in the full of her powers. Everywhere she was breaking new ground. Her "Up in the Blue Ridge," which appeared one month before Charles Egbert Craddock's first Tennessee Mountain sketch, stands at the head in point of time of a notable list of Southern Mountain tales, just as her dialect sketch, "King David," antedates the negro dialect stories of Page and Harris.

After her mother's death in 1879, Miss Woolson went abroad, and the remainder of her life was connected chiefly with Italy. Again she tried to open a new literary area; she wrote what were gathered into two volumes of stories of Italian life, but on the whole they fall below her earlier work. Distinctly was she the portrayer of wild fresh American backgrounds and of pathetic survivals and exceptions living in environments strange and even startling.

Her work has not fulfilled the expectations of the 'seventies and the 'eighties. In 1887 Henry James could include her in his *Partial Portraits* along with George Eliot, Stevenson, Daudet, Maupassant, and Turgenieff. All the fields in which she was a pioneer have been more richly tilled by the later workers who followed her lead. Not in many ways was she significant; in some important details she was actually a retrogressive force. She never wholly outgrew, for instance, the earlier lessons she learned from her first enthusiasm, Charlotte Brontë. There is a conventional diction, too, and a conventional manner about much of her work that are real defects: she lacked Harte's powers of innovation, his startling twists of adjective and phrase, and she made little use of the humor that undeniably was a part of her endowment. Her characters are inclined to be as over declamatory even as Cooper's: their talk is often stiltedly bookish. Surely, even the most ardently patriotic of Southern girls would not talk in such theatric strain as this:

"Shall I, Bettina Ward, set my name down in black and white as a visitor to this cemetery, where lie fourteen thousand of the soldiers who killed my father, my three brothers, my cousins? . . . Shall I forget these things? Never! Sooner let my right hand wither by my side!"

Neither would little Felipa, "the small, dark-skinned, yellow-eyed child, the offspring of the ocean and the heats, lithe and wild, shy yet fearless," utterly ignorant and scarce twelve years old, introduce herself in the diction of Henry James:

I have seen only three women in all my life, and I like women. I am a woman, too, although these clothes of the son of Pedro make me appear as a boy; I wear them on account of the boat and the hauling in of the fish. The son of Pedro being dead at a convenient age, and his clothes fitting me, what would you have? It was a chance not to be despised.

The speech of Harte's M'liss was doubtless as unreal, but somehow it carries conviction; but this speech on the very face of it seems impossible.

In all that concerns short-story form Miss Woolson was strong. She had learned much from her studies in French fiction. "The Lady of Little Fishing," for instance, greatly surpassed in short-story art Harte's "Luck of Roaring Camp." The motif of Harte's piece centers about the abnormality of a group of men isolated completely from all feminine and domestic influences and the grotesque extremes to which such a group may go when such an element appears suddenly among them. Harte shows this excellently well, but he shows only this. Miss Woolson does all that Harte does, and then she adds a touch that makes her work a model short story, as Harte's is not. All the men but one are in love with the Lady, and she is forced to choose one from among them. She chooses Mitchell, who refuses her absolutely, and then explains himself to the amazed group whom she had rejected:

"I never gave in to her influence; I was never under her thumb. *I* was the only man in Little Fishing who cared nothing for her."
"And that is the secret of *her* liking" murmured the doctor. "O woman! woman! the same the world over!"

That is the real motif of the story; not the mere grotesqueness of an abnormal situation presented merely for entertainment and wonder. The story is not finished when the reader has read it: it becomes with him a haunting suspicion, a peep into the heart of life. Not always is she so happy in her art, but all in all she must be rated with James and Aldrich as a strong influence toward more careful short-story workmanship at a moment when such influence peculiarly was needed.

III

From still another quarter there came into the decade a touch of French artistry and romance. The French, to quote Howells, have touched America "with romance whenever they have touched it at all as soldiers, priests, exiles, or mere adventurers."

That there was a French population in Louisiana partly descendants of the Creoles who had displaced the original Spaniards and
partly the descendants of the Acadians who had been transported
from Nova Scotia as told in *Evangeline,* was in 1870 almost totally
unknown in America, at least in the North. Edward King, sent by
Scribner's Monthly to report in a series of papers the condition of
"The Great South" seven years after the war, brought back
nothing more strange or more significant than the two or three
short stories which he had found in the hands of a young New
Orleans warehouse clerk whose acquaintance he had made almost
by accident. Published at length in *Scribner's,* these stories seemed
to the North like something utterly foreign. Both in background
and in treatment they were exotics, strange tropic fruit to come
floating down the staid current of American fiction. In 1880 after
The Grandissimes novel had followed the early short stories, the
New York *Nation* could remark of their author, "considering his
nativity, his appearance just now is almost to be called sensational." That a writer of real power could come out of the South
was indeed sensational news in 1880. George Washington Cable
must be ranked first of all as a pioneer: he was the first literary
voice of the New South.

It was by no means a precocious phenomenon that had been
discovered, not at all a genius unexplained and dominating: he
was twenty-nine when his first story, "'Sieur George," appeared
in *Scribner's;* he was thirty-six when *The Grandissimes,* his second
book, brought him wide recognition. His apprenticeship had
been as long and exacting as even Hawthorne's. And yet, like
Harte, he seemed to have come full fledged. To read him to-day
one begins with no callow material: there is no *Fanshawe* in his
list. One finds in his first volume, *Old Creole Days,* what is really
his best work, and it is because he mastered his art in obscurity
and did not—could not—publish until he had reached his highest
form. He was not a Creole as at first was reported—there was
in him no French or Spanish strain; he was not even an unmixed
Southerner—his mother was of New England stock: it accounts
for a Puritan quality within him; it accounts for his later forced
exile from the South. And yet he was by no means a Northerner.
He had been born and reared in *ante bellum* New Orleans; the mark
of the old city was broad upon him: an exotic strangeness, a Gallic
predilection to artistry, a tropic efflorescence in style and diction,

an unhurried lingering over the amenities of life, a patrician fastidiousness that avoided as by instinct the unlovely and the coarse.

There had been little schooling in the boy's life and no college
to make him conventional. To a large degree he was self-educated.
The death of his father had thrown him at twelve into the world of
work—any work he could get to do. At seventeen the war broke
into his life and he gave the period that should have been his
college years to the Confederate Army. And after the war, had
come at length employment by a firm of cotton factors, a Charles
Lamb-like position held until he was thirty-five years of age—
these are the externals of his early biography.

But he was no ordinary boy and no ordinary clerk. As a cavalry-
man he had carried Latin books in his saddle-bags, and as an
accountant he had spent his spare hours with books far different
from those upon his office desk.

Yes, I read some French literature, and I believe it had its influence on
me, tho not as much as Dickens, Thackeray, Poe, or Irving. My French-
men were Hugo, Mérimée, and About. I also read many of the old
Relations of the priest-explorers and much other French matter of early
historical value.

Unusual employment for a city clerk. It led him to the archives
of the old Spanish-French-American metropolis. He delved in
them with all the zest of an antiquarian, and found them excitingly
rich in strange history and romantic tradition—how rich, indeed,
one has but to open *The Grandissimes* or the *Strange True Stories
of Louisiana* to realize. And he brooded over them as Hawthorne
had brooded over the Puritan traditions, and he wrote them at
length into romance. "Money, fame, didactic or controversial
impulse I scarcely felt a throb of. I just wanted to do it because
it seemed a pity for the stuff to go so to waste."

Material it was that it was hardly possible to treat realistically.
It covered not one *ancien régime*, but three: the era of Spanish
beginnings, the era of French domination with its pirates in the
gulf, its indigo planters, its Creoles and its Acadians, and the era
of American domination after 1804, ended dramatically by the
storm of the war which made even the days of Cable's youth
seem like romance. There is no sharpness of line in the stories
that make up *Old Creole Days:* all is mellowed and softly tinted
and idealized. In his own words, descriptive of a tale by one of

his characters, "There shone a light of romance upon it that filled it with color and peopled it with phantoms." So with his own work. The exquisite dialect effects, the impressionistic backgrounds, the dainty etchings of Creole femininity, the humorous Dutchmen and chivalrous Gulf pirates seemed to the North the very essence of realism, but old New Orleans did not at all accept them as photographs. A little later Grace King turned to fiction for no other purpose than to correct Cable's picture and to show to the North what Creoles really are.

Cable was a romancer with a manner all his own. He had learned his art in solitude in a corner of the world, and it was unconventional in the extreme. Nowhere else in American literature, save in Lafcadio Hearn, may one find a tang so individual. It is like mangoes or alligator pears: one must acquire the taste. Everywhere a suggestion of French influence—in the artistry, in the lightness of line, in the style: often paragraphic, elided of verbs, subtly suggestive. The technique shows faintly the influence of Poe. The early short stories have uniformity of tone, atmosphere, culminating effect; they are strong in characterization; they bring out a certain unique or single effect. They lack, perhaps, what Poe called momentum—the fault with which he had charged De Béranger: they are beautiful, sparkling, brilliant, but they move slowly, they have a Southern disregard for rush and immediacy. The backgrounds are etched in without regard to proportion, the character descriptions go to extremes: in "Madame Delphine" a chapter of analysis and description is given to each character.

It was caviar to Northerners when it first came, and they acquired the taste slowly. After five years only seven of his stories had found place in the magazines, and when in 1879 they were published as *Old Creole Days* there was no excitement anywhere, no real enthusisam, though to-day we realize that the book was a classic. *The Nation* ignored the volume: short stories, however brilliant, did not in 1879 interest Godkin. A year later, when *The Grandissimes*, a bulky novel, appeared, he gave it two pages of review. It was *The Grandissimes* that gave Cable his entrance to the Valhalla of American fiction. In 1880 the novel was still the supreme literary form: the short story was still an amusing trifle.

Undoubtedly it was his materials rather than his art that gave

Cable his first vogue. His own confession that he was led to write simply because of his materials and his reaction after his success with *The Grandissimes* are both significant. After his first two or three volumes, which are the real Cable untouched by outside opinion, we find him turning more and more to merely picturesque presentation. He wrote for *Scribner's* a long series of articles on Creole life and character, legends of Louisiana which are not short stories, but histories, papers on the moral and economic problems of the South. His short-story fountain dried up almost in a moment. His total product is less than a dozen if we count only his real achievements: it includes the seven in *Old Creole Days*, later swelled to eight by the inclusion of "Madame Delphine," "Père Raphael," and perhaps the three parts of *Bonaventure*, which undoubtedly are of short-story texture. Little that he wrote in later days really matters. When he left the South in 1879 he became like a tropic tree transplanted into Northern soil: he lost somehow that indescribable tang that had made his early work so distinctive.

His influence upon the American short story, however, has been a marked one. He helped to swell the stream of dialect and local peculiarity that was slowly gathering now, to break shortly in a veritable flood; he called attention anew to style as an essential of short-story art, and by the great success of his work he inspired new writers everywhere to search for the unique and to put the emphasis upon material and characterization. In quantity he did little for the form, but the little he did do is distinctive. He is one of the rare few of whom, even while he is living it may be said, he added a permanent volume to the none too large library of American masterpieces.

IV

The growing popularity of unique local settings and highly individualized characters as material for fiction brought to light a new area in the much-cultivated New England environment. The literary beginnings of Sarah Orne Jewett were almost exactly contemporaneous with those of Harte and Miss Woolson and Cable, her first story, indeed, "Mr. Bruce," appearing in *The Atlantic* as early as 1869. Unlike any of these three, however, she was indigenous to the region she portrayed, for generations indigenous; she wrote always with complete knowledge and with perfect sympathy. South Berwick, Me., was her birthplace, a distinctive old town, not far removed from Portsmouth, N. H., which once, to quote her biographer, had "seemed the capital of New England and the governors and clergymen thereof rulers and potentates." The legends of a glorious past lay over the region like a Washington Irving atmosphere. She tells us that not long after her twentieth year she awoke to the fact that the New England of her early favorite authors, Mrs. Stowe, Mrs. Cooke, Lowell, and the rest, was rapidly becoming a New England of tradition only, and that the New England even of her own childhood before the War was passing, if not already gone. Her native town had once been a prosperous deep-sea port with busy wharves and wealthy merchants, and there had been a courtly society in its richly furnished manor houses, "Judges and Governors and grand ladies," and in these same mansions now so decayed and pathetic, even yet there were to be found survivals of this aristocracy, families fallen on evil times because the shipping had left the old harbor for more prosperous ports, yet a group that still preserved "the best traditions of culture and of manners, from some divine inborn instinct toward what is simplest and best and purest."

A frail child, she had been taken much by her father, a country doctor, on his professional rounds over a wide territory, and from him she had learned the story of every family in the region, had gathered the wisdom of a kindly and much-experienced soul, and had come to know the lives of her people with a peculiar intimacy. She had no suspicion at first that she was gathering material for literary use; she did not enter literature deliberately and with aforethought, with the beginner's perplexity as to what her field was to be. Her work came to her almost as a matter of duty. By 1870 a new social movement had come into American life—the modern summer-vacation ebb and flow had begun.

The steady inflow of immigration, and the way in which these cities had drawn to themselves, like masses of quicksilver, much of the best life of the remotest villages, had made necessary a reflex current that set countryward in summer. This presently showed itself to be of unsuspected force and significance: it meant something more than the instinct for green fields and hills and the seashore; crowded town and the open country were to be brought together in new association and dependence upon each other. . . . The increase of wealth, and of the number of persons who had houses in town and country both—all these causes brought about great and almost sudden changes in rustic life. Old farmhouses opened their doors to the cheerful gayety of summer; the old jokes about the respective aggressions and ignorances of city and country cousins gave place to new compliments between the summer boarder and his rustic host.

The summer boarder had arrived and he was penetrating into the remotest districts. He was portrayed by Howells in his earlier novels as a new type. His arrival in numbers in her native Berwick filled the daughter of the country physician with something akin to resentment. To many of them countrymen were mere "hayseeds," rustics, peasants—or to put it in her own words:

> The young writer of these Deephaven sketches was possessed by a dark fear that townspeople and country people would never understand one another, or learn to profit by their new relationship. She may have had the unconscious desire to make some sort of explanation to those who still expected to find the caricatured Yankee of fiction, striped trousers, bell-crowned hat, and all, driving his steady horses along the shady roads. It seemed not altogether reasonable when timid ladies mistook a selectman for a tramp, because he happened to be crossing a field in his shirt sleeves. At the same time, she was sensible of grave wrong and misunderstanding when these same timid ladies were regarded with suspicion, and their kindnesses were believed to come from pride and patronage. There is a noble saying of Plato that the best thing that can be done for the people of a state is to make them acquainted with one another. It was, happily, in the writer's childhood that Mrs. Stowe had written of those who dwelt along the wooded seacoast and by the decaying, shipless harbors of Maine. The first chapters of "Pearl of Orr's Island" gave the young author of "Deephaven" to see with new eyes, and to follow eagerly the old shore paths from one gray, weather-beaten house to another where genius pointed her the way.

Deephaven was the result, a bundle of sketches, as she herself termed them, loosely bound into a kind of unity as experiences during a summer vacation. The book attracted but little attention. From its first story, "Shore House," in *The Atlantic* in 1873, to the final collection was four years, and the short stories that followed the book came only two or three or four in a year. It was not until well into the eighties that her position as a writer was at all fixed. She refused to yield to the demands of the time. "What shall I do with my 'White Heron,' now she is written?" she once asked concerning one of the most typical of her sketches. "She isn't a very good magazine story, but I love her." She wrote to please herself, to satisfy her own artistic requirements. Her stories are etchings made *con amore*, centering always about a character or a group of characters and seldom about a situation or a culminating action. Material came first—her neighbors in the little circle that she loved, and then the background of "the country of the pointed firs," which to her was the whole world. With her a short story was not, as with Poe, a deliberate thing of form, of impression, of effect upon the reader: it was a sympathetic study in individuality. She worked always with emotion, with real people in mind, perhaps in view, and as a result her unit of measure was short. Her genius was lyric and not epic; it was essentially feminine and not masculine. Charles Egbert Craddock, she once observed, was able to take time and to build elaborately on broad foundations "a good big *Harper's* story," but "not S. O. J., whose French ancestry comes to the fore and makes her nibble all around her stories like a mouse. They used to be as long as yardsticks, they now are as long a spools, and they will soon be the size of old-fashioned peppermints, and have neither beginning nor end, but shape and flavor may still be left them."

Faithful as her pictures are to the environment she knew so well, she is not to be counted as a realist or a local-color worker dominated by her material. Her own definition is illuminating: "the trouble with most realism is that it isn't seen from any point of view at all, and so its shadows fall in every direction, and it fails of being art." She tells always truth, but not the whole truth. Her Deephaven undoubtedly had in it the same average amount of vulgar democratic unloveliness and coarse sin as might be found in any other town in America East or West, but she recorded only the things lovely and of good report. Her pages are as free from the harsh and the harrowing as even Irving's. In her senile captains and forlorn feminine survivals, her house-wives on isolated farms and far-off coast islands, her David Berrys and Miss Chaunceys and Miss Debbys and Sister Wisbys, she sees only the heroic. For her, romance lay in the commonplace, even in humble little farmhouses and grimy fish houses. "Mr. Howells thinks that the age frowns upon the romantic, that it's no use to write romance any more; but, dear me, how much there is left in everyday life, after all." Her humble characters cast, all of them, long shadows in a single direction, and over them always is the golden light of a vanished past, faint sometimes and evanescent, yet akin always to the glow that tints the far hillsides of romance.

In a way both Cable and Miss Jewett were reactionary influences. Mark Twain and his like were adding epic fling to American fiction, the sweep and vastness of the American frontier, and its coarseness and its democratic abandon, and he was to be followed by the Kipling school, raucous, masculine, far-flung in its materials. Miss Jewett worked always patiently, lovingly, in the small, with subdued passion, with grace and refinement and artistry and perfection of style. She was of the eighteenth century rather than the nineteenth, a Mrs. Gaskell, a Jane Austen, a White of Selborne. In our vulgar, headlong democracy she found only refinement; surrounded by our democratic coarseness and crudeness, she yet made sketches that are patrician in their fastidious beauty. She worked always with emotion, but seldom does she topple over into the sentimental. She prolonged the feminine influence upon American fiction and she prolonged the Washington Irving softness and sentiment that still was keeping one area free from the tumult and the shouting of the "Goths from over the mountains." The best of her stories may be chosen, perhaps, from the eight selections made from all her books and published with the title *Tales of New England:* "Miss Tempy's Watchers," "The Dulham Ladies," "An Only Son," "Marsh Rosemary," "A White Heron," "Law Lane," "A Lost Lover," and "The Courting of Sister Wisby."

BIBLIOGRAPHY

1871. *Oldtown Fireside Stories*, Harriet Beecher Stowe.
    "The Ghost in the Mill"; "The Sullivan Looking-Glass"; "The Minister's Housekeeper"; "The Widow's Bandbox"; "Captain Kidd's Money"; "'Mis' Elderkin's Pitcher"; "The Ghost in the Cap'n Brown House"; "Colonel Eph's Shoe-Buckles"; "The Bull-Fight"; "How to Fight the Devil."

1873. *South Sea Idylls.* Charles Warren Stoddard.

1873. *Saxe Holm's Stories.* First series. Helen Hunt Jackson.
    "Draxy Miller's Dowry," *Scribner's,* May–July, 1872; "The Elder's Wife," *Scribner's,* April–May, 1873; "Whose

Wife Was She?" *Scribner's*, Sept., 1871; "The One-Legged Dancers"; "How One Woman Kept Her Husband," *Scribner's*, Feb., 1872; "Esther Wynn's Love Letters," *Scribner's*, Dec., 1871.

1878. *Saxe Holm's Stories.* Second series. Helen Hunt Jackson.
"Four-Leaved Clover," *Scribner's*, June, July, 1874; "Farmer Bassett's Romance," *Scribner's*, Feb.–May, 1877; "My Tourmaline," *Scribner's*, Nov.–March, 1874–75; "Joe Hale's Red Stocking"; "Susan Lawton's Escape."

CONSTANCE FENIMORE WOOLSON

1875. *Castle Nowhere: Lake-Country Sketches.*
"Castle Nowhere"; "Peter the Parson," *Scribner's*, Sept., 1874; "Jeannette," *Scribner's*, Dec., 1874; "The Old Agency," *Galaxy*, Dec., 1874; "Misery Landing," *Harper's*, May, 1874; "Solomon," *Atlantic*, Oct., 1873; "Wilhelmina," *Atlantic*, Jan., 1875; "St. Clair Flats," *Appleton's*, Oct., 1873; "The Lady of Little Fishing," *Atlantic*, Sept., 1874.

1880. *Rodman the Keeper: Southern Sketches.*
"Rodman the Keeper," *Atlantic*, March, 1877; "Sister St. Luke," *Galaxy*, 23; "Miss Elizabetha," *Appleton's*, 13; "Old Gardiston," *Harper's*, April, 1876; "The South Devil," *Atlantic*, Feb., 1880; "In the Cotton Country," *Appleton's;* "Felipa," *Lippincott's;* "'Bro,'" *Appleton's;* "King David," *Scribner's*, April, 1878; "Up in the Blue Ridge," *Appleton's*, Aug., 1878.

1895. *The Front Yard and Other Italian Stories.*
"The Front Yard," *Harper's*, Dec., 1888; "Neptune's Shore," *Harper's*, Oct., 1888; "A Pink Villa," *Harper's*, Nov., 1888; "The Street of the Hyacinth," *Century*, May, June, 1882; "A Dancing Party"; "In Venice," *Atlantic*, April, 1882.

1896. *Dorothy and Other Italian Sketches.*
"Dorothy," *Harper's*, March, 1892; "A Transplanted Boy," *Harper's*, Feb., 1894; "At the Château of Corinne," *Harper's*, Oct., 1887; "A Florentine Experiment," *Atlantic*, Oct., 1880; "The Waitress."

GEORGE W. CABLE

1879. *Old Creole Days.*
"'Sieur George," *Scribner's*, Oct., 1873; "'Tite Poulette," *Scribner's*, Oct., 1874; "Belles Demoiselles Plantation";

"Jean-Ah Poquelin," *Scribner's*, May, 1875; "Madame Délicieuse," *Scribner's*, Aug., 1875; "Café des Exilés," *Scribner's*, March, 1876; "Posson Jone'," *Appleton's*, 1878; "Madame Delphine" [not in first edition], *Scribner's*.

1888. *Bonaventure.*
"Caranco"; "Grande Pointe"; "Au Large."

1899. *Strong Hearts.*
"The Solitary"; "The Taxidermist," *Scribner's*, **13: 679**; "The Entomologist," *Scribner's*, **25: 50.**

1909. *Posson Jone' and Père Raphael.*
"Posson Jone'," "Père Raphael," *Century*, **1901.**

SARAH ORNE JEWETT

1877. *Deephaven.*
"Kate Lancaster's Plan," *Atlantic*, Sept., 1873; "Brandon House and Lighthouse"; "My Lady Brandon"; "Deephaven Society," *Atlantic*, Sept., 1875; "The Captains"; "Danny"; "Captain Sands"; "Circus at Denby"; "Cunner-Fishing"; "Mrs. Bonny," *Atlantic*, Sept., 1876; "In Shadow"; "Miss Chauncy"; "Last Days at Deephaven."

1878. *Play Days. A Book of Stories for Children.*

1879. *Old Friends and New.*
"A Bit of Shore Life," *Atlantic*, Aug., 1879; "Mr. Bruce," *Atlantic*, Dec., 1869; "A Lost Lover," *Atlantic*, March, 1878; "Miss Sydney's Flowers"; "Lady Ferry"; "Late Supper"; "A Sorrowful Guest."

1881. *Country By-Ways.*
"Andrew's Fortune," *Atlantic*, July, 1881; "Good Luck"; "Miss Becky's Pilgrimage," *Independent*, Sept. 1, 1881; "Driftwood," *Atlantic*, Oct., 1881; "A Winter Drive"; "An October Ride"; "An Autumn Holiday," *Harper's*, Oct., 1880; "From a Mournful Villager," *Atlantic*, Nov., 1881.

1883. *The Mate of the Daylight and Friends Ashore.*
"The Mate of the Daylight," *Atlantic*, July, 1882; "A Landless Farmer," *Atlantic*, May, June, 1883; "A New Parishioner," *Atlantic*, April, 1883; "An Only Son," *Atlantic*, Nov., 1883; "Miss Debby's Neighbors," "Tom's Husband," *Atlantic*, Feb., 1882; "The Confessions of a House-Breaker"; "A Little Traveller."

1886. *A White Heron and Other Stories.*
"A White Heron"; "The Gray Man"; "Farmer Finch," *Harper's*, Jan., 1885; "Marsh Rosemary," *Atlantic*, May,

1886; "The Dulham Ladies," *Atlantic*, April, 1886; "A Business Man"; "Mary and Martha"; "The News From Petersham"; "The Two Browns," *Atlantic*, Aug., 1886.

1888. *The King of Folly Island and Other People.*

"The King of Folly Island," *Harper's*, Dec., 1886; "The Courting of Sister Wisby," *Atlantic*, May, 1887; "The Landscape Chamber," *Atlantic*, Nov., 1887; "Law Lane," *Scribner's*, Dec., 1887; "Miss Peck's Promotion," *Scribner's*, June, 1887; "Miss Tempy's Watchers," *Atlantic*, March, 1888; "A Village Shop"; "Mère Pochette, *Harper's*, March, 1888.

1890. *Strangers and Wayfarers.*

"A Winter Courtship," *Atlantic*, Feb., 1889; "The Mistress of Sydenham Plantation," *Atlantic*, Aug., 1888; "The Town Poor," *Atlantic*, July, 1890; "The Quest of Mr. Teaby," *Atlantic*, Jan., 1890; "The Luck of the Bogans," *Scribner's*, Jan., 1889; "Fair Day," *Scribner's*, Aug., 1888; "Going to Shrewsbury," *Atlantic*, July, 1889; "The Taking of Captain Ball," *Harper's*, Dec., 1889; "By the Morning Boat," *Atlantic*, Oct., 1890; "In Dark New England Days," *Century*, 1890; "The White Rose Road," *Atlantic*, Sept., 1889.

1893. *A Native of Winby and Other Tales.*

"A Native of Winby," *Atlantic*, May, 1891; "Decoration Day," *Harper's*, June, 1892; "Jim's Little Woman," *Harper's*, Dec., 1890; "The Failure of David Berry," *Harper's*, June, 1891; "The Passing of Sister Barsett," *Cosmopolitan*, May, 1892; "Miss Esther's Guest"; "The Flight of Betsy Lane," *Scribner's*, Aug., 1893; "Between Mass and Vespers," *Scribner's*, May, 1893; "A Little Captive Maid," *Scribner's*, Dec., 1891.

1895. *The Life of Nancy.*

"The Life of Nancy," *Atlantic*, Feb., 1895; "The Guests of Mrs. Timms," *Century*, Feb., 1894; "Fame's Little Day," *Harper's*, March, 1895; "Hilton's Holiday," *Century*, Sept., 1893; "All My Sad Captains," *Century*, Sept., 1895; "The Neighbor's Landmark," *Century*, Dec., 1894; "A Second Spring," *Harper's*, Dec., 1893; "A War Debt," *Harper's*, Jan., 1895; "Little French Mary"; "Only Rose," *Atlantic*, Jan., 1894.

1896. *The Country of the Pointed Firs.*

"The Return"; "Mrs. Todd"; "The Schoolhouse"; "At the Schoolhouse Window"; "Captain Littlepage"; "The Waiting Place"; "The Outer Island"; "Green Island";

"William"; "Where Pennyroyal Grew"; "The Old Singers"; "A Strange Sail"; "Poor Joanna"; "The Hermitage"; "On Shell-Heap Island"; "The Great Expedition"; "A Country Road"; "The Bowden Reunion"; "The Feast's End"; "Along Shore"; "The Backward View."

1899. *The Queen's Twin and Other Stories.*
"The Queen's Twin," *Atlantic*, Feb., 1899; "A Dunnett Shepherdess," *Atlantic*, Dec., 1899; "Where's Nora?" *Scribner's*, Dec., 1898; "Bold Words at the Bridge," *Mc-Clure's*, April, 1899; "Martha's Lady," *Atlantic*, Oct., 1897; "The Coon Dog," *Century*, Aug., 1898; "The Night Before Thanksgiving."

CHAPTER XII

I

The 'eighties in the history of the American short story were ruled by the "local colorists." It was the period of dialect stories, of small peculiar groups isolated and analyzed, of unique local "characters" presented primarily for exhibition. The short-story writer now thought first of materials, often only of materials. Reviewers now spoke much of "realism," a comparatively new term in American criticism. After Howells had reviewed James in the *Century Magazine* (1882), the words "romanticism" and "realism" became shibboleths of opposing camps, with realism in the lead. Maurice Thompson, himself a romanticist, wrote, in October, 1884, "No matter how much the theorists differ at other points, they all agree that towards realism is the strongest trend of to-day's fiction literature." "Realism" in the 'eighties meant selected bits of nature pictorially presented, native stuff unidealized, ordinary folks—never extraordinarily ideal or extraordinarily repulsive—in the ordinary sequences of life; no elaborate plots, no heroes, no heroines, no inflated diction. The age was turning more and more to the concrete and the practical. As a result of the enormous activities and the material expansion that had followed the war, pragmatism was beginning to displace the old idealism. But the reading masses were conservative; the generality of them clung to the romantic; the two forces were in conflict. Even Howells was not strictly a realist in the 'seventies and early 'eighties; he chose with fastidious care the social areas he depicted; there was much in the world about him that he never permitted himself to see at all. So with James, so with Miss Woolson, so with Miss Jewett: they sentimentalized life, they looked only for the good in humanity and idealized it. It was a compromise: it satisfied fully neither side. Then had come the discovery that it was possible to produce all the effects of realism, to appear to be working scientifically in the actual ma-

268

terials of common life, and yet to be as romantic in fundamentals
and effects as the most deliberate of romanticists. There were
unexplored social areas in America where the bare truth was
stranger than any romance. After the success of Harte and Eggleston and Cable, great numbers of writers turned from the old
worked-out claims of fiction to prospect in new and startling
environments. Studies of local uniqueness began increasingly to
appear in the magazines. Following the vogue of *The Hoosier
Schoolmaster*, dialect began to run to extremes. The *Century
Magazine* received Page's story, "Marse Chan," written entirely
in the negro dialect, as early as 1880, but it was not until 1884
that they had the courage to publish it. The appearance of this
instantly acclaimed dialect piece and the publication the same
year of Charles Egbert Craddock's *In the Tennessee Mountains*
stands as the high-water mark of the local color flood. Its sub-
sidence began in the later 'eighties.

The new fad at one time or another seems to have affected
every writer of the period. Even a romanticist as radical as the
young Maurice Thompson, of Indiana, fell for a moment under the
dialect spell. His *Hoosier Mosaics* (1875) on the surface is crudely,
even baldly, realistic. Its dialect is as uncouth and its characters
are as radically Pikes as anything in Eggleston's Hoosier fiction.
The story, "Trout's Luck," for instance, presents in photographic
detail the side-show life of a rural Indiana fair. It is convincing.
Jack, the farmer boy, loses to the first "faker" he meets the
circus money he had been accumulating for months, then spends
the day in the agony of seeing his girl taken into show after show
by his more lucky rival. No happy ending to this grim tragedy
in parvo. This is the last sentence of it: "Jack slipped to his
room and went supperless to bed, often during the night muttering,
through the interstices of his sleep—'Bill's got me.'" It is a
story of a bumpkin abysmally far from being a hero; it is relieved
by no golden atmosphere; it presents no final triumph of the good
and the deserving. It is a bit of unrelieved realism, gripping,
depressing, yet done with materials so fresh and picturesque that
even *The Lamplighter* reader might not turn from it.

Thompson undoubtedly had been influenced by Harte and
Eggleston; not so Philander Deming, graduate of the University
of Vermont, and court reporter at Albany, New York, who as
early as 1873 began to contribute to the *Atlantic* austere little

tales of farm life in the isolated valleys of the Adirondacks. Here was a realist who used no subterfuges, a primitive realist untouched by forbears, a writer, like the author of "Life in the Iron Mills," made realist by the poverty and the grimness of his materials. One may compare him with no one save Mary E. Wilkins, who a decade later modeled her Millet-like figures from the same clay. The style of both was puritanic, repressed, parsimonious—stripped of all ornament; in both the asthmatically short sentence, the almost total abandonment of the connective:

They had a local insurance company in town. They had seen enough of large companies; the mutual affair at home was better. Jacob's policy was in the home company. As soon as Jacob told his story, Silas said it was all right. The committee came the next day. They awarded Jacob a hundred dollars. It was satisfactory.

Even his name he signed "P. Deming," and his titles he reduced to "Lost," "Lida Ann," "Rube Jones," "Willie," "Joe Baldwin," "Benjamin Jacques,"—one thinks of *The Spoon River Anthology*. The stories, he said, were not fiction: they were actual happenings without addition or coloring, and the reader is inclined to believe it. They deal with the grimness and the sordidness of country life; they are realism uncolored, unselective, shrinking from no gruesome detail: little Willie killed in the pasture by a vicious ram and his mangled body found by children at play; Ike's wife whipping an incorrigible child, then, charged with brutality by the neighbors and brooding over it in Mary E. Wilkins manner till she hangs herself to the kitchen door; the baby running away into the woods and perishing while the whole countryside searched, then the sinister whisper that the father has murdered the child; Jacob accused of burning his buildings for the insurance and becoming a social pariah, though totally innocent. They take one by the throat as life takes one by the throat. This, indeed, is country life stripped of all its idealism: sordid, suspicious, narrow, peasant-like—it is a prophecy of the work of Hamlin Garland in the next decade. They are sketches rather than short stories, artless and unstudied, and yet a sketch like "Mr. Toby's Wedding Journey" has a real surprise ending that must have been carefully planned, and another, "Tompkins," closes grippingly, as a short story should, with an end that for the reader is a beginning. Philander Deming must be counted as a pioneer force in the gathering realistic movement of the 'seventies and early 'eighties; when the flood came of richer and more picturesque material from the South and the West he was forgotten, and to-day he is almost totally unread.

II

The final avalanche of dialect which came with the 'eighties was precipitated by a curious bit of uncontracted-for advertising. In 1878 a story had come in to *The Atlantic* from the Southwest over the unheard-of name of "Charles Egbert Craddock." There was dialect in the very title, "The Dancin' Party at Harrison's Cove," and large parts of it were told in an argot, a leisurely tedium of barbarous wordiness, strange to Northern readers.

Ef he don't want a bullet in that pumpkin head o' his'n he hed better keep away from that dancin' party what the Harrisons hev laid off ter give, 'kase Rick say he's a-goin' ter it hisself, an' is a-goin' ter dance too; he ain't been invited, Mis' Darley, but Rick don't keer fur that. He is a-goin' ennyhow, an' he say ez how he ain't a-goin' ter let Kossute come, 'count o' Kossute's sass an' the fuss they've all made 'bout that bay filly that war stole five year ago,—'t war five year an' better. But Rick say ez how he is agoin', fur all he ain't got no invite, an' is a-goin' ter dance too, 'kase you know, Mis' Darley, it's a-goin' ter be a dancin' party; the Harrisons hev determinated on that. Them gals of theirn air mos' crazed 'bout a dancin' party. They ain't been a bit of account sence they went ter Cheatham's Cross-Roads ter see thar gran'mother, an' picked up all them queer new notions. So the Harrisons hev determinated on a dancin' party; an' Rick say ez how he is goin' ter dance too; but Jule *she* say ez how she know thar ain't a gal on the mounting ez would dance with him; but I ain't so sure 'bout that, Mis' Darley; gals air cur'ous critters, ye know yerself; thar's no sort o' countin' on 'em; they'll do one thing one time, an' another thing nex' time; ye can't put no dependence in 'em.

The sketch manifestly had been accepted on account of its unusual materials and the wild new atmosphere which enveloped it. Of plot there was practically none: the inevitable fight between Rick and Kossute, prevented forcibly by a man-handling old circuit preacher who had been Rick's regimental chaplain during the war—that was all: the rest was local color of a rather startling variety. Other sketches followed at long intervals; the public responded as slowly as a few years earlier they had responded to

Cable's southern sketches. After six years, eight of them had accumulated, enough for a small volume. *In the Tennessee Mountains* was the title decided upon, and in the spring of 1884 the author went to Boston to make final arrangements. Then had come the climax: to the amazement of T. B. Aldrich, the *Atlantic* editor, and of Oliver Wendell Holmes, who happened to be in the office, Charles Egbert Craddock proved to be a woman— Miss Mary Noailles Murfree, of the historic family that had given its name to Murfreesboro', Tennessee. The story of this dramatic moment, spread broadcast over America, advertised the new book tremendously. Perhaps no collection of American short stories, save only the *Sketch Book* and *The Luck of Roaring Camp*, was ever launched with more of impetus or was awaited by the reading public with more of curiosity. Its success precipitated a veritable downpour of local-color fiction.

Miss Murfree's rank as a writer of short stories must be determined almost solely by this single volume. She followed her success with a series of Tennessee Mountain novels, and it is as a novelist rather than a short-story writer that she must finally be judged. Short lengths of fiction were imperative for her during the uncertain days when she was acquiring a market: most of the young writers of the period were forced to try the currents with skiffs before launching the five-decked galleons of their dreams; later, when her popularity had declined and she was no longer sure of a market, she again was forced to use the smaller unit. Strictly speaking, her short stories are not short stories at all save in the one element of shortness. She records simple, everyday incidents in their natural sequence and stops when the space allotted to her has been filled. She moves leisurely from incident to incident in the monotonous vacuity of mountain life, as a minutely written journal might move.

In all of her fiction, materials come first. Her titles are usually expressed in terms of landscape: "T'other Mounting," "Lonesome Cove," "Sunrise Rock," "Chilhowee," "Harrison's Cove," "Witch-Face Mountain"—the setting first and then the action. On the cover of her first edition was the impressionistic design of a ragged landscape with an eagle hovering above it in mid-foreground. Everywhere the strikingly novel: barbarous locutions, strange fashions of dress, manners, traditions: wild mountain passes and coves and ravines, savage and forbidding—everywhere the unique. The reader is in charge of a competent guide who calls attention constantly to local peculiarities and is voluble with his explanations. Manner—art, plot—is secondary. She begins with landscape, a landscape always in some vague extreme of beauty, or vastness, or wildness: she introduces characters to match, sometimes whole neighborhood clans, each individual minutely described—impressionistically—in terms of his uniqueness; and then rambles on and on until the reader loses himself in an atmosphere that at last is like nothing he has ever known before. She has created a new world and it all seems curiously real at first, and yet a second reading in cold blood is very apt to reveal an artificiality that is repellent. It is a trick of style we feel, not an actuality, that has captured us.

It was this impressionistic manner of presenting materials, this wild mountain haze over all things, this new conception of landscape, that made Charles Egbert Craddock so important a figure in the fiction of the 'eighties in America. Part of it undoubtedly was her own personality, but part of it was Thomas Hardy, whose *Return of the Native* was contemporary with her first tales in *The Atlantic*. In both writers the landscape is used symbolically, impressionistically; it becomes in reality the leading character in the tale, the ruling motif in the plot. Cynthia Ware is but the human counterpart of Lost Creek. The grim mountain range held her in its grip just as Egdon Heath held Eustacia Vye and Wildeve till they died. "Whether the skies are blue or gray, the dark, austere line of its summit limits the horizon. It stands against the west like a barrier. It seemed to Cynthia Ware that nothing which went beyond this barrier ever came back again." And at the close of the tale, her hopes of escape forever blasted, "it seems to her that the years of her life are like the floating leaves drifting down Lost Creek, valueless and purposeless and vaguely vanishing in the mountain."

Her minute pictures of mountain life, for all their minuteness, cannot be classed as realistic. She was not a mountaineer herself; she studied the region not sympathetically, but curiously, as a summer visitor who went about with a notebook. She heightened all her pictures. Her mountains are hills, but she makes them tower into the very skies. In the words of an early reviewer, "they are purpler, bluer, and yellower than any other mountains; they are at times more remote and forbidding, at times more close and tender, than the peaks and summits of other ranges; their moon is distinctly superior, and, unlike other moons, constant. Their inhabitants bear little resemblance to the natives of other altitudes and gorges." She is a colorist splashing with broad strokes: she dashes all her pages with a profusion of lurid adjectives—her imagination runs riot amid her materials. Her genius is epic rather than dramatic or lyric: she works at her best with the sweep of great mountain vistas and elemental men and elemental passions. "Behind the crowd was the immensity of the unpeopled forests; below, the mad fret of the cataract; above, the vast hemisphere of the lonely skies; and far, far away was the infinite, stretching o'er those blue ranges that the Indians called the Endless"—this is her setting. She is wholly masculine in her treatment of the sentimental and the feminine. She is almost without humor—as austere, indeed, and as cold as her mountain ranges and her lonesome coves. She is at her best when describing desolation, *genre* pictures with impressionistic detail.

One is never moved by the tales of Charles Egbert Craddock except perhaps intellectually. One may exclaim, *This is vivid*, or, *This is well-nigh poetry*, or, *This is Johnsonian English, rare at this late day*, but there is no other emotion. We feel that she is self-conscious, that she is adding ornament to ornament with deliberation, that she is exhibiting rather than sharing. A style that alludes to cows as "bovine vagrants," that describes a scene in terms of "interfulgent sunbeams," that, instead of "dancers," has "sinful votaries of Terpsichore," that can begin a paragraph with, "There was a prolonged silence in the matutinal freshness," or, again, with "The hairy animal, whose jeans suit proclaimed him man, propounded this inquiry with a triumphant air. There was a sarcastic curve on the lips of his interlocutor"—a style that is everywhere like this can hardly carry conviction. At a dramatic moment in the action she pauses for a page, two pages, to paint a picture.

The sudden flight of a bird cleft the rainbow; there was a flash of moisture on his swift wings, and he left his wild sweet cry echoing far behind him. Beetling high above the stream, the crags seemed to touch the sky. One glance up and up these towering, majestic steeps—how it lifted the soul! The Settlement, perched upon the apparently inaccessible heights, was not visible from the road below. It cowered back affrighted from the verge of the great cliff and the grimly yawning abysses.

And so on and on. A touch of this now and then may be used
with Shakespearean effect to relieve the emotional tension or to
show how nature harmonized with the mood of the moment or
was in contrast with it, but after page after page of such material,
inserted at every possible point, we feel that with her the picture
was first and the drama incidental. It is artificial: it does not
move us.

Unquestionably her work is not of short-story texture. It may
be even used, brilliant as it is at times in its impressionism, as a
warning and as an example of fundamental rules ignored and
broken. Even had she been more perfect in her technique, from
the very nature of her material, she was headed toward ultimate
failure. Her material was even more attenuated than Harte's.
The California mines *did* afford a variety of characters drawn from
the whole of the civilized and the uncivilized world, but the
Tennessee Mountains had only one variety, and their social
system was austerely uncomplex. A half dozen sketches she
might make, a half dozen motifs for fiction there might have been:
the primitive murder for revenge or jealousy, the outlaw adventurer and his deeds, the drama of the moonshine still raided by
revenue officers, the shooting of strangers who had wandered for
various reasons into the mountains—there could be little variety.
It was not long after her first book that reviewers were charging
her with "plowing ground which already she had plowed to
barrenness." She lived to see herself forgotten save by a few of
her early readers, and her books unable to command for any
length of time a uniform publisher. Yet in the history of American
fiction she is still notable. At a single moment in the drama she
was the central figure, and she created a profound impression.
Her influence upon the rising young school that was to rule the
'nineties cannot be overlooked by one who would write the history
of the closing years of the century.

III

The dominance of fashion is not confined to matters of dress:
it affects everything of a period, even its literature. Thomas
Wentworth Higginson in 1887, writing of "the recent swing of the
pendulum in favor of what is called realism in fiction," could
declare that "it is very possible that if Hawthorne's *Twice-Told*

Tales were to appear for the first time to-morrow they would attract no more attention than they did fifty years ago." Every generation has its own ideals. Most undoubtedly the local-color fad of the 'eighties made fashionable more than one writer who otherwise never would have been known at all. Richard Malcolm Johnston, of Georgia, was nearly sixty when the North discovered that he was a writer and started him on a voluminous career. He had published in Georgia, in 1864, *Georgia Sketches by an Old Man*, and in 1871 and 1874 had reissued enriched editions of it in Baltimore over the title *Dukesborough Tales* by Philemon Perch. The book had fallen unnoticed, but a decade later the Harpers discovered it and issued it with loud trumpetings, and in 1892 the Appletons issued it still again in sumptuous form. Johnston, neglected all his life till now, found himself at sixty in step with the new generation, and in fifteen years produced no less than twelve volumes, the most of them collections of sketches that had made their first appearance in the magazines.

His decline has been as sudden as his rise, and yet in one respect he is a notable figure in the history of the short-story form: *Dukesborough Tales* in its various editions shows the evolution of the American *genre* sketch from the primitive Longstreet model, coarse and brutal, which so greatly influenced the 1864 first edition, through the Baltimore period with the softening and artistic influence of Sydney Lanier, to the final Appleton edition, of the early 'nineties, reduced to six sketches carefully subdued and finished.

From any other standpoint, however, his work may be passed over quickly. Even at his best he can hardly be classed as a short-story writer, certainly not if the definition is to be in terms of the French *conte*. He may be taken as the type-representative of a large group of writers which filled the magazines of a decade—local colorists like John Habberton, whose sketches issued separately in 1877 with such titles as "The Brandon Experiment," "The Scripture Club of Valley Rest," "The Jericho Road," drew from E. L. Burlingame a contemporary estimate that, with small change, might be applied to them all: "They deal with the hard, prosaic, and angular life of villages on the Western lakes and rivers; life that has grown up on moral and social lines as rigid and ungraceful as 'fever an' ager' ever made the gaunt contours of those who have ft. . . . We are almost sorry to see them clothed in the dignity of volumes, instead of passing their ephemeral lives between the covers of the magazines." One may single from the group such representative figures as Sarah Pratt Greene, who followed her *Cape Cod Folks* with much broadly splashed sketch work; and Harry Stillwell Edwards with his humorous Georgia sketches, like "Elder Brown's Backslide"; and Rowland E. Robinson, of Vermont, whose work, as he explained in *Danvis Folks*, was written "with less purpose of telling any story than of recording the manners, customs, and speech in vogue fifty or sixty years ago in certain parts of New England." The name of this group is legion; it is needless to present even a check-list. Some of them worked as exhibitors, some as humorists, some tried to reproduce with loving minuteness characters and localities that had become a part of their own lives. "Sketches, which I have ventured to call tales," is Johnston's characterization of his own work, and it characterizes all of it. *Dukesborough Tales* is dedicated "To memories of the old times: the grim and rude, but hearty old times in Georgia." The work of all may be classified as rambling talks about folks and places and manners, with little thought of manner —sketches that meander on and on like one of Sam Lawson's fireside tales and stop only when the narrator has exhausted his material.

IV

Far more significant was the work of another Georgia storyteller, Joel Chandler Harris, who also served as a link between his own day and the Longstreet beginnings, and who also told with sympathy and fidelity of the homely life from which he sprang. He was thirteen, a diffident, almost totally uncultured country lad, when the accident happened that turned him to literature. This is his own version:

> It so happened that I was in the post office at Eatonton reading the Milledgeville papers, when the first number of the "Countryman" was deposited on the counter where all the papers were kept. I read it through, and came upon an advertisement which announced that the editor wanted a boy to learn the printer's trade. This was my opportunity, and I seized it with both hands.

He applied for the position and was accepted promptly because of the quality of his letter. The editor was J. A. Turner, of Turnwold plantation, nine miles away, "a miscellaneous genius," who, in addition to the management of a large farming establishment with one hundred and twenty slaves, found time for other exacting activities, among them the editing of a newspaper, the only one ever published on a plantation. He was a scholar, a discriminating reader with a library of four thousand volumes, a finished writer of Johnsonian English, and an orator who had made himself heard even in the state legislature. Under his direction the boy found training that was better than school or college. The isolated plantation was a little world, patriarchal in its régime, where were to be observed the workings of negro slavery under its best conditions. The primitive little printing office where he learned to set type and work with a press, and where early his ambition to write and to publish was gratified, the helpful criticism from the exacting Johnsonian who passed upon his articles and directed him to carefully selected models, the wholesome family life with the negroes always a contributing part, all of this was an education that later in his literary life was to furnish him not only with materials, but the ability to handle those materials effectively.

His career at Turnwold ended as abruptly as it had begun: the plantation lay in the path of Sherman's army. The youngster still in his 'teens found himself adrift, a journeyman printer now seeking employment. Until he was twenty-two he was a workman in many offices, but by 1870 he had risen until he was able to command the position of assistant editor and humorous columnist of the *Savannah Morning News*, the editor of which was no less a personage than Colonel W. T. Thompson, author of the early Georgian classic, *Major Jones's Courtship*. The partnership of the two men during the six years that followed—the veteran depicter of Georgia scenes and the young columnist who was soon to be quoted all over Georgia, as a witty paragraphist, cannot be overlooked. When in 1876 Harris was transferred to the *Atlanta Constitution* staff, he went with a reputation as a humorist, a brilliant editorial writer, and a general utility man who could contribute with distinction to any department of any paper.

For the next thirty years he gave the major part of his activities to the *Atlanta Constitution*. From whatever angle one approaches him one must remember that first of all he was a journalist. Cable and Craddock and Johnston and Page turned to literature deliberately; they wrote with literary intent, but Harris when fame

came to him was simply about his ordinary tasks as a staff worker
upon a city daily. It was a long time before he could realize that
he had produced anything that could be called literature: he had
only been grinding out copy to fill the insatiable maw of the press.

The story of the beginnings of the Uncle Remus papers has been
variously told. A study of the files of the *Constitution*, however,
reveals these facts, that on the 6th of July, 1879, there was printed
a short negro sketch entitled "Uncle Remus and the Fourth."
Six weeks later appeared a brief paragraph entitled "Uncle
Remus Makes a Confession," and two weeks later still, "Uncle
Remus. The Old Man and His Deceitful Jug. An Aged Piece of
Earthenware. Brer John Henry's Mistake. Why the Negroes
Will Refuse to Emigrate." In mid-October came "Christmas
Play-Song. As Sung by Uncle Remus. (Myrick Place, Putnam
County, 1858)" and on November 16th, "Brer Rabbit, Brer Fox,
and the Tar Baby." This last seems to have struck fire. It was
followed weekly by an Uncle Remus column, the papers numbered
in a series, the series ending May 16th, with "How the Rabbit
Lost His Fine Bushy Tail." The sketches manifestly had been
started merely as a humorous venture to fill the lighter columns
of the journal and to be varied with other material, and they had
suddenly come to life in the hands of their creator. The New York
Evening Post and the Springfield *Republican*, sensitive to novel
literary tangs and fresh American *genre* effects, quickly discovered
the new *Constitution* folk tales and gave them wide publicity in
their columns. The reaction in the North was electric in its suddenness. The Uncle Remus book which appeared in December, even
before its ink was fairly dry, was hailed everywhere as a classic.
In later years, when the tales had everywhere been accepted
as real classics, Harris in an article for *Lippincott's*, entitled
"An Accidental Author," added new details as to their origin:

The "Countryman" was published on a plantation, and it was on this
and neighboring plantations that I became familiar with the curious
myths and animal stories that form the basis of the volumes accredited
to "Uncle Remus." I absorbed the stories, songs and myths that I
heard, but had no idea of their literary value until, some time in the 'seventies, Lippincott's magazine published an article on the subject of negro
folklore, containing some rough outlines of some of the stories. This
article gave me my cue, and the legends told by "Uncle Remus" are the
result.

The strength of these narratives lies first of all in their genuineness. "Not one of them," he wrote the London *Folk-Lore Journal,* "is cooked, and not one, nor any part of one, is an invention of mine. They are all genuine folklore tales." He was not making literature *about* the negro; he was making the negro alive for his reader as he himself had known him on the old plantation. He worked not from books, but from life: no writer of the period, not even Deming, was less affected by the work of others. His negro was a new creation in literature. It had been conventional, for instance, from the earliest days of negro minstrelsy to associate the darky with the banjo and the bones, but there are no banjos and no bones in Harris's tales.

I have seen the negro at work and I have seen him at play; I have attended his corn shucking, his dances and his frolics; I have heard him give the wonderful melody of his songs to the winds; I have heard him fit barbaric airs to the quills; I have seen him scrape jubilantly on the fiddle; I have seen him blow wildly upon the bugle, and beat enthusiastically on the triangle; but I have never heard him play on the banjo.

This is the key to all he did. He was unconventional; he was writing only of what he knew, of what he had himself actually seen and felt.

He was inclined to believe that it was the freshness and the strangeness of his materials that had given him his sudden vogue. To Mark Twain he wrote in 1881, in the first wonder days of the original Uncle Remus book: "I am perfectly well aware that my book has no basis of literary art to stand upon; I know it is the matter and not the manner that has attracted public attention and won the consideration of people of taste in the North," and in reply Mark Twain had gone completely to the other extreme! "The stories are only alligator pears—one eats them merely for the sake of the dressing. 'Uncle Remus' is most deftly drawn." The truth lies midway. Undoubtedly Harris wrote all of his work without thought of literary art. "'Art,' 'unity,' 'harmony' and all the other literary catchwords were bugaboos to him," wrote his biographer. "He had an amusing, and perhaps morbid, horror of waxing pedantic and getting away from simple things and plain ways." Yet unconsciously, as Twain had perceived, he was genuinely an artist, and it was his art which gave his work much of its power. After his first book he began to explore the region for folklore themes. To one of his friends he wrote: "All I want is a reasonably intelligent outline of the stories as the negroes tell them." He could himself add the distinctive Uncle Remus style and atmosphere—he could supply the art. It was a spontaneous thing: an impassioned recording from memory and imagination. Uncle Remus and the rest to him, indeed, were not mere characters in a story: they were individuals actually alive before him. To Mr. Burlingame he wrote, while creating the *Chronicles of Aunt Minervy Ann:* "I have been intensely absorbed in the series. . . . There have been moments when I could hear her voice as plainly as I now hear the youngsters talking in the sitting room." Uncle Remus is one of the most vital creations in modern literature. The sly, unobtrusive humor of the old man, the little touches almost imperceptible that accumulate until the little boy to whom the stories are told stands alive before the reader, the whole social régime of the plantation that unobtrusively he unfolds and makes grippingly real, the uniform atmosphere enveloping the whole work, each tale and all the tales, until one awakes at last to the world of the real with a bit of a start, the steady progress of the narrative to the quaint and inevitable climax —never a studied and conscious dénouement, but a mere following of nature, a mere recording of the negro's innate dramatic instinct, his love of startling climax craftily led up to—all this is art and art in its subtlest forms. His object, as he wrote to Gilder in 1886, was not literary; it was an attempt to "invest his characters with a certain nobility of purpose, a certain pathos, that shall relate them to human nature, or to a series of incidents that belong to human nature." And by an artlessness that is the soul of art, and that eludes analysis, he accomplished his purpose with animals rather than men as characters. Harris's "Brer Rabbit," as often has been observed, is the negro himself: he acts, he talks, he thinks like a negro, and in A. B. Frost's illustrations he *is* a negro, though at the same time he is unmistakably a rabbit. Harris himself has written the best commentary on the subject:

It needs no scientific investigation to show why he (the negro) selects as his hero the weakest and most harmless of all animals and brings him out victorious in contests with the bear, the wolf and the fox. It is not *virtue* that triumphs, but *helplessness;* it is not *malice*, but *mischievousness.* Indeed, the parallel between the "weakest" of all animals who must, perforce, triumph through his shrewdness, and the humble condition of the slave raconteur, is not without its pathos and poetry.

The Uncle Remus tales are not fables or anecdotes; they are short stories: there is more to them than the mere narrative. The action with its simple animal actors moves to its culmination, but it leaves with the reader more than rabbits and foxes and bears: it leaves the vast shadow of a race in slavery, of a great social system destroyed and looming romantic as it disappears; it leaves a single pathetic figure that must be added to the small gallery of creations which contains "My Uncle Toby" and "Parson Andrews," and the "Vicar of Wakefield." The genius of Harris was poetic; he worked only in the golden light of his subject. His was the same type of genius that created the old ballads: the Uncle Remus Tales in places remind one strongly of this primitive minstrelsy. And it may be remarked in passing that the modern short story follows more of the canons of the ballad art than any other form. His temperament, his journalistic training, his methods of composition—usually in hours stolen from the exacting round of his profession—unfitted him for any literary form save the short, the intense, the episodic. His novels were failures— at least as novels. He was at his best only with short units of humble life treated with feeling.

After his earliest Uncle Remus collections Harris turned to the Longstreet area of Georgia life and began to make broad sketches of the mountain crackers. Using the same materials that Charles Egbert Craddock had discovered on the westward slopes of the same Appalachian ridges, he made a series of pictures that is greatly different from the epic canvases of his contemporary worker. Like her, he wrought with seriousness, and like her, and Hardy before her, he believed that with humble materials he could get at the soul of the life of his time; that even with Georgia crackers he could study the meanings of all America.

No matter what phase of American life the novelist may choose to depict, he cannot fail to reproduce the true American type if he but faithfully portray the human nature that underlies all types of life; the human nature (to take an instance at random) that makes Mrs. Poyser as common to Georgia as to New England, to Maine as to Kansas.

While such sketches as "At Teague Poteet's," "Free Joe," and "Trouble on Lost Mountain" are not strictly realistic—they are chosen instances softened and idealized—they are as near to realism as the South has ever got. To quote Thomas Nelson Page, who speaks with authority, literary work in the South has never been based on any purely literary standard. It has rather been "based on public opinion, which in its turn was founded on the general consensus that the existing institution was not to be impugned, directly or indirectly, on any grounds or by any means whatsoever." Longstreet in later years made strenuous efforts to suppress his "Georgia Scenes" because in his youth he had been over realistic. New Orleans criticized with bitterness George W. Cable because he was inclined to tell harsh truths, and one might cite other instances. The fiction from the South has been almost uniformly romantic: the dialect dress of much of it has been only a seeming yielding to the demand for reality.

Harris in his tales of mountain life, then, surpassed Craddock first of all in genuineness. Craddock was a craftsman who was able to create a world of her own, marvelous in its beauty and its seeming verisimilitude; Harris worked with emotion in the materials from which he had sprung. One reads Craddock for her atmosphere, her epic sweep, her strangeness of setting; one reads Harris as one reads *Scenes from Clerical Life,* for his truth to life, his pathos, his human touch. One closes "The Mystery of Witchface Mountain" with an impression of mountains, weird and wild, and among them picturesque men with uncouth dialect; one closes "Trouble on Lost Mountain" with a single picture seared into one's soul of the Lear-like old father, his murdered daughter in his arms, sobbing in an agony that overtopples at last his very reason, "Why, gentermen, how *kin* she be dead?" The one is art; the other is more than art: it is life.

V

By the close of the decade the South seemed to be dominating not only the short story, but the novel. The New York *Nation* in 1888 spoke of the sudden appearance "within half a dozen years of a host of Southern writers" as one of the most interesting phenomena in the history of American fiction.

They have not worked slowly upward from the rank and file, but have rushed to the front and won the prize of public favor almost without a struggle. Uncritical readers have devoured everything descriptive of distinctly Southern scenes, life and character, and professed critics seem to have agreed to declare each newborn Southern story-teller to be the greatest living master of his art.

The *Nation* was inclined to see in the movement a rebuke to realism. The critics, it believed, "were getting tired of abetting the Northern realists in their efforts to show how, in fiction at least, something can be made out of nothing." This, however, was not the root of the matter. The South took the lead because it had the materials, and the writers who understood those materials, and it made full use of its opportunity. To Henry James the leading canon of the art of fiction was "the cure of souls, the subjection and, if need be, the exclusion of the picturesque," but with the Southern writers the picturesque element overshaded all else. They had a strange new world to exhibit that was as romantic as anything created by Scott: an *ancien régime* in the new world with a system of slavery, with vast landed estates and a society almost feudal to match—an aristocracy, exclusive, proud as any in older lands—and all this suddenly destroyed, blotted out utterly and forever as by a convulsion of nature. It was the very substance of romance, and yet it was so near at hand that it might be treated seemingly with all the methods of realism: dialect, local color lavish and dominating, humble characters, even former slaves given the speaking rôles.

The literary voice of this Southern aristocracy was Thomas Nelson Page, a Virginian of the old stock, an inheritor of all the proud traditions of his class. He was eight when the war broke upon the South, old enough to have seen and felt something of the old régime; he was thirteen when it closed, young enough to be able to adapt himself without bitterness to the new order. The war had ruined the family fortunes; it was necessary for him to turn to a profession for support, and he chose the law, fitting himself for it first at Washington and Lee University, where he remained for three sessions, and then in the legal department of the University of Virginia. His professional career at Richmond and Washington and his ambassadorship to Italy during the German war we need not follow. With him literature has been, as with Harris and as with so many other American writers, the avocation of a man exceedingly busy with an engrossing profession.

Page began his literary career, like Harte and Cable and Craddock and Harris and others, by striking twelve with his first

creations. The short stories, "Marse Chan," "Unc' Edinburg's
Drowndin'," "Meh Lady," and "Polly"—written painstakingly
and feelingly during the leisure periods of his early legal practice,
he never equaled in later years. The sweeping success of this early
work hastened him into voluminous production: stories, novels,
essays, biographies, juveniles, histories. Like the rest of his
school, he mistook the voice of his decade for the voice of permanence and poured out in profusion what the decade desired.
He was too much dominated by his materials. His novels became
treatises, source books, defenses of the Southern position, picture
books; his later short stories, like those, for instance, in *Pastime
Stories*, became collections of anecdotes and episodes of the old
régime.

One need linger only with the collection *In Ole Virginia*, which
first appeared in 1887. *Bred in the Bone*, the name of one of his
later books, might have been used as its secondary title and indeed
as the secondary title of nearly every tale he ever wrote. "All
the stories," he explains in the preface of the book bearing the
name, "are founded on traits of character which have appeared
to the author to be bred in the bone." These lines from the lips
of the old slave in his poem, "Marse Phil," might serve as the text
for all he wrote:

> Blood is jes like pra'r is, hit tain' gwine nuver fail—
> Hit's sutney gwine to come out soon or late.

Always he deals with thoroughbreds. His typical hero is tall and
distinctive of bearing, the scion of a proud old race, rushing into
duels to defend his honor, utterly fearless, punctilious to the bounds
of absurdity, at every point, chivalric, cavalier in manners and
ideals, in love to madness with a maiden equally as thoroughbred
and equally as proud, plunging into the war like a crusader to the
Holy Sepulcher, and at last brought home from battle dead, the
tragedy of his passing blighting every life it touches. With only
these tales for evidence, one might gather that the Southern
chivalry to the last man perished in the war and that the South
to-day is but a land of memories. The stories are all emotional,
though not effusively so; they are at every point romantic; they
are wrought of materials selected with fastidious care and softly
idealized. That there could have been anything that was not
holy or altogether lovely about the civilization that centered in

slavery one gathers not a hint from the fiction of Thomas Nelson Page. Whatever of harshness there was in the old life came from elements brought in from without—from the North, whose unholy hands destroyed the only aristocracy America has ever achieved.

In one respect the tales stand unique among American short stories: their point of view. They are told in their entirety by the negro survivors of the tragedy; they are told in dialect from end to end; their perspective is the perspective of a former slave who tells in his own simple way of what he saw of the perished era. It is as if a traveler in the desert had come upon a wretched descendant of the slaves of Ozymandias, king of kings, and through him was able to reconstruct the glory that once was. The contrast adds to the pathos of the tale; the faithfulness of the slave to his dead master and the old régime adds a touch that could be brought in no other way. "Marse Chan" is an exquisite bit of artistry and feeling; it stands in the all-too-small list of great American short stories. Its author never equaled it: its subject and its manner would not bear reproduction. Like Harte and the rest of the school, its author could only make replicas ever less and less distinctive.

VI

By no means was the dialect story of the period confined to the South. As early as 1887 the *Nation* was waxing sarcastic over the phenomenon of the fiction of an era "written mostly in corrupt English," and it was praising but seldom even the best of the output. "The South," it sneered, "has not been permitted to monopolize the attraction of jargon in fiction. The West competes closely." It might have added New England as well and New York. Hardly a writer of the period who at one time or another was not affected. Rose Terry Cooke was rediscovered and her really excellent tales for the first time were issued in book form. Her earliest collection, *Somebody's Neighbors*, came in 1881, and her latest, *Huckleberries Gathered From New England Hills*, a decade later. Elizabeth Stuart Phelps also entered upon a new period with her "Jack the Fisherman" and "A Madonna of the Tubs." What might have been the result had John Hay and not Bret Harte been fated to direct the course of the short story through the 'seventies we may judge, perhaps, from his strong tale "A Blood Seedling," *Lippincott's*, March, 1871, and that later story of his, "A Foster Brother," which so influenced Bronson Howard's drama "Moorcroft." As it is, two decades in the history of the short story form must be denominated the era of Bret Harteism—an era on the whole of small advance.

The short sketch of local manners, touched with sentiment and ingenious in its display of quaint localisms in the speech of its characters, was peculiarly adapted to the feminine pen. A veritable army of women that a generation before would have voiced itself in verse now turned to the production of these sketches in color—short stories the most of them could hardly be called. Following the example of Miss Murfree, some of them wrote with masculine names—Katharine Sherwood MacDowell, for instance, whose collections, *Dialect Tales* and *Suwanee River Tales* (1884), were signed "Sherwood Bonner," and the young woman of North Georgia who posed as "Matt Crimm." Others concealed themselves behind feminine pen names. Alice French signed her stories of the Arkansas canebrakes "Octave Thanet." Her first collection, *Knitters in the Sun*, 1887, was by its earliest readers rated even with *Old Creole Days* and *In Ole Virginia*, but it has been lost, together with the volumes that followed it, in the dialect jungle of which it formed a part. Others, like Annie Trumbull Slosson, Mary Hallock Foote, and Lillie Chase Wyman, author of *Poverty Grass* (1886), signed their own names to their work. It is a region that grows more dim now with every year; one need not explore it further.

The period closed some time in the early 'nineties. In 1898 Harris, writing to *Scribner's Magazine*, felt he should apologize for sending them sketches in dialect: "That sort of stuff," he wrote, "has seemed to be under the ban." For new writers certainly it had been under the ban for a decade.

BIBLIOGRAPHY

MAURICE THOMPSON, 1844–1901.

1875. *Hoosier Mosaics.*
"Was She a Boy?"; "Trout's Luck"; "Big Medicine"; "The Venus of Balhinch"; "The Legend of Potato Creek"; "Stealing a Conductor"; "Hoiden"; "The Pedagogue"; "An Idyl of the Rod."

PHILANDER DEMING. 1829–1915.

1880. *Adirondack Stories.*

"Lost," *Atlantic*, 1873; "Lida Ann," *Atlantic*, 1874; "John's Trail," *Atlantic*, 1874; "Joe Baldwin"; "Willie," *Atlantic*, 1874; "Benjamin Jacques," *Atlantic*, 1874; "Ike's Wife"; "An Adirondack Neighborhood."

1884. *Tompkins and Other Folks. Stories of the Hudson and the Adirondacks.*

"Tompkins," *Atlantic*, 1883; "Rube Jones," *Atlantic*, 1882; "Jacob's Insurance," *Atlantic*, 1882; "Mr. Toby's Wedding Journey"; "Hattie's Romance"; "The Court in Schoharie"; "An Adirondack Home."

MARY NOAILLES MURFREE ("Charles Egbert Craddock"). 1850.

1884. *In the Tennessee Mountains.*

"Drifting Down Lost Creek," *Atlantic*, April, 1884; "A-Playin' of Old Sledge at the Settlemint," *Atlantic*, Oct., 1883; "The Star in the Valley," *Atlantic*, Nov., 1878; "Electioneerin' on Big Injun Mounting," *Atlantic*, Jan., 1880; "The Romance of Sunrise Rock," *Atlantic*, Dec., 1880; "The Dancin' Party at Harrison's Cove," *Atlantic*, May, 1878; "Over on T'other Mounting," *Atlantic*, June, 1881; "The 'Harnt' That Walks Chilhowee," *Atlantic*, May, 1883.

1895. *Phantoms of the Footbridge.*

"Phantoms of the Footbridge," *Harper's*, 1893; "His 'Day in Court,'" *Harper's*, Dec., 1887; "The Moonshiners at Hobo-Hebee Falls"; "The Riddle of the Rocks"; "Way Down in Lonesome Cove," *Harper's*, Dec., 1885.

1895. *The Mystery of Witch-Face Mountain and Other Stories.*

"The Mystery of Witch-Face Mountain," *Atlantic*, 1895; "Taking the Blue Ribbon at the County Fair"; "The Casting Vote," *Century*, 1893.

1897. *The Young Mountaineers.*

1899. *The Bushwhackers and Other Stories.*

1904. *The Frontiersmen.*

1912. *The Raid of the Guerilla and Other Stories.*

RICHARD MALCOLM JOHNSTON. 1822–1898.

1864. *Georgia Sketches by an Old Man.*

1871, 1874, 1883, 1892. *Dukesborough Tales.*

1888. *Mr. Absalom Billingslea and Other Georgia Folk.*

1891. *The Primes and Their Neighbors.*

1892. *Mr. Billy Downs and His Likes.*

1892. *Mr. Fortner's Marital Claims und Other Stories.*

1894. *Little Ike Tomplin and Other Stories.*

JOEL CHANDLER HARRIS. 1848–1908.

1880. *Uncle Remus, His Songs and His Sayings.*

1883. *Nights With Uncle Remus: Myths and Legends of the Old Plantation.*

1884. *Mingo and Other Sketches in Black and White.*
"Mingo: Sketch of Life in Middle Georgia," *Harper's*, Dec., 1882; "At Teague Poteet's: a Sketch of the Hog Mountain Range," *Century*, May, June, 1883; "Blue Dave"; "A Piece of Land."

1887. *Free Joe and Other Georgian Sketches.*
"Free Joe and the Rest of the World," *Century*, Nov., 1884; "Little Compton," *Century;* "Aunt Fountain's Prisoner," *Scribner's*, March, 1887; "Trouble on Lost Mountain," *Century*, Jan., 1886; "Azalia," *Century*, Aug.–Oct., 1887.

1889. *Daddy Jake the Runaway and Short Stories Told After Dark.*

1891. *Balaam and His Master and Other Sketches and Stories.*
"Balaam and His Master," *Century*, Feb., 1891; "A Conscript's Christmas," *Century*, Dec., 1890; "Ananias," *Harper's*, April, 1888; "Where's Duncan?"; "Mom Bi"; "The Old Bascom Place," *Century*, Aug.–Oct., 1889.

1892. *Uncle Remus and His Friends.*

1898. *Tales of the Home Folks in Peace and War.*

1899. *Chronicles of Aunt Minervy Ann.*

1900. *On the Wings of Occasion.*

1905. *Told by Uncle Remus: New Stories of the Old Plantation.*

THOMAS NELSON PAGE. 1853—1922.

1887. *In Ole Virginia; or, Marse Chan and Other Stories.*
"Marse Chan: A Tale of Old Virginia," *Century*, April, 1884; "Unc' Edinburg's Drowndin': a Plantation Echo," *Harper's*, Jan., 1886; "Meh Lady: a Story of the War," *Century*, June, 1886; "Ole 'Stracted," *Harper's*, Oct., 1886; "'No Haid Pawn,'" *Scribner's*, April, 1887; "Polly: a Christmas Recollection," *Harper's*, Dec., 1886.

1891. *Elsket and Other Stories.*
"Elsket," *Scribner's*, Aug., 1891; "A Soldier of the Empire," *Century*, Oct., 1886; "George Washington's Last Duel,"

Cosmopolitan, April, 1890; "P'laski's Tunaments," *Harper's*, Dec., 1890; "Run to Seed," *Scribner's*, Sept., 1891.

1894. *The Burial of the Guns.*
"My Cousin Fanny"; "The Burial of the Guns," *Scribner's,* April, 1894; "The Gray Jacket of 'No. 4'," "Miss Dangerlie's Roses," *Scribner's*, Nov., 1892; "How the Captain Made Christmas," "Little Darby."

1894. *Pastime Stories* (23 in all).

1904. *Bred in the Bone.*

1907. *Under the Crust.*

1913. *The Land of the Spirit.*

ALICE FRENCH ("Octave Thanet"). 1850.

1387. *Knitters in the Sun.*
"The Ogre of Ha Ha Bay," *Atlantic*, Oct., 1885; "The Bishop's Vagabond," *Atlantic*, Jan., 1894; "Mrs. Finlay's Elizabethan Chair," *Century*, March, 1884; "Father Quinnailon's Convert"; "Schopenhauer on Lake Pepin"; "'Ma' Bolin'," *Harper's Weekly;* "Half a Curse," *Scribner's*, Feb., 1887; "Whitsun Harp, Regulator," *Century*, May, 1887.

1891. *Otto the Knight and Other Trans-Mississippi Stories.*
"Otto the Knight," *Scribner's*, Aug., 1888; "The Conjured Kitchen"; "The First Mayor," *Atlantic*, Nov., 1889; "Sist' Chaney's Black Silk"; "The Loaf of Peace"; "The Day of the Cyclone," *Scribner's*, March, 1888; "Trusty No. 49," *Century*, June, 1890; "The Plumb Idiot," *Scribner's*, Dec., 1890; "The Governor's Prerogative," *Century*, Feb., 1888; "The Mortgage on Jeffy," *Scribner's*, Oct., 1887.

1893. *Stories of a Western Town.*

1897. *The Captured Dream and Other Stories.*

1897. *A Book of True Lovers.*

1898. *A Slave to Duty and Other Women.*

ANNIE TRUMBULL SLOSSON

1890. *Seven Dreamers.*
"How Faith Came and Went"; "Botany Bay"; "Aunt Randy"; "Fishin' Jimmy"; "Butterneggs"; "Deacon Pheby's Selfish Natur"; "A Speakin' Ghost."

1898. *Dumb Foxglove and Other Stories.*
"Dumb Foxglove"; "Apple Jonathan"; "Anna Malann"; "Davy's Christmas"; "Clavis"; "A Transient"; "Aunt Liefy."

CHAPTER XIII

THE DISCOVERY OF THE "SHORT-STORY"

I

The term "short story" (hyphenated as Matthews advised, or unhyphenated) as used to designate an independent literary form and not "a story that is merely short," is a new addition to critical terminology, as recent, indeed, as the eighteen-eighties. Irving wrote "sketches" and "tales." Poe travestied the *Blackwood's* type of tale under the title, "How to Write a Blackwood *Article*." *The North American Review* in 1822 discussed Dana's *The Idle Man* and similar story collections in a critique entitled "*Essay Writing*." Poe and Hawthorne wrote "tales"—*Tales of the Folio Club, Tales of the Grotesque and Arabesque, Seven Tales of My Native Land, The Twice-Told Tales.* Poe in his much-quoted critique laid down rules not for the short story, but for "the tale proper," "the short prose narrative requiring from half an hour to one or two hours in its perusal." The terms persisted almost to our own times. *Scribner's Monthly*, for instance, in the early 'seventies, reviewed *Mrs. Skagg's Husbands*, as "lively sketches," *Coupon Bonds and Other Stories*, as "clever *sketches*," and *Marjorie Daw and Other People*, as distinctive "short prose tales." Howells reviewed "Marjorie Daw," as a "Sketch." The name "short story" began to be used more and more during the 'sixties and the 'seventies, but never in a generic sense; always the emphasis on the first word. It connoted simply that for general magazine purposes fiction must be severely shortened. That the tale, or the short story, was a distinct *genre*, necessarily short as a lyric is necessarily short, following laws distinct from those ruling the novel and its abbreviated form the novelette, had been realized in its fullness by no one, save perhaps Poe. Unity of various kinds most of the early tales possessed and suspense and dénouement, but these are only the fundamental requirements of all narrative, long or short. Sometimes the writer actually produced a short story in the modern sense of the term, but never was it, even in the case of Hawthorne, a premeditated effect. The tale, the short story, to most of the American writers, was an inferior thing, a fragment, a convenient, apprentice exercise, a stepping stone to better things—the dignified novel and the stately romance. Stories shortened to magazine lengths were good pot-boilers and useful exercises for those denied the gift of construction in the large, but not things to be lingered over and thought of in terms of artistry or finality. As late as 1880 *Scribner's Monthly* could say of one of Bret Harte's creations: "Short story though it be, it is an honor to American literature," and seven years later the editor of *The Critic* could make the generalization, "As a rule the short story is produced in youth, while the novel is a product of experience."

Aldrich had been a maker, doubtless because of his innate sense of form and his long training as a lyrist, of exquisite "Short-stories," to use the Brander Matthews method of designation, but he had made no definition and he had suggested no laws for other workers. The first after Poe at all prominently to make this definition, though he, too, advanced no laws, was Frederick B. Perkins, in the preface to his collection, *Devil-Puzzlers* (1877). "The claims," he declared, "of this particular kind of literature to artistic dignity as a class or department had not been appreciated." He had read, it appears, Poe's critique, and he had read the German tale writers. "I think highly of the art of writing short stories," he went on. "My idea is that a good short story possesses all the merits of a long one, and others of its own besides. A short story, in short, is to a long one what a diamond is to a mountain." The form had been used, he explained, by Hoffman, Fouqué, Goethe, Tieck, Novalis, and Zschokke, and there were none in English to compare with these save Poe and Hawthorne. Mrs. Stowe and Willis came next. The short story was the lyric among prose forms, and he defined the lyric as "a single pang of high and passionate emotion." "The prose tale, or short story, is not the highest order of prose composition, any more than the lyric of the poetical; but it is entitled, like the lyric, to high rank. It compares with other prose compositions as the lyric does with the epic, or narrative, or dramatic poem; as a melody with an opera or a sonata. A really fine short story (after the grade of Poe, Hawthorne, or the other masters I have named) is the product of a faculty lofty, unique and rare. It is a thing of power or beauty or fantastic pleasure, as fully as an oration, a melody, a picture, a statue, or an edifice."

Near the beginning of the 'eighties, both in England and in America, the general technique of fiction writing became a subject of increasing interest. Henry James analyzed with brilliancy contemporary French novelists, Howells interpreted James and explained realism in fiction, Walter Besant delivered a lecture much discussed on the subject of novel making, and Robert Louis Stevenson defended romance. At the height of the debate an anonymous writer in the London *Saturday Review* added a new element. "With all its extension," he wrote, "the discussion did not include one important branch of the art of fiction: it did not consider at all the minor art of the short story," and "the short story," he believed, "properly and technically so called, is a work of art of a distinct kind, and the writing of short stories is a distinct department of literary art." There was no distinctive name in English for the new art form. There was the word "*conte*—which is almost the exact French equivalent for short story as *nouvelle* may be taken to indicate the story which is merely short," and there was precedent for taking it over as a critical term as the term "*vers de société*" had been taken over in poetic criticism, but he suggested an alternative: he would discriminate between the *conte* form and the *nouvelle* form by writing the former with a capital S and a hyphen—"Short-story."

That was in 1884. A year later the paper, elaborated and revised by its author, Brander Matthews, appeared in the October issue of *Lippincott's Magazine*, with the title "The Philosophy of the Short-story"; in 1888 it was reissued as a part of the collection of essays entitled *Pen and Ink*, and three years later still it was published as a separate volume, with an appendix in which its author wrote that he believed himself to have been the first "to make explicit what is more or less implicit in Poe's review of *Twice-Told Tales*."

The claim is not extravagant. The short story in America, though its creators undoubtedly were all unconscious of the fact, had become in their hands a new literary entity with a form of its own and laws of its own, and Brander Mathews was the first to perceive the fact and to formulate those laws in a preliminary canon. The short story, he maintained, in distinction from the novel, must possess some seven or eight requisites, each a *sine qua non: originality, unity, compression, brilliancy of style, action, form, substance,* and, if possible, *fantasy.* His laws might be codified as follows:

1. *Originality:* "The one absolutely indispensable quality is ingenious originality. The short story demands an originality which we do not ask of the novel."

2. *Unity:* "The short story has what the novel cannot have, the effect of 'totality,' as Poe called it, the unity of impression. A short story deals with a single character, a single event, a single emotion, or the series of emotions called forth by a single situation."

3. *Compression:* "Compression is needed almost as much as ingenuity and originality—compression not merely in the telling of the story, but also in the style of the writer. No digression is tolerable."

4. *Brilliancy of Style:* "The short story should have brevity and brilliancy. In no class of writing are neatness of construction and polish of execution more needed. The style must be direct and vigorous, however subtle it may be in suggestion."

5. *Action:* "While a sketch may be still life, in a short story something always happens. A sketch may be an outline of character, or even a picture of a mood of mind, but in a short story there must be something done, there must be action. A short story is nothing if there is no story to tell."

6. *Form:* "The writer of short stories must have the sense of form which Mr. Lathrop has called 'the highest and last attribute of a creative writer.' The construction must be logical, adequate, harmonious."

7. *Substance:* "Important as are form and style, the subject of the short story is of more importance yet. What you have to tell is of greater interest than how you tell it."

8. If possible, *Fantasy:* "If the writer of short stories has a touch of Fantasy, so much the better. 'To mingle the marvelous rather as a slight, delicate and evanescent flavor than as any actual portion of the substance,' to quote from the preface to the 'House of the Seven Gables,' this is, or should be, the aim of the writer of short stories whenever his feet leave the firm ground of fact."

This in 1884 was startlingly new. Even the French had taken no such advanced position. It may be doubted if "*conte*" at this period connoted with them more than its name denotes—brief

tale, no more and no less. The French excellence in this department had come not from any formulated theory, but from their
sheer sense of form. Few sided with the young critic. The *Nation*
in an editorial challenged his statements and later dismissed the
finished essay as it appeared in *Pen and Ink* with a single word:
it was "over ingenious."

II

The next addition to short-story criticism came from Howells,
who in 1887 devoted an "Editor's Study" paper to the new rising
tide. The essay by Matthews apparently he had not read: he
spoke indiscriminately of sketch and tale and short story. He was
inclined to view the flood of single-number magazine fiction with
something like alarm. Was it not threatening the very foundations
of the novel? The astounding volume of the flood, he wrote,
"gives one question whether a branch of art tempting to such
profusion ought to be encouraged." The rich materials for the
American novel were being squandered, fiction was being written
in the small rather than in the large. "The motives that are both
great and simple are not so many that the profession can afford to
waste them in the narrow limits of a tale or a sketch." The magazine forms were inferior forms, the product, for the most part, of
youth or the apprenticeship period, or of women who as a rule
were restricted to them "by reason of their more restricted lives
and necessarily narrower outlook on the world." The short story
had come not, as many believed, as a result of the American
temperament, the American proneness to rush and hurry. Its
phenomenal success had been won simply because of "the success
of American magazines, which is nothing less than prodigious.
American magazine readers must have short stories, and by the
operation of the law of supply and demand, the short stories
abundant in quantity and excellent in quality are forthcoming
because they are wanted." Many of the tales and sketches, he
admitted freely, had been remarkable, and he proceeded to take
stock of them and their writers, producing thereby the first survey
of the short story made with anything like completeness since
Griswold's attempt in the mid-century.

Howells himself, after his volume, *Suburban Sketches* (1871), had
confined himself almost exclusively to the novel, and yet at one
point he enters prominently into American short story history:

beginning with "The Parlor Car" (1876), he produced first and last no less than sixteen "farces" or "parlor comedies," or, in the terminology of to-day, one-act plays. In all save dress these are "short stories" obedient implicitly to the first seven canons of the new code. Matthews in his essay had observed that "In dramatic composition, the equivalent of the Short-story is the one-act play, be it drama or comedy or comedietta or farce," and he might have added that the rules for both are practically the same. Howell's farces were light and humorous creations with sparkling dialogue, severely abbreviated description, and skillfully managed dénouement—mere anecdotes, amusing situations, depending almost wholly for their interest upon the manner of the telling. Never were they successful as acting dramas; their appeal is literary: they were written to be read, not acted. Their remarkable vogue during two decades had its effect upon the short story: they impressed the meaning and the value of form, and, what is more, they schooled young writers in that artistry that works with lightness of line rather than heavy splashings of color, with daintiness and suggestion and refinement of theme.

III

To what extent Matthews's critique was precipitated by Frank R. Stockton's "The Lady or the Tiger?" which, after 1884, became the most-talked-of short story of the period, it is impossible to say. Matthews himself admits its probable influence. Here was a tale, sensationally acclaimed as a masterpiece, yet depending for its success entirely upon the manner of its telling. It came at the height of the dialect era, yet it was totally detached from American geography; it came at a time when characterization was a short-story fad, yet its central figure was an abstraction—*a* woman; it had, moreover, nothing of sentiment in its make-up and nothing of pathos: it was merely a whimsical anecdote skillfully managed, an unusual situation led swiftly to an *impasse* and abandoned with a tantalizing challenge to its victim. It had more than a mere surprise ending: it stung its reader and then injected an irritating drop that lingered. It set young writers, always observant of new literary currents, to thinking of fiction in terms of manner.

The story was by no means Stockton's salutatory. He had as early as 1869 published his *Ting-a-ling Stories*, a collection in the

Alice in Wonderland manner, and he had followed it with a series of similar books—curious whimsies of goblins and griffins and the wonder world, often with a jump at the end. When at length he began to contribute real "grown-up" tales to *Scribner's Monthly*, he changed but little his method. His specialty was the marvelous, the absolutely impossible situation treated with all seriousness as if it were the dreariest of commonplaces. He would surfeit his reader with plausibility after the Edward Everett Hale manner, and then, after he had lulled his suspicions, would lead him with all gravity through adventures as utterly absurd as any Alice ever experienced in the land beyond the rabbit hole. Unlike Poe, however, and Hale, he made no attempts to unfold in detail his pseudo-science. Fitz-James O'Brien in his "How I Overcame My Gravity" used up nearly his whole space explaining the mechanism of his gravity-neutralizing machine, but Stockton, using the same theme in his "A Tale of Negative Gravity," (*Century Magazine*, December, 1884), simply tells, as if it were the most natural thing in the world, the amazing adventures and misadventures of an elderly couple equipped with the device. The story explains the story-teller: Stockton's stock in trade was negative gravity—the opposite always of what the reader expects. In "The Transferred Ghost" it is the ghost that is haunted. Everywhere the topsy-turvy; all that he wrote is as nonsensical as Edward Lear.

In other words, Stockton was a humorist, and American humor from the first has expressed itself prevailingly in brief narratives. It has been always a type of humor that has depended for its effect upon its form. The "point" of the story, the "nub" of the joke, the climax where the laugh comes, must be skillfully led up to and then revealed suddenly in the last sentence. Mark Twain's "The Jumping Frog" is completely typical of this American manner. It is an orgy of incongruity, it rambles in sublime contempt for every short-story canon, but nevertheless it works steadily toward the explosion point, the delicious moment when the would-be joker discovers the ingenious trick that has been played upon him. It is not a short story: it is a whimsical anecdote intent only upon producing a moment of laughter, yet it is a long step toward the true short story: nearly all of its effectiveness as a narrative depends upon the manner of the telling. Mark Twain, like most of the other humorists of his day, wrote few pieces that may strictly be classed as short stories. He lacked compression, he lacked restraint, he lacked patience and architechtonic skill. He wrote humorous sketches lawless and sprawling. Books like *Tom Sawyer* and *Huckleberry Finn* are simply the glorified ramblings of a boy's day and a boy's dreams. American humor has always been unrestrained: everything too much—exaggeration even to coarseness, color splashings with a white-wash brush.

After Aldrich, Stockton was the first writer of short stories to be humorous without being grotesque, to be incongruous and yet to be artistically incongruous, to have restraint and refinement and yet to be really and truly funny. To him manner was immeasurably more than matter. He evolved for himself a humorous style that may be recognized as his wherever it may be found: always original conceits of situation, always quaint predicaments, always whimsical unexpectedness. He was the antithesis of the local colorists who were everywhere working about him. He was making parables with no thought of actual landscape or actual people. Often he was preaching sermons in motley, though few of his readers suspected it. In the greater number of his tales a good-natured irony, subtle, evanescent, the mere aura of a suspicion, yet enough to tickle the fancy and suggest unconsciously a gentle correcting of life's follies and cruelties. Stockton was a humorist, but at the same time he was an artist.

He wrote unconscionably too much; it is doubtful indeed if any other generation in American literary history would have paid money for such a mass of absurdity as that which from first to last he put forth. Save for a very few of his tales, like "The Lady or the Tiger?" "The Transferred Ghost," and "The Remarkable Wreck of the *Thomas Hyke*," he has already receded far into the shadow, the gloom of which bids fair to become total. His influence, however, cannot be overlooked: it was greater than his work. At a single moment in the history of the short-story form, while all around him were modeling in the coarse colored clay of strange, unliterary regions, he chose to stand with Aldrich for manner rather than materials, and to turn, with him, American humor into forms refined and artistic.

IV

The first—at least, the first after Poe—to write the short story with conscious technique were Brander Matthews and Henry

Cuyler Bunner, two of the younger school who collaborated for a time in their studies and their literary output. Matthews was a scholar, a graduate and a post-graduate of Columbia, a student of literature in London and Paris, and at twenty-nine the author of *French Dramatists of the Nineteenth Century*. The drama was his specialty and his enthusiasm. Late in New York he reviewed dramatic books for the *Nation* and posed as a critic and literary free-lance. Literary forms appealed to him: *vers de société*, dramatic varieties, and at length the short story which had attracted him because of the art of "Marjorie Daw":

> My model was then the ingeniously invented tale of Thomas Bailey Aldrich, with an amusing twist of surprise at the end of it; and a little later still I came under the influence of the less artificial cleverness of Ludovic Halévy. When Bunner and I became intimate [1875] we had never-ending discussions over our favorite story-tellers; and I discovered that he admired the dexterity of Aldrich as much as I did— although I doubt if mere dexterity was ever as satisfying to him at any time as it was to me then.

In collaboration with Bunner he wrote two short stories, "The Documents in the Case," the form of it suggested by Aldrich's tale, and "The Seven Conversations of Dear Jones and Baby Van Rensselaer," and in 1884 the two put forth a collection entitled *In Partnership: Studies in Story-Telling*. The title is significant: the stories were all of them experiments in form; they were conscious efforts. Of the leading story, "The Documents in the Case," Matthews himself has written, "It is a most artificially contrived story, owing its sole merit not to its veracity, but to its novelty of construction." The same observation may be made upon the other stories of his earlier period: "In those days I was more keenly interested in the form than in the content." Study of the French drama had made him keenly alive to the value of manner. "I still find in my short stories of these 'prentice days an ingenuity in plot-making and a neatness of construction which I am inclined to ascribe to a constant study of the deft play makers of Paris."

A decade later, when local color had become a dominating motif, Matthews had another inspiration: why not treat New York City as Cable had treated New Orleans or as Craddock had treated the Great Smoky Mountains? Why should local color be

confined to wild unknown areas? "I began to write short stories
saturated with local color. I attempted to catch certain aspects
and attributes of New York—snap shots of the metropolis. When
I had written a dozen of these urban impressions, scarcely solid
enough in texture to be called short stories, I gathered them into
a volume called *Vignettes of Manhattan* and published in 1894."
N. P. Willis had been the pioneer sketcher in the field, Richard
Harding Davis and O. Henry were to follow, and to the work of
all of them might be applied the verdict of Matthews himself upon
the tales of Aldrich: sparkling, artistic, refined, yet lacking "the
sweep of emotion which touches the heart and the depth of char-
acter-delineation which lingers in the mind." And again of his
own work, "In all these essays in fiction the frame now appears to
me to be more prominent than the picture itself."

The most distinctive work of the school was done by Bunner, a
later Aldrich—a maker of exquisite *vers de société*, a lyrist of
distinction, a wit, a journalist. From the age of twenty-two until
he died at forty-one he was the editor of *Puck*—the statement is
enlightening. His short stories, almost all of them, he shaped for
the columns of his humorous weekly. They must be short and
inexorably condensed; they must be timely, sparkling, alive;
they must be restrainedly humorous. In the words of the advertising that first described them, they were "modern to the very
latest minute," they did not "much resemble short stories published elsewhere," and they were "trifles in size but treasures in
literary art."

Bunner is more like Maupassant than any other American, not
excepting even O. Henry of the later period. H. S. Canby has
noted "the rare power of perfect focus combined with perfect
restraint by which Bunner, like Maupassant, could make six pages
tell a story as complete as *Vanity Fair*." It was partly, to use
Bunner's own words concerning another, "inherent in his genius,"
a gift closely akin to his lyric power; it was partly unremitted
practice from early boyhood—few men have ever lived more constantly and more conscientiously with their craft and few have
ever mastered it more completely; and partly it was close study
of models like Aldrich and Maupassant and close study also of the
literary currents of the time. The Frenchman in particular fascinated him: they were kindred souls. In his *"Made in France":
French Tales Retold With a United States Twist*, Americanized

versions of ten of Maupassant's *contes*, he sought to reproduce, as he expressed it, "the marvelous conciseness and directness of his story-telling," to give the equivalents for his ingrained Frenchiness and local color, an element almost invariably lost in translation, and to add to it "the characteristic of a remarkable susceptibility, sensitiveness, and sympathetic changeableness of literary style which makes Maupassant in every instance subtly suit his manner of telling to the subject matter of his story." One is tempted to quote still further from the introduction to the tales:

> In this present book I have selected a few ethical situations from among the brightest of Maupassant's inventions, and have tried to reproduce them, not as translations, but as English, or rather American stories, based on a Frenchman's inspiration—and have done this with the sole hope of making that inspiration clear to people who will not or cannot read Maupassant in the original.

Certainly the tales are not translations; certainly they have suffered a sea change into something peculiarly Bunner-like and strange, yet no translation has ever presented the spirit and even the form of the brilliant French *conte* maker more perfectly. And there are those who contend that, for Americans, at least, they surpass in humor and vivacity and even in structure the originals upon which they are based.

At one point, however, they conspicuously fail, and it is a failure that marks also the *Short Sixes* collections, which contain the best of his work: they lack distinction of style, they lack that undefinable final touch which Aldrich, almost alone of American short-story writers, was able to give. The mark of the journalist is upon the tales. They are as flimsy of texture as Paris creations, they are marvelously clever in construction, with surprise lurking everywhere, especially in the endings, they have unity and compression, as was imperative from their brevity and their journalistic intent, and they are played over always with a lambent gleam of humor that is delightfully entertaining, but more one may not say. They have no depth of earth; they are ephemeral things made for the most brilliant yet the most transient of all literary vehicles, the humorous weekly of a great metropolis.

Bunner's influence, however, has been considerable. From him as much as from Aldrich has come that type of sparkling anecdotal story that came to its full growth in O. Henry. Bunner taught the possibilities of brevity. It was only after his short-story work in the columns of *Puck* that the latter-day humorous weekly *Life* could conduct its contest based upon the very up-to-date question, "How short can a short story be?"

V

A different type of the anecdotal or episodic short story was furnished by Ambrose Bierce, who issued his first collection as late as 1891. A caustic wit, intellectual, egocentric, disillusioned, he wrote tales without humor and without sentiment, bitter anecdotes for the most part, illustrative of life's ironies and the squalor in general of the human farce. It has been conventional to rate him in terms of Poe, but except that he wrought with intellect in the materials of horror there is little of likeness. He lacked Poe's imaginative sweep and his romanticism and his lyric soul.

Bierce is to be rated first of all as an individualist, a man deliberately out of step and defiant. He was of Puritan descent, though born in Ohio, and congenitally he was a dissenter even to balkiness. Childhood and youth in the solitude of a Western farm, with almost nothing of formal education, nurtured his individualism. Instead of college there were four years of army life during which he took active part in the bloodiest campaigns of the war—it meant disillusion, it meant a hardening of the sensibilities. At twenty-four he was in San Francisco, editor of a local sheet that allowed full exercise of his impetuous youthfulness and his egotism. It was breezy, it was bitter with personalities, it was cocksure. A little later he was in England, a literary adventurer, boon companion of Tom Hood the younger, and Sala, and Captain Reid, and the whole Bohemian set, writing satire vitriolic that startled even London. "Bitter Bierce" they called him, and "Bitter Bierce" he was again in San Francisco when for ten years after 1876 he edited the column "Prattle" for the *Examiner*— "the most wickedly clever," says a contemporary, "the most audaciously personal, and the most eagerly devoured column of causerie that probably ever was printed in this country." Like every columnist since Eugene Field, he was versatile and cleverly witty. No literary form but he essayed it with brilliance and no species of wit, but he pressed it to its limits.

That Bierce should have been attracted to the short-story form so increasingly in demand by all readers was inevitable: his training had peculiarly fitted him for its technique. His success in England had been won by a unique variety of satiric fable, short and pointed: collected as *Cobwebs From an Empty Skull*. It is his most original and typical work. Later in San Francisco he evolved again his own type of the short story, following no one, and throwing into it, as into all his work, his own fierce individualism and self-expression. The magazines were afraid of his gruesome tales. Bailey Millard, who speaks from his own personal knowledge of Bierce, is authority for the statement that "Beginning with the early 'eighties, he wrote story after story, but nearly all were considered by magazine editors to be impossible for their pages; and when he sent a lot of manuscript tales to book publishers they would have none of him." The preface to his first collection, *Tales of Soldiers and Civilians*, San Francisco, 1891, later changed to *In the Midst of Life*, is unique certainly: "Denied existence by the chief publishing houses of the country, this book owes itself to Mr. E. L. G. Steele, merchant, of this city." His second collection, *Can Such Things Be?* came two years later. It is upon these two volumes that his rating as a short-story writer must depend.

Brief tales—that is one's first impression of the volumes. The second contains forty-two stories, each averaging nine large-print pages. With so abbreviated a unit a writer can do almost nothing toward humanizing and making individual his characters. The death of the central figure in his tale—and in Bierce he invariably dies—is simply the death of *a* person. The reader may be harrowed, may be terrified, even, just as he might be harrowed and terrified in a morgue or a slaughter house, but the reaction is simply physical, and as such the lowest accomplishment of art. If it is a friend one finds on the slab, the horror is vastly different. In all of his tales merely the intellectual: their author prided himself upon the fact. They are like machine-made stuff, mechanically perfect, yet lacking the human element. The motto of the Cavaliere San Giorgio, patron saint of fencers, was, "*To the Heart: Always Strike at the Heart!*" Bierce strikes always for the head. His tale, for instance, "A Baby Tramp," which in other hands would have been a moving human document, stripped as it is of all pathos, becomes a mere curious happening, a tragic coincidence.

One's next observation, especially if one has approached the tales by way of the fiction of the 'seventies, is that in all of them there is an utter absence of the love element and an utter absence of good women. Matthews in his critique had pointed out what then was a new and startling idea, that the short-story writer "may do what he pleases, but from him a love tale is not expected," but it was for Bierce to illustrate this thesis at its extreme. Women are introduced into his stories only as remote instances, and then usually with a cynical sneer. Note the subtle ending of "Killed at Resaca." Herman Brayle in battle after battle has been brave even to foolhardiness. He has become the admiration not only of his whole division, but of the enemy as well. Finally in a mad forlorn-hope charge he is killed. On his body is found a letter. It was evidently from his "sweetheart":

Mr. Winters, whom I shall always hate for it, has been telling that at some battle in Virginia, where he got his hurt, you were seen crouching behind a tree. . . . I could bear to hear of my soldier-lover's death, but not of his cowardice.

A year later his superior officer places the letter in the hands of its writer.

"You know, doubtless, that he fell in battle. Among his effects was found this letter from you. My errand here is to place it in your hands."

She mechanically took the letter, glanced through it with deepening color, and then, looking at me with a smile, said:

"It is very good of you, though I am sure it was hardly worth while." She started suddenly and changed color. "This stain," she said, "is it—surely it is not—"

"Madam," I said, "pardon me, but that is the blood of the truest and bravest heart that ever beat."

She hastily flung the letter on the blazing coals. "Ugh! I cannot bear the sight of blood!" she said. "How did he die?" . . .

"He was bitten by a snake," I replied.

The man was an artist, cold, cynical, conscious of his art. He was not bound by rules: he was heedless sometimes even of fundamentals. He tells a story often in relays: two or three pages of headlong narrative, then a total break and a new line of action, the jump of a generation, perhaps, or the introduction of a secondary set of characters, then on for two or three pages, then another break, to resume the first situation. If is the method of the novel and with a lesser artist such work would be fatal. But always he succeeds in his main endeavor: he leaves one vivid impression. There are various ways for instance, of making the reader realize a battle. In his "Chickamauga" we do not see the fighting at all or even hear it: we see rather a writhing group of mangled men crawling along in silence to a water hole like black beetles. A baby has run away from home, and, thinking the men are playing, jumps astride one of them, but is hurled off with a ghastly hiss. The man's lower jaw has been shot away. It is not realism; Stephen Crane, born years after the war, did work as vivid and convincing. It is impressionism: a hundred ghastly details selected and brought into one focus. The mechanism is too evident. The baby in the last sentence is revealed to the reader as deaf and dumb. Why? Otherwise it would have heard the battle and been terrified. One has no sympathy even for the baby: it is a mere spectacle, a deliberate attack upon the reader's nerves. "The Damned Thing" is a clever creation, but it is cold and it leaves the reader cold: one does not feel with the terror that is of the soul the invisible thing as one does Maupassant's "La Horla" or even O'Brien's "What Was It?" Everywhere deliberately manufactured surprise endings. In "An Occurrence at Owl Creek Bridge" the reader in the last sentence learns to his horror, that the man actually *was* hanged, and that the details of his escape were but his mental reactions during the instant before he dropped. "The Man and the Snake" was written solely for the sake of the last sentence. The man had died in ghastly contortions from the basilisk gaze of the snake under his bed, and yet "It was a stuffed snake; its eyes were two shoe buttons."

And right here lay Bierce's real power. Artificial as was the material in which he worked, and deliberate and ironic as were his motifs, nevertheless he was able to create situations hauntingly suggestive. Many of his stories really begin for the reader where the last sentence ends. His ghost stories, totally unexplained, recorded with circumstance as actual history, nevertheless have within them suggestions of an abnormal psychological world, possible within each of us, and thus are more terrifying than even a supernatural apparition. It is the last touch of art: it is the art that compels the reader to search his own soul.

When, however, one studies the history of the American short-story evolution, not from the point of view of what might have been or what should have been, but of what actually happened, one is compelled to the conclusion that Ambrose Bierce was a vivid episode rather than a positive force. He was read by very few; his stories were too horrible, too physically repulsive at times, as, for instance, "The Coup de Grâce," where a herd of hogs is pictured on the battlefield, rending the putrid bodies. A few, however, he influenced—two or three who themselves, were to be compelling forces. His story, "The Famous Gilson Bequest," to take but a single example, points unmistakably back to Harte, but still more unmistakably does it point forward to O. Henry. It is impossible that O. Henry had not read it. In the school of the anecdotal short story, brilliant, witty, climactic, Bierce undoubtedly is the transition figure. The steps in the evolution of the form that seems to have culminated in the volumes of short-story yearbooks edited by O'Brien, are, therefore, Harte and Aldrich, Matthews and Bunner, Ambrose Bierce and O. Henry.

BIBLIOGRAPHY

FREDERICK B. PERKINS.   1828–1899.

1877. *Devil-Puzzlers and Other Stories.*
"A Chat by the Way of Preface"; "Devil-Puzzlers"; "The Manufactory"; "Childhood: a Study"; "The Compensation Office"; "My Forenoon With the Baby."

WILLIAM DEAN HOWELLS.   1837–1919.

1872. *Suburban Sketches.*
"Mrs. Johnson"; "Doorstep Acquaintance"; "A Pedestrian Tour"; "By Horse Car to Boston"; "A Day's Pleasure"; "A Romance of Real Life"; "Scene"; "Jubilee Days"; "Some Lessons From the School of Morals"; "Flitting."

One-Act Plays or Farces.
1876. "The Parlor Car," *Atlantic*, Sept., 1876.
1883. "The Sleeping Car."
1884. "The Register."
1885. "The Elevator."
1886. "The Garoters."
1886. "The Mouse-Trap," *Harper's*, Dec., 1886.
1891. "The Albany Depot."

1892. "A Letter of Introduction."
1893. "The Unexpected Guests."
1893. "Evening Dress."
1897. "A Previous Engagement."
1900. "Room Forty-Five."
1900. "The Smoking Car."
"A Likely Story."
"Five O'Clock Tea."
"Parting Friends."

FRANK RICHARD STOCKTON. 1834–1902.

1884. *The Lady or the Tiger and Other Stories.*
"The Lady or the Tiger?" *Century*, Nov., 1882; "The Transferred Ghost," *Century*, May, 1882; "The Spectral Mortgage," *Century*, Feb., 1883; "Our Archery Club," *Scribner's*, Aug., 1879; "That Same Old 'Coon," *Scribner's*, June, 1878; "His Wife's Deceased Sister," *Century*, Nov., 1884; "Our Story," *Century*, 26: 762; "Mr. Tolman"; "On the Training of Parents," *Century*, Oct., 1884; "Our Fire Screen"; "A Piece of Red Calico"; "Every Man His Own Letter Writer."

1886. *A Christmas Wreck and Other Stories.*

1887. *The Hundredth Man.*

1887. *The Bee-Man of Orn and Other Fanciful Tales.*

JAMES BRANDER MATTHEWS. 1852.

1884. *In Partnership: Studies in Story-Telling.*
"The Documents in the Case" (Matthews and Bunner); "Venetian Glass" (Matthews); "The Red Silk Handerchief" (Bunner); "The Seven Conversations of Dear Jones and Baby Van Rensselaer" (Matthews and Bunner); "The Rival Ghosts" (Matthews); "A Letter and a Paragraph" (Bunner); "Playing a Part" (Matthews); "Love in Old Cloathes" (Bunner).

1893. *The Story of a Story and Other Stories.*

1894. *Vignettes of Manhattan.*

1896. *Tales of Fantasy and Fact.*

1898. *Outlines in Local Color.*

HENRY CUYLER BUNNER. 1855–1896.

1890. *Short Sixes: Stories to Be Read While the Candle Burns.*
"The Tenor"; "Colonel Brereton's Aunty"; "A Round-Up"; "The Two Churches of 'Quawket," *Puck*, Aug., 1890;

"The Love Letters of Smith," *Puck*, July, 1890; "Zenobia's Infidelity"; "The Nine-Cent Girls," *Puck*, Aug., 1890; "The Nice People," *Puck*, July, 1890; "Mr. Copernicus and the Proletariat"; "Hector"; "A Sisterly Scheme," *Puck*, Sept., 1890; "Zozo"; "An Old, Old Story."

1891. *Zadoc Pine and Other Stories.*

1893. *"Made in France."*

1894. *More Short Sixes.*

"The Cumbersome Horse"; "Mr. Vincent Egg and the Wage of Sin"; "The Ghoollah"; "Cutwater of Seneca"; "Mr. Wick's Aunt"; "What Mrs. Fortesque Did"; "'The Man With the Pink Pants'"; "The Third Figure in the Cotillion"; "Samantha Boom-de-ay"; "My Dear Mrs. Billington."

1896. *Love in Old Cloathes and Other Stories.*

AMBROSE BIERCE. 1842–1914.

1891. *In the Midst of Life: Tales of Soldiers and Civilians.*

"A Horseman in the Sky"; "An Occurrence at Owl Creek Bridge"; "Chickamauga"; "A Son of the Gods"; "One of the Missing"; "Killed at Resaca"; "The Affair at Coulter's Notch"; "The Coup de Grâce"; "Parker Adderson, Philosopher"; "An Affair of Outposts"; "The Story of a Conscience"; "One Kind of Officer"; "One Officer, One Man"; "George Thurston"; "The Mocking Bird"; "The Man Out of the Nose"; "An Adventure at Brownville"; "The Famous Gilson Bequest"; "The Applicant"; "A Watcher by the Dead"; "The Man and the Snake"; "A Holy Terror"; "The Suitable Surroundings"; "The Boarded Window"; "A Lady From Red Horse"; "The Eyes of the Panther."

1893. *Can Such Things Be?*

CHAPTER XIV

THE REVOLT OF THE 'NINETIES

During the 'eighties and far into the 'nineties the most discussed topic connected with the short story was the alleged prejudice of the reading public against short-story collections. That a piece of literature should be popular when published in a magazine and unpopular when published with others like it in a volume was a seeming paradox much reasoned upon by critics. Howells gave perhaps the most ingenious explanation. In 1901, *apropos* of Harper's "Portrait Collection of Short Stories," he wrote:

A reader can read one good short story in a magazine with refreshment and a pleasant sense of excitement, in the sort of spur it gives to his own constructive faculty. But if this is repeated in ten or twenty stories, he becomes fluttered and exhausted by the draft upon his energies; whereas a continuous fiction of the same quantity acts as an agreeable sedative. A condition that the short story makes with the reader, through its limitations, is that he shall subjectively fill in the details and carry out the scheme which in its small dimensions the story can only suggest, and the greater number of readers find this too much for their feeble powers, while they cannot resist the incitement to attempt it.

Undoubtedly collections of short stories during the 'seventies and early 'eighties could not compete on even terms with the novel, intrenched as it was by centuries of tradition. Moreover, the English novel was then at its highest tide. During the 'fifties and the 'sixties had appeared the chief work of Dickens and Thackeray and George Eliot, of Kingsley and Reade and Trollope, of Mrs. Gaskell, and Charlotte Brontë and George Meredith, not to mention lesser figures. English novels for years had been run serially in American magazines as the chief literary feature of each issue. The short story had been regarded as distinctively a minor form, at least as compared with the novel, a form ephemeral, thought of always in connection with the magazine and the newspaper rather than in connection with the bound volume of fiction.

309

Yet in spite of all this there was not a publishing season for decades after the Civil War when short-story collections did not make up an appreciable percentage of the fictional output. By the mid-'eighties the volume began to increase. In 1884-85 the Scribners published in ten volumes a series of "Stories by American Authors," "the best short stories of American fiction," declared by its first reviewers to be "the only undertaking of its kind," and following it had come other compilations in increasing numbers. The authors of the younger school were making their first appearance almost without exception with a volume of short stories reprinted from the magazines. In 1891, Howells in the September number of *Harper's Monthly*, thought it worthy of record that "however it has come about, it is certain the result has come, and publishers are fearlessly venturing volumes of short stories on every hand; and not only short stories by authors of established repute, but by new writers who would certainly not have found this way to the public some time ago." A year later, *The Atlantic* in a single issue reviewed the short-story volumes of fifteen different writers, and three years later still *Harper's Weekly*, after reviewing a dozen or more of such collections, remarked that it was indeed a thing to record that two of the first publishing houses of the country had in one season printed more volumes of the American short story than volumes of the American novel.

The causes for the increased production were many. "The Lounger," in the *Critic* of August, 1890, gave perhaps the contemporary explanation:

The short story is having its day again. There was a time within the past ten years when authors objected to writing short stories. They agreed that as much plot went to the making of a short as of a long story, and that if they took a little more time to elaborate it, they would have a manuscript worth one thousand dollars instead of one worth fifty or a hundred. This left most of the short story writing to be done by second-rate writers, and the reading public began to complain that the short stories dealt out to them were, with rare exceptions, not worth reading. This aroused the editors, so they offered prices for short stories which brought forth much good work; now quite a crop of good short story writers has sprung up. Guy de Maupassant, also, has been a marked influence on the younger generation of writers. He has taught them what can be done with very little plot by one who has a mastery of the art of story-telling.

The era of sensational prize contests had begun. Short story writing became to many an enormously profitable vocation. S. S. McClure's "one hundred short stories by one hundred authors in one hundred days" had been followed by the syndicated short story and the unlimited market, with standard prices and often with small fortunes as prizes. The result was inevitable: in mere quantity at least the product became really astonishing.

With the 'nineties had come a new generation of short-story writers, contemporaries of Rudyard Kipling and later greatly to be influenced by his art, a vigorous original group that had been reared on Harte and Aldrich and Cable and now considered them antiquated—"crumbling idols" to be left behind in the forward march of "art." Harte and Howells and their followers, they announced, had told the truth, but not the whole truth. They had been enamoured of the merely literary rather than of Life; their realism was not true realism at all—it was a selective realism, a deliberate choosing of only those things that suited the writer's taste or ideals or ultimate design. The writer of fiction, they believed, should follow Truth, lead where it might, "selecting nothing, rejecting nothing, scorning nothing." This was the challenge of the young Frank Norris:

I never truckled; I never took off the hat to fashion and held it out for pennies. By God! I told them the Truth. They liked it or they didn't like it. What had that to do with me? I told them the Truth; I knew it for the Truth then, I know it for the Truth now.

The same challenge, at least in implied substance, came from the pens of Hamlin Garland and Mary E. Wilkins and Stephen Crane and a dozen others. Most emphatically a new group of short-story writers had arisen, one to be ruled by "the god of things as they are." The demand was for zest, pointedness, actuality, science. Poe had considered his own age intolerant of surplusage and awkwardness, but with the closing years of the century the demands had become imperative. Charlotte Porter in the *Century Magazine* of 1885, gave this as the new American attitude toward fiction:

The modern reader will not sit easily in his chair while the novelist pursues pet digressions, elaborates irrelevant details, and blocks the progress of his chief characters with a throng of supernumeraries. The long-winded narrative of Fielding and Richardson, indulged with innocent zest, suited the old-school manners of a departed age. But the average magazine reader will have none of it, under any circumstances. He must come to the point, understand the clearly marked issue, and get about his own business shortly.

II

Young James Lane Allen, of Kentucky, was one of the first of the new school to protest against the mechanistic conventionalism that was beginning to rule the short stories of the times. Dialect seemingly had become dialect for mere dialect's sake. His cry, in effect, was *Back to Hawthorne*. In January, 1886, when he had published only the tale, "Too Much Momentum," in *Harper's*, he put forth his literary creed:

Fiction is not the proper literary form in which to furnish the reader miscellaneous information of flora, climate, and other scientific features of an unknown region.

Local color was not to be condemned in its totality: it was to be modified. The fiction writer must perforce be scientifically accurate in his settings, but local color must not dominate his art:

From an artistic point of view the aim of local color should be to make the picture of human life natural and beautiful, or dreary, or somber, or terrific, as the special character of the theme may demand; from a scientific point of view, the aim of local color is to make the picture of human life natural and—*intelligible*, by portraying those picturable potencies in nature that made it what it was and must go along with it to explain what it was. The novelist must encompass both aims.

Moreover, the writer of fiction must strive interminably for distinction of style. "The utmost felicity" in fiction can come only

When the writer chooses the most suitable of all colors that are characteristic; when he makes these available in the highest degree for artistic presentation; and when he attains and uses the perfection of coloring in style.

A country boy, without literary environment, educated in school and college largely by his own efforts, attracted early to authorship as a lifework, yet for years, by seemingly adverse fates, rejected by magazines and publishers, he was handicapped at the start, yet handicapped, we can see now, completely to his own advantage. He studied the art of fiction as the musician studies the organ; with patience and toil he evolved a style for himself that seems like a rare exotic when viewed against the average magazine style of its day; and he wrote and rewrote and, like Hawthorne, destroyed much of his early product. As a result his earliest work, as found in his first volume, *Flute and Violin*, contains few immaturities. His master undoubtedly was Hawthorne. Such sketches as "Part of an Old Story" *The Century*, 1887, "The White Cowl," and "Posthumous Fame" are redolent of the great romancer.

Allen's chief service to the short story was his stand against the tyranny of local color, and his insistence upon beauty of style and substantiality of substance. The short fiction of the 'eighties was dealing prevailingly with picturesque externals: like Hawthorne, he would center upon internal factors. Working without humor or picturesqueness in the deeper problems of sin and of passion and of "Nature," he would give no happy endings, and, though he wrote wholly of Kentucky life and legend, he would paint no backgrounds that with little change might not be transferred to any other environment. He sought to deepen the channel of the short story, and he sought also to give to the form the literary distinction it had in the days of Irving and Hawthorne. The promise of this first volume impressed all who reviewed it. He is "the one man in the South," declared the New York *Critic*, "capable of lifting its fiction above the level of negro-dialect stories." The volume, however, remains alone among his works. Two other undisputed masterpieces he wrote in the shorter unit. "A Kentucky Cardinal," and its sequel, "Aftermath," in all save length, are true short stories, but the rest of his literary output was in the field of the novel and the romance.

III

The revolt of Hamlin Garland took a different direction. He was "a son of the middle border," born in Wisconsin and reared on a succession of wild new claims beginning in Iowa and ending in the Dakotas. Inspired at length, like the Cary sisters and others of the early middle West, with a longing for the things of art and letters, which for him were centered in Boston as the youthful Washington Irving's had been centered in London, he worked his way East. After a starvation period in the heart of New England culture he began to write. At first he produced realistic sketches, studies in the prevailing fashion of the time, later to be reproduced in *Boy Life on the Prairie*. At the high tide of the local color era there was a market for such material.

My fictional inspiration did not come till two years later, when, having saved up something like ninety-eight dollars, I felt enabled to make a midsummer trip back to my old home in Osage, Iowa, and to my father's home in Ordway, Dakota. This was an epoch-making experience to me, for my three years in Boston had given me perspective on the life of the prairie farmer. I perceived with new vision the loneliness and drudgery of the farmers' wives. All across northwestern Iowa and up through central Dakota I brooded darkly over the problem presented, and this bitter mood was deepened by the condition in which I found my mother on a treeless farm just above Ordway.

It was in this mood of resentment that I began to write (immediately after returning to Boston), the stories which later made up the first volume of *Main-Travelled Roads*. My second trip to Dakota, in 1889, added to my savage resentment, for while on the farm I saw my mother suffer a paralytic stroke which seemed at the moment to be the end of her life. During these years, 1887–89, I wrote nearly all of the stories which are now brought together in final form in the two volumes of *Main-Travelled Roads*.

The distinction of these stories lies in their genuineness and their spontaneous freshness. They are photographically true to the middle Western environment in the decades immediately following the war, but for the most part they were not written with thought of local color. They were written with passion by one who knew. They are vivid cantos in the vast epic of the winning of the West, or, as Garland himself would express it, each is a single scene in the colossal drama of the Western settlement:

For forty years an infinite drama has been going on in these wide spaces of the West—a drama that is as thrilling, as full of heart and hope and battle, as any that ever surrounded any man; a life that was unlike any ever seen on the earth, and which should have produced its characteristic literature, its native art chronicle.

For him in the first period of his inspiration "the native art chronicle" of the westward movement took the form of vividly presented episodes, short stories, single flashes of light thrown into this angle and that angle of the settlement era, until the whole vast meaning of it—its heroisms, its tragedy, its colossal abuses, its grinding toil—was understood. He would not poeticize it, he would not select here and there its romantic episodes and ignore the rest. He would tell all of it as it actually existed and actually exists, for "farm life in the West is still a stern round of drudgery. My pages present it—not as the summer boarder or the young lady novelist sees it—but as the working farmer endures it." The people of the East should know precisely what it had meant to his father and mother and his old neighbors to farm the raw prairie often as renters and to live in sod huts and shanties in the first squalid days of the settlement.

He scorned the word "realist." Henry James and the local colorists had softened and sentimentalized the word—he was a "veritist":

Veritism puts aside all models, even living writers. Whatever he may do unconsciously, the artist must consciously stand alone before Nature and before Life. . . . I do not advocate an exchange of masters, but freedom from masters. Life, Nature—these should be our teachers. . . . Art is not necessarily a thing far away, and select, and very civilized. . . . I believe in the mighty pivotal present . . . In all that I have written upon local literature, I have told the Truth as I saw it.

His little volume, *Crumbling Idols* (1894), was a demand for genuineness, for an abandonment of local color for merely exhibition purposes, for originality, for Americanism. "It is intended to weaken the hold of conventionalism upon the youthful artist."

The spirit of the reformer was often stronger in Garland than his sense of art. Especially was this true in his earlier period. In the heat of his anger—that same breed of Western anger that had created the Populist political party and other similar movements— he wrote tales that fundamentally are propaganda, like "Under the Lion's Paw" and "Up the Coulée." Lucretia Burns is not an individual only: she is a type representing a class, and is painted with all the depressing details at the author's command that the reader may feel and pity, and may condemn with emphasis the system that made her possible. But even Garland refused to go with the Russian veritists to the extremes of the manner.

Perhaps it was the Puritan soul within him that held him back; more probably it was his publishers. In one of his autobiographic fragments he remarks naïvely of this period of his life, "My stories, the more cheerful of them, were beginning to be bought by the magazines," which would imply that even in the early 'nineties the less cheerful, the products of unmodified veritism, were not marketable commodities in American publishing houses. Two decades later we find Jack London complaining that when he wrote of life as he himself really had experienced life no magazine would accept his work. The publishers, he declared, were afraid of the reading public: they did not dare to give them the Truth. Whatever the cause, it is true that even the most depressed of Garland's tales ends happily. Julia, the enslaved Norse girl, finds a lover and elopes at midnight; Agnes flees from her brute of a husband with Will Hannan, her old lover; and even Lucretia Burns finds at the end something, in a degree at least, to ameliorate her lot.

Garland turned away from the short-story field after three years of intense production, and, with few exceptions, did the rest of his work in the longer forms of fiction. "I had put together," he wrote in his *Daughter of the Middle Border*, "in *Main-Travelled Roads* and its companion volumes, a group of thirty short stories (written between 1887 and 1891), in which I expressed all I had to say on that especial phase of Western life." Unlike Harte and Craddock and other depicters of raw local areas, he awoke early to the realization that his material was limited and to continue would be only to repeat with constantly diminishing freshness and power. He turned, therefore, to other literary fields and for the most part to other literary forms. His permanence, however, rests almost wholly upon these thirty short stories of his first inspiration. How much of their value depends upon the materials used, upon the fact that they record with truth the spirit of a vanished epoch, that was enormously picturesque, it is perhaps too early to determine. Undoubtedly they are documentary in intent, written deliberately to exhibit conditions in the life of an area during an intense period of its development. To the extent that this is true they fall short of real greatness as literature. That they also, some undoubtedly more than others, express truth universal through a local medium is also perfectly true. The balance is hard to strike. That they are still read a generation after their first publication by readers who care no more for the West than they do for the South or the East, who are bored even by reference to the Populist propaganda of the 'seventies, and who think of the settlement of the middle border just as they think of the settlement of New England in the days of Miles Standish, argues strongly on the side of their permanence. A love story like "Among the Corn Rows" is not a local episode of the 'seventies: it is universal and timeless.

VI

To realize the change that came over the short story in the early 'nineties one has but to place the work of Sarah Orne Jewett beside that of Mary E. Wilkins Freeman. Both dealt with New England life and character, but so differently that it is hard to realize that the two sets of pictures can both of them be true.

Unlike Garland and Norris, Miss Wilkins made no attempt to classify herself, uttered no literary dictums, formulated no rules, and followed no laws. She simply wrote what was native to her personality, and with New England conscience she told the truth as best she could concerning the life she knew, leaning ever, unconsciously, it may be, toward the romantic, since in soul she was a Puritan. Thrown for support upon her own resources, incapacitated for teaching and for other professions even then open to women, she turned to the short story as a desperate last resort and wrote with little technical knowledge of literary art tales that she hoped would be purchased by the magazines.

What directed me to the short story? I think the answer is very simple. The short story did not take so long to write, it was easier, and, of course, I was not *sure* of my own ability to write a short story, much less a novel. I consider the art of the novel as a very different affair from that of the short story. The latter can be a simple little melody; the other can be grand opera.

The quality of her work — its style, its subject matter, its angle of view—came from herself alone. No other short-story writer of her period, save Deming, perhaps, was at the start so little affected by masters and models. Like Emily Brontë, whom she resembled in her lyric intensity, her seclusion from the main currents of life, and her imaginative vividness, she spun from her own soul.

Concerning any influence of other writers, it may seem egotistical, but there was none. I did, however strange it may seem, stand entirely alone. As a matter of fact, I would read nothing which I thought might influence me. I had not read the French short stories; I had not read Miss Jewett's stories. I will add that, although I have repeatedly heard that I was founded on Jane Austen, I have never read any of her books.

She was a part of her own materials. Since Colonial days her family on the father's side had aged and ripened and individualized in old Salem, Massachusetts. One of the earliest members of it, Bray Wilkins, had been in authority during the witchcraft period and had been harsh in his punishments: the shadow of it affected somberly her imagination as a similar shadow had affected Hawthorne. One finds it in her tragedy, *Giles Corey, Yeoman*. One finds it in the grim depths of many of her tales. Her father, the first to break from the Salem environment, had married into another old Massachusetts family and had settled down in his wife's native village, Randolph, not far from Boston. The main street of this decaying old Puritan town, the accumulated memories of her little home circle, the surroundings of the Vermont village to which her family later removed, furnished the material from which her stories grew. Her life had been repressed and introverted more than is usual even in the rural areas of New England. Ill health from early childhood had forced her into a world as restricted in its physical bounds, yet as boundless in its unseen reaches, as that in which had moved that other New England nun, eager of soul, pale ghost of Puritanism—or rather pale, ghostly flower sprung up amid the moldering ruins—Emily Dickinson. The death of her sister and then of her mother had affected her profoundly. For years she lived a dreamy, secluded life devoted to her invalid father, and when he died she returned to the ancestral home, to the old mansion in Randolph which her maternal grandfather had built with his own hands. There she lived almost alone and there she began to write her short stories, the earliest of them, "Two Old Lovers," "A Humble Romance," and the like, finally finding refuge in Harper's Magazines. But wide recognition came slowly. There were no trumpets even after the 1887 collection, *A Humble Romance and Other Stories*. Perhaps her arrival might have been as delayed as Hawthorne's had not the English critics now found her work. In 1890 the New York *Critic* suddenly announced, "There is something like a craze in England over Mary E. Wilkins." Her second collection, which appeared a year later was hailed in England with superlatives. The London *Spectator* went to extremes like this: "The stories are among the most remarkable feats of what we may call literary impressionism in our language, so powerfully do they stamp on the reader's mind the image of the classes and individuals they portray without spending on the picture a single redundant word, a single superfluous word." Recognition in America now came like a flood. The book became instantly a classic, and after a generation it is still rated as a classic. Since then she has written voluminously and in many varieties, very often in the longer forms of fiction, but her most distinctive work undoubtedly lies in these two volumes of her first inspiration.

Accustomed as we are to-day to the type of work for which she stands, we can hardly realize how fresh and strange these early tales seemed to the readers of the early 'nineties. It was a new tang, a wild native flavor from Nature and not at all from art. To open a love story and to find the heroine described at the very start as Garland had described Lucretia Burns was a new sensation. This is the opening paragraph of "A Humble Romance":

She was stooping over the great kitchen sink, washing the breakfast dishes. Under fostering circumstances, her slenderness of build might have resulted in delicacy or daintiness; now the harmony between strength and task had been repeatedly broken, and the result was ugliness. Her finger joints and wrist bones were knotty and out of proportion, her elbows, which her rolled-up sleeves displayed, were pointed and knobby, her shoulders bent, her feet spread beyond their natural bounds—from head to foot she was a little discordant note. She had a pale, peaked face, her scanty fair hair was strained tightly back and twisted into a tiny knot, and her expression was at once passive and eager.

And this astonishing hired-girl heroine runs away with a grizzled old tin peddler whom she has never seen or heard of ten minutes before her flight, a man, moreover, with a wife still living—not conventional material surely. Yet humble though it is, and truthful to the verge of veritism, it nevertheless is a romance even as its author terms it. Seldom are her stories harrowing to the bitter end, seldom are they without those deeper shadows that only romance may throw.

Though her manner is traceable to no originals, nevertheless she

was affected deeply by her era. She wrote for the magazines, and
the magazines of the mid-'eighties were demanding sharply
defined characters, unique personalities graphically presented—
Colonel Starbottles, Huckleberry Finns, Uncle Remuses, Marse
Chans—and in no area could more individualized characters be
found than among the moldering ruins of the old Puritan theoc-
racy with its survivals, and its abnormalities of the New England
conscience, that ghostly reminder of an age of spiritual laws as
inflexible as Nature herself. And she gave the times what the
times demanded. She gave dialect in abundance in her earliest
tales, and yet she never gave it for mere local color effect: it was
an organic part of her material and inseparable from it, so much
so that one to-day may read the tales and not think of the dialect
within them. One sees only her intensely presented men and
women, hauntingly alive, compelling. Alone of all the New
England writers she has left out the ancestral element. She was
not working upon the surface. Tales like a "A Village Lear" and
"Louisa" are studies not in the local, but the universal.

To study her methods and her materials, open to what is perhaps
the most embracingly typical of all her tales, "Gentian." Note
first the Scotch-like parsimony as to title and note in her indexes
that it is a mannerism: "Silence," "Louisa," "Luella Miller,"
"Sister Lyddy," "Eglantina,"—one is reminded of P. Deming,
who also was a New Englander. Note that the sentence structure
is as bare as the title. The characters are introduced at once,
curtly, gaspingly, as by one with the asthma:

The women were sisters. Hannah was Hannah Orton, unmarried,
Lucy was Mrs. Tollet. Alfred was her sick husband. Hannah's long,
sallow face was deeply wrinkled. Her wide mouth twisted emphatically
as she talked—

An unpromising *dramatis personæ* for a tale—only three in all, a
man and wife married fifty years and the wife's dismal old-maid
sister. The parsimony extends even to the style: repressed at
every point, stripped like a Puritan of all ornament and color and
shorn even of conjunctions. The New England conception of the
sphere of woman, Abrahamic in its narrowness and severity, is
everywhere in evidence. One finds it in all her tales. "Alfred
Tollet, ever since she had married him, had been the sole autocrat
of all her little Russias; her very thoughts had followed him like

sheep." Sick all the spring, he refuses in balky sullenness to have a doctor, and the women are worried, especially his wife:

"Well, I know one thing; ef he was my husband he'd *hev* a doctor."

"No, you couldn't make him, Hannah; you couldn't, no more'n me. Alferd was allers jest so. He ain't never thought nothin' of doctors, nor doctor's stuff."

"Well, I'd make him take somethin'. In my opinion he needs somethin' bitter."

"Lor'! he wouldn't take it, you know, Hannah."

"He'd hev to. Gentian would be good for him."

"He wouldn't tech it."

"I'd make him, ef I had to put it in his tea unbeknownst to him."

"Oh, I wouldn't dare to."

Nevertheless, though in palpitating terror, she not only put it in his tea, but mixed it with his food, explaining the bitter taste to him with the theory that the bitter was in his mouth, an accompaniment of the disease. And the man improved until by summer he was entirely well again; but as he improved his wife seemed to decline. She had deceived her husband and her New England conscience, like a hair shirt, grew daily sharper and sharper. At last, no longer able to contain her awful secret, against Hannah's earnest advice, she poured out upon her husband a flood of confession. With a face like a flint he spoke not a word, but left the room, followed by her piteous little bleating explanations: "Oh, Alferd, don't look at me so! I meant it all fer the best. I was afeard you wouldn't git well without you hed it, Alferd. I was dretful worried." But he spoke not a word and the next morning went to the store for supplies for his breakfast, announcing that he was going to know hereafter what had been put into his food and henceforth would do his own cooking. Heedless of her elaborately prepared meals, day by day he ate his own half-cooked food, saying not a word, and at last, unable to bear it longer, she went down to Hannah's to live. Summer and winter passed and then on a day in the spring the flood broke. He stood at Hannah's door, where his wife awaited him with tremulous eagerness:

"I've come to ask you to come home, Lucy. I'm a-feelin' kinder poorly this spring, an'—I want you ter stew me up a little gentian. That you give me afore did me a sight of good."

"Oh, Alferd!"

It ends as abruptly as it began. It is a story of the life within rather than of the life without, a story of repression, something held grimly within the soul without an outward sign of yielding, and gathering and gathering until the dam breaks at last, sweeping all before it. It is the theme of "A Village Singer," "The Revolt of Mother," "Sister Liddy," "Amanda and Love," "Evelina's Garden," "The Givers," "The Cloak Also," "The Liar," and of the novels *Pembroke* and *Jane Field*, and of other stories besides.

More than any other American short-story writer she may be compared with Hawthorne. Both worked in the deeper and more somber areas of New England life, with the emphasis always upon character rather than action. Of the two, Miss Wilkins is the more human: her tales often are tremulous with pathos, often are illuminated with heat-lightning flashes of humor; of the two, however, Hawthorne was the most perfect artist, the most Grecian in his sense of literary values and the limits of tragedy. His smoothness is the smoothness of current denoting the depth of his genius. Both worked with restraint in the somberest of materials; without the Puritan régime both would have been impossible. Had she had the will of a Hawthorne, the ability to starve in a garret rather than surrender to the magazines, she now might stand, perhaps, even at his high level. Her confession of surrender is not without its touch of pathos:

The most of my work is not really the kind that I myself like. I want more symbolism, more mysticism. I left that out because it struck me people did not want it, and I was forced to consider selling qualities.

Thus for mere bread she surrendered and for years wrote serials for the lady's books of her day. In later years, after her fame was secure enough to dominate to a degree her market, she attempted often pure symbolism as in *Understudies*, and once, at least, the area of ghostly mysticism. Her ghost stories in *The Wind in the Rose Bush* are among the best New England has ever produced—unconventional, unexplained, unreduced, yet seemingly natural and wholly convincing.

Her later short-story work stands on the whole at higher levels than the similar later work of any other American of her period. Her material was richer and more varied: she drew for her characters and motifs not upon a limited and accidental area of rawness and picturesque exceptions: she recorded the decay of an

entire civilization, a complicated social régime in many ways the
richest America has yet produced.   She has written upwards of
two hundred and thirty-eight short stories, not to mention a long
list of novels and novelettes, and yet as late as 1909 the New York
Nation reviewing her book of that year *The Winning Lady and
Other Stories*, could call it the best of all her collections.   Her later
work is often more finished, more artistically self-conscious,
more perfect in form, and yet taken altogether the stories in her
first two collections must be the work upon which her foundations
are to stand.   It is fresh and unconventional, intense in feeling,
spontaneous, the first flow of her inspiration.   In it she stands
peculiarly external to her material, detached, irresponsible,
recording often in shuddery horror, often in tears, the human
tragedy that passes before her eyes.   With *The Luck of Roaring
Camp, Old Creole Days, Main-Travelled Roads*, and a few others,
A New England Nun and Other Stories must be placed upon the
all too slowly growing list of modern American classics.

V

What Allen attempted to do for Kentucky, Grace Elizabeth
King, daughter of a leading barrister and plantation owner of
New Orleans, herself partly Creole, sought to do for Louisiana.
Cable, she believed, had misrepresented her people.   He had
known them only as an observer from without, but she, reared in
the heart of Creole exclusiveness, educated in the fashionable
Creole *pension* of the Mesdames Cenas—scene of "Monsieur
Motte" and "Pupasse"—knew the soul of the old New Orleans,
the richness, the timidity, the passion, the exotic strangeness of a
social régime more French, more Spanish, indeed, than American,
a régime of which Cable could only conjecture and only paint the
picturesque surfaces visible to the observer from without.
The French language was as inevitable for her as the English.
After the school of the mesdames, had come two years of finishing
at Paris, years that gave her pen its Gallic point.   No other
native American short-story writer has been so thoroughly French.
Her tales are like well-made translations from the school of Flaubert and Daudet.   Like Norris and Garland, she affected veritism:
it was in the air of the times; she had learned of Zola to tell the
Truth, but not after the manner of Zola.   Cable she believed had

romanticized New Orleans beyond toleration and misrepresented it: she would present the charming side of her people, their pride, their uniqueness, their distinction, their lovable unselfishness. If romance came into her tales it would be only because romance in New Orleans was the Truth, or to use her own words:

> I am not a romanticist, I am a realist *à la mode de la Nouvelle-Orleans*. I have never written a line that was not realistic, but our life, our circumstances, the heroism of the men and women that surrounded my early horizon—all that was romantic. I had a mind very sensitive to romantic impressions, but critical as to their expression.

The beginning of her *Monsieur Motte*, a chaotic kind of novel made up of short-story episodes in the life of the Creole maiden Marie Modeste, appeared in *The New Princeton Review* in 1886, and the collection was published in final form in 1888. Two other collections she issued during the next five years, and then after 1893 she turned to other literary forms. Like Cable, she had reached the limits of her material and to go on was to repeat what earlier she had done with more freshness and enthusiasm.

Her weakness lay in her technique: she conceived of her material in terms of the novel. Her short stories are chapters. The first section of *Monsieur Motte* contains all the elements of a perfect *conte*, but in section two the story sprawls like a mountain stream that has lost itself in a marsh. *Balcony Stories* are sketches with documentary design like Cable's *Strange True Stories of Louisiana*. Her power lay in her lightness of touch, her dialogue—French in its rapidity and brilliancy, her restraint, her ability by touches of suggestion to do in a sentence what a heavier hand might do in a page, and finally in her characterization, her Creole femininities with their shrinking timidity, their tropic passion and intensity, their piquancy, their simplicity and folly, their innate gentility—Bon Maman, Misette, Madame Josephine, Marie Modeste, Madame Lareveillère. They are as intensely alive as are the creations of Miss Wilkins in her world which is so utterly different. A tale like "Bon Maman" is unique among American short stories: it is as native as even "A Humble Romance" or "Up the Coulée," but it reads like an exotic, like a translation from another tongue.

In technique, however, in spontaneous humor, and in universality of appeal she was surpassed by her contemporary, Kate

Chopin, who in American short-story chronicles must be rated as
a vivid episode, as brief and intense as a tropic storm. Her two
volumes of short tales, *Bayou Folk* and *A Night in Acadie*, are still
in their original editions and totally unread, and her name is
forgotten save by a few, and yet there are few pieces in the American short-story collections that surpass in restrained intensity,
in finesse, in the inevitableness of startling climax, some of the
best of her tales.

To no novelist of her period, not even to Miss Wilkins, was
fiction-writing a more spontaneous thing. She was of Celtic
temperament, her father pure Irish, her mother partly French.
Nothing in her early years, save, perhaps, this racial inheritance,
prepared her for art. She left the convent school in St. Louis at
nineteen to be married to a New Orleans cotton factor, and for
years in Louisiana there was little that might be called literary in
her surroundings. When her husband died, the family—there
were six children—was living in the remote French hamlet of
Vloutiersville in the Natchitoches parish on the Red River. When
a year later, she moved to St. Louis with her children, she was
thirty-six and literature was as far from her thoughts as playing
the organ in the city cathedral. Then wholly by accident had
come the inspiration to turn her experiences among the 'Cadians
and the Creoles of the remote Louisiana bayou villages into fiction
for the market. The magazines were full of studies of remote
regions not half as strange and picturesque. She began with a
novel, *At Fault* (St. Louis, 1890), following it as she could with a
flight of short stories, and by 1894 the leading publisher of Boston
was issuing them in a collection. This seems to have been her
crowning achievement. From this moment, for some reason, began
her decline. She never won popularity; her later books were issued
by various publishers, and when, in 1899, her novel, *The Awakening*, was greeted with hostile criticism, she abandoned literature
as temperamentally as in the first place she had entered it.
She must be rated as a genius, taut, vibrant, intense of soul,
yet a genius in eclipse, one, it is to be feared, that is destined to
be total.

The materials in Mrs. Chopin's two volumes are more strange
even than those used by Cable and Miss King, but the tales are
far more than mere strange materials. Without a thought, undoubtedly, of what she was really doing, she struck always uni-

versal chords. The tales are more than mere snapshots in the Red River canebrakes: they are glimpses into the universal heart of humanity. Open, for instance, to the tale "Athénaïse." The young Creole maiden, after only two months of marriage, has run away from her husband, though he has done not a thing that even the most assiduous divorce lawyer could find against him. And this is her explanation:

No, I don't hate him. It's jus' being married that I detes' an' despise. I hate being Mrs. Cazeau, an' I want to be Athénaïse Miché again. I can't stan' to live with a man; to have him always there; his coats and pantaloons hanging in my room; his ugly bare feet—washing them in my tub, befo' my very eyes. Ugh!"

And she simply deserted him even as you and I may have dreamed, in our own lives, and what came of it is what might have come to you and me had we dared, like her, to go to the extremes of our impulses.

Despite Cooper-like crudenesses—she can even write passages like this: "He noticed that they were handsome eyes; not so large as Elvina's, but finer in their expression. They started to walk down the track"—nevertheless, in a few of her stories she has been surpassed in technique not even by Aldrich or Bunner. Local color she used with restraint only to intensify her characterization. Here, as with Miss King, was a chief source of her strength. Like Dickens, she could make even the most insignificant of her characters intensely alive. The reader knows them and feels them and sees them. Madame Celestin with her unconscious coquetry, her pathetic helplessness, her wavering, her delicious femininity, completely fascinates the solid old judge. He becomes young again, he will get her divorce—he is certain of it, he will marry her himself—he goes to propose to her, but Madame Celestin—the astounding last sentence of the story, so natural yet so dramatically final, is the very soul of art—and of life.

Her sense of dramatic values was strong. Unconsciously to the reader, she worked ever toward some unforeseen climax. The culmination of the story, "Désirée's Baby," is peculiarly effective. The young planter, Armand Aubigny, rich, handsome, proud of his family name, married the beautiful Creole Désirée, who had come as a stranger into the community, and the two lived in a heaven of love and happiness until the baby was born. Then came a ghastly suspicion, growing with every day into more complete certainty: manifestly there had been a reversion to a negro ancestor. The neighborhood began to whisper and the love of Armand turned swiftly into hate. His wife had deceived him. Without defense or explanation, her head held high, her dainty wedding slippers on her feet, Désirée, her baby in her arms, marched into the swamp along the bayou and was never seen again, and in sullen rage Armand burned all traces of the woman and her child, even the costly wedding finery and the dainty layette. She had brought the first blot upon the proud family name. The tragedy is over; the reader is about to close the book, when Armand, who is clearing the old bureau of all of Désirée's belongings, happens upon an old letter in his mother's handwriting. It had been written to his own father: "But, above all," the letter ended, "night and day, I thank the good God for having so arranged our lives that our dear Armand will never know that his mother, who adores him, belongs to the race that is cursed with the brand of slavery." The sentence closes the story, but not for the reader.

Without models, without study or short-story art, without revision, and usually at a sitting, she produced what often are masterpieces before which one can only wonder and conjecture.

VI

The short story offered a peculiarly rich field for feminine writers and their increasing numbers and the excellence of their product was a noteworthy phenomenon of the period. In 1895 Howells, reviewing eight current short-story collections, was struck with the fact that "the artistry of the women seems finer than that of the men," but "whether this is because the slighter form lends itself more willingly to their touch" or because of some other reason, he was undecided. In his volume, *Criticism and Fiction*, he returned to the subject:

An interesting fact in regard to the different varieties of the short story among us is that the sketches and studies by the women seem faithfuller and more realistic than those of the men, in proportion to their number. Their tendency is more distinctly in that direction, and there is a solidity, an honest observation, in the work of such women, which often leaves little to be desired.

The New England environment, especially in its rural areas, furnished a surprisingly rich field for feminine study. A score of five-foot shelves would hardly hold the literary ventures of women in this area so suited to their powers. Annie Trumbull Slosson, Mrs. Chace Wyman, Anna Fuller, Kate Douglas Wiggin, Eliza Orne White, Alice Brown, are but the beginning of the list of feminine writers who have continued the traditions of Mrs. Stowe, Mrs. Cooke, Miss Jewett, and Mrs. Freeman. Their work, though much of it is well done, has added little that need detain the student of the American short-story evolution.

One may pause, however, before the later volumes of Alice Brown, who in many ways is the most significant figure of the later group. In her earlier "Tiverton" period she was a local colorist, reminiscent, inclined to the sentimental, selective. Like most of the women writers of the day, she was intent upon picturization, upon the collection of local peculiarities, types, quaint dialect perversions. Her tales were sketchy and loose of structure; often they read like the opening chapter of a novel, leisurely, undramatic. One feels that until even past the eighteen-nineties the short-story form was not grapsed by her in its artistic bearings, that her ambitions lay rather in the field of the novel. She worked in various forms: only a comparatively small section of her final shelf of books is occupied by short stories. But with the awakening of the new decade to the new sense of short-story form she also seemed to awake. Unconsciously, perhaps, to herself, she began to deepen and broaden, and to plan with artistic restraint and proportion. Almost alone among American short-story writers, she has done her best work last. In her volume, *Vanishing Points*, and the stories that had followed it she has worked with an artistry sonnetlike in its form and finish and with materials and motifs not merely localized, but universal. She has more humor than Mrs. Freeman and more grace of style, but she lacks her dramatic power and her lyric intensity. She lacks, too, even in her best tales, a certain robustness and trail-breaking originality, and, lacking it, must fall into secondary place. By nature she is prone to sentiment, prone to a gentle mysticism, to an avoidance of the harsh and the brutal, to a deliberate shutting of the eyes to those injustices of life that are never righted, those false balances so common all about us that weigh and record and mock their victim's despair. Her kinship is with Howells and Miss

Jewett. Beside the work of the latter-day school of tale writers, the Mrs. Whartons and the Dreisers and the Hergesheimers and all the revolters from the sentimental and the provincial, her short stories seem spineless and mid-Victorian, and yet it may be recorded that none of the New England group since Hawthorne, save only Mrs. Freeman, has thrown more light upon the New England soul than has she in her sketches and tales.

Two other women writers stirred deeply the imagination of the mid-eighteen-nineties: Margaret Deland and Mary Hartwell Catherwood, the first a native of Pennsylvania, the second a native of Ohio and the first woman in America to approach fiction with a college degree—a degree, it may be noted, won in a trans-Allegheny college. Mrs. Deland is fundamentally a novelist, but her creation of Old Chester—an idealization of her native Manchester, Pennsylvania—and of Dr. Lavendar, about whom the stories center, places her securely in the inner circle of American short-story writers. To have added a character to the small roll of distinctively American fictional types is surely distinction. She has worked without dialect and without local color, prevailingly with ethical basis, in the more refined materials of village life. Her inclination constantly is toward problems—problems social, ethical, religious—and her Dr. Lavendar is the *deus ex machina,* the supreme court of appeal in her little world, and his kindly solutions are always Solomonlike and final.

Mrs. Catherwood also was primarily a maker of Scottlike romance: but at times she turned to the smaller canvas. Her field was Parkman's French and Indian area about the St. Lawrence and the Great Lakes in the days of the *voyageurs* and the *coureurs de bois.* Her *Mackinac and Lake Stories* are more historical in material than Miss Woolson's tales of the same region, more rapid, more intense, and more exciting. She had the imagination of the historical romancer and she had learned from her master, Parkman, to make her materials from the dead past compellingly alive. The full tide of a century of French romance flows through the tales. They lack short-story condensation at times, and often they are like mere chronicles—colorful chapters in a Parkman history, narrated episodes in the complete story of an era, but in power of characterization and in ability to create the atmosphere of a time or place that holds the reader to a unity of impression from the first moment and makes him feel, as, for example, the horror of superstition in "The Windigo" tale, in Cooperlike management of headlong action that does not culminate till the last sentence, she stands alone among the later writers of fiction. The wave of historical romance that gathered and broke in the late 'nineties after the swift collapse of the Spanish-war venture, expressed itself almost exclusively in fiction of Waverley-novel length. Mrs. Catherwood almost alone of the romancers of the period sought to turn the tide into the short-story inlets and bays. It was a doubtful experiment. Historical romance needs room, perspective, spread of canvas: the short story is a vividly presented moment of to-day, without past and without future save as the imagination of the reader may create them for himself after the story has been told.

BIBLIOGRAPHY

STORIES BY AMERICAN AUTHORS. TEN VOLUMES. 1884.

[Arranged alphabetically by Authors.]

Alvey A. Adee, "The Life Magnet," Vol. 8.[1] *Putnam's*, Aug., 1870.

George Arnold, "Why Thomas Was Discharged," Vol. 5. *Atlantic*, June, 1863.

Henry A. Beers, "Split Zephyr," Vol. 8. *Century*, June, 1883.

Edward Bellamy, "Lost," Vol. 7. *Scribner's*, Dec., 1877.

Park Benjamin, "The End of New York," Vol. 5. *Fiction*, Oct. 31, 1881.

William Henry Bishop, "One of the Thirty Pieces," Vol. 1. *Atlantic*, Jan., 1876.

H. H. Boyesen, "A Daring Fiction," Vol. 10. New York *Commercial Advertiser*, Nov., 1884.

Noah Brooks, "Lost in the Fog," Vol. 4. *Overland*, Dec., 1868.

H. C. Bunner, "The Documents in the Case" (with Matthews), Vol. 1. *Scribner's*, Sept., 1879.

H. C. Bunner, "Love in Old Cloathes," Vol. 4. *Century*, Sept., 1883.

Frances Hodgson Burnett, "A Story of the Latin Quarter," Vol. 3. *Scribner's*, May, 1879.

Lizzie W. Champney, "The Heartbreak Cameo," Vol. 6. *Galaxy*, Jan., 1877.

Roland F. Coffin, "How Old Wiggins Wore Ship," Vol. 9. New York *World*, Nov., 1878.

Rebecca Harding Davis, "Balacchi Brothers," Vol. 1. *Lippincott's*, July, 1872.

J. W. DeForest, "An Inspired Lobbyist," Vol. 4. *Atlantic*, Dec., 1872.

---

[1] This in each case refers to the number of the volume in the set.

J. W. DeForest, "The Brigade Commander," Vol. 8. New York *Times*.
Charles De Kay, "Manmat'ha," Vol. 10. *Atlantic*, Feb., 1876.
John Eddy, "A Dinner Party," Vol. 2. *Atlantic*, Nov., 1872.
Lina R. Fairfax, "The Misfortunes of Bro' Thomas Wheatley," Vol. 6.
  Scribner's, Sept., 1881.
Margaret Floyd, "Passages From the Journal of a Social Wreck," Vol. 7.
  Harper's, Oct., 1882.
Mary Hallock Foote, "Friend Barton's Concern," Vol. 4. *Scribner's*,
  July, 1879.
Harold Frederic, "Brother Sebastian's Friendship," Vol. 6. Utica
  Observer, 1879.
Charles S. Gage, "Mr. Bixby's Christmas Visitor," Vol. 9. *Appleton's
  Journal*, Dec., 1871.
Lucretia P. Hale, "The Spider's Eye," Vol. 3. *Putnam's*, July, 1856.
J. S. of Dale, "Mrs. Knollys," Vol. 2. *Century*, Nov., 1883.
Mary Putnam Jacobi, "A Martyr to Science," Vol. 2. *Putnam's*, Aug.,
  1869.
Henry James, "A Light Man," Vol. 5. *The Galaxy*, July, 1869.
T. A. Janvier, "Pancha," Vol. 10. *Century*, Sept., 1884.
Virginia W. Johnson, "The Image of San Donato," Vol. 7. *Harper's*,
  Jan., 1879.
Leonard Kip, "Xmas Has Come," Vol. 9. *Overland*, Jan., 1870.
George Parsons Lathrop, "Two Purse Companions," Vol. 3. *Scribner's*,
  Aug., 1878.
David D. Lloyd, "Poor Ogla-Moga," Vol. 3. *Harper's*, April, 1882.
James T. McKay, "Stella Grayland," Vol. 7. *Scribner's*, March, 1877.
Brander Matthews (with H. C. Bunner), "The Documents in the Case,"
  Vol. 1. *Scribner's*, Sept., 1879.
Brander Matthews, "Venetian Glass," Vol. 3. [Hitherto Unpublished.]
F. D. Millet, "Yatil," Vol. 5. *Century*, March, 1883.
E. P. Mitchell, "The Tachpomp," Vol. 5. *Scribner's*, March, 1874.
E. P. Mitchell, "The Ablest Man in the World," Vol. 10. New York
  Sun, May, 1879.
Thomas Nelson Page, "Marse Chan," Vol. 9. *Century*, April, 1884.
Elizabeth Stuart Phelps, "Zerviah Hope," Vol. 8. *Scribner's*, Nov. 1880.
Julia Schayer, "The Story of Two Lives," Vol. 10. *Swinton's Story-Teller*,
  Oct. 31, 1883.
Milicent Washburn Shinn, "Young Strong of the Clarion," Vol. 9. *Over-
  land*, Sept., 1884.
Harriet Prescott Spofford, "The Mount of Sorrow," Vol. 2. *Harper's*,
  June, 1883.
C. A. Stephens, "Young Moll's Peevy," Vol. 10. *Scribner's*, April, 1875.
Frank R. Stockton, "The Transferred Ghost," Vol. 2. *Century*, May,
  1882.

Louise Stockton, "Kirby's Coals of Fire," Vol. 7. *Atlantic*, Dec., 1875.

Elizabeth D. B. Stoddard, "Osgood's Predicament," Vol. 8. *Harper's*, June, 1863.

Bayard Taylor, "Who Was She?" Vol. 1. *Atlantic*, Sept., 1874.

Octave Thanet, "The Bishop's Vagabond," Vol. 7. *Atlantic*, Jan., 1884.

Celia Thaxter, "A Memorable Murder," Vol. 3. *Atlantic*, May, 1875.

Mary Agnes Tincker, "Sister Sylvia," Vol. 2. *Lippincott's*, Dec., 1878.

Albert Webster, "An Operation in Money," Vol. 1. *Appleton's*, Sept., 1873.

Albert Webster, "Miss Eunice's Glove," Vol. 6. *Atlantic*, July, 1873.

C. H. White, "The Village Convict," Vol. 6. *Scribner's*, August, 1881.

C. H. White, "Eli," Vol. 9. *Century*, Nov., 1881.

N. P. Willis, "Two Buckets in a Well," Vol. 4. *People I Have Met.*

Constance Fenimore Woolson, "Miss Grief," Vol. 4. *Lippincott's*, May, 1880.

JAMES LANE ALLEN. 1849–

1891. *Flute and Violin and Other Kentucky Tales and Romances.*
"Flute and Violin," *Harper's*, Dec., 1890; "King Solomon of Kentucky," *Century*, June, 1889; "Two Gentlemen of Kentucky," *Century*, 1888; "The White Cowl," *Century*, Sept., 1888; "Sister Dolorosa," *Century*, Dec., 1890, Jan., Feb., 1891; "Posthumous Fame; or, a Legend of The Beautiful," *Century*, March, 1890.

1894. *A Kentucky Cardinal: a Story.*

1895. *Aftermath: Part Two of a Kentucky Cardinal.*

1910. *The Doctor's Christmas Eve and Other Stories.*

HAMLIN GARLAND, 1860–

1891. *Main-Travelled Roads: Six Mississippi Valley Stories.*
"A Branch Road"; "Up the Coulé"; "Among the Corn Rows," *Harper's Weekly*, June, 1890; "The Return of a Private," *Arena*, Dec., 1890; "Under the Lion's Paw," *Harper's Weekly*, Sept., 1889; "Mrs. Ripley's Trip," *Harper's Weekly*, Nov., 1888.
Added to later editions: "The Creamery Man"; "A Day's Pleasure"; "Uncle Ethan Ripley"; "God's Ravens," *Harper's*, June, 1894; "A 'Good Fellow's' Wife."

1893. *Prairie Folks: or, Pioneer Life on the Western Prairies, in Nine Stories.*
"William Bacon's Man"; "Elder Pill, Preacher"; "A Day of Grace"; "Lucretia Burns"; "Some Village Cronies";

"Drifting Crane"; "Daddy Deering"; "Black Ephram";
"The Wapscypinnuon Giger"; "Aidgewise Feelin's"; "The
Sociable at Dudley's."

1897. *Wayside Courtships.*

1910. *Other Main-Travelled Roads.*
"William Bacon's Man"; "Elder Pill, Preacher"; "A Day
of Grace"; "Lucretia Burns"; "Daddy Deering"; "A
Stop-Over at Tyre"; "A Division in the Coolly"; "A Fair
Exile"; "An Alien in the Pines"; "Before the Low Green
Door"; "A Preacher's Love Story."

1916. *They of the High Trails.*

MARY E. WILKINS FREEMAN. 1862–

1887. *A Humble Romance and Other Stories.*
"A Humble Romance"; "Two Old Lovers"; "A Symphony
in Lavender"; "A Tardy Thanksgiving"; "A Modern
Dragon"; "An Honest Soul"; "A Taste of Honey"; "Brakes
and White Vi'lets"; "Robins and Hammers"; "On the
Walpole Road"; "Old Lady Pingree"; "Cinnamon Roses";
"The Bar Light-house"; "A Lover of Flowers"; "A Far-
away Melody"; "A Moral Exigency"; "A Mistaken
Charity"; "Gentian"; "An Object of Love"; "A Gatherer
of Simples"; "An Independent Thinker"; "In Butterfly
Time"; "An Unwilling Guest"; "A Souvenir"; "An old
Arithmetician"; "A Conflict Ended"; "A Patient Waiter":
"A Conquest of Humility."

1891. *A New England Nun and Other Stories.*
"A New England Nun"; "A Village Singer"; "A Gala
Dress"; "The Twelfth Guest"; "Sister Lyddy"; "Calla-
Lilies and Hannah"; "A Wayfaring Couple"; "A Poetess";
"Christmas Jenny"; "A Pot of Gold"; "The Scent of the
Roses"; "A Solitary"; "A Gentle Ghost"; "A Discovered
Pearl"; "A Village Lear"; "Amanda and Love"; "Up
Primrose Hill"; "A Stolen Christmas"; "Life Everlasting";
"An Innocent Gamester"; "Louisa"; "A Church Mouse";
"A Kitchen Colonel"; "The Revolt of Mother."

1892. *Young Lucretia and Other Stories.*

1898. *Silence and Other Stories.*
"Silence"; "The Buckley Lady"; "Evelina's Garden";
"A New England Prophet"; "The Little Maid at the Door";
"Lydia Hersey of East Bridgewater."

1898. *People of Our Neighborhood.*

1900. *The Love of Parson Lord and Other Stories.*
"The Love of Parson Lord"; "The Tree of Knowledge";
"Catharine Parr"; "Three Old Sisters and the Old Beau";
"One Good Time."

1901. *Understudies.*

1903. *Six Trees: Short Stories.*

1903. *The Wind in the Rosebush.*
"The Wind in the Rosebush"; "The Vacant Lot"; "Luella
Miller"; "Shadows on the Wall"; "The South-West
Chamber"; "A Lost Ghost."

1904. *The Givers.*

1907. *Fair Lavinia and Others.*
"The Fair Lavinia"; "Amarina's Roses"; "Eglantina";
"The Pink Shawls"; "The Willow Ware"; "The Secret";
"The Gold"; "The Underling."

1909. *The Winning Lady.*

1914. *The Copy-Cat and Other Stories.*

1918. *Edgewater People.*

GRACE ELIZABETH KING.   1852–

1888. *Monsieur Motte.*
"Monsieur Motte"; "On the Plantation"; "The Drama of
an Evening"; "Marriage of Marie Modeste."

1892. *Tales of a Time and Place.*
"Bayou L'Ombre"; "Bonne Maman"; "Madrilene; or,
the Festival of the Dead"; "The Christmas Story of a
Little Church"; "In the French Quarter."

1893. *Balcony Stories.*
"The Balcony"; "A Dream of Three"; "La Grande De-
moiselle"; "Mimi's Marriage"; "The Miracle Chapel";
"The Story of a Day"; "Anne Marie and Jeanne Marie";
"A Crippled Hope"; "'One of Us'"; "The Little Convent
Girl"; "Grandmother's Grandmother"; "The Old Lady's
Restoration"; "A Delicate Affair"; "Pupasse."

KATE CHOPIN.   1851–1904.

1894. *Bayou Folk.*
"A No-Account Creole"; "In and Out of Old Natchitoches";
"In Sabine"; "A Very Fine Fiddle"; "Beyond the Bayou";
"Old Aunt Peggy"; "The Return of Alcibiade"; "A Rude
Awakening"; "The Bênitous's Slave"; "Désirée's Baby";

"A Turkey Hunt"; "Madame Celestin's Divoroo"; "Love on the Bon-Dieu"; "Loka"; "Boulôt and Boulotte"; "For Marse Chouchoute"; "A Visit to Avoyelles"; "A Wizard From Gettysburg"; "Ma'ame Pélagie"; "At the 'Cadian Ball"; "La Belle Zoraïde"; "A Gentleman of Bayou Têche"; "A Lady of Bayou St. John."

1897. *A Night in Acadie.*

ALICE BROWN. 1857–

1895. *Meadow-Grass. Tales of New England Life.*
"Number Five"; "Farmer's Eli's Vacation"; "After All"; "Told in the Poorhouse"; "Heman's Ma"; "Heartsease"; "Mis' Wadleigh's Guest"; "A Righteous Bargain"; "Joint Owners in Spain"; "At Sudleigh Fair"; "Bankrupt"; "Nancy Boyd's Last Sermon"; "Strollers in Tiverton."

1899. *Tiverton Tales.*
"Dooryards"; "A March Wind"; "The Mortuary Chest"; "Horn-o'-the-Moon"; "A Stolen Festival"; "A Last Assembling"; "The Way of Peace"; "The Experience of Hannah Prime"; "Honey and Myrrh"; "A Second Marriage"; "The Flat-Iron Lot'"; "The End of All Living."

1904. *High Noon.*

1906. *The Country Road.*

1910. *Country Neighbors.*

1911. *The One-Footed Fairy and Other Stories.*

1913. *Vanishing Points.*

1918. *The Flying Teuton.*

MARY HARTWELL CATHERWOOD. 1847–1902.

1894. *The Chase of Saint Castin and Other Stories of the French in the New World.*

1897. *The Spirit of an Illinois Town.*

1899. *The Queen of the Swamp and Other Plain Americans.*

1899. *Mackinac and Lake Stories.*
"Marianson"; "The Black Feather"; "The Cobbler in the Devil's Kitchen"; "The Skeleton on Round Island"; "The Penitent of Cross Village"; "The King of the Beaver"; "Beaver Lights"; "A British Islander"; "The Cursed Patois"; "The Mothers of Honore"; "The Blue Man"; "The Indian on the Trail."

MARGARET DELAND. 1857–

1893. *Mr. Tommy Dove and Other Stories.*
1898. *Old Chester Tales.*
1903. *Dr. Lavendar's People.*
1908. *R. J.'s Mother and Some Other People.*
1915. *Around Old Chester.*

CHAPTER XV

I

By the later 'nineties the short story had become so established an article of merchandise that the production of it became a recognized industry with numberless workers. The coming of the fifteen-cent magazine and the Sunday supplement stimulated greatly the quantity of the output. By 1900 the short-story stream had become a flood and syndicates had been established to handle it. Each magazine and paper had its own definition of short-story excellence and to get what it wanted paid often unheard-of prices. The New York *World* paid O. Henry one hundred dollars a week for his story contribution, whatever it might be, to the Sunday issue, and later the *Saturday Evening Post* paid for each of its short stories more than many of the great English novelists a generation before received for complete novels that have become classics.

Magazine and newspaper offices now became schools for short-story writing. Young reporters and copy readers and editors, stimulated by the success of Kipling and other popular writers, grown adept in the rules of the game, became themselves producers. The new generation of writers came largely from this journalistic training school. One needs cite but the names of Richard Harding Davis, Lafcadio Hearn, Stephen Crane, Harold Frederic, George Ade, William Allen White, Thomas Janvier, John R. Spears, Alfred Lewis, and such modern instances as Theodore Dreiser, Willa Cather, James Branch Cabell, Edna Ferber, Irving Cobb, Freeman Tilden, Zona Gale, Sinclair Lewis—it is needless to extend the roll.

Frank Norris in his "Salt and Sincerity" papers in *The Critic* of 1902 caught the literary pitch of the new century. The writer of fiction, he believed, must be like the writer of news for the morning journal, in closest touch with the great democratic mass called "the American people." He should make it his constant study to give them precisely what they want, for "in the last analysis the people are always right." American literature must be democratized literature. "A literature that cannot be vulgarized is no literature at all and will perish." The new young school of fiction writers was awake to this fact. "The 'language, institutions and religion' of fiction writers are at present undergoing the most radical revolution in the history of literature." More and more it was being recognized that the novelist must be a journalist; he must "be in the midst of life. He cannot plunge too deeply into it." No more Hawthornes, no more Henry Jameses, no more Mary E. Wilkinses sitting apart and watching the currents of life:

If the modern novelist does not understand the Plain People, if he does not address himself directly to them intelligibly and simply, he will fail. But he will never understand them by shutting himself away from them. He must be—and here one comes to the conclusion of the whole matter— a Man of the World. None more so. Books have no place in his equipment, have no right to be there; will only cumber and confuse him. His predecessor never read the newspapers, but for him the newspaper is more valuable than all the tomes of Ruskin and all the volumes of Carlyle. And more valuable than all are the actual vital Affairs of Men.

The short story under the new conditions was to be, he believed, like the fifteen-cent magazine and the daily newspaper, a thing brilliantly done, timely to the moment, and completely ephemeral. The life of a short story, no matter what its quality, was a month. "If very good, it will create a demand for another short story by the same author, but that one particular contribution, the original one, is irretrievably and hopelessly dead." It was impossible to galvanize it into life by issuing it with others in book form. Successful collections were startlingly few and always the work of masters of fiction, and the masters of fiction more and more were using the short-story form only as a makeshift:

If a writer is one of the "best men" working for a "permanent place," he will turn his attention and time, his best efforts, to the writing of novels, reverting to the short story only when necessary for the sake of boiling the Pot or chasing the Wolf. He will abandon the field to the inferior men, or enter it only to dispose of "copy" which does not represent him at his best. And, as a result, the quality of the short story will decline more and more.

Norris himself was too multitudinous and headlong, too epic of soul, to appreciate the possibilities latent in the restricted area of the short story, or to work with patience upon art in the small. Several collections he published, but his shorter pieces are fragments of novels, preliminary studies like "A Deal in Wheat," or dashed-off "pot-boilers." He was a novelist. He thought not in units of single situations nor even in units of whole novels: he thought in trilogies, in vast epic cycles that involved not America alone, but the whole world. He died early, before he had blocked out more than the ground plan of his great fictional cathedral. Perhaps no other American novelist has been so little endowed by nature for working with the short story form.

II

Another shaping force came with the 'nineties—doubtless was created by the spirit of the 'nineties: Rudyard Kipling, East Indian journalist and cosmopolitan reporter, who almost alone, both in England and in America, swung the short-story form into a new orbit. The decade was his. He had appeared with its opening year—the first mention of his name in the New York *Critic* was March, 1890—and by the middle of it he was as widely known to the English-speaking world as even Thackeray. His tremendous vogue fired the imagination of America. He had settled in America, near Brattleboro, Vermont, the early home of Mary E. Wilkins, and he was making contracts with American magazines and publishing houses that seemed to the little world of Hawthorne and Poe and Longfellow nothing short of amazing. His vigorous narratives of India and the Indian army came like a breath from a new world, as Bret Harte's had come a generation before. Harte, indeed, had been the source of his inspiration. He had borrowed all the elements of the elder writer's uniqueness: his strangeness of materials and settings, his impressionism that made alive a character by an epithet or a stroke of the pen, his compression, his melodramatic vigor and momentum; but swiftly the readers of *Plain Tales From the Hills* forgot the elder master in the freshness and strangeness of the new genius. Here was power; here was lavish creative energy let loose upon a new world, the youthful Anglo-Indian empire behind which lay a civilization that had been ancient before history had received its name.

And he called his creations "Plain Tales"—the young Frank Norris school hailed the term as a definition, for to be a *plain* tale the narrative must be stripped of all the conventional embroideries: sentimentalism, propagandic purpose, false romanticism, mere literary veneer, and every variety of that fastidious squeamishness as to theme and *dramatis personæ* which had rendered effeminate so much of the Victorian fiction. A plain tale told the plain truth, no more and no less, and to tell the plain truth the teller must have had concrete and vicarious experience with the material in which he worked. One could not read a page of the early Kipling without feeling its creator's nearness to his subject. He had been on the spot, and he had seen and he had felt; he was writing from the inside; he was a part of what he wrote—"*et quorum pars magna fui.*"

To leaf through the magazines of the later 'nineties is to be increasingly in the presence of the Kiplingized short story. The novelist was becoming, even as Norris was demanding, a man of action in the thick and the center of things, a special correspondent returned from the ends of the earth or from behind the locked doors of mystery to report upon what he had seen. The era of the specialized short story, the new plain tale, had begun. And with it came a new short-story manner. The narrative must move at every point with vigor, it must have brilliancy and "snap"; it must be fresh and new and picturesque; and it must be the work of a specialist with whom it might have been—probably was—a personal experience. Jack London at the beginning of his amazing literary sixteen years gave this as the demand of the times:

Make it concrete, to the point, with snap and go and life, crisp and crackling and interesting. . . . Be terse in style, vigorous of phrase, apt, concretely apt, in similitude. Avoid platitudes and commonplaces. Get the atmosphere, the color, strong color, lots of it. Dig right in with both hands, and get the essence of it, the spirit, the significance. What does it mean? Find out what it means. That's what you're there for. Exercise selection. Seize upon things salient, eliminate the rest and you have pictures. Paint those pictures in words. Then put a snapper at the end, so if they are crowded for space they can cut off your contents anywhere, reattach the snapper, and the story will still retain form.

Such was the art Jack London was practicing after the grilling apprenticeship he has described in *Martin Eden*. One finds a perfect illustration of it in the work of Stephen Crane, inspired reporter, literary *coureur de bois* equipped for every emergency— poetry *à la mode*, prose artistic or plain, mere fiction worth cabling under oceans for its news value, war letters that read like *contes*. Never was there more intense and headlong and artistically creative worker for the press: he was dead at twenty-nine, with fourteen volumes published, not to speak of multitudinous newspaper work done in various stormy areas of the world.

The first canon of Crane's art was avoidance of the conventional. If he described a battle he would leave out all the pomp and circumstance of war—the heroic, the melodramatic, the merely ghastly—and dwell upon the seemingly useless movements of a few type figures. Their remarks, their conjectures, their perplexity as to the meaning of the parts they were playing in the colossal drama, their rushings here and there, their behavior when wounded —that is all the war any individual soldier can ever know; no one, not even the general in command, ever sees the *battlefield* during the action: it is a sum of infinitesimal minor parts, and Crane paints with care these infinitesimal parts. "The Open Boat" is a study, chiefly psychological, of four shipwrecked men in a dory that is constantly on the point of capsizing—their running remarks, their conjectures, their expedients suggested or tried, their hopes and fears, their actions during the night, their fundamental characters slowly emerging under the strain, their final battle with the surf—a thousand minutiæ, each insignificant, but gradually working toward a finished whole that makes the reader feel as if the adventure had been his own, as indeed it had been the author's own during the filibustering days before the war in Cuba.

Crane's second canon concerned sentiment—"sentiment is the devil" had been Flaubert's phrasing. Avoidance of it became an obsession: it was the chief enemy of Truth. He would not even assign names to his characters; he made them symbols: the captain, the cook, the oiler, the freckled man, the assassin, and the like. The death of one of them, however, realistically pictured, stirs no emotions save momentary horror. The death of the oiler is recorded as one would record the destruction of a machine:

Suddenly the man cried: "What's that?" He pointed a swift finger. The correspondent said, "Go."

In the shallows, face downward, lay the oiler. His forehead touched sand that was periodically, between each wave, clear of the sea.

That is all.

"The Open Boat," perhaps his most praised story, is the day's work of a newspaper correspondent intent only on reproducing graphically the experience through which he has just passed. The style is staccato, short of sentence, compressed like a night letter, stripped bare of all but essentials. Every detail must be made vivid by an epithet or a picturing phrase. Details seemingly trivial are made important. Impressionism is pushed to the extreme; the picture is everything:

Canton-flannel gulls flew near by. Sometimes they sat down on the sea, near patches of brown seaweed that rolled on the waves with a movement like carpets on a line in a gale.

Or this from his story, "The Bride Comes to Yellow Sky":

A man in a maroon-colored flannel shirt, which had been purchased for purposes of decoration, and made, principally, by some Jewish women on the east side of New York, rounded a corner and walked into the main street of Yellow Sky. In either hand the man held a long, heavy, blue-black revolver. Often he yelled, and these cries rang through the semblance of a deserted village, shrilly flying over the roofs in a volume that seemed to have no relation to the ordinary vocal strength of a man. It was as if the surrounding stillness formed the arch of a tomb over him. These cries of ferocious challenge rang against walls of silence. And his boots had red tops with gilded imprints, of the kind beloved in winter by little sledding boys on the hillsides of New England.

This defect, not always so conspicuous in Crane's work, became with his followers a mannerism that spoiled much otherwise good narrative. If *every* detail has been made vivid it becomes like music played wholly in *fortissimo;* if every epithet and color stroke has been heightened to its extreme the result is monotony. There is no contrast; the straining is too evident; the work is a *tour de force.*

Whether this Stephen Crane type of short narrative is a short story or not depends wholly upon definitions. Of plot, as plot is usually defined, it has none; of love element, of women, indeed, none; of problem, or of dramatic dilemma, or of struggle between contrasted forces, none at all. It is a running series of moving pictures, each picture vivid and intense; it is a forced growth in the field of modern journalism.

The influence of Kipling spread swiftly, even into the most conservative literary areas. The young Owen Wister, of Philadelphia, encouraged by Howells, and set to dreaming over his Stevenson, was all at once, to quote his own words, given "a shove from the genius of *Plain Tales From the Hills.*" It sent him "on a long and broad wandering through the Platte Valley, Powder River, Buffalo, Cheyenne, Fort Washakie, Jackson's Hole and the Park." And then, after "a final push" by Prosper Mérimée, it set him to writing his plain tales of the Northwest, culminating in *The Virginian,* a novel written originally as short stories, "our last glimpse," to quote Henry Mills Alden, "of the pioneer in the plainsman and the cowboy types, then passing and now gone."

The craving of the reading public for this specialized brief fiction—vivid narrative work by writers who drew not upon imagination, but upon positive knowledge—was gratified by a whole school of writers. F. Hopkinson Smith, artist, engineer, cosmopolitan, in such sketches as those in his *The Under Dog, At Close Range,* and *Forty Minutes Late and Other Stories,* told of travels with dragoman on Balkan railroads and in Oriental hotels, or of the adventures of a lecturer hurled from place to place in winter over the American map, or again of the battles of a lighthouse architect on the reefs of the Atlantic; John Fox, Jr., recounted with vivid details vendetta episodes in the southern Cumberlands; William Allen White, country editor, told of people and of politics behind the scenes in Kansas; John R. Spears, practical sailor, wrote *The Port of Missing Men and Other Stories of the Sea;* James Brendan Connolly recorded with grim realism the life of the Gloucestermen on the deep-sea fishing grounds; F. Marion Crawford, traveler and cosmopolitan, turned from his novels to prepare a series of ghost stories of the ocean, and with his "The Upper Berth" succeeded in producing one of the most creepy tales in later literature; Frank H. Spearman pictured life in the engine cab and the roundhouse; Stewart Edward White drew from full experience savage materials from the wilds of two continents, centering especially upon the Michigan lumber camps and the life of the river man, perhaps a new character in American fiction; and Jack London transported his readers to the Klondike and the Solomon Islands. Much of the work of this school must be classed as sketches, or as adventure "yarns," or as mere "news stories," but among the astonishingly voluminous mass may be found here and there genuine short stories, often so distinctive in quality and in form that, had they appeared a generation earlier, they would have been singled out as masterpieces. As it is, for the most part they have been swept by the flood into the rubbish heap of forgotten periodicals.

III

The undoubted leader of the school of literary special correspondents, the most picturesque figure, perhaps, in a peculiarly picturesque era, was Richard Harding Davis, son of Rebecca Harding Davis, author of the remarkable tale of the 'sixties, "Life in the Iron Mills." The biography of a professional newspaper correspondent is, to a large extent, a list of his reportorial assignments and of his adventures while following instructions. Of these Davis had more than commonly falls to the lot of one man. At twenty-two, after a brief college career, he became a reporter on Philadelphia dailies, and until his death was in the employment of great metropolitan journals. For twenty-five years he lived in the storm centers of the world. "No one," said Charles Dana Gibson, "ever saw more wars in so many different places." He reported the Cuban war, two Balkan wars, the Russo-Japanese war, various South American and Central American disturbances, the Boer War, the early phases of the World War, and he was sent to report at various times upon conditions in the Congo, in Mexico, in the Mediterranean regions, and elsewhere. In a single year, to quote the words of his biographer "he reported the Coronation at Moscow, the Millennial Celebration, the Spanish-Cuban War, the McKinley Inauguration, the Greek-Turkish War and the Queen's Jubilee." The whole world—its thousand cities, its roadways and carriers, its passwords and rituals, its "waiters, generals, actors, princes," to quote Mr. Dunne, became to him a twice-told tale. In a casual letter he could mention as a mere episode in his work such a tremendous itinerary as this: "I have been in Spain, France, Italy, Germany, Austria, Hungary, Serbia, Bulgaria, Turkey, Greece, Egypt and Morocco. I have sat on the rock of Gibraltar, sailed on the Nile and the Suez Canal, and crossed through the Dardanelles, over the Balkans, the steppes of Hungary and the Danube and the Rhine"—this for a single series of newspaper articles, finally gathered as *The Rulers of the Mediterranean*.

As to the quality of his literary product the first remark concerns his father and mother: he was reared in an atmosphere of letters; from early boyhood, literature as a profession was to him a foregone conclusion; and the guidance of the home from first to last was steadily in the direction of the older and more conservative definitions of art. The second remark concerns his later training in the rigid technique of metropolitan journalism. The two forces together made up the Richard Harding Davis that we know: a reporter in kid gloves, a Van Bibber on Newspaper Row, an art molder in wood pulp. He had by nature the news sense; his judgment of what the people would read was infallible, and as a result his popularity was uniformly great. He was keenly aware of all the literary newnesses of his generation and he tried them all. He wrote "Zenda" books, and swashbuckling novels, and adventure tales, and short stories in every key—his final shelf of fiction is surprising in its heterogeneousness. Like the journalist he was, he took ever the color of the moment and pleased his day.

As a genius he falls short. He was a clever workman with an eye always on the sales sheet. Literature to him was a thing for to-day's consumption: to-morrow it might be as old as yesterday's paper; he was not writing for to-morrow. There had been no ripening period in his life; no Hawthornelike study of life's meanings. He was a reporter, and the reporter must work always amid excitement, with rapidity and dash and brilliancy. To him the world existed to be recorded in news dispatches, in cabled correspondence sent hot from scenes of action, in moving stories of contemporary life dashed off for the monthly magazines. He was not a realist like Norris or an impressionist like Crane. There was a touch of the romantic in his nature verging upon the sensational; there was a touch, too, of the melodramatic and the theatric. He delighted in posing before the camera dressed faultlessly for the part he was playing. If he reported the English boat races he would be in boating costume, if it were the yacht-club races he would be faultless as a yachtsman. He announced his engagement to the world by sending his fiancée a ring by messenger boy eight thousand miles altogether, with orders to break all records, and then issuing to the press of two continents daily bulletins of the boy's progress. These elements appear in his fiction. He is smart, cocksure, omniscient; he has been everywhere, in his ears have been whispered the secrets of five continents, the rituals of the whole world he knows by heart.

Superficial is the adjective that comes first to one's pen; artificial is the second. His stories have the perfection of Japanese paper flowers. One thinks of the stage with its painted scenery, its costumes and deftly managed lights, its clever illusions. It is not life: it is the simulacrum of life.

Davis was a latter-day N. P. Willis, vain, theatric, brilliant, journalistic. His readers, like those who bought so eagerly the creations of Willis, opened his pages because that through them they were to be admitted behind doors that were closed. Davis wrote of the New York idle rich as his predecessor had written of the English aristocracy. Willis had traveled everywhere, his readers knew, and had seen everything; in like manner Davis could draw upon the whole world for his materials and motifs. His first story, "Gallegher," admitted its reader to the reporter's quarters and the press rooms of a great city daily; his story, "The Trailer for Room No. 8," transported him to the heart of the criminal area of New York City; "Her First Appearance" personally conducted him through the unknown world behind the asbestos curtain; "The Exiles" showed how defaulters fare in South American cities; "In the Fog" told of his own experience one memorable night in London, and one might go on with tales of Cairo or Cuba or Monte Carlo or Tangier, or the African mines, or the trenches of the World War. Like Willis, he has been there; he is doubtless telling his own adventures; and he is doing it with gentility and vivacity, and with just enough of sentiment and spice and melodrama and movement.

As with Willis's earlier sketches, the tale skims always gracefully over the surface of life, dwelling upon manners and costumes and small talk, and the minutiæ of contemporaneousness. Upon all of it is the stamp of youth. As with Willis, his charm lay in his zest, his delight in the human show, his vivacity, his D'Artagnan-like high spirits and absorption in the moment. It is better done work than Willis's: its author had half a century the advantage of his older rival. He had learned short-story art from his contemporaries and from his newspaper training. In the matter of form he was exquisite. His openings and his closings may be used as models; his dialogue is often distinctive and his climaxes are skillfully managed. He had learned his trade. But the short story is more than technique and more than vivacity and more than headlong movement. Like Willis, he created no living character: Van Bibber is but a lay figure with opera hat and cane. There is no distinction of style, no depth of soil, no philosophy of life, nothing of the fundamental stuff of which all great literature has been made. It is journalism: a thing of the moment, to be thrown aside with the wood-pulp carrier that contained it. It may place its creator even at the head of the notable reporters of his generation, but it can do little more.

The criticism is severe, but it is the arraignment not of an individual alone, but of a school. The Richard Harding Davis type of short story was quickly to give place to the O. Henry type, which was to dominate the second decade of the new century as Kipling had dominated the first.

IV

The decade following the war with Spain was in American literary history the period of picturesque personalities and of stirring fiction from the pens of adventurers. This was the age of Roosevelt and the strenuous life, the age of "men with the bark on," of fiction "red blooded" and near to the Anglo-Saxon elementals. It was the golden age of the war correspondent and the literary soldier of fortune: Crane, Davis, Thomas A. Janvier, John Fox, Jr., Chester B. Fernald, Ralph D. Paine, Harold Frederic, Julian Ralph, Jack London; and of the literary cowboy and the wilderness hunter: Owen Wister, Frederic Remington, Stewart Edward White, O. Henry. These are but the most notable figures of the school, and from all of them came a copious by-product of magazine short stories and sketches.

The most compellingly interesting of the group and perhaps the one of them all most sure of literary permanence was Jack London of California. Few arrivals in all literature have been so startling, so impossible. One's first impulse is to dismiss him with a line. His crudeness, his unrevised prolixity and chaotic story structure, his red-flag socialism often rampant, more often thinly concealed as propaganda, his cave-man philosophy, barbarous and brutal, his supermen and superwomen, wild dreams of adolescence—all of this seems hardly material for permanent literature. It is easy to criticize him, it is easy to deplore him and even despise him, but it is impossible to avoid him. For a decade and more he held the whole middle of the literary road in America and in parts beyond. No literary historian but sooner or later must reckon with Jack London, for, like Davis, he represented more than an individual: he was the product of a literary condition in America. To understand the opening years of the new century one must study Jack Londonism.

Two men more radically unlike than Davis and Jack London it would be hard to find. The whole continent lay between their birthplaces and an even wider gulf lay between their training and their ideals. Davis was of the extreme East, softly reared in the circles of the Philadelphia aristocracy, surrounded by books and art, and instructed by the counsels of a literary father and mother; Jack London was born on the last frontier of the Great West, of pioneer stock that for a century and more had gambled with the horizon and lost. He was reared in poverty on a squalid farm remote from schools, where everything within him save the physical was dwarfed and starved. When he was nine the family removed to the city and there he became a street gamin, selling papers and sweeping out saloons and attending as he could the city schools. A little later he broke from all restraint and became a "tough," a "drunken bum," in the waterfront saloons and dives of Oakland. At sixteen he was leader of a gang of desperadoes. "I had earned," he records, "the title of 'Prince,' but this title was given me by a gang of cutthroats and thieves, by whom I was called 'The Prince of the Oyster Pirates'"—a gang made up of the most desperate human elements of a Pacific terminal port. For months at a time, he records, he "drew not a sober breath." Then at eighteen, by sheer chance, he signed for a sealing voyage to the north Pacific and Japan. Returning after months of brutal hardship, the liquor driven from his system, he determined to reform. For a short time he was a common laborer in the city. "I worked in canneries and factories and laundries; I mowed lawns and cleaned carpets and washed windows," but with the opening spring the wanderlust in his blood became overpowering. Work was intolerable, impossible. "I became a tramp, begging my way from door to door, wandering over the United States and sweating bloody sweats in slums and in prisons. . . . At the age of eighteen I was beneath the point at which I had started. I was down in the cellar of society, down in the subterranean depths of misery about which it is neither nice nor proper to speak. I was in the pit, the abyss, the human cesspool, the shambles and the charnel-house of our civilization. . . . The things I saw there gave me a terrible scare. I was scared into thinking."

The rewards of the world, he reasoned, went not to the muscle worker, but to the men of schooled and trained minds. He would try brain work; he would go to college. By working as a janitor he was able to complete a year at high school, but two years more would be required before he was prepared for college. He would enter at once. By toiling nineteen and twenty hours a day, without a day of respite, or a moment, he completed in three months the two years' work and passed the entrance examinations of the University of California. And then had come his freshman year at college—a year of disillusion. The pace was too slow, the course was too unpractical, the professors were namby-pamby and conventional, failures in life and therefore teachers. He settled down to conduct with strenuous practicability his own private university course, precisely as he has recorded it in *Martin Eden*— "I myself was Martin Eden," he has declared—but in the midst of it had come a flash of news that changed his whole career; gold had been discovered in Alaska, and he was off with the first wave of adventurers. Returning a year later with no gold, he sat down to enter by sheer force the realm of literature, just as earlier he had forced himself into the state university. Whatever one may think of his writings, one cannot but admire the pluck and the desperate toil and the bulldog hang of the man during this period of his preparation. *Martin Eden* at this point is autobiographical. For years he was the most rejected author in America. He rushed at every gate in the literary domain: poetry, essays, philosophy, romance, fiction in every key, and at last he broke through at the identical spot where Harte and Kipling had made their first success. The *Overland Monthly*— strange repetition—late in 1898 accepted his Klondike tale, "To the Man on Trail," and during the following year published seven others: "The White Silence," "The Son of the Wolf," "The Men of Forty Mile," "In a Far Country," "The Priestly Prerogative," "The Wife of a King," and "The Wisdom of the Trail"—and then a year later the *Atlantic Monthly*, attracted by the series, accepted the tale, "An Odyssey of the North," and the publishing house that had issued *The Luck of Roaring Camp*, published the nine tales as a volume, *The Son of the Wolf*. The parallel with Harte breaks at this point: Boston did not further encourage Jack London. Success was far from won: his first five books bear the imprint of five different publishing houses, each of which, save the last, dropped him from their list after a single volume. It was not until *The Call of the Wild* in 1903 that he won his fight and that publishers began to seek him with eagerness instead of his seeking them. And then by leaps and bounds his popularity became enormous: at the end of his sixteen years his work had appeared in eighty different magazines and at prices that even now seem impossible.

London did not create in the reading public that lust for "the abysmal brute" in man that seemed to possess the world before the German eruption in 1914: simply he found it and fed it raw meat. By training and temperament and experience with life he was peculiarly fitted to be the American Gorky. In 1901, during his period of experiment before he had fully realized his field, we find him defending with superlatives the "Bitter One" who had just put forth his *Fomá Gordyéeff:* "He writes because he has something to say which the world should hear. From that clenched fist of his, light and airy romances, pretty and sweet and beguiling, do not flow, but realities—yes, big and brutal and repulsive, but real." And a month before, he had blazed out in wrath because a Chicago reviewer had announced that Kipling, "the prophet of blood and vulgarity, prince of ephemerals, and idol of the non-elect," was dead. Kipling, he declared, was not only not dead, but was the most vital force in modern literature: he had told of things as they are: "he has seen life as it is, 'taken it up squarely' in both hands and looked upon it," and he had seen and painted without reservation the naked Anglo-Saxon, "a pirate, a land robber and a sea robber. Underneath his thin coating of culture he is what he was in Morgan's time. . . . He possesses a primitive brutality all his own. . . . Kipling as no one else, has sung the hymn of the dominant bourgeoisie, the war march of the white man round the world, the triumphant pæan of commercialism and imperialism."

Into this Kipling-Gogol world London plunged like a nihilist.

He was young, physically perfect, eager of temperament, the son of a long line of pushers into the untrodden West, and he painted a young world of adventure peopled only with youth physically perfect. Like Byron, he could work only with himself as the central figure, himself and wild adolescent idealizations of himself and his desires. His Alaska he made the land of "the blond beast," of the superman who ruled by sheer physical might and brutality, like Buck, the leader of the wolf-pack. Later, when his Alaska material began to grow repetitious, he transferred his blond beasts and supermen and their supermates to the last frontier of the world, the islands of the South Seas. His creative energy and the sheer amount of his literary product were amazing. In sixteen years he published eighteen collections of short stories, nineteen novels, and eleven other books, not to mention abundant war correspondence and other material for the daily press.

His enduring work lies undoubtedly among his one hundred and fifty-two short stories. He was too impatient, too crowded with thick coming materials, to succeed with the novel. The long book thrown off a thousand words a day without rereading or revision, became at last a heap of materials rather than a unit, but the short story was narrowly limited in space by magazine requirements; it could be but a single episode, and single episodes he could handle with intensity and dramatic climax. Action—fights, battles, races, typhoons, forlorn-hope dashes, mutinies, exciting moments—he could make alive with masterly skill. His was the genius of the raconteur. Broadly splashed backgrounds —arctic nights, snow-covered desolations, the aurora borealis, tropic atolls, and reeking jungles and far sea rims—and then action that halted not a moment. He had a Gorkylike power to make his reader feel things of physical horror—starvation, Indian torture, cannibalism, leprosy, and smallpox—all the coarseness and primitive hells latent in man and let loose in the areas of savagery.

His greatest power, next to his sheer narrative skill, lay in the atmosphere that he could throw about his creations. There is an epic quality to some of his best Klondike short stories, rare indeed in modern literature. *The Call of the Wild*, which might have been named "Six Episodes in the Life of the Super-Dog Buck," marks his highest reach. Here he broke loose from Harte and Gogol and Kipling, from Karl Marx and Nietzsche and Spencer, and worked with imagination in the materials of his own genius. It is not realism, it is not even truth to life: it is an epic dream of the heroic age of the North, expressed at times even in poetic terms. It is this epic quality that will give its author, many and glaring as are his deficiencies, a permanent place after Davis and the rest of his school have passed from sight.

As a short-story writer London lacked the power to create living human characters. His gallery of supermen and super-women has about it the myth atmosphere of the older world. His Indian women, as in *The God of His Fathers* volume, dedicated "To the daughters of the wolf who have bred and suckled a race of men," his gigantic "Burning Daylights," and even his monstrous dogs, are demigods, not creatures of the actual twentieth century. It is a new Northern mythology and the stories of their deeds have the quality of sagas. Contrary to his own belief, he was not a realist at all. His tales were not written on the spot, but after they had mellowed for years in his imagination. Everywhere exaggerations, poetizations, utter marvels described as common-places, superlatives in every sentence. It is not the actual North: it is an epic dream of the North, colored by an imagination adoles-cent in its love of the marvelous, of fighting and action, and of headlong movement.

There is more than adventure in the best of his work, though adventure is the web and woof of it; there is more than the mere materialism that the reader at first sight finds dominant. At his best, London gave to his work—if we may use the term without being misunderstood—soul. The short-story writer, he believed, should be more than a mere skillful raconteur: he should give to his tale an underrunning motif, never conspicuous, often a mere evanescent suspicion felt only by the more sensitive, yet never-theless always present. And with London the motif came first. In his autobiographic *Martin Eden* he declared that to him it "was always the great universal motif that suggested plots." A tale like "The God of His Fathers," to cite but a single example, coarse and wild though it be in background and materials, con-tains, none the less, a glimpse into the human heart is subtle as anything in Hawthorne.

And he had, when at his best, as in his early Klondike tales, especially in *Children of the Frost* and *The Call of the Wild*, a style all his own as distinctive as Kipling's. When he describes the arctic night and the aurora borealis and the wild lament of wolf dogs in the snow, or when in later work he is deeply moved by the romance of the tropic seas, he comes near to poetry; and everywhere, as did the early Kipling, he planned, to quote his own words, "phrases that bit like acid and scorched like flame, or that glowed and were mellow and luscious in the midst of the arid desert of common speech."

Jack Londonism, which was a wider thing by far than Jack London, was antisentimentalism, was in reality revolt against the aftermath of Preraphaelitism, "the esthetic movement," Oscar Wildeism, Aubrey Beardsleyism, and all the decadent squeamishness and ultracivilization of the closing years of the Victorian century. Jack London was its most penetrating voice. It was a call of the wild, a prophet cry in the soft decade before the German deluge: "Man is to-day the same man that drank from his enemy's skull in the dark German forests, that sacked cities and stole his women from neighboring clans like any howling aborigine. The raw animal crouching within him is like the earthquake monster pent in the crust of the earth." Be not asleep! Prepare for the reign of the brute. And the reign of the brute came—is still here, and large areas of its fiction are ruled by jungle ideals and jungle codes, without a spark of London's honest idealism or his faith in the ultimate coming of right.

BIBLIOGRAPHY

RICHARD HARDING DAVIS. 1864–1916.

1891. *Gallegher and Other Stories.*
1891. *Stories for Boys.*
1892. *Van Bibber and Others.*
1894. *The Exiles and Other Stories.*
1896. *Cinderella and Other Stories.*
1899. *Episodes in Van Bibber's Life.*
1899. *The Lion and the Unicorn.*
1901. *In the Fog.*
1902. *Ranson's Folly.*
1903. *The Bar Sinister.*
1910. *Once Upon a Time.*
1911. *The Man Who Could Not Lose.*
1911. *The Red Cross Girl and Other Stories.*
1913. *The Lost Road.*

1915. *Somewhere in France.*
1917. *The Deserter.*
1917. *The Boy Scout and Other Stories.*

THOMAS ALLIBONE JANVIER. 1849–1913.

1885. *Color Studies.*
1891. *The Uncle of an Angel and Other Stories.*
1814. *At the Casa Napoleon.*

FRANCIS HOPKINSON SMITH. 1838–1915.

1892. *A Day at Laguerre's and Other Days.*
1895. *A Gentleman Vagabond and Some Others.*
1899. *Gondola Days.*
1899. *The Other Fellow.*
1903. *The Under Dog.*
1905. *At Close Range.*
1905. *The Wood Fire in No. 3.*
1907. *The Veiled Lady and Other Men and Women.*
1909. *Forty Minutes Late and Other Stories.*

HAROLD FREDERIC. 1856–1898.

1893. *The Copperhead and Other Stories of the North During the Civil War.*
1894. *Marsena and Other Stories of the War Time.*
1897. *In the 'Sixties.*
1898. *The Deserter and Other Stories: a Book of Two Wars.*

FRANCIS MARION CRAWFORD. 1854–1909.

1911. *Wandering Ghosts.*
"The Dead Smile"; "The Screaming Skull"; "Man Overboard"; "For the Blood Is the Life"; "The Upper Berth"; "By the Waters of Paradise"; "The Doll's Ghost."

JOHN RANDOLPH SPEARS. 1850–

1896. *The Port of Missing Ships and Other Stories of the Sea.*

JULIAN RALPH. 1853–1903.

1896. *People We Pass: Stories of Life Among the Masses of New York City.*

OWEN WISTER. 1860–

1896. *Red Men and White.*
1903. *Philosophy 4, a Story of Harvard University.*
1911. *Members of the Family.*

JOHN FOX, JR. 1863–1919.

1896. *A Cumberland Vendetta and Other Stories.*
1897. *'Hell fer Sartain' and Other Stories.*
1904. *Christmas Eve on Lonesome and Other Stories.*
1917. *In Happy Valley.*

WILLIAM ALLEN WHITE. 1868–

1896. *The Real Issue and Other Stories.*
1899. *The Court of Boyville.*
1901. *Stratagems and Spoils: Stories of Love and Politics.*
1906. *In Our Town.*
1909. *A Certain Rich Man.*
1916. *God's Puppets.*
1918. *The Marital Adventures of Henry and Me.*

CHESTER BAILEY FERNALD. 1869–

1896. *The Cat and the Cherub and Other Stories.*
1899. *Chinatown Stories.*
1903. *Under the Jackstaff.*

STEPHEN CRANE. 1871–1900.

1896. *The Little Regiment and Other Episodes of the American Civil War.*
1898. *The Open Boat and Other Tales of Adventure.*
1899. *The Monster and Other Stories.*
1900. *Wounds in the Rain; War Stories.*
1900. *Whilomville Stories.*
1921. *Men, Women and Boats.*

ALFRED HENRY LEWIS. 1842–1914.

1897. *Wolfville.*

FREDERIC REMINGTON. 1861–1909.

1898. *Crooked Trails.*

FRANK HAMILTON SPEARMAN. 1859–

1901. *Held for Orders: Being Stories of Railroad Life.*

BENJAMIN FRANKLIN NORRIS. 1870–1902.

1903. *A Deal in Wheat and Other Stories.*
1906. *The Joyous Miracle.*
1909. *The Third Circle.*

STEWART EDWARD WHITE. 1873–

1904. *Blazed Trail Stories and Stories of the Wild Life.
Arizona Nights.*
1918. *Simba.*

RALPH DELAHAYE PAINE. 1871–

1906. *The Praying Skipper and Other Stories.*
1909. *College Years.*

JACK LONDON. 1876–1916.

1900. *The Son of the Wolf.*
1901. *The God of His Fathers.*
1902. *Children of the Frost.*
1904. *The Faith of Men.*
1905. *Tales of the Fish Patrol.*
1906. *Moon Face.*
1907. *Love of Life.*
1909. *Lost Face.*
1910. *When God Laughs.*
1911. *South Sea Tales.*
1912. *Smoke Bellew.*
1912. *A Son of the Sun.*
1912. *The House of Pride.*
1913. *The Night Born.*
1914. *The Strength of the Strong.*
1916. *The Turtles of Tasman.*
1918. *The Red One.*
1919. *My Hawaiian Aloha.*

CHAPTER XVI

O. HENRY AND THE HANDBOOKS

I

The final major figure in the history of the American short story, the last individual able, single-handed, to influence the direction of its current, was "O. Henry," or, to use his own name, seldom mentioned now save in textbooks, William Sydney Porter. His swift rise to dominance has been one of the sensations of the new century. In 1899, when his first story appeared in *McClure's*, he was totally unknown; in 1910 he was dead, but in the eleven years he had captured the reading public with short stories alone as no other writer anywhere has ever done it, and he had made his pen name almost as familiar, in America at least, as "Mark Twain," the most widely known pseudonym in all literature.

Until he was thirty-five his life was unliterary and undistinctive. He was born in the little town of Greensboro, North Carolina, he was almost totally unschooled; at fifteen he was set to learn the drug business in his uncle's store, and at twenty, threatened with tuberculosis, he was sent to a Texas ranch, where, for a brief period, he caught a glimpse of the vanishing cowboy—this was his boyhood. Then for ten years he had lived in Austin, Texas, working in various ordinary capacities: office clerk, draftsman, bank teller, and finally newspaper man—editor of a comic journal that made haste to expire, and then, at Houston, columnist for *The Daily Post*.

And there he might have remained interminably, pouring his daily cupful into the bottomless pit of a Texas daily, had not good fortune in the guise of total annihilation forced his life suddenly into melodrama: accused of embezzling funds while employed in the Austin bank, he made a dash for South America by way of New Orleans and Honduras, lived for nearly a year with criminals and adventurers in various cities of refuge from extradition, and then, learning of the critical illness of his wife, returned to Texas, surrendered himself to the authorities, and was given five years in the Federal penitentiary at Columbus, Ohio. For three years and three months—1898 to 1901—he was in prison: but for this experience the O. Henry that the world knows never would have been.

From the first he seems to have been treated more as an employee than as a prisoner: he was made prison druggist, given leisure and unusual freedom, and allowed a room, not a cell. He read much, kept up with the current magazines, and was permitted to converse with prisoners, many of them extraordinary characters whose stories furnished rich material in later days. To his little daughter in Texas, who knew nothing of her father's disgrace, he wrote the jolliest of letters. He would send her presents and money, but to earn money in prison is manifestly not easy. It would have to be with his pen. He had sold newspaper jokes in his earlier days and he had written whole issues of *The Rolling Stone:* why not write stories for the magazines? He could sign them with a fictitious name and market them, perhaps, through a friend in New Orleans. The plan worked: the greatest short-story writer of his generation had found his occupation; and magazine readers were soon reading with delight stories written by a Texas convict with years of his sentence yet to serve. Sensational surely.

The twelve of his stories which are known to have been written during this prison period are manifestly apprentice work.[1] They deal for the most part with adventure in strange regions—the Southwest, the Southern mountains, and the lands below the Caribbean. They are for the most part more elaborate in plot, more studiously conventional, than his later work. Curiously enough, his first master seems to have been Frank Norris, whose parodies and striking sketches were appearing in the *San Francisco Wave* and other magazines. The "gentle grafter" brand of "tall talk," for instance, impossible on any human lips save on the vaudeville stage, is identical in the two writers. There are

[1] The twelve stories are as follows: "Whistling Dick's Christmas Stocking," in *Roads of Destiny;* "Georgia's Ruling," in *Whirligigs;* "An Afternoon Miracle," in *The Heart of the West;* "Money Maze," in *Cabbages and Kings;* "No Story," in *Options;* "A Fog in Santone," in *Rolling Stones;* "A Black-jack Bargainer," in *Whirligigs;* "The Enchanted Kiss," in *Roads of Destiny;* "Hygea at the Solito," in *The Heart of the West;* "Rouge et Noir," in *Cabbages and Kings;* "The Duplicity of Hargraves," in *Sixes and Sevens;* "The Marionettes," in *Rolling Stones.*

traces, too, of Harte and Kipling, especially Kipling, but one quickly forgets all influences and all crudenesses as one swings into the current of his tales.

From this time on the short story was his profession: he did nothing else. Released from prison, he drifted in 1902 to New York City, writing, as the mood or the need was upon him, stories of South America or the Southwest, or else "gentle grafter" tales from the materials he had collected in the Ohio penitentiary. Popularity came suddenly even as it had come to Jack London, and for much the same reason: his materials were wild and strange and manifestly first hand. His first story, "Whistling Dick's Christmas Stocking," had attracted the attention of *McClure's* because of its materials: it was the story of the Southern tramp migration at the end of the Northern summer and it was told evidently by one who himself had been a tramp. All that was known of him was rumor: he had been a cowboy, a tramp, perhaps a yeggman, certainly a soldier of fortune in Honduras and South America, and he was writing with strangely graphic pen of his own experiences. The demand for his work came almost exclusively from the new popular magazines of the journalistic type, tremendously alive, up to date, and so thickly spread over the news stands of the world that they could be sold for ten and fifteen cents. One story forced itself into *Harper's* "Editor's Drawer," another into *The Century*, and a third into *The Outlook*, but all the rest had their start in the wood-pulp journals. He wrote, as he once phrased it, for Mr. Everybody. From first to last *Everybody's Magazine* published twenty-two of the tales, *Munsey's* fourteen, *McClure's* ten, *The Cosmopolitan* six, *The American* and *Hampton's* four each, and the rest found lodgment in such periodicals as *Ainslee's*, *Collier's*, *The Black Cat* and *Short Stories*.

The period of his apprenticeship may be said to have ended in December, 1903, when the New York *World* added him to its staff as short-story writer for its Sunday edition. The result was one hundred and thirteen stories in some thirty months—the heart of O. Henry. Never was writer seemingly so irresponsible, so whimsical, so chattily heterogeneous. He had been given perfect freedom, and his stories had shaken off all traces of models and conformity to standards and were pure O. Henry. Maupassant he read constantly, but it was only to stimulate his own

sense of form, for behind his seeming lawlessness were art requirements the most rigid. His chattiness, his familiarity with the
reader, his seeming digressions, his monstrous exaggerations, all
held rigidly to one end: he would win his reader—completely,
put him utterly off his guard, and then bring him up rigid at the
last sentence, and the newspaper requirements were that he should
do it in the compass of a page. His stories of this period average
2,500 words. Entertainment was his only thought—entertainment of the vaudeville variety, won at any cost, even the sacrifice
of truth and reality. He was a reporter sent out each week for a
"story" from the Babylon of New York and he was to tell this
story so that the jaded and *blasé* and sensation-surfeited readers
of Sunday papers would be attracted to it, would be held on and
on to the end of it, and would even be thrilled and rendered
exclamatory by the totally unexpected climax of it, so much so
that they would turn to the same page on the following Sunday.
It was superlatively good journalism. No longer was it strange
background and Jack-Londonlike adventure from first hand
experience that won his readers: he was working now with New
York City stuff concerning which until a few months before he
had had absolutely no first-hand knowledge. His vogue now
came not from his materials, but from his manner.

The elements of his art were not many. One notes first of all
that his stories are generally trivial as stories—mere anecdotes.
Any one of his *World* pieces may be reduced to the compass of a
commercial traveler's "good one." And not even this figment of
plot is the vital thing about the story: it is the style of the telling
—O. Henry stands first of all for manner, and the chief ingredient
of this manner is humor. He should be rated first of all as a
humorist, as much so as even Artemus Ward or Mark Twain. He
was a born humorist: his biography is larded with Eugene Field-
like practical jokes, with cartoons and caricatures and outrageous
drolleries. He had been early the contributor of a column of
jokes to the Burlington, Iowa, *Free Press;* for months he had
written alone each number of *The Rolling Stone,* a Texas comic
magazine, in which one may find all the elements that later were
to appear in his short-story work; and finally at Houston he had
settled down to newspaper column writing as a permanent
vocation. Given perfect freedom now, with an assured market,
he gave free rein to the Momus within him and produced work

that primarily is humorous. The point is an important one: it illumines much more than O. Henry.

The second element of his art came from his journalistic sense. He knew the public for which he was writing—Mr. Everybody— and catered to his whims. To his boon companion, Al Jennings, train robber and yeggman with literary aspirations, he wrote in 1902 this advice: "We have got to respect the conventions and delusions of the public to a certain extent. . . . In order to please John Wanamaker, we will have to assume a virtue that we do not possess. Comment on the moral side of the proposition as little as possible. Do not claim that holding up trains is the only business a gentleman would engage in, and, on the contrary, do not depreciate a profession that is really only financiering with spurs on." He knew precisely how much of the sugar of senti- mentality the great average reading public must have, and how much of the pepper of sensation, and the salt of facts, and the salad dressing of romance. He had, moreover, the newspaper man's horror of heaviness, of surplusage, of the commonplace. The story must have "snap," "go," up-to-dateness to the moment; a "punch" in every sentence.

The third conspicuous element in his art is closely allied to the second—form, technique. He studied Maupassant, but Maupas- sant in turn might have added a certain glow to the cold finish of his own tales, could he have studied O. Henry. The American certainly was the more original of the two. Not enough has been made of the ingrained Americanism of the man. No one, not even Mark Twain, was more a product of our own soil. He was a finished oral story-teller of the Western hotel-foyer type before he had ever written a word of fiction. In every company "mixed" and "unmixed," there are stories, anecdotes *apropos*, Abraham- Lincolnlike modern instances cleverly told—it is a peculiar evo- lution of our Western civilization. A "good one" is followed by "another one" and still another and better one, and the soul of them all is humor, and the technique is the technique of the short story. The "nub" of the narrative is held to the last moment and then greeted with a roar of laughter. The embroidery of the tale, the skill in concealing the final crux, and the color and the momen- tum of it all depend upon the narrator. O. Henry is the crowned chief of the ancient American order of *That Reminds Me of An- other*. To read him is at times almost to feel his physical presence.

He slaps you on the shoulder, asks your advice on points of grammar and the wording of quotations, and you can almost hear his laugh when he springs his final ending. His art is the art of Poe: he has no thought beyond the immediate effect of his tale upon his reader. Poe often left his audience quivering with horror; O. Henry leaves them chuckling with laughter.

The last distinctive element in his art is the strangest of all the strange paradoxes connected with O. Henry. In this unschooled druggist, this cowboy and Main Street clerk, this Texas funny man, one would hardly expect to find verbal precision and wide range of vocabulary. Modern slang he used with outrageous abandon, but everywhere amid the slang are felicities of expression and strange verbal flavors that amaze one. Not even Henry James could choose words more fastidiously or use them more accurately. And yet should one attempt to illustrate this quality of his style one could find only sentences or at most paragraphs. Not one of his stories as a whole can be singled out for its distinction of phrase and its uniformity of beautiful style. The Momus that ruled his pen suffered few serious interludes. One can never trust him. A paragraph of beauty ends in a caper; one reads a whole page at the height of Emerson, only to find its author grinning through a horse collar at the end; one may discover what seems at last a completely serious story of real life—yet beware! Until its closing sentence "The Guardian of the Accolade" is a beautiful tale of the Old South, but the last sentence turns the whole of it into vaudeville—a whole story written beautifully with no other intent than deliberate preparation for a single vulgar moment of surprise. What he might have done had he dropped his harlequin pen and done serious work at the height of his powers we may not say. We know, however, that he had, whenever he deigned to use it with seriousness, a vocabulary like a backwoodsman's rifle: every word striking the red with a precision that gives to the reader a continual thrill.

But brilliant as were the possibility of his powers, and distinctive as was his technique, his final place can never be high even among the writers of short stories. He did not take literature seriously: he was a victim of Momus and the swift ephemeral press. His undoubted powers were completely debauched by it. He became exclusively an entertainer, with no thought but of the moment, and no art save that which brought instant effect upon his reader. To accomplish that he would sacrifice everything, even the truth. One never reads his tales for their material— incident for its own sake—as one does Jack London's or Kipling's; nor do we read them because of the characters as one does Mary E. Wilkins's or Alice Brown's; nor for seeing life exactly as life is as one reads Garland or Norris: one reads them for the narcotic effects they produce. These tales of South America, of picaresque adventurers and New York shop girls—two hundred and forty-five of them in all—are not necessarily the truth: they are *opera bouffe*. His gentle grafters may have been suggested by actual men he had met in the Ohio prison, but they are not alive: they never could have been alive. Open at random and hear them talk. Or if one is no judge of the argot of grafters, then open at random again. Here are two ordinary college professors talking together on the street what O. Henry reports as the ordinary daily talk of college professors. Listen to them:

"Oh, come off your perch!" said the other man, who wore glasses. "Your premises won't come out in the wash. You wind-jammers who apply bandy-legged theories to concrete categorical syllogisms send logical conclusions skallybootin' into the infinitesimal ragbag. You can't pull my leg with an old sophism with whiskers on it. You quote Marx and Hyndman and Kautsky—what are they?—shines! Tolstoi?—his garret is full of rats. I put it to you over the home plate that the idea of a co- operative commonwealth and an abolishment of competitive systems simply takes the rag off the bush and gives me hyperesthesia of the roop- teetoop. The skookum house for yours!"

Satire? Perhaps so. Then turn back a few pages. An ordinary man has come to the ordinary law office of Mr. Gooch to consult him in all seriousness concerning certain matrimonial legalities. How would such a man address such a lawyer, a perfect stranger to him, when he entered his office? O. Henry makes this his greeting:

"You are a divorce lawyer. You handle all the various ramifications of busted-up connubiality. You are a surgeon, we might say, who extracts Cupid's darts when he shoots 'em into the wrong parties. You furnish patent, incandescent lights for premises where the torch of Hyman has burned so low you can't light a cigar at it. Am I right, Mr. Gooch?"

Enter some city law office and try this opening speech on the head of the firm if you wish to appreciate the utter artificiality of O. Henry.

He worked without truth, without moral consciousness, and without a philosophy of life. He created no characters: he worked with puppets, lay figures without souls—we see them moving before us, but we know them not at all; they are x, y, and z in his rambles in absurdity. He was a harlequin Poe with modern laughter in place of gloom: much that we have charged up against him we have also charged up against the creator of the "Gold Bug" and "The Black Cat," but he was utterly without Poe's reverence for the literature of power, he was without his simplicity, without his universality, without his ability to stand with the great serious literary creators of the world.

II

With the opening decade of the new century short-story art in America began to be exploited as if it were an exact science. It had been impossible to ignore the rising tide of short fiction, even though one considered it a trivial form of literature, and impossible not to speculate as to its final direction. The critical journals of the 'nineties made much of the problem. It peculiarly fascinated Howells, who returned to it again and again and it engaged the attention of such authoritative writers as Harte and Higginson and the English Frederick Wedmore, all of whom contributed to the magazines careful papers. Then had come a shoal of lesser critics who went to extremes. The short story, they discovered, was a new and distinct literary form that had been evolved from the peculiar conditions of American life, and it was ruled by laws as definite and as elaborate as those governing the sonnet. These laws they proceeded to codify and promulgate.

The first decade of the new century was the era of the short-story handbook. The first textbook worthy of noting was that by Charles R. Barrett, whose *Short Story Writing* bears the date 1898. Others followed until every educational publishing house had its book. In the multitude of them one may note as distinctive Bliss Perry's chapter in his *A Study of Prose Fiction* (1902), and H. S. Canby's scholarly brochure, "The Short Story," *Yale Studies in English*, the same year. In 1904 came C. S. Baldwin's *American Short Stories*, with an illuminating introduction; in 1907 came Brander Matthews's collection also with a distinctive preliminary study, and in 1909 H. S. Canby's definitive *The Short Story in English*.

By 1910 the short story had become a distinct subject for study in American colleges and universities. Dr. C. Alphonso Smith, while exchange professor, even lectured on the short-story form in a German university, and later, in 1912, issued his lecture as a textbook. Short-story art was found to be peculiarly teachable: it seemed to have all the elements of an exact science, with laws as arbitrary and as multitudinous as those governing bridge whist, and it had, moreover, the added stimulus of contemporaneousness and of personal conjecture. Why not be an O. Henry yourself and make money? Here were the rules. College professors of the short story advertised their courses by statistics of the number of stories sold by the class the preceding year. Correspondence schools in short-story writing sprang up, and their students were assured a lucrative market after a given number of lessons by mail. Everywhere the emphasis was upon the mechanistic, upon manner, upon a technique that one might learn from books. It is noteworthy, however, that none of the makers of these elaborate handbooks have also made short stories of distinction.

From the various treatises one may deduce what we may denominate the ten commandments of the art, the canons most insisted upon now in college courses and in short-story correspondence schools. We may venture to formulate them thus:

A SHORT STORY MUST HAVE

1. *Shortness.* Its problem is substantially that of tragedy, the length of which, according to Aristotle, is "determined by the conditions of stage presentation and by the power of attention in an audience." Poe's definition of it as what can be read at a single sitting prolonged to not over two hours and a half is known to all. By Howells it was defined as a story that is complete in a single magazine number.

2. *Compression.* There must be no excrescence, no digression, no picture presented merely for pictorial effect, no Greek-chorus observations and moralizings. Backgrounds should be sketched in impressionistically with only detail enough that the reader may realize vividly the genius of the place and so better understand the characters in the foreground.

3. *Unity,* or, in Poe's words, "a certain unique or single effect to be wrought out." A short story is a single dynamic effort, with

a single group of characters, a single line of action, a single situation, a single impression, and a single atmosphere from beginning to end.

4. *Immediateness.* The story must have effectiveness from the very start. Again to quote Poe, "If his first sentence tend not to the outbringing of this effect he has failed in his first step." What the dramatist calls the "exposition" must be handled without surplusage. The reader must be started strongly and must be given the situation and the nature of the characters in as few as possible of the opening paragraphs.

5. *Momentum.* The story must move without intermission. It must be like a ballad, which is a ride on a winged steed, not necessarily headlong in its movement, but never alighting and never resting until the end.

6. *Characterization.* "Homer," says Aristotle, "makes his personages live before us." The characters are the main thing in a short story. They must be not types, but individualities that the reader can feel. They must be drawn from life and not from the imagination, they must reveal themselves and not be presented by exposition, and they must be consistent throughout the story. There can be no character development: that belongs to the novel.

7. *Verisimilitude.* The story must impress the reader as natural and true; the dialogue used should have the quality of seeming inevitableness. Everything should combine to project the reader into a world that seems perfectly plausible at every point, that is not fiction for him, but life.

8. *Style.* There must be distinction in phrase, epithet, sentence structure, diction, and there must be "totality of effect." There must be beauty, originality, atmosphere with light and shadow, and perspective.

9. *Culmination.* The story should have an objective toward which it constantly moves. It should suggest more than it tells. It should leave the reader with stimulated imagination, eagerly continuing the tale even at the finish and powerless instantly to dismiss it.

10. *Soul.* The story must have character, or, to quote Aristotle, "*ethos.*" It should shed light in some way upon the human

tragedy or human comedy. The reader should feel that fundamentally he has read a section of what might have been his own life.

The deadly sin, according to the editors of the period, was heaviness: the tale must move trippingly, with modernness in every sentence. A critical test was the dialogue: of all things it most clearly revealed the artisan. It must seem perfectly natural, inevitable, indeed, and yet it must be in reality the perfection of the artificial. It must be stripped to the barest essentials, relieved to the last possible degree of the childish "tags," of older days, like "said he" and "replied she," and it must move with brilliance and vivacity. In Robert W. Chambers, the most skillful exponent of the ultramodern methods, the dialogue often leaves the reader breathless. The characters talk cracklingly, in fragments of sentences often, in epigrams, exclamations, sudden dramatic thrusts and parries. It is rapier work. This for example:

"I was in love with you once."
She bent her head and looked down gravely at her slender hand, which lay across his.
"That was very dear of you," she murmured.
After a silence.
"And—you?" he asked.
"Do you mean, was I ever in love with you?"
"Yes."
"I—don't—know. I loved your letters. I adored you. I do now. Perhaps, if you had come back——"
"I wish I had!"
"Do you?" She lifted her eyes to him curiously. "You know, Jim, I must be honest with you. I never did love anybody—but, if you—had come home—and if you had told me that you cared for me—that way——"
"Yes."
"Well, I was just a girl. You had my affections. I could have been taught very easily, I think—to care—differently——"
"And—now?"
"What?"
"Is it too late to teach you, Steve?"
"Why, yes—isn't it?"
"Why?"
"I'm married."

Chambers had begun his work after a long residence as an art student "in the Quarter" at Paris. His second volume, *The King in Yellow*, shadowy unrealities, tales of weird terror treated with what seemed like dawning power, appeared in 1895. Remarkable facility he had and lightness of brush with a French quality of taste that promised well, but—read Mrs. Wharton's caustic tale "The Pot-Boiler." The girl wooed by the penniless genius Stanwell and by the unbelievably-paid panderer to vulgarians, Mungold, chose the latter, for Mungold was using the best that was in him:

"I can take money earned in good faith—I can let Caspar live on it. I can marry Mr. Mungold because, though his pictures are bad, he does not prostitute his art."

The tale explains the quality of one whole area of later fiction.

III

The tendency of the period has been more and more in the direction of manner. O. Henry affected it strongly, but he was not alone the moving cause of it. His artistry was so striking and his methods so evident that even the novice was inspired to codify his laws and imitate his devices. But O. Henry had himself been an effect; he had been created by his times and others had been swept along with the same current. The age of the enormously multiplied daily newspaper, of the million-copied popular weekly like *The Saturday Evening Post* or *The Ladies' Home Journal*, of the magazine of light entertainment whose hundred varieties loaded all the news stands, was an age of brilliancy that tolerated only excellence of workmanship, and that hesitated at no cost to secure the new, the sparkling, the surprisingly turned—every possible device for the entertainment of a public overentertained and increasingly *blasé*.

The emphasis pre-eminently was upon the mechanistic, upon technique, upon the external and striking rather than upon the internal workings of character. The popular demand, as indicated by the quantity of the output seemed to be for the strongly emphasized motion picture, preferably with strange atmosphere and background, for slashing records of business *finesse*, for broad characterizations with cartoonlike exaggeration. Montague Glass with his "Potash and Perlmutter" creations may be cited as a typical example, or Octavus Roy Cohen with his very modern negroes, or Edna Ferber with her Mrs. McChesney, the latest word in business femininity. The colors are vivid and startlingly splashed, the humor is broad, the characters stand out like caricatures. Everything is keyed for the Main Street multitude whose reading centers in *The Saturday Evening Post* and whose ideals of art are satisfied by the moving pictures. The primary object is entertainment, gross entertainment—laughter, sensation, the exhilaration of success won through difficulties, eternal newness, adventure, the thrill of movement, always movement. To quote the New York *Nation*, "Our short stories move rapidly, but it is a form of speed that is confined within the limits of each paragraph. Every sentence must have 'go' in it and stimulate the desire for the next sentence as an object in itself, and only secondarily because it brings us nearer to the end of the anecdote." Instead of plot or real movement, there must be action which is something far different from "movement." "For the latter means progress toward the point of the story, whereas action means agitation in any direction, provided only there is 'something doing' in each paragraph. '*From the beginning*,' that is the secret of short-story writing to-day. You must start at the crack of the pistol, not necessarily to tell your story, but to seize the attention."

A few there have been who have not fought the new journalistic tendency and yet have not yielded to its grosser influences. George Ade, for instance, has been strong enough to plunge into the new current and compel it to carry him into regions worth visiting. He has been as broadly humorous as O. Henry and as up-to-date and as brilliant, and yet he has given to much of his work, despite its seeming triviality, genuineness, and truth and moral purpose. His *Fables in Slang* are uniquely American: they are unliterary, they are uncouth in dress, yet fundamentally they are as serious of purpose as even Hawthorne's dissections of the Puritan heart, and often as illuminating. Booth Tarkington, too, among the younger group must be counted with those who have not surrendered wholly to the vulgarians. Primarily is he a novelist, yet once at least he entered the short-story field with real distinction. By more than one critic "Monsieur Beaucaire" has been rated as one of the most brilliant short stories of its period. If it be a short story, it certainly deserves this high rating. Nothing its author has done can compare with its cleverness, its dainty artistry, its Gallic verve and sprightliness. But discussion of it, as indeed discussion of many of Henry James's later creations, or of Edith

Wharton's "Ethan Frome" and "Madame de Treymes," must begin with the questions, "Is it a short story, after all? Is it not a novelette?" Tarkington himself has been inclined to class it as a novel:

I recall that when I wrote "Monsieur Beaucaire" I thought I was writing a short story and intended to write a short story. It ran out to 11,000 words and was instantly rejected by most of the magazines of that time. I think they no more than looked at its length, which was too great for one installment. I suppose it might be considered an "intensive" romantic novel. Howells called me an "intensivist," and in my later talks with him I think he seemed to favor "intensivism."

"Intensivism" is the soul of the short story, and the constant insistence upon it by generations of short-story writers has had a marked effect, almost a revolutionary effect, indeed, upon the novel. In the mid-nineteenth century "Monsieur Beaucaire" and "Ethan Frome" would have been lengthened into two volumes. Dickens, for example, as read to-day, is diffuse even to tediousness. When confronted by what may be called short-story conditions he realized himself his lack of "intensivism." *Putnam's Magazine* of March, 1854, has this suggestive paragraph:

He lopped off instinctively, in the reading, under the pressure of a public ordeal, everything to which the knife of the critic would be applied; curtailing his needless amplifications, omitting passages of mere description that have nothing to do with advancing the main purpose, and subduing the exaggerations and overcolorings—so that the story as received was shorter, and far more interesting, than as originally published.

In other words, unconsciously he applied the rules that govern the modern short story. A similar process has been increasingly in operation in American fiction for half a century. Undoubtedly it has been this conscious and unconscious mastery of short story art that has tended to shorten our recent novels and free them of much that in the language of criticism may be denominated as "lumber." It has been observed that more and more the novel is approaching the short story form.

IV

During the last decade the increase in quantity of the short-story product has been, perhaps, the most striking American literary phenomenon. The demand by the magazines for tales fresh and original and moving has been nothing short of marvelous, and the demand has constantly outrun the supply. According to Brander Matthews in a recent review, this is a state of affairs "peculiar to the United States. Nothing of the sort is to be observed in England or in France. The British periodicals (in so far as they rely on fiction) depend rather upon their serials; and the circulation of a London monthly or weekly rises and falls with the popularity of the novel it is publishing in installments. . . . Thirty or forty years ago a popular English novelist explained to me that he could not afford to write short stories, since a subject strong for a brief tale was likely to be adequate for a full-length novel." Whether or not this prodigality of the Americans in their reckless use of material for short stories that with patience and frugality might have been made into novels has been a sign of weakness or of strength, whether it indicates more widespread creative genius or the prostituting of power in the creation of a trivial and scattering literary form it is not the province of the historian to argue.

He who would study the problem has now an abundance of material at easy command. Beginning with the year 1915 Edward J. O'Brien has issued an annual volume of what he considers the twenty leading short stories of the year. Then in 1919 began another and similar annual publication entitled *O. Henry Memorial Award Prize Stories, Chosen by the Society of Arts and Sciences.* The same year, too, the managing editor of *Life* issued a volume of eighty-two stories that had been submitted in its contest to determine how short a short story may be. And with every year came volumes of up-to-date work like, for instance, R. W. Pence's *Short Stories by Present-day Writers* (1922).

It is interesting to read the varying standards of these latter-day anthologists, these self-constituted appraisers of the yearly product in an intensively cultivated field. O'Brien set this as his standard:

The first test of a short story in any qualitative analysis is to report upon how vitally compelling the writer makes his selected facts or incidents. This test may be known as the test of substance.

But a second test is necessary in this qualitative analysis if a story is to take high rank above other stories. The test of substance is the most vital test, to be sure, and if a story survives it, it has imaginative life. The true artist, however, will seek to shape his living substance into the

most beautiful and satisfying form, by skillful selection and arrangement
of his material, and by the most direct and appealing presentation of it
in portrayal and characterization.

His findings and awards need not detain us. Some of them are
surprising. In 1917, for instance, he singled out three writers,
"whose sophistication is the embodiment of a new American
technique. Katherine Fullerton Gerould, Wilbur Daniel Steele,
and H. G. Dwight have each attained a distinction in our contemporary literature that places them at the head of their craft."

The first *O. Henry Memorial Award* committee agreed that for
a short story "the first requisite was *struggle*." Then "the judges
sought originality, excellence in organization of plot incidents,
skill in characterization, power in moving emotions." A good
short story, also they added, "always compels belief: the longer
the period of belief the greater the story." They insisted strongly
upon the value of "atmosphere" and they were "not insensible to
style. But expert phrasing, glowing appreciation of words and
exquisite sense of values, the texture of the story fabric—all
dropped into the abyss of the unimportant after the material they
incorporated had been judged."

The editor of *Life* in his comment upon the picturesque contest
to determine how short a short story can be and still be a short
story, gave this as the general body of rules agreed upon by the
judges of the contest:

A short story must contain at least two characters, for otherwise there
would be no contrast or struggle. A situation must be depicted in which
there are two opposing forces.

A short story must be a picture out of real life which gives the reader a
definite sensation, such as he gets upon looking at a masterpiece of painting. While it must be complete in itself, the art of it lies in what it suggests
to the reader beyond its own limits. That is to say, it must convey an
idea much larger than itself. This is the open sesame to the golden
principle.

Every short story must of necessity deal with human beings, either
directly or indirectly. It must reveal in the briefest manner possible—
as it were, like a lightning flash—a situation that carries the reader
beyond it. It is, therefore, inevitable that the supreme test of the short
story lies in its climax. The climax must gather up everything that has
gone before, and perhaps by only one word epitomize the whole situation
in such a way as to produce in the reader a sense of revelation—just as if

he were the sole spectator of a supremely interesting human mystery now suddenly made plain.

The technique of the short story should be such that no word in its vocabulary will suggest triteness or the fatal thought that the author is dependent upon others for his phrasing. When, for example, we read, "With a glad cry she threw her arms about him," "A hoarse shout went up from the vast throng," "He flicked the ashes," we know at once that the author is only dealing in echoes.

Thus the American short story in its most modern demands.

V

As to the writers of the later school which has filled the magazines and the short-story annuals of the past two decades, the number of even the excellent technicians is surprisingly large. Miss Blanche Colton Williams, in her survey of *Our Short Story Writers* (1920), singles out twenty and gives to each a chapter. This in alphabetical order is her list: Alice Brown, James Branch Cabell, Dorothy Canfield, Robert W. Chambers, Irvin Shrewsbury Cobb, James Brendan Connolly, Richard Harding Davis, Margaret Wade Deland, Edna Ferber, Mary Wilkins Freeman, Hamlin Garland, William Sydney Porter, Joseph Hergesheimer, Fannie Hurst, Jack London, James Brander Matthews, Melville Davisson Post, Mary Roberts Rinehart, Booth Tarkington, Edith Wharton. R. W. Pence two years later would add Susan Glaspell, Lincoln Colcord, Wilbur D. Steele, Octavus Roy Cohen, and Henry van Dyke. O'Brien and the O. Henry Award committees have attempted to give prominence to others like Benjamin Rosenblatt, Richard Matthews Hallet, Arthur Johnson, Rupert Hughes, and Margaret Preston Montague. It is useless as yet to do more than record names in this contemporary group. The work of most of them, if not all of them, is too near for focus. To attempt to determine their final place among the American writers is simply to display one's own prejudices and hobbies. Some are merely brilliant technicians with no fixed moral realities, some are distinctively humorists with a striving for exaggerated types and unexpected turns, some are to be classed with the creators of cubist and futurist art, and some have done distinctive work that may be compared to advantage even with the best that America has yet produced. This product time infallibly will select and make prominent. The rest will disappear like the underbrush when the pines begin to overshadow it.

The leader, however, of the group formed since the opening of the new century it is not too early to name. Concerning the work of Edith Wharton there no longer is question; it shines among the mass of writings of the period like a diamond in a tray of beads. Inflexibly she has held to fundamental standards, refusing to be hurried, refusing to popularize her work or to surrender to mere manner or to journalism or to the canons of a moving-picture age, or again to sentimentalism. Mere popularity has concerned her no more than it concerned Henry James, her earliest model.

To treat of her fiction without mention of James has been possible to no critic who has considered her work, and it is so not alone because of his influence upon her in the days of her apprenticeship or again because of the friendship of the two in later years, a friendship that is one of the charming episodes in later literary annals. There are deeper reasons. There is suggestive parallelism in their biographies, their natures, their training, their attitudes toward life. Both were born in New York City in homes of wealth and culture; both were carefully educated by private tutors; both traveled much abroad and became clever linguists, especially in French, which became to both like a mother tongue; both settled down for a period in the center of New England culture; and both in their later years lived much abroad, surrounded by all that is best in European art and refinement.

It was inevitable that Mrs. Wharton, like James, should write much of New England society, of international episodes, and of life in the artistic and literary circles of the Paris and the Italy which she knew, and it was inevitable that she should be a fastidious craftsman, repressed, finished, brilliant, sprightly, Gallic in her lightness of touch and her clever finesse. Her "Madame de Treymes" is as perfect a short story as American literature contains: a rigidly single motif—an attempt to pierce the inflexible wall of French social tradition; characters that reveal themselves until one sees their very souls; a struggle that grips the reader's sympathies and will not loose its hold; a dénouement sudden, unlooked-for, yet inevitable, and so skillfully presented that the reader is powerless to stop with the last line, but reads on and on in his own soul and cannot clear himself of its effects for days. "Ethan Frome" again has all the characteristics of a Greek tragedy save the chorus, but before he is aware of it the reader finds that he himself is the chorus. Ethan Frome is as blind and as powerless in the grip of fate that hurries him to doom as was even Œdipus, the King. And there is not a word too much, or a turn of the screw neglected, or a single pause in the swift movement, and at the end there is a surprise that even the most practiced of short-story readers could not have foreseen, a surprise that takes one by the throat like a hand out of the dark.

Not all of her stories have the distinction of these two, but all of the fifty-two or more that she has written have stood with refinement and restraint and artistic finish upon moral bases and upon a Hawthornelike knowledge of the human heart. Each has been an expression of a state of society often ironic and frequently satirical, and she has known her materials and spoken with conviction. She is not so pyschologically analytical as Henry James nor yet so scientific of method: where he worked notebook in hand she works with intuition, and often with more glow and passion. In rapidity, too, she greatly surpasses him, as she does in simplicity and naturalness of style. To call her a feminine Henry James is perhaps fanciful, is possibly ludicrous, but the comparison certainly works no injustice to Henry James and certainly it does not attribute too much to Mrs. Wharton.

VI

We close our study with the question that already has been suggested. The short story has been the one literary form that America has evolved and presented to the world; it has taken a place in America at least where it threatens all other literary forms: what of its value? Has our America evolved an inferior form of expression because of our restlessness and our lack of time as readers to devote to the longer and more elaborate forms of art? Has our climate rendered us scant of breath and capable only of short dashes? Can one see life steadily and see it whole if one may look at it only for the space of a *conte?* Howells asked such questions more than once in his later years. "Is it because American life is scrappy and desultory," he asked, "and instinctively seeks its expression in the sketch, the little tale, the miniature romance; or because the short story seems in all literatures to find its development earlier than the full-sized novel? Did our skill in writing short stories create the demand for them in the magazines or did the demand of the magazines foster the skill?" He ventured no answer.

Henry James, at least once, *did* express an opinion. In one of his autobiographical moments, a mere passing mood it may have been, he declared that when at length he passed from the short story to the novel he drew a sigh of relief: it was like passing from a frail craft that momently threatened collapse to the firm deck of a ship of the line. Others unconsciously have admitted the inferiority of the form. Hawthorne and a whole school of later novelists abandoned the short story at the first promise of an assured market for their longer fiction. Mary E. Wilkins confessed that she made use of the shorter form at the start because it was more easily marketed. To write eight or ten short stories she believed was a much safer venture at least at the start, than to spend the same amount of time on a novel that might not find a publisher. Even a critic as recent as Carl Van Doren can advise Miss Willa Cather to continue writing novels and express the hope that she will consider her volume of short stories, "striking though it is, but an interlude in her brilliant progress."

These questions, we say it again, it is not the province of the literary historian to discuss or even to venture an opinion. They are questions, however, that the thoughtful student is sure to ask himself, and concerning which, after his study of the evolution of the American short story form, he is sure to have an opinion.

BIBLIOGRAPHY

WILLIAM SYDNEY PORTER, "O. HENRY." 1862–1910.

1904. *Cabbages and Kings.*
1907. *The Heart of the West.*
1908. *The Gentle Grafter.*
1908. *The Voice of the City.*
1909. *Options.*
1909. *Roads of Destiny.*
1909. *The Four Million.*
1910. *The Trimmed Lamp and Other Stories of the Four Million.*
1910. *Strictly Business: More Stories of the Four Million.*
1910. *Whirligigs.*
1911. *Sixes and Sevens.*
1912. *Rolling Stones.*

NOTABLE BOOKS AND ARTICLES ON SHORT-STORY HISTORY AND TECHNIQUE

1842. Poe's Review of Hawthorne, *Graham's Magazine.*
1876. Friedrich Spielhagen, *Novella oder Roman?*
1884. Brander Matthews, "The Philosophy of the Short-Story."
1891. W. D. Howells in *Criticism and Fiction.*
1892. T. W. Higginson, "The Local Short-Story," *The Independent.*
1898. Frederick Wedmore, "The Short Story," *The Nineteenth Century,* March.
1898. Charles R. Barrett, *Short Story Writing. A Practical Treatise on the Art of the Short Story.*
1899. Bret Harte, "The Rise of the Short Story," *Cornhill Magazine,* July.
1900. W. M. Hart, *Hawthorne and the Short Story.*
1902. W. D. Howells, "Anomalies of the Short Story," *Literature and Life.*
1902. Bliss Perry, "The Short Story," Chapter XII, *A Study of Prose Fiction.*
1902. H. S. Canby, "The Short Story," *Yale Studies in English.*
1902. Lewis Worthington Smith, *The Writing of the Short Story.*
1903. Alexander Jessup and Henry S. Canby, *The Book of the Short Story.*
1904. Charles S. Baldwin, *American Short Stories.*
1905. William Patten, *Short Story Classics,* American. Five Volumes.
1906-1907. W. D. Howells and H. M. Alden, *Harper's Novelettes.* Eight volumes.
1907. Brander Matthews, *The Short Story: Specimens Illustrating Its Development.*
1907. W. P. Trent and J. B. Henneman, *Best American Tales.*
1908. Clayton Hamilton, *Materials and Methods of Fiction.*
1908. H. W. Mabie, *Stories New and Old.*
1909. J. B. Essenwein, *Writing the Short Story: A Practical Book on the Rise, Structure, Writing and Sale of the Modern Short Story.*
1909. Evelyn M. Albright, *The Short Story: Its Principles and Structure.*
1909. Henry S. Canby, *The Short Story in English.*
1909. G. W. Gerwig, *The Art of the Short Story.*
1910. G. R. Chester, *Art of Short Story Writing.*
1910. W. J. Dawson and Coningsby W. Dawson, *The Great English Short Story Writers.*
1912. Elias Lieberman, *The American Short Story.*
1912. W. B. Pitkin, *The Art and the Business of Story Writing.*
1912. C. Alphonso Smith, *The American Short Story.*
1913. Henry S. Canby, *A Study of the Short Story.*

1913. Essenwein and Chambers, *The Art of Story-Writing*. (For Correspondence School Work.)
1913. Carl H. Grabo, *The Art of the Short Story*.
1913. Carolyn Wells, *The Technique of the Mystery Story*.
1914. Stuart P. Sherman, *A Book of Short Stories*.
1914. E. A. Cross, *The Short Story*.
1914. Robert W. Neal, *Short Stories in the Making*.
1914. Lilian Notestein and W. H. Dunn, *The Modern Short Story*.
1915. Fred L. Pattee, *A History of American Literature Since 1870*. Chapters XI and XVI.
1915. Ina Ten Eyck Firkins, *Index to Short Stories*.
1915. L. B. Moulton, *Short Stories*.
1915. Edward J. O'Brien, *The Best Short Stories of 1915*. (A similar volume for each year since, seven volumes in all.)
1915. E. E. Hale and F. T. Dawson, *The Elements of the Short Story*.
1916. T. L. Mason. *Short Stories From "Life": The Eighty-one Prize Stories in "Life's" Shortest Story Contest*.
1916. W. Patterson Atkinson, *The Short Story*.
1916. Barry Pain, *The Short Story*.
1916. H. T. Baker, *The Contemporary Short Story*.
1917. Blanche Colton Williams, *A Handbook on Story Writing*.
1918. Francis J. Hannigan, *Standard Index of Short Stories. 1900–1914*.
1918. Clayton Hamilton, *A Manual of the Art of Fiction*.
1918. Robert W. Neal, *To-Day's Short Stories Analyzed*.
1920. *O. Henry Memorial Award. Prize Stories 1919 Chosen by the Society of Arts and Sciences*. (Similar volumes for 1920, 1921.)
1920. Alexander Jessup, *American Humorous Short Stories*.
1920. W. D. Howells, *The Great Modern American Stories*.
1920. B. A. Heydrick, *Americans All*.
1920. Blanche Colton Williams, *Our Short Story Writers*.
1921. Robert L. Ramsay, *Short Stories of America*.
1922. Fred Lewis Pattee, *A Short History of American Literature Based Upon the Cambridge History of American Literature*. Chapter IX, "The Short Story."
1922. R. W. Pence, *Short Stories by Present-Day Writers*.
1922. Alexander Jessup, *Representative American Short Stories*. (With very complete bibliography of short stories by years and by authors.)
1923. Fred Lewis Pattee, *The Development of the American Short Story: an Historical Survey*.

EDITH WHARTON. 1862–

1899. *The Greater Inclination*.
"The Muse's Tragedy"; "A Journey"; "The Pelican";

"Souls Belated"; "A Coward"; "The Twilight of the Gods"; "A Cup of Cold Water"; "The Portrait."

1901.   *Crucial Instances.*
"The Duchess at Prayer"; "The Angel at the Grave"; "The Recovery"; "'Copy': A Dialogue"; "The Rembrandt"; "The Moving Finger"; "The Confessional."

1904.   *The Descent of Man and Other Stories.*
"The Descent of Man"; "The Mission of Jane"; "The Other Two"; "The Quicksand"; "The Dilettante"; "The Reckoning"; "Expiation"; "The Lady's Maid's Bell"; "A Venetian Night's Entertainment."

1907.   *Madame de Treymes.*

1908.   *The Hermit and the Wild Woman.*
"The Hermit and the Wild Woman"; "The Last Asset"; "In Trust"; "The Pretext"; "The Verdict"; "The Pot-Boiler"; "The Best Man."

1910.   *Tales of Men and Ghosts.*
"The Bolted Door"; "His Father's Son"; "The Daunt Diana"; "The Debt"; "Full Circle"; "The Legend"; "The Eyes"; "The Blond Beast"; "Afterward"; "The Letters."

1911.   *Ethan Frome.*

1916.   *Xingu and Other Stories.*
"Xingu"; "Coming Home"; "Autres Temps"; "Kerfol"; "The Long Run"; "The Triumph of Might"; "The Choice"; "The Bunner Sisters."

INDEX

INDEX OF CRITICAL TERMS

THE END